THORSTEIN VEBLEN
ANd
THE AMERICAN
way of life

This work is dedicated to

Mary Gordon, my companion of many years

Patricia Patsouras, my daughter

and

Gerhart Alexander Hirsch, dear friend

THORSTEIN VEBLEN
and
the AMERICAN
way of life

Louis Patsouras

Montréal/New York/London

Black Rose Books No. HH325

National Library of Canada Cataloguing in Publication Data
Patsouras, Louis
Thorstein Veblen and the American way of life / Louis Patsouras

Includes bibliographical references and index.
Hardcover ISBN: 1-55164-229-8 (bound) Paperback ISBN: 1-55164-228-X (pbk.)
1. Veblen, Thorstein, 1857-1929. 2. Socialism--United States--History. I. Title.

HB119.V4P38 2003   320.53'1'092   C2003-904159-X

Cover design: Associés libres

BLACK
ROSE
BOOKS

C.P. 1258	2250 Military Road	99 Wallis Road
Succ. Place du Parc	Tonawanda, NY	London, E9 5LN
Montréal, H2X 4A7	14150	England
Canada	USA	UK

To order books:

In Canada: (phone) 1-800-565-9523 (fax) 1-800-221-9985
email: utpbooks@utpress.utoronto.ca

In United States: (phone) 1-800-283-3572 (fax) 1-651-917-6406

In the UK & Europe: (phone) London 44 (0)20 8986-4854 (fax) 44 (0)20 8533-5821
email: order@centralbooks.com

Our Web Site address: http://www.web.net/blackrosebooks

A publication of the Institute of Policy Alternatives of Montréal (IPAM)

Printed in Canada

Contents

Preface

A PLETHORA OF WORKS HAVE APPEARED ON Thorstein Veblen, one of America's out-standing economic and social thinkers, the classic being Joseph Dorfman's *Thorstein Veblen and His America*. To be sure, my work on Veblen has been greatly influenced by earlier ones, but is somewhat different from them in that it not only presents Veblen's socialism, but also that of other socialists, which are contrasted to a select conservativism representing the status quo, continuing the debate to the present, importantly indicating that the differences between them are essentially the same as when Veblen flourished. Furthermore, this study presents an extensive background on socialism, including anarchism, to better appreciate the debates which follow.

The work itself is in two parts. The first ("The Making of a Revolutionary Socialist") is an historical progression of Veblen's life and intellectual activity, related to the various forces, socioeconomic, political, intellectual, and others within the American experience, and his responses to them, climaxing with his avid support of the 1917 Bolshevik Revolution in Russia. The second part ("Veblen and Problems of Socialism") basically involves the ongoing differences between socialism and capitalism, with Veblen properly situated in this continuum, in the key areas of the human drama, self-explanatory in the chapter headings.

PART I

THE MAKING OF A REVOLUTIONARY SOCIALIST

I   Thorstein Veblen: An Overview

THORSTEIN BUNDE VEBLEN WAS BORN IN 1857 on the frontier at the Cato Township of Mantiwoc County, Wisconsin, the sixth of twelve children of Thomas Anderson Veblen, a carpenter, and his wife, Kari (née Bunde), land-starved Norwegian immigrants who came to America in 1847. The Veblens soon became successful farmers, and further improved their lot with the purchase of a three-hundred-acre farm in a Norwegian enclave near Nerstrand, Minnesota.

Quite normally, as immigrant outsiders, with their own subculture in a largely rural setting—schools, churches, and so forth—Norwegians were somewhat isolated from their Anglo-Saxon neighbors, who considered them as social inferiors, enduring their usual ethnic slights, including comparing them to Native- and African-Americans. But as Northern Europeans, middle-class farm owners, and Protestants, Norwegians rapidly entered the mainstream of American life, the Veblen family itself with its emphasis on education being in the forefront.

Among 19th-century immigrants, the Norwegians, Swedes, and Germans, especially those who had the economic wherewithal to purchase farms, fared much better than those who were poverty stricken, forced to usually work in the eastern seaboard cities, and were Catholic (historically, Catholicism was Protestantism's great religious enemy), like the Irish, the despised immigrant group of the mid-19th century. The lowly position of the Irish in a white-dominated caste society, which relegated blacks to the nether world, was so deep that "No Irish Need Apply" advertisements for work were a common sight in the mid-to-late 19th century, blacks being preferred to them. But over time, the Irish by their very large numbers and various networks, like religious, economic, and political, were able to improve their status; the bottom rung among whites was then to be occupied by the later immigrants, Southern and Eastern Europeans.

Americanization, with its implied social mobility, was furthered by Veblen's attending nearby Carleton College from 1874 to 1880, graduating with a BA degree. Carleton's curriculum was sufficiently broad and rigorous to allow Veblen successful egress to America's top colleges.

After a one-year teaching position at a Lutheran school in Wisconsin in 1881, Veblen entered the Johns Hopkins graduate school to study history and philosophy, but soon afterward left for Yale, majoring in philosophy under its president, Noah Porter, and attending the economics classes of the controversial social Darwinist, William Graham Sumner. He graduated in 1884 with a Ph.D. in philosophy, with a strong letter of recommendation from Porter and one from Sumner in 1889. A successful academic career seemed likely, but disappointment intervened.

When Veblen attended college, philosophy classes included not only what is now considered philosophy, but also religion and much of what today is social science, involved as it was in understanding the larger society, the influence of Greek philosophy being apparent. Also of note was Veblen's mastery of many languages. In addition to Norwegian, which he learned before English, he was familiar with classical Greek and Latin (invariably taught in high school/college in the 19th century), the other Scandinavian languages, Old Norse, German, French, Italian, and later Russian. Veblen was simply a brilliant student before becoming one of America's outstanding thinkers.

For seven years, from 1884 to 1891, Veblen ignominiously lived either at the family farm or those of relatives as he was unable to procure a position as a college teacher. During this trying period, he was afflicted with a psychosomatic illness (he claimed that he was recuperating from malaria contracted in the Eastern seaboard), which, although excusing him from performing strenuous farm work, fortunately allowed for omnivorous reading. His failure to secure an academic appointment was basically related to ethnic and religious prejudices: As Joseph Dorfman, Veblen's leading biographer, stated, "No faculty wanted a 'Norskie,' particularly one suspected of agnostic leanings." The rebel and outsider was paying his dues.

Veblen, however, would ultimately return to academia: His marriage to Ellen Rolfe, from a Yankee/Congregationalist family of wealth and position (they were classmates at Carleton), might have been decisive in this because, in all likelihood, she would not have relished living with him on a farm. Thus it was that in 1891 Veblen entered the graduate school at Cornell University to pursue post-graduate studies in history and economics, finally opting to concentrate on the latter.

In 1892, Veblen received a fellowship and subsequently an assistant professorship at the newly founded University of Chicago whose leading patron was John D. Rockefeller. He left Chicago in 1906 to become an associate professor of economics at Stanford, but was forced to resign in 1909. He then became a lecturer in economics, with no tenure, at the University of Missouri from 1911 to 1918. His academic career was marked by a forced retreat from the first two universities for amorous activity involving faculty wives. After the Veblens divorced in 1912, he soon married a former student, Ann Bradley Fessenden, who was devoted to him. The marriage was a happy one, but tragedy struck in 1918 when Ann was hospitalized for psychological problems, and died in 1920.

After securing a leave of absence from the University of Missouri, Veblen served in the first half of 1918 as a statistician at the Food Administration in Washington, D.C. In the course of his duties, he prepared several reports suggesting that government prosecution of Industrial Workers of the World (IWW) members be lifted and that they be allowed to operate democratically run farm-worker units. When this and other proposals were ignored, he resigned.

The 1918-19 period was a tumultuous one for Veblen since he not only enthusiastically championed the Russian Communist Revolution of November 1917, but, also, decided to live in New York, the radical capital of the United States, as an associate professor of economics, from 1919 to his retirement in 1926, at the newly established New School for Social Research, a haven for radical scholars. There, he was known as one of the "Big Four," along with the historians Charles A. Beard and James Harvey Robinson, and the economist Wesley C. Mitchell. Other distinguished faculty included the political scientist Harold J. Laski, the philosopher/educator John Dewey, the historian Harry Elmer Barnes, and Graham Wallas, a political scientist and psychologist.[1]

A controversial thinker, Veblen invariably went against the grain. Two views by eminent scholars on this, David Riesman, a social scientist, and Henry Steele Commager, an historian. For the former:

> He [Veblen] had a compelling sympathy for the outcast: with immigrants, Jews, workers, farmers, Wobblies, primitive tribes, the small Scandinavian countries, the embattled Soviets, women and cats (as against dogs).[2]

For the latter:

> Although Veblen's immigrant background is important in understanding him, the environment was more important—the Middle Border that produced in his generation Lester Ward and Frederick Turner, Vernon Parrington and Charles Beard, Simon Patten, and John R. Commons.

And:

> For all his sophistication, his esoteric learning, his muffled echoes of Marx, he
> can be better understood in terms of agrarian radicalism than of eastern progres-
> sivism or of the revolutionary economics of central Europe.[3]

Veblen's intellectual output was indeed prodigious, authoring ten books, several of which were collections of his articles. It notably included *The Theory of the Leisure Class* (1899); *The Theory of Business Enterprise* (1904); *The Instinct of Workmanship and the State of the Industrial Arts* (1915); *The Higher Learning In America* (1916); *The Engineers and the Price System* (1921); and *Absentee Ownership and Business Enterprise in Recent Times* (1923). These works displayed the thought of not only one of America's foremost econo- mists, but also of one of its most notable social scientists, and perhaps its most acerbic social critic. Although the early works feigned a scientific detachment, the later were of a decid- edly polemical nature as Veblen's socialism became more insistent and revolutionary.

Toward the end of his life, Veblen again hoped for a revolutionary cycle when the 1926 British General Strike erupted, but once more tasted disappointment. He died in 1929, a few months before the great stock market crash.

In his vignettes of representative Americans who best personified American life, John Dos Passos, in his magnificent trilogy *USA*—in *The Big Money* volume—presented a mem- orable portrait of Veblen. An excerpt:

> Socrates asked questions, drank down the bitter drink one night when the first
> cock crowed, but Veblen drank it in little sips through a long life in the stuffiness
> of classrooms, the dust of libraries, the staleness of cheap flats such as a poor in-
> structor can afford. He fought the bogey all right, pedantry, routine, timeservers
> at office desks, trustees, college presidents, the plump flunkies of the ruling busi-
> nessmen, all the good jobs for the yesmen, never enough money, every broaden-
> ing hope thwarted. Veblen drank the bitter drink all right.[4]

Veblen himself profoundly influenced a number of students, literary and public figures: Wesley Mitchell, a distinguished economist; Dos Passos, one of the eminent novelists of the 20th century; Henry A. Wallace, Secretary of Agriculture and Vice President under Franklin D. Roosevelt; and Howard Scott, an engineer who founded Technocracy Incorporated dur- ing the Great Depression.[5]

Notes

1. The most comprehensive study on Veblen's life and work is by Joseph Dorfman, *Thorstein Veblen and His America* (New York: Viking Press, 1935). Other notable works, including anthologies and compilations of Veblen's work, are: Wesley C. Mitchell, ed., *What Veblen Taught* (New York: Viking Press, 1936); R.L. and William M. Duffus, *The Innocents at Cedro* (New York: Macmillan, 1944); Max Lerner, ed., *The Portable Veblen* (New York: Viking Press, 1978); David Riesman, *Thorstein Veblen: A Critical Interpretation* (New York: Charles Scribner's Sons, 1953); Bernard Rosenberg, *The Values of Veblen* (Washington, D.C.: Public Affairs Press, 1956); Lev E. Dobriansky, *Veblenism: A New Critique* (Washington, D.C.: Public Affairs Press, 1957); Douglas F. Dowd, *Thorstein Veblen* (New York: Washington Press Square, 1966); Carlton C. Qualey, ed., *Thorstein Veblen* (New York: Columbia University Press, 1968); David Seckler, *Thorstein Veblen and the Institutionalists: A Study in the Social Philosophy of Economics* (Boulder CO: Colorado Associated Press, 1975); John P. Diggins, *The Bard of Savagery: Thorstein Veblen and Modern Social Theory,* (New York: Seabury Press, 1978); and Rick Tilman, *Thorstein Veblen and His Critics, 1891-1963: Conservative, Liberal, and Radical Perspectives* (Princeton, NJ: Princeton University Press, 1992). On when Veblen learned English, cf. Dorfman, *Veblen*, p. 11, with Tilman, *Veblen*, pp. 4-5. On the Dorfman quotation, see his *Veblen*, pp. 4-5. On ethnic slights comparing Norwegians to African- and Native-Americans, see Dorfman, *Veblen*, pp. 4-5. Prejudice against non-Protestant and poor Europeans settling in the cities was even greater than that directed against Norwegians, as, for instance, the Catholic Irish. On this, see Noel Ignatiev, *How the Irish Became White* (New York: Routledge, 1995), pp. 1-3, 92-121, 178-88. To become fully qualified as "white" immigrants must acquire the various prejudices against African-Americans.

2. Riesman, *Veblen*, p. 139.

3. Henry Steele Commager, *The American Mind: An Interpretation of American Thought and Character Since the 1880s* (New Haven: Yale University Press, 1959), pp. 237ff.

4. John Dos Passos, *The Big Money* (Vol. III of *USA*) (Boston: Hougnton Mifflin, 1960), p. 84.

5. Dorfman, *Veblen*, pp. 506-07 ff. Walter B. Rideout, *The Radical Novel in the United States: Some Interrelations of Literature and Society* (New York: Hill and Wang, 1956), pp. 156-61 on Dos Passos.

II   Selective Background on Radicalism and Socialism

Background

TO BETTER UNDERSTAND THE THOUGHT OF VEBLEN, America's premier economic and social thinker, and the lineage of radical and socialist thought in the debates that follow between left and right, it is necessary to selectively present a background of Western radicalism and socialism.

It is a truism that with the advent of civilization, well-defined ruling elites emerged oppressing the majority. Lewis Mumford, a noted neo-anarchist American social philosopher, drawing deeply from Veblen, utilized the term "mega-machine" for this condition; and others, like Robert Morrison MacIver, a professor of political science and sociology at Columbia University delineated this phenomenon in great detail: one of interrelated socioeconomic, political, and religio-cultural institutions in bureaucratic modes, run by elites usually grouped around leaders subordinated to a maximum one invested with the magic of some form of absolute authority, usually regarded as an exalted godlike figure, invariably to be respected and obeyed, disobedience being the worst of all possible crimes/sins.[1]

The first civilizations, Sumer and Egypt, were well-developed mega-machines, setting the tone for the following ones, like the classical Greek and Roman, which had, however, some popular male participation in government for extended periods (the first more so than the second). Until quite recently, the usual mega-machines were capped by kings, supported by a not numerous nobility and wealthy capitalists, along with a priestly class, followed by the overwhelming majority, the masses, mostly farmers, with only a minority being urban workers, usually in a state of harsh economic and political servitude, the very bottom consisting of serfs and slaves, the last a large minority. This pattern in the last few centuries was supplanted by the rise of capitalism, with the bourgeoisie in the superior position, the proletariat their subalterns.

Radicalism and Utopian Socialism

Socialism before the mid-19th century, when it became a mass movement, was called "utopian socialism" after Sir Thomas More's *Utopia* because it involved small-scale socialist experiments or works on socialism in literature. But first, a general definition of socialism: It is a bundle of ideas/practices advocating a general socioeconomic, political, gender, and cultural equality, in which the technology is in the hands of cooperative and public bodies in various proportions. Although not against the private ownership of small individual/family property, socialism is against employing the labor of others for profit. It also believes in the freedoms that have largely been won by the progressive bourgeoisie and workers, of speech, press, religion, and assembly, and insists on the cooperative brotherhood of all people—it is internationalist. Veblen himself views socialism as "an organization [based] on industrial as contrasted with business lines, and "of industrial coherence…not on lines given by pecuniary conjunctures and conventional principles of economic right and wrong," but on "economic stability."[2]

Forms of socialism have been the norm of the human condition, certainly until the New Stone Age beginning ten to twelve thousand years ago, Marx's "primitive communism." But with the advent of civilization or class oppressive societies, at about 3500 B.C.E., the first large-scale attempt for a general equality, a form of radical liberalism or proto-socialism occurred in the 8th and 7th centuries B.C.E. with the Hebrew Prophetic Revolution. Its principal social critics and visionaries, like Amos, Micah, and Isaiah (the last being three persons), spearheaded a sustained attack against a society based on a divisive socioeconomic and political inequality, viewing it as an abomination displeasing God, leading to the destruction of Israel and Judah through foreign conquest, although a righteous remnant would be ultimately saved to live in a society of equality and abundance, of peace and joy.

This was the first recorded instance of the millenarian social psychology of the oppressed poor employing God as a vehicle to aid them in establishing a just society. Several examples of prophetic social criticism: Of Amos, a "herdsman and fruit picker" who characterized the rich and powerful, as those who "lie on ivory beds surrounded with luxury," who "trample on the poor and steal their smallest crumb by…taxes, fines, and usury." Of Isaiah, "How dare you grind my people in the dust like this," and, "You buy property so others have no place to live. Your homes are built on great estates so you can be alone in the midst of the earth."

The great *Old Testament* law codes, of Deuteronomy and Leviticus, outgrowths of the Prophetic Revolution, called for progressive measures (applicable only to Hebrews), as in abolishing interest on loans, canceling all debts every seven years (for instance, if one borrowed money in the fifth year it would be canceled in the seventh), freeing of debt slaves after six years, with resources to begin a new and independent life, a tithe to aid the indigent, election of officials ("Judges") by the people, and restoration of property to owners/descendants every fifty years. Although these laws (some may have been practiced for a generation) permitted private property, it was of the small-type variety, ensuring a general equality. The Prophets also envisioned a world without war in which nations "beat their swords into plowshares and their spears into pruning forks."

The second major instance in the West of social criticism and desire to institute a world of equality was in the Hellenic and Greco-Roman worlds. (We should also note the existence of a progressive Zoroastrianism in Persia, a religion that influenced Judaism and Christianity.) It began with the 6th century B.C.E. Greek mathematician, social reformer and mystic—he believed in reincarnation—Pythagoras who called for a virtuous elite to live pacifically, ascetically (celibacy was de rigeur), and communistically (no private property) to avoid the contamination of exploiting others, organized along the lines of brotherhoods and sisterhoods. A principal maxim of Pythagoras was of no forgiveness for those possessing wealth, which itself sprang from social injustice while poverty existed; another was that if you were more capable than others, there was no excuse in having others work for you; yet another was "From each according to his ability, to each according to his need"—made famous by Marx as the basis of his communism.

The Pythagorean tradition was well ensconced in the Socrates-Plato-Antisthenes-Diogenes of Antiope axis in the 5th to 4th centuries B.C.E. Socrates, the greatest of the Greek philosophers, like Jesus of Nazareth, never wrote anything; we know of him only through his brilliant pupil Plato, but his other devoted student Antisthenes (the founder of the Cynics), and his student, in turn, Diogenes of Antiope, were also of importance to socialism, especially anarchism.

Plato, although an elitist and arch anti-democrat (an admirer of Spartan aristocracy), was basically in the socialist tradition. In *The Republic*, whose central character was Socrates, he well understood that in a world of economic inequality, the consequent class struggle could only weaken the city-state, one between a grasping ruling wealthy elite (more wealth equaled less virtue) and the many average citizens. To remedy this, he sought a society based on justice leading to social harmony and happiness.

Its basic outlines: Power was firmly lodged in the hands of a communist elite or guardian class composed of two status groups, the highly intelligent/educated philosophers or intellectual elite embodying reason, and the military, somewhat less intelligent and less schooled symbolizing courage; they numbered less than ten percent of the people. Since the two represented the two highest Platonic virtues—reason and courage—they would rule. Because they were economically unselfish as individuals, the guardians would reject the evils of the private nuclear family and private property for a collective family/property one, their children belonging to the group, brought up communally, apart from their biological parents.

To be sure, the guardians would compete with one another in the educational arena, in examinations, for honors, the more successful becoming philosophers. They would even eschew gender inequality, the only exception being the male top generalship.

The basis for this elite would be their superior intelligence manifested in tests, itself related to genetic superiority of parents. But this popular prejudice of many philosophers has been undermined by present scientific knowledge emphasizing the importance of environment, especially in the early lives of children, in fostering general intelligence and psychological stability. Plato's elite children generally would obviously perform better than the others in that they were nourished communally in an enriched intellectual environment with its many benefits, including great social solidarity.

As for the appetite class, the average people (about ninety percent of the population, of unexceptional intelligence and utterly selfish as they worked only for private gain), they were occupied in the ordinary occupations, like farming and crafts; their lifestyle demanded the private family and private property, although the latter element was to be rigorously controlled by the guardians lest a large landowner class emerge to challenge them for political power.

This society would allow for some social mobility based exclusively on biological fitness, with a few elite children having mental or physical handicaps—there is some genetic imperfection within the elite—falling to the lower class, while a few appetite-class children, again because of biological good fortune, ascending to the guardian level, a unifying element between the classes.

Plato attempted to resolve the antagonistic social relations of class society based on an insufficient economic surplus to give everyone the good life. But, in his social diagram, the appetite class was still exploited by the guardians who had the time to cultivate their intellectual and military "virtues." Furthermore, it is historically impossible for the "virtuous" few, be they philosophers or Communist bureaucrats in authoritarian societies to long remain egalitarian, as the Soviet Communist experiment has proven, for they are not hermetically sealed from the inherent socioeconomic tensions of societies with insufficient technological development/economic surpluses and the specter of war. To be sure, Plato confirms the truism that even in societies malformed by economic scarcity/steep labor division, the possibility of communism, although a deformed one, still exists.

It should be added that Plato well indicated the problem of labor division involved in class rulership, the minority guardians representing mental labor as opposed to the manual one of the masses, most employed in agriculture.

One of the followers of Socrates, Antisthenes, whom Plato characterized as "Socrates gone mad," may be regarded as the father of anarchism. He urged that distinctions between Plato's guardians and masses be erased in a communist society without formal government, private property, marriage, and religion; everyone would live like Plato's guardians in an ascetic milieu.

Antisthenes' disciple, Diogenes of Sinope, who lived in a tub, also urged the Greeks to stop enslaving others and promoted pacifism. For him, like Plato, societies which stressed wealth as the principal goal of life lacked virtue. He attacked the rich and powerful on this basis, while condemning the poor for wishing to attain wealth as they envied the rich. Under these circumstances, he rejected political democracy and autocracy, preferring a philosopher "ruler" who would foster an educational system to promote his egalitarian communism based on a simple life style.

To be sure, a general ascetic lifestyle, even in technologically backward societies by our standards, could allow a rather decent life for all, but there remained the element of the class-related labor division and technology nexus and resultant social and other antagonisms that simply could not be resolved at this time.

These socialist ideas were then taken up by the stoic Zeno of Citium who was greatly influenced by the Cynics. In his ideal world, in the Golden Age of humanity, in the state of nature, everyone was equal as brotherly love prevailed, underscored by a community of goods or communism, which atrophied in later ages, as in his contemporary Iron Age characterized by war and inequality, most of humanity in misery, this because of avarice related to the rise of private property.

In contrast to Plato's elitist communism there were also the contemporary democratic and egalitarian views of the Sophists, the most notable one being Protagoras who championed the democratic and egalitarian aspirations of farmers and workers and was against slavery, war, and the ethnic exclusiveness of the Greeks. It was he who proclaimed that "man is the measure of all things," or that such ideals as beauty, truth, justice, goodness, and so forth were simply relative to the needs and interests of individuals and societies, thus there being no absolute standards of right and wrong. In this relativistic stance, he saw the senses as the source of knowledge and socio-ethical standards in the different societies, morality having human not supernatural standards of the gods. In thus stressing the importance of the environment in human affairs, it would, thus, be possible to remake societies by changing the environment, especially of the children, thus offering hope for a more just world. He was also considered the principal father of dialectics in which the truth emerged from the clash of opposites, obviously influenced by Heraclitus.

It should also be noted that during the Hellenistic Age, with the destruction of the Greek city-states and their liberties by large empires (of Alexander the Great, his successors, and Roman), there were a plethora of utopias. One was Iambulus' *Isles of the Blessed* or *Island of the Sun* which described austere communist societies partly abolishing labor division in that all performed manual labor, in a pacific world. This escapism at once denoted intense alienation, but also a thirst for social justice.

The third great historical force in the West to promote an egalitarian society of brotherhood was Christianity, a multistoried religion most heavily influenced in its ethical and millenarian conceptions by the Hebrew Prophetic tradition but also by Pythagoreanism, Buddhism, Zoroastrianism, and Greek mystery religion, by the last's insistence on a man/god.

Christianity's rise was certainly a resultant of the class struggles among the Roman Empire's free and slave masses and its equestrian and patrician elites capped by divine emperorship. Indeed, Christianity wished to establish a world of equality within one replete with inequality and oppression. Lest it be forgotten, Christianity was an underground millenarian religion in its early centuries, with its own counterculture to the dominant institutions of Rome, whose man/god, Jesus of Nazareth, would soon return to destroy the world of privilege and power symbolized by the man/god Roman Emperor. It was with good reason that the Roman authorities viewed early Christians as subversives.

But by the 4th century of the C.E., the overwhelming economic and other powers of the military/landed elites transformed Christianity into a state religion, the Constantinian Church. But despite the many conservative strictures in the *New Testament*, as of slaves to obey their masters (perhaps ruses to appease the authorities), many revolutionary parts condemning wealth and power remained: The story of Jesus and the rich man, including the famous "It's easier for a camel to squeeze through a needle's eye [a small door] than for a wealthy man to get into God's domain," Mark 10:17-31, Matthew 19:16-30, and Luke 18:18-301; in Matthew 6.24, of not being able to "serve two masters, God and money"; in Timothy 6:10, "For the love of money is the root of all evils"; in Luke 6:20 ff., where the poor inherit "the kingdom of God," but not the wealthy; in the Epistle of James 5:1, where the rich are cursed with "miseries that shall come upon you. Your riches are corrupted and your garments are moth eaten. Your gold and silver is cankered; and the rust of them shall be a witness against you and will eat your flesh like fire." Furthermore, there was the millenarian communism of the early Jewish Christians in Jerusalem (the "Ebionites" or the poor) as described in the Acts of the Apostles, waiting for the Messiah and quick end of the present world.

(It should also be noted that Christianity has a strong tradition of a human-only revolutionary Jesus of Nazareth. The synoptic gospels, Mark, Matthew, and Luke, emphasize this Jesus who in the Gospel of John was transformed into a divine savior of the world. There is also a fifth Gospel, that of Thomas, which nowhere mentions Jesus' divinity. For interested readers on the complexity of the Christian Gospels, see *The Search for the Authentic Words of Jesus: The Five Gospels by the Jesus Seminar*, which involved the collaborative work of seventy-four biblical scholars.)[3]

To be sure, the principal figure of Christianity, Jesus of Nazareth, may also be seen as particularly being part of the anarchist tradition, fighting the established religion and power structure as in driving out the money changers from the Temple and condemning the rich, living by begging with his followers, while calling for a new world of equality and joy to come quickly with the aid of a revolutionary God. (Not surprisingly, there is Christian Anarchism in the 19th and 20th centuries, for instance, as practiced by Leo Tolstoy and the Catholic Worker movement led by Dorothy Day and Peter Maurin.)

In the Middle Ages, three instances of socialism/anarchism were in evidence from the 12th to 14th centuries. The first was Joachim of Fiore, a Calabrian abbot who averred that a new age was dawning, "Age of the Holy Spirit," in which wealth, property, and work would be done away with as humans would become spiritual, not needing food, forming a free community without ecclesiastical or temporal authority. The second was St. Francis of Assisi who hated to see anyone poorer than himself. He founded an order based on the absence of personal and collective property (for him property required the use of weapons to retain it) whose members would work with their hands and beg to show their solidarity with the oppressed masses. The third was in the 1381 English Peasant's Revolt when one of its leaders, the defrocked priest John Ball attacked both hierarchy and inequality in proclaiming: "When Adam delved and Eve span who was then the gentleman?"

Christian Socialism received a great boost forward with the advent of the Protestant Revolution or Reformation in the 16th century. Specifically, its left wing, exemplified in the millenarian Anabaptist/Pietistic tradition (many elements being closely related to the 1524-1525 German Peasants' and Workers' Revolt, a series of *spontaneous* uprisings by peasants and workers against the nobility and bourgeoisie), envisaged a society along the lines of general socioeconomic equality, either through the predominance of small property or communism. The influence of this left-wing Protestantism on American utopianism is not negligible.

The best known leader of these revolts was Thomas Münzer, a former priest who was associated briefly with Martin Luther. He advocated a class war by the masses against the ungodly wealthy and powerful to usher in a communist society. A mystic who regarded suffering as the road to redemption, he directly communicated with God.

It was during the late Renaissance and the early period of Protestant Revolution and Catholic response, a time of social turmoil, leading to social revolution in Germany, that the prototypical modern utopia—soon to be followed by others—appeared, More's statist *Utopia* (from Greek *outopos*, "no place"). It presented a detailed account of a communist society without Plato's starkly elitist diagram, featuring a general socioeconomic and gender equality linked to democracy, although there was a status difference between a minority composed of the intelligentsia, elected to the magistracy, and the general public. Contrary to Plato's guardians, More allowed for the nuclear family's existence, satisfied that the other institutions encircling it would prevent any undue selfishness in favoring one's progeny over those of others. This progressive utopia also abolished wage labor since work was regarded as integral to a way of life, not as a commodity or cost of production. The workday itself was of six hours.

More, an acute social critic, who well understood the various levers of power—economic, political, and social—pictured government as a "conspiracy of the rich, who in pretense of managing the public only pursue their private ends." This paradigm pitted the nobility and wealthy few ('drones') against the farmers and workers, or the poor, who, laboring "as hard as a beast at labor," lived like "draft animals," and were "worn out by age and sickness." Furthermore, echoing Jesus of Nazareth and Plato, he opined, "while money is the standard of all things, the most unworthy tend to acquire most of the wealth."

Other well-known utopias of this period included Tommaso Campanella's *City of the Sun* and Valentin Andrea's *Christianapolis*. Like More, Campanella and Andrea rejected private property and wage labor and favored democracy; and Andrea was the first to discuss integrated labor or the combination of manual and intellectual labor to transcend the curse of labor division and consequent general inequality.

The English Revolution of the 1640s also promoted human liberation through its principal progressive current, the Levellers whose main spokesperson, John Lilburne, representing the lower-middle class, tried to ring in power and privilege by popular democracy and the widespread distribution of property, along with religious tolerance. This movement properly inaugurated modern radical republicanism. But socialist ideas were not forgotten during this revolution. Gerrard Winstanley, a perceptive thinker, in *The New Law of Righteousness* and *Law of Freedom*, in a pantheistic and rationalist vein, sketched the outlines of an Anarcho-Communist society without private property and wage labor, with production based on separate households sharing a common storehouse, and annual parliamentary elections through universal suffrage. For him, private property, the origin of sin and evil, disturbed love with its authority, corrupting all human relations and inevitably leading to strife, including class warfare, a pattern of thought common to anarchists in general.[4]

In the 18th century, a mature Enlightenment dominated the intellectual scene, a movement propelling the forward thrust of the progressive American and French revolutions. Although there was a socialist current in it, the principal left one was radical republicanism represented by luminaries like Rousseau, Diderot, Robespierre, Hébert, and Roux in France, and Jefferson, Franklin, and Paine in America.

The socialist side of the Enlightenment was particularly active in France. It included Jean Meslier, a former priest-turned-atheist, in *Testament; The Abbé Morelly in Code de la nature*; and the Abbé Gabriel de Bonnot de Mably in *Le Droit et les devoirs du citoyen*. The three proposed socialist societies, either limiting or abolishing private property, with attendant fraternity and equality. The first of these utopias even urged the end of formal government, definitely in the anarchist tradition.

Before observing radical republicanism and its leading exponents mentioned, an examination of the views of John Locke, the principal father of Liberalism, is in order. Basically a political conservative, he was against monarchical absolutism, monarchy to share power with the nobility/bourgeoisie in the House of Lords and House of Commons. He was no democrat. In fact, he authored the *Fundamental Constitution for Carolina*, constructing a semi-feudal society ruled by a nobility and ancillary bourgeoisie resting on slavery. But in his theoretical works, as *Two Treatises of Government, Essay Concerning Human Understanding,* and *Letter Concerning Toleration,* Locke was a progressive thinker. In the first, he formulated a social-contract theory based on human natural goodness resulting in a natural law justifying the rights of life (protection from the incursions of others), liberty (freedom of action), and property as foundation for limited government resting on popular sovereignty or majority rule to protect these rights. In the second, despite some contradictions, his sensationalist psychology held that since the mind at birth was a *tabula rasa* or blank slate, the environment was the key to understanding human actions, opening the possibility for progress and future equality in education and other areas. The third, urging religious toleration, except for the religiously intolerant, was a step forward in tolerance, especially within Protestantism.[5]

Jean-Jacques Rousseau, the neurotic and brilliant scion of lower-middle-class Protestants from Geneva, was the outstanding radical-liberal thinker of the period, indeed a proto-socialist and an inspirer of the French Revolution, with two seminal works justifying equality, *Discourse on the Origins of Inequality* and *The Social Contract*. In the first, he expressed that large private property arose only with the rise of civilization and the state, the latter an instrument of the strong and wealthy. Thus, since property was not "natural," but conventional, it might be regulated by society. Furthermore, in this work, he viewed the individual and the collective society existing peacefully and cooperatively in a socioeconomic construct of general equality, not being cursed by large private property. Only with the advent of civilization from the Agricultural Revolution leading to sedentary agriculture and metals, did large private property originate and with it the train of class division, war, and subsequent social oppression and misery. In this pattern, he followed the Stoics.

In the second, he challenged the privileges of monarchs, nobility, and capitalists in the name of equality, liberty, and popular sovereignty, which he associated with the concepts of "social contract," and "general will," both linked to small private property. For him, human beings consented to a social contract for establishing government or sovereignty whose legislation was under the aegis of the general will or the majority in the context of a general socioeconomic and political equality, in which small nonexploitative property dominated, i.e., an individual owning only what he directly worked on. Ideally, political decisions were made on the basis of direct democracy, but he also accepted a representative one. In the milieu of a general socioeconomic equality, he believed that individual interests were similar to the public one or common good, but in class-ridden societies, the common good was subverted by the economically strong who inordinately manipulated the political process to further their interests at the expense of the many. He defended general equality also on the basis that an individual alone, without society, could not achieve much, that humans were social animals, and that a general equality furnished the optimum conditions for liberty, itself only formal with great socioeconomic inequality.

For Geroge Lichtheim, Rousseau is the major precursor of modern socialism. For some, Rousseau is a totalitarian, because of his "general will" concept. This is a false view because the general will is based on a general socioeconomic and political equality; nothing can be more libertarian than that. Indeed, this equality would buttress general tolerance with respect to art and other areas as well as foster a proper individualism, one devoid of an antisocial egoism, itself the mark of an alienated individual.[6]

Perhaps the central figure of the Enlightenment, the son of a lower-middleclass skilled worker, Denis Diderot was an audacious thinker who at once embraced atheism/materialism and the social ethics of Jesus of Nazareth. An archenemy of organized religion, with its intolerance and distorted view of social and physical reality, of kings and nobility, Diderot favored an egalitarian republican society of small property owners. His view of human nature, influenced by the sensationalism of Protagoras and Locke, which modern socialism generally follows, was of a good human nature: "Nature has not made us vicious; it is bad education, bad examples and bad legislation that have corrupted us." He supported the American Revolution. His most enduring contribution to humanity was his general editorship of the seventeen-volume *Encyclopedia* (with eleven volumes of illustrations), which assembled the knowledge of the past "to change the general way of thinking."

The general left in the French Revolution were the Jacobins led by the indomitable Maximilien Robespierre, the principal actor of the Committee of Public Safety in the 1793-94 period, when the revolution reached its furthest left point: A disciple of Rousseau, he wished to abolish not only the aristocracy based on birth/wealth, but all large existing socioeconomic inequalities by progressive taxation, to be further erased at death with a steep testamentary one. Property itself, for him, was a creature of social convention, not a natural right, thus allowing for its widespread use, all citizens to enjoy it with its corollary, the right to work. He also promoted democracy, of male universal suffrage in a one-house legislature, the last being enshrined in the 1793 Constitution. But he was aware that these principles were not easily arrived at because the masses, lacking education—thus importance for state education—and being poverty stricken, were under the cultural hegemony of wealth, the normal enemy of the revolution, this in his confidential *Catechism.* A deist, he favored religious liberty. But he was against workers' unions—indeed all corporate bodies—as is evidenced by his being for the *Le Chapelier* law. There was only a minuscule workingclass at this time.

To the left of Robespierre were the Hébertists named after Jacques-René Hébert, and the *Enragés* whose leaders, principally Jacques Roux and Jean-François Varlet, represented the *sans culottes* or the workers of Paris, savaged by high food prices, while wealthy speculators enriched themselves. They would extend the revolution by alleviating workers' discontent through deepening the class struggle against the rich by more democracy and mass action.

As for a purely socialist current in the Revolution, there was the Society of the Equals—the first modern secular communist group—founded in 1796 by François-Noël Babeuf and others, who influenced many of France's leading 19th-century socialists, like

Louis Blanc and Louis-Auguste Blanqui. Its May 1796 revolt in Paris was suppressed by Napoleon Bonaparte, Babeuf and thirty others being guillotined and twenty-four being deported.[7]

Not only was Thomas Jefferson the author of the "Declaration of Independence" and third President of the United States, but he was also an outstanding intellectual, one of the principal luminaries of the American Enlightenment. A deist and fighter for religious freedom, he was also an opponent of privilege and slavery (although a racist), favoring a general socioeconomic equality made somewhat possible by the frontier mixture of inexpensive land and sparse population. To maintain a general equality and democracy: For the former, he recommended equal testamentary laws, progressively higher taxation on larger amounts of wealth to prevent the formation of a hereditary wealthy class; and for the latter, in local matters a direct democracy, and in state and federal ones a representative one—to be undergirded by an extensive system of public-school education for an educated and democratic citizenry whose individualism was further protected by the Bill of Rights, in which religious freedom, freedom of speech, assembly, and so forth were vigorously protected. To be sure, he opposed an absolute socioeconomic equality, positing the need for a "natural aristocracy," based on talent and public service, as opposed to an "artificial aristocracy," resting on "wealth and birth," but lacking "virtue or talent."[8]

Benjamin Franklin was yet another advocate of general socioeconomic equality and democracy. A deist, who believed in religious freedom, and determined opponent of slavery (president of the Pennsylvania Society for Promoting Abolition of Slavery), he also advocated the widespread diffusion of property (private property itself being "a creature of society…subject to the calls of that society, whenever its necessities shall require it, even to its last farthing"). Then, too, as an ardent democrat for the time, he favored unrestricted male suffrage, a one-chamber legislature and annual elections for its representatives in Pennsylvania. Finally, he was sympathetic to debtors, viewing poverty as being related to the fact that much of commerce was involved with the making of luxury goods for the wealthier classes, a notion very similar to Veblen's concept of "conspicuous consumption," to be examined later.[9]

Thomas Paine, from an English working-class family, was a noteworthy 18th century revolutionary, participating in both the American and French Revolutions, more active in the first. His *Common Sense*, the key broadside in launching the American Revolution, cogently explained why the colonists would be better off without the yoke of monarchy's oppressive practices, and his *Crisis* pamphlets (sixteen in all) bolstered American resolve for independence.

The socioeconomic and political views of Paine, as enunciated in *The Rights of Man* and *Agrarian Justice*, endeavored to establish a society of general equality, holding that monarchy invariably exploited the masses and that the power of hereditary and privileged rulers ensured their being corrupt. Under the aegis of popular sovereignty, Paine proposed a single governing legislature chosen by a broad electorate in which executive power, if any, was minimal. As for property or wealth, like other radicals, he held that it was conventional, not a natural right, the earth and its resources being the common patrimony of everyone; he would limit its accumulation through inheritance and progressive income taxes to secure its broad diffusion. Democratic government itself would provide for a whole host of services in the name of commonality—public-school education, maternity benefits, unemployment relief, and old-age pensions. Like other radical liberals, Paine was not only against slavery, but also favored deism: "My religion is to do good."[10]

In the early 19th century, utopian socialism's most vigorous expression in the West was in the United States, a frontier society, which despite its tradition of slavery and accompanying racism and bourgeois elitism, also, had strong egalitarian and democratic currents. Both religious (like the Shakers, Oneida Community, and Rappites) and secular (like Robert Owen's New Harmony, Etienne Cabet's Icarians, and Brook Farm) utopias were then in vogue. We only examine the secular utopias, but note that apart from the intellectual narrowness of some of the religious ones, like the Rappites and Shakers, they all invariably stressed the principles of cooperation and general equality.[11]

The secular utopias were associated with three prominent utopian socialists, Owen, Charles Fourier, and Cabet—all flourished in the first half of the 19th century—and Transcendentalism.

But before delving into them, Claude Henri de Rouvroy Saint-Simon, an older contemporary of the three utopians, and the Saint-Simonians, contemporaries of the three, and Transcendentalism, should be mentioned because of their influence on anarchism, Marxism and Veblen. Saint-Simon was a thinker and activist who might be considered a thoroughgoing historical materialist in that he conceptualized history as being propelled forward by economic/technological forces, the social and political institutions being their reflections. He emphasized the importance of production through efficient large-scale economic planning as the key for the good society. His historical conceptions importantly involved a class struggle between the "parasites" (the ruling nobility, other large landowners, government officials, and military) and "producers" (bankers, industrialists—he accepted large private property—scientists and skilled workers). Under a centralized, technocratic and hierarchic setting characterized by extensive labor division, with no democracy, the large industrialists and scientists would provide work for all in an expanding economy fueled by scientific discoveries.

Saint-Simon's disciples, however, led by Barthélemy Prosper Enfantin, Pierre Leroux, and Saint-Armand Bazard, became full-fledged state socialists, recognizing that in the history of civilized humanity there was a continuing class struggle between masters and slaves, patricians and plebeians, nobility and serfs, capitalists and workers; workers now were simply exploited by capitalists in the exchange of labor for wages, resulting in poverty for the former and riches for the latter. Thus, although espousing large industry under a scientific and technical elite open to talent, the Saint-Simonians also demanded a society based on social ownership of the means of production and exchange, rejected the inheritance of property, thus eliminating large-scale inequality, and guaranteed work for all, calling for an "association of workers." As for gender relations, they were based on equality. The Saint-Simonians had much influence among educated Europeans, like the novelist Georges Sand, the composer Franz Liszt, the poet Heinrich Heine, and the great man of letters and writer, Goethe.

The father of British socialism, Owen, born into a Welsh working-class family, was a benevolent capitalist who became interested in establishing utopian communities, his most noteworthy one—basically anarchist—being New Harmony, Indiana which lasted from 1825 to 1827. Its existence might be divided into two phases: In the cooperative half, in which Owen remained sole proprietor, colonists were compensated through a system of labor credits to purchase necessities. On July 4, 1826 (the 50th Anniversary of the American Declaration of Independence), the communist one was inaugurated by Owen's speech condemning private property, organized religion, and traditional marriage. Key elements of this period were gender and wage equality, as well as direct or participatory democracy. But despite the valiant efforts of Owen and others, the experiment failed for the differences among the disparate colonists were simply too irreconcilable to overcome. Owen lost as much as four-fifths of his fortune in the fiasco.[12]

Another notable utopian was the Frenchman Cabet, a lawyer greatly influenced by Babeuf and Owen; he met the latter in his English exile. His well-known utopian novel, *Voyage en Icarie* (*Voyage in Icaria*), pictured a democratic communist society of fifty million inhabitants in which gender equality was emphasized in the context of the nuclear family thoroughly socialized by communal dining halls. In an anarchist vein, a pervasive democracy elected managers and other officials who were also required to work alongside others, necessitating that others aid them in their supervisory duties, thus lessening their administrative power. Education was deemed important inasmuch as it was vital for economic development and to ensure a well-rounded individual. The workday was rather long, seven hours in the winter, six in the summer, and retirement for women was at age fifty, for men at sixty-five.

Cabet and his followers came to America in 1849, purchasing Nauvoo, Illinois from the Mormons. The enterprise soon failed because of internal bickering and the Panic of 1857, a splinter group continuing in Corning, Iowa until 1895.[13]

A most interesting early 19th-century French utopian socialist was Fourier, who promoted a generally egalitarian society, which, however, had some capitalist elements. After a minimum subsistence for everyone, capital, labor, and managerial talent shared the remainder; but since everyone participated in at least two of the three categories and since the rate of capital return diminished with more individual investment, economic differences were not pronounced.

The ideal communities of Fourier, Phalanxes or Phalansteries, comprised sixteen hundred members on approximately five thousand acres of land, agriculture being more important than industry. They were run on the basis of universal suffrage, resting on gender equality, absence of marriage, frequent job rotation to obviate boredom, and a form of wage labor, everyone receiving a basic wage supplemented by additional compensation through meritorious work.

These ideas found an enthusiastic audience in America, especially among the intelligentsia. Fourier's chief American disciple, Robert Brisbane, in *The Social Destiny of Man*, cogently delineated the guiding principles of Fourierism (he excluded free love), influencing many Transcendentalists and Horace Greeley to accept this basically anarchist doctrine. In the 1840s, there were more than forty Phalanxes in America, the chief two being Brook Farm near Boston and the North American Phalanx at Red Bank, New Jersey. Only the first will be examined.[14]

Brook Farm, which thrived from 1841 to 1847, along with New Harmony, was the most celebrated of American utopias. That this is so should not be surprising since it involved the most important American literary and philosophical movement of the 19th century, Transcendentalism, most of whose luminaries either participated in the experiment or encouraged it; among the former were Nathaniel Hawthorne, Charles A. Dana, and Isaac Hecker; among the latter, Ralph Waldo Emerson, Bronson Alcott, Theodore Parker, Margaret Fuller, and Orestes Brownson, along with Greeley.

The chief inspirers of Brook Farm were the indomitable and thoroughly cheerful Transcendentalist George Ripley, a Unitarian minister, and his wife, Sophia. Ripley summarized the *raison d'etre* of this fraternally cooperative experiment in the shibboleth: "A better life, here and now." This endeavor was financed as a joint-stock company whose membership owned stock and performed individual labor, economic return based on the number of hours worked and shares held. The farm became a Fourierist Phalanx midway in its existence with scarcely any changes in its basic outline.

An intense community life, characterized by a high intellectuality—scintillating conversation, the norm—and a contagious spontaneity, associated with the fraternity of equality based on equal wages and frequent job rotation, provided an environment highly stimulating to intellectuality. Emerson described this ambiance thus: "In Brook Farm...each was a master or mistress of his or her actions; happy, hapless, anarchists."

But even paradise had its bad moments as the usual arguments erupted and not everyone was completely enchanted by the various utopian aspects. For instance, Hawthorne, in *Blithedale Romance*, recounted his many difficulties with other members and distaste in performing the obligatory but often irksome manual labor. But in the last chapter, he redeemed himself by opining, "posterity may dig it up and profit by it."

This noble experiment in the art of communal living—basically anarchist—was tragically cut short by two closely occurring disasters, a fire which destroyed what was to be the main building, and a smallpox epidemic.[15]

There is no dispute about the utopian-socialist content of Transcendentalism or that its generally socialist-anarchist stance railed against the various oppressions of its day—war, slavery, and a plutocratically-controlled government.[16] Four individuals best represented this spirit: The two great sages of American civilization: Emerson and his friend, Thoreau, and two other friends of Emerson's, Parker and Wendell Phillips.

Emerson, to be sure, was a complex figure, having both conservative and socialist-anarchist personas. His conservatism, expressed in essays, like "Power" and "Wealth," celebrated the competitive self-made man who commanded respect, since "in a free and just commonwealth, property rushes from the idle and imbecile to the industrious, brave, and persevering"; this undoubtedly reflected the views of his wealthy family, his father being a clergyman, his mother, the daughter of a successful merchant.

But the conservative and elitist Emerson also had radical liberal and utopian socialist-anarchist views. In essays, like "Man the Reformer," "Fourierism and the Socialists," "The Young American," and "Essay on Politics," his individualism favored a general egalitarianism ensconced in a pervasive democratic setting in which the progressive intellectual played a proper role: To serve humanity through an "audacious mental outlook," able to reach the higher reality behind the "fact world," to, perforce, inspire the majority "the uninventive or accepting class," held down by "gravity, custom, and fear," to change society for the better.

Ever the reformer, Emerson opposed slavery, favored democracy ("democracy has its roots in the sacred truth that every man hath in him the divine reason"), and a positive role for government ("set up for the protection and comfort of all good citizens"), which, based on the "spirit of love for the common good," would play a leading role in education, "supply the poor with work," and "mediate want and supply." A democratic government not doing this was a "feudal" one, under the thumb of an "aristocracy of trade." Furthermore, the "state exists to educate the wise man and with the appearance of the wise man the state expires," but "I ask, not at once for no government, but at once a better government."[17] Not surprisingly, he supported Brook Farm: a "noble and generous" experiment, the harbinger of a new socialism, combining "the union of labor and capital in the same individual" through the "scientific analysis of the cooperative principle." This "beneficent socialism," a "friendly omen," had already manifested itself in the various utopian experiments in America and in the "communism of France, Germany, Switzerland." Ultimately, for him, socialism was "founded in love and labor," substituting "harmonious for hostile industry."[18]

A world-renowned figure, influencing such giants as Leo Tolstoy, Mohandas K. Gandhi, and Martin Luther King, Jr., Henry David Thoreau lived his life in Concord, Massachusetts and its neighboring countryside. A philosophical anarchist and friend of Emerson and other Transcendentalists, he critiqued society and delved into the beauty and wonder of nature and human existence.[19]

Walden or Life in the Woods (1854) is the classic American Individualist-Anarchist utopia, not only extolling the virtues of rigorous self-reliance, but condemning an economically, unjust social system, thus rejecting the private utopia of individual wealth existing at the general expense of the community, to echo Lewis Mumford in *The Story of Utopia*. From the summer of 1845 to the summer of 1847, Thoreau largely lived alone on the banks of Walden Pond near Concord, leading an austere life based on his motto of "simplicity, simplicity, simplicity," to allow time for needed self-cultivation. This obviously dictated that the scholar/poet/essayist also be his own worker/farmer, transcending the usual barriers demarcating manual from intellectual labor.

Thoreau himself was acutely aware that this experiment was forced upon him by economic necessity since he was not one of the wealthy in a classist society, which he incessantly castigated in the "Economy" section of *Walden*. Thus, the workers, for him, being particularly exploited by their bosses, existed in a most pitiful state:

> Actually, the laboring man has not leisure for a true integrity day by day; he cannot afford to sustain the manliest relations to men; his labor would be depreciated in the market. He has not time to be anything but a machine.

And:

> Where is this division of labor to end? And what object does it finally serve? I cannot believe that our factory system is the best ode by which men get cloth-

ing. The condition of the operatives is becoming every day much like that of the English; and it cannot be wondered at, since, as far as I have heard or observed, the principal object is, not that mankind be well and honestly clad, but, unquestionably, that the corporations may be enriched.

The results of this, for him, were evident, for instance, in the housing of poor workers:

To know this I should not need to look farther than to the shanties which everywhere border our railroads, that last improvement in civilization; where I see in my daily walks human beings living in sties, and all winter with an open door, for the sake of light, without any visible, often imaginable, wood pile, and the forms of both old and young are permanently contracted by the long habit of shrinking from cold and misery, and the development of all their limbs and faculties is checked.

And, he observed that these obscenities were symptomatic of a society where "the luxury of one class is counterbalanced by the indigence of another. On the one side is the palace, on the other are the almshouse and 'silent poor'." In this over-arching wasteland, not unexpectedly, "the mass of men lived lives of quiet desperation."

In accordance with his disdain for wealth, riches, and power over others, Thoreau deliberately glorified the common, painstakingly describing his labors to provide basic necessities, the setting up of his small hut, of farming, of the sights and sounds of nature, and of his impressions of people.

Thoreau's anarchist position was ultimately based on a high intellectuality that rested on these ethical and socioeconomic foundations: Simplicity, analogous to Veblen's strictures against "conspicuous consumption," and not exploiting others economically: "If I devote myself to other pursuits and contemplations, I must first see, at least, that I do not pursue them sitting upon another man's shoulders. I must get off him first, that he may pursue his contemplations, too."[20]

In *Civil Disobedience*, Thoreau emerged as the enemy of a repressive state dominated by wealth, not only condoning slavery, but also launching war against a helpless Mexico. Because he resolutely opposed these twin evils, he could not in good conscience pay a poll tax, resulting in his arrest and incarceration for a night. (This practice of passive or nonviolent resistance to morally reprehensible positions has influenced many reformers changing the world through moral example.) Thus, for him, good citizenship at times demanded going against the majority, for morality superseded expedience: "I was not born to be forced. I will breathe after my own fashion. Let us see who is the strongest. What force has a multitude?" He thus linked the absolute of conscience to the necessity for ultimate freedom or the absence of government. Although, in the short run, he wished for a better and wiser government, he favored the dictum "that government is best which governs not at all." Thoreau, the critic of wealth, again, was much in evidence. One instance of this: "But the rich man…is always sold to the institutions which make him rich. Absolutely speaking, the more money, the less virtue."[21]

An even angrier Thoreau appeared in *John Brown's Body*, a speech delivered in Boston, in October, 1859, to defend his friend who went to the gallows for the raid at Harpers Ferry to end slavery, the first prominent American to do so at a time when even the *Liberator*, the leading abolitionist journal, called the raid "wild and insane," his speech at once a defense of Brown's character and a condemnation of a society living with slavery. He now passed from passive to active resistance against unjust laws and institutions: "I do not wish to kill or be killed, but I can foresee circumstances in which both these things would be by me unavoidable."[22]

A courageous and brilliant Unitarian minister and close friend of Emerson and Ripley, Parker fought for a society devoid of slavery, bigotry, and steep socioeconomic inequality. Utterly fearless and ever the reformer, he informed conservatives "I am not afraid of men, I can offend them. I care nothing for their hate or their esteem. I am not very careful of my reputation."[23]

An acute observer of the social problem. Parker was obviously aware of the great concentration of wealth in the Boston of his day. (In 1845 Boston, 4 percent of the people owned more than 65 percent of the wealth, much of it in real estate bringing lucrative rent from hated Irish immigrants who also enriched the wealthy Yankee factory owners as cheap labor.[24])

Specifically, Parker stated that:

> Here in America the position of this class [the merchant class—it includes factory owners] is the most powerful and commanding in society. They own most of the property of the nation. The wealthy men of this class; in practical skill, administrative talent, in power to make use of the labour of other men, they surpass all others. Now, wealth is power, and skill and power—both to a degree unknown before. This skill and wealth are more powerful with us than any other people, for there is no privileged caste, priest, or king, or noble, to balance against them.[25]

A mordant critic of plutocracy, Parker posited that the capitalist class "controls the state" whose "effects…appear in our legislation." This class "buys up legislators, consciously or not, and pays them for values received,"[26] and greatly influenced the mindset of the society through control of religious expression (ministers usually being its hirelings, "ecclesiastical blowbags"), newspapers and the educational system.[27]

In contradistinction to his opposing big business, Parker defended the rights of workers, whom he pictured as being economically dependent on their employers, a condition inimical to proper individual independence and freedom. He further lamented the tragic condition in which the advent of machinery still did not reduce the workday, insisting that high unemployment and capitalism were synonymous.

Parker's social vision ultimately called for replacing the present timocracy ("irrational and unchristian"), with an egalitarian democratic and Fourierist near-anarchist socialism as practiced at Brook Farm, an experiment, which he heartily endorsed.[28]

The most noted American radical and socialist of the 19th century was Phillips. Born into a wealthy Boston Yankee family (his father was a mayor of Boston), a graduate of Boston Latin School, Harvard University, and Harvard University Law School, he was a member of the American elite, personally close to Emerson and Parker. He eschewed mere wealth and high political office to become a dedicated reformer, an "agitator," aided and abetted by his wife, Terry Anne Greene, the daughter of a wealthy Boston merchant.

Phillips began his radical odyssey as one of the stalwarts of abolitionism, easily one of its most impressive exponents. A believer in human equality, after African-Americans were emancipated during and after the Civil War, he urged that the government grant them land, education, and full civil liberty. He was also concerned with and supported the full gamut of human emancipation: women's rights, including the vote and equal education, justice for Native-Americans, Irish independence, well-being and rights for the mentally ill, unions and workers' ownership of productive sources, and end of the wage system, pitting workers against one another. In this vein, he steadfastly maintained that as long as capitalism existed, there was wealth for the few and poverty for the many. He joined the fledgling Workers' Party in Massachusetts, ran on its electoral ticket as governor, and almost became the presidential candidate of the National Labor Union in the 1872 elections. Phillips' socialist views were similar to those of anarchism in many respects and in this vein he supported the Paris Commune of 1871.[29]

After the Transcendentalist upsurge, notable examples of American socialist writing were works of Henry George, Edward Bellamy and William Dean Howells. All three intersected with Veblen's life. The first two will be covered later as their works are involved in Veblen's early defense of socialism. The third, a Christian utopian socialist and one of the leading American novelists and literary critics of the late 19th and early 20th centuries, was related to Veblen through his two favorable reviews of *The Theory of the Leisure Class* in *Literature* in April and May, 1899, acquainting middle-class readers with Veblen's work.

Howells was born into a radical middle-class family in Ohio, his father a newspaper editor greatly influenced by Owen. Howells' socialism itself was an amalgam of wide reading, in which More's *Utopia* and Campanella's *City of the Sun* were in evidence, but the two most significant influences of his socialism were Owen and the Christian anarchism of Leo Tolstoy of *War and Peace* and *Anna Karenina* fame. His largely anarchist concerns were much in evidence in such novels as *Annie Kilburn* and *A Hazard of New Fortunes*, and in his two utopian socialist novels, *A Traveller from Altruria* and *Through the Eye of the Needle*. Let's observe his first utopia.

In *A Traveller from Altruria*, when Mr. Aristides Homos, from an imaginary Greek-island utopia, Altruria, in the Aegean Sea, visited the United States, he quickly suffered from culture shock in viewing the horrendous socioeconomic inequality and savage competitive individualism of American life, since Altruria was based on the precepts of early Christianity: "No man owned anything, but every man had the right to use anything that he could use: when he could not use it, his right lapsed." Furthermore, everyone was "equal on duties and rights," "the whole people control affairs, no man works for another and no man pays another" (wage labor had been eliminated), and all shared equally.

In this utopia, the nuclear family and a brief workday were two key norms: Along with Bellamy and others, Howells did not see any inconsistency between the private family and a socialist society, provided that the family was properly socialized. For instance, he at once envisioned a family whose privacy was strictly respected as also being highly sociable, eating in common dining halls where "joking and the friendly give and take of witty encounters" naturally occurred. His workday, along with most utopians, was brief, of three hours, necessary not only for self-cultivation, but also for strengthening community.

In this largely decentralized society, the large cities of the past, with their many problems, were mostly evacuated for the safety and sanity of the small town, where the latest technological innovations were employed, but not at the expense of human happiness. But even so, the "large mills and shops are beautiful as well as useful." And although the work was done cooperatively, if one wished "to work alone," it was permissible. Furthermore, creativity and aesthetic temperament were given free reign. But good taste forbade the manufacture of useless articles for beauty was related to their being "honest and useful." Money and crime, of course, did not exist as equality reigned. Even mental illness had largely disappeared since the psychologically destructive elements of economic uncertainty and competition had been removed.

The government itself was truly democratic since all citizens were so educated that they invariably participated in running it, public officials serving only for a year, reminiscent of classical democratic Athens.

The religion was Christian, but of a form without denominations, permitting religious differences to be "aesthetic and temperamental rather than theologic and essential." The yardstick for religiosity was the conduct of one's life, not religious profession. Death, for this religion, was regarded as "just and natural," with hope for an afterlife predicated on the belief in "faith of the risen Christ." But being a religion based primarily on reason, there was no interest in the supernatural.

Much of the work was an acerbic criticism of American society in which a murderous economic struggle to succeed was contrasted to an idealized earlier America of community and equality. In writing the work in the depression-plagued 1890s, Howells had a character remarking: "I notice that wherever 5,000 men strike in the forenoon, there are 5,000 men to take their place in the afternoon." In this vein, he mercilessly lampooned the social Darwinist mentality of the period, which extolled the virtues of the wealthy and condemned the poor for their supposed vices, and he committed the unpardonable sin of questioning the validity of the great American myth, equality of opportunity.

For Howells, American society was controlled by the wealthy ("the accumulation,") whose monopoly profits allowed them to live in "palaces," while the "poor swarmed in squalid tenements" and endured the indignity of high unemployment. In this backdrop, he foresaw the rise of socialism as inevitable, but not before the plutocracy attempted to disenfranchise the workers and even contemplated armed resistance against them.[30] To be sure, this utopia was in the anarchist tradition.

Why the persistence of utopia? For the German sociologist Karl Mannheim in *Ideology and Utopia*, utopia expressed the inner longings of the exploited masses for equality. Despite a powerful "religion" of inequality so very fashionable among bourgeois ideologues, the utopian egalitarian spirit has persisted. As Herbert Marcuse stated in *Eros and Civilization,* in the chapter titled "Phantasy and Utopia":

> Imagination envisions the reconciliation of the individual with the whole, of desire with realization, of happiness with reason. While this harmony has been removed into utopia by the established reality principle, phantasy insists that it must and can become real, that behind the illusion lies *knowledge*.[31]

Since Veblen's thought is clearly in the anarchist tradition, a short history of anarchism outside the United States is presented. But before doing so, it should be asserted that many of the utopias just mentioned can not be neatly categorized, with some exceptions as Plato's *The Republic*, as either statist socialist or anarchist, especially those insisting on pervasive egalitarian and democratic norms, although capped by some form of leadership, severely circumscribed by the institutional contours just described. It is now known that a general socioeconomic equality without some form of participatory democracy and widespread civil liberties, as in the former Soviet Union and China, inexorably leads to the ossification of Communist bureaucracies and restoration of capitalism. Or, lack of political equality inevitably progresses to socioeconomic inequality.

A definition of anarchism as employed by George Woodcock, a distinguished historian of anarchism, is now given with a brief prologue. To begin, anarchism in the main is in the socialist tradition; as a movement with the "anarchist" name, it appeared only after the demise of the First International in the late 1870s, among the followers of Michael Bakunin and Pierre-Joseph Proudhon to distinguish themselves from Marxists. Whereas Marxists would abolish the state gradually after the arrival of socialism, anarchists would abolish it rapidly. Thus it is that anarchism "is a system of social thought, aiming at fundamental changes in the structure of society and particularly, for this is the common element uniting all its forms, at the replacement of the authoritarian state by some form of governmental co-operation between free individuals." Proudhon was the first to call himself an "anarchist" in his 1840 work *What Is Property?* with the answer of "Property is theft."

A brief background of European anarchism is now in order as it furnished the major thinkers, works, and currents of modern anarchism. At the end of the 18th century, a well-defined anarchist work appeared by an outstanding English intellectual, William Godwin, *Enquiry Concerning Political Justice*. It contrasted a rational and sociable individual with an authoritarian-exploitative society/government and hoped that the good society would proceed through democracy and discussion; once consummated, it would be based on "parishes" or local self-governing units in which decision making would be handled by the community as a whole through direct democracy. To be sure, property was to be held in common, no wage labor existed, and common warehouses would distribute goods freely to everyone.

By the 1860s, the advanced sections of the French proletariat were greatly influenced by Mutualism, which formed the central thrust of the social ideas of Proudhon, the principal founder of modern anarchism and the single most important personage in French socialism. He—Owen was another—was one of the few prominent socialist thinkers to have come from a working-class family. A printer, Proudhon did not view the proletariat as an abstraction, but as a living and vibrant historical reality in which he was immersed. He early became involved in a clandestine workers' organization in Lyon during the early 40s. In 1844, Proudhon met Michael Bakunin and Karl Marx. He formed a lifelong friendship with the former, but soon broke with the latter, presaging the acrimonious debates between anarchists and Marxists in the First International.

Proudhon's Mutualism envisioned a society largely based on the economic activity of self-employed farmers and artisans. Although the existence of property allowed for socioeconomic inequality (intensity and longevity of work would vary according to individual effort), there was, nonetheless, a general equality in that one could not exploit the labor of others. Economic activity between individuals and/or groups would be legitimized through contracts. Formal government was minimal since local autonomous communes would federate only under a common constitution. Two important buttresses of this system were a strong family, the wife clearly subordinate to the husband, and the national bank operating on the national level. The peaceful change from capitalism to anarchism would come thus: With workers and farmers gaining political power, they would impose a levy on the bourgeoisie by having a national bank make low-term or interest-free loans to them, as individuals or associations, to begin their self-managed enterprises.

With the demise of the Paris Commune in 1871, Mutualism in anarchist circles gave way to the Revolutionary Collectivism of Bakunin. From a noble Russian family that was Westernized (his father had a Ph.D. from the University of Padua), he became a revolutionary while a young Hegelian in Berlin and soon afterward met and was influenced by Proudhon. He participated in the February 1848 Revolution in Paris, and in the 1849 Dresden Revolution with Richard Wagner. Bakunin's involvement in the latter adventure led to his forcible return to Russia, and consequent imprisonment and banishment to Siberia, from where he escaped.

Bakunin's ideas differed from Proudhon's in several key respects. Whereas Proudhon emphatically rejected the revolutionary overturn of society in one fell swoop, Bakunin envisaged a cataclysmic revolution from the activities of a small, secret, and highly disciplined organization which would create the necessary conditions through propaganda-by-deed, terrorist acts, such as bombings and assassinations, to be launched against the power structure in order to ignite revolt among the people. For this end, he founded the International Social Democratic Alliance in 1868. In the economic sphere, in contradistinction to Proudhon's stress on small and privately owned property, Bakunin foresaw the importance of agricultural and industrial collectives, probably influenced by the increasing industrialization of Europe which Proudhon had not sufficiently anticipated. Despite the differences noted between them, they agreed as anarchists on the importance and necessity of the local autonomous commune as the bedrock of future anarchist society. The communes obviously would federate.

Despite the setbacks in the 70s, from a theoretical perspective, anarchism progressed when Bakuninist collectivism was refined by a further advance, Anarcho-Communism. Its first consistent modern advocates, Elisée Reclus, his brother

Elie, and a Genevan worker François Dumartheray added the free distribution of goods and elimination of wage labor to Bakunin's views.

The most prominent thinker of Anarcho-Communism, a member of the Russian nobility, was Peter Kropotkin (1842-1921). This sensitive, but forceful, idealist was acutely aware of the social injustice which permitted the nobility to enjoy great privileges at the expense of social misery for the masses. After graduating in 1857 from the exclusive Corps of Pages attached to the Czar, he enrolled in an army regiment spending five years in Siberia. There, in numerous expeditions, he was thoroughly impressed by the fact that their success depended more on voluntaristic cooperation than on authoritarian discipline.

In 1872, Kropotkin made his first trip to Western Europe. While in Switzerland, he noticed a striking difference between anarchists and other socialists: In the formally organized socialist groups, socioeconomic and intellectual differences between leaders of middle-class origin with few exceptions, and followers, usually blue-collar workers (some of whom, however, were skilled), were so marked that a truly egalitarian spirit did not exist between them. In the Swiss Jura federation, however, among Bakuninist anarchists, generally economically independent and educated craftsmen, a spirit of general equality prevailed.

Returning to Russia, Kropotkin joined a revolutionary circle whose aim was to propagate revolutionary socialist ideas among the people. In 1874, he was imprisoned for his role in this activity, but soon afterward escaped and went to London. In 1877, after a brief stay in Paris, he arrived in Geneva, the center of the important anarchist Jura Federation, to write for *L'Avant Garde*, the leading anarchist newspaper of the period, in the course of which he effectively developed his Anarcho-Communism.

Another Anarcho-Communist thinker of note was Jean Grave who flourished in the 1880-1920 period, an editor of *La Révolte* and *Les Temps Nouveaux*, a pioneer in combining art and literature in these journals to anarchist theory and the social struggle, and author of many works, the most known being *La Société Mourante et L'Anarchie (The Dying Society and Anarchy)*.

Another anarchist current, especially noticeable in France, were the Individualists whose leading figure circa 1900 was Albert Libertad. He claimed that he was the son of a high government official. Libertad, who would not have been out of place in the American counterculture of the 1960s, was an emaciated cripple, who wore sandals and had long hair, he supposedly resembled Christ. An excellent orator, unafraid of physical danger, often involved in brawls, he drew to himself a group of followers, soiled and unkempt, who were in a perpetual state of rebellion.

Two of Libertad's better known followers were Victor Kilbatchiche and Ernest Armand. The first, Le Rétif from 1909 to 1919, later became well known as Victor Serge, a disciple of Leon Trotsky, serving in the Soviet government before fleeing with him from the Soviet Union. The second had earlier been a Christian anarchist and succeeded Libertad after his death as editor of *L'Anarchie,* the journal of the Individualists.

The Individualists were greatly influenced by the following thinkers: (1) Johann Kaspar Schmidt, a German teacher better known by his pen name of Max Stirner, who was one of their leading founders. He praised the free individual who realized himself through conflict with others (the individual was part of a union of egoists who were against the general society), even committing crime, including murder. The individual/small group, however, would not have any power over others. Obviously, these contradictory views have a powerful antisocial element. (2) Friedrich Nietzsche, who glorified the egoistic individual in constant revolt, who despised the many, forged his own morality, and lived dangerously. Nietzsche, against socialism, was for a group of superman (an intellectual and military elite à la Plato's *The Republic*) to rule over the masses. (3) Félix Le Dantec, a teacher of the biological sciences at the University of Paris and author of numerous scientific-philosophical works, who extolled the virtues of a stridently antisocial individualism. In a typical work, *La Lutte universelle,* living organisms are in constant struggle to survive.

Both Anarcho-Communists and Individualists were for individual sovereignty as against the primacy of the group; both had a deep fear of and antipathy to any social organization based on hierarchy; and both regarded the state as the very negation of freedom. Also, despite the fact that the Individualists were against Anarcho-Communist collective property, many approved the individual ownership part of Proudhonian Mutualism, allowing for some ideological affinity. But the Individualists saw the individual and the small in-group which one is part of and society as forever in conflict.

These differences reflected antithetical mindsets in such areas as the possibility for revolution and the class struggle. Contrary to Anarcho-Communist general optimism with respect to the revolutionary potential of the people, the Individualists, viewing the future as bleakly as the present, regarded them as apathetic to change; they rejected class struggle and sympathy for proletarian unions for the primacy of the egotistic individual and individual or small in-group action. Thus, for example, whether one was a worker or a bourgeois had no consequence concerning revolution. As for unions, Individualists regarded them as authoritarian and capitalist organizations which promoted a narrow craft mentality tied to parochial economic interests, in which majority rule impinged on individual autonomy. Revolution, therefore, would have to be undertaken by the individual and like-minded comrades. Kilbatchiche has Libertad saying in this respect: "Do not wait for revolution. Those who promise revolution are practical jokers. Make your own revolution. Be free and live in camaraderie."

Anarchist participation in trade unions led to the founding of Anarcho-Syndicalism in the 1880s. A key activist and theoretician of this movement in France was Fernand Pelloutier, one of the founders of the Bourses du Travail (Labor Exchanges Union) in 1892, and its general secretary until his death in 1901. He himself never saw any significant differences between Anarcho-Communism and Anarcho-Syndicalism. In 1902, the Bourses united with the Confédération Générale du Travail (CGT), with the name of the latter designating the new union. It was the GGT that carried forward the doctrine of Anarcho-Syndicalism which technically became Revolutionary Syndicalism in the first decade of the new century, now not relying on Anarcho-Communist intellectuals.

The theory of Anarcho-Syndicalism as propounded by Pelloutier was essentially a mixture of Proudhonian Mutualism, Bakuninist revolutionary élan (he approved of sabotage during strikes and the slogan of "Bad Pay, Bad Work" to intensify the class struggle), and Anarcho-Communist insistence to end wage labor, with the addition of unions forming the key cells of the new society. Unions, for him, embodied a "free association of free producers" of "no laws, no statutes, and no rules which force an individual to submit to any punishment not previously determined." Although aware that authoritarian tendencies might arise within unions, especially in the federal bureaucracy (unions federate nationally), he insisted that recall provisions of elected officers could effectively control this problem. Freeing itself from Anarcho-Communist intellectuals was the essentially similar Revolutionary Syndicalism whose most important thinker was Georges Sorel, a contemporary of Veblen. His *Reflections on Violence,* emphasized the importance of the myth of the general strike (similar to Christian millenarianism) to inspire workers to topple capitalism for socialism, in the course of which they would become the future aristocracy.

On the whole, anarchism, with its closely related Anarcho-Syndicalism/Revolutionary Syndicalism current, has played a not inconsiderable role in the last hundred or so years in such nations as France, Italy, Spain, Russia, and the United States. Anarchism played an important role in French intellectual and artistic spheres and in the trade union movement, was a strong element in Italian labor, developed a powerful mass base in Spain, formed a significant segment of the Russian revolutionary tradition, well-ensconced in the Socialist Revolutionary Party, and had modest success in the United States among pockets of German, Jewish, and Italian immigrants, in addition to being involved in its labor movement, principally in the IWW.

Anarchist influence in the preceding nations was tied to certain socioeconomic and cultural patterns. In France, the persistence of small enterprise, coupled to a powerful revolutionary tradition, inevitably fostered among workers a desire to control industry. In Italy, Spain, and Russia, which had traditional rural societies, characterized by deep class division and endemic social oppression, anarchist revolutionary fervor attracted many workers and peasants. In the United States, the alienation experienced by politicized immigrants and the normal labor violence of a tempestuous frontier nation, which stressed individualism, formed the requisite crucible for anarchist penetration.

Anarchist success in these nations and social settings, however, did not equal that of democratic socialism, including its Marxist component. As industrialization became more widespread, it brought in its train increased labor differentiation which divided the proletariat into various status groups, thus diminishing its solidarity; it promoted hierarchical relations in the normal milieu of the large factory; and it further pacified the proletariat by higher living standards. The rise of representative democracy also aided in deflecting proletarian revolution for its very essence is gradualism. These developments favored democratic socialism, including Marxism, at the expense of anarchism. The former was in mass electoral parties which basically advocated piecemeal reform, whereas the latter was in relatively small and informally organized groups stressing immediate revolution.[32]

Karl Marx was the principal founder of revolutionary communism; he was ably assisted by Frederick Engels. Their theoretical views stressed the importance of the class struggle in the unfolding of history, one which would end when the working class would overthrow the middle class led by capitalists and inaugurate a classless society. Previously the principal class struggles involved slaves versus masters and serfs and freemen versus the nobility. There is a technological component in this class struggle in that as technology expands the productive forces, the possibility for socialism advances. Thus it is that the Industrial Revolution allowed for the creation of a large working class to challenge its capitalist masters.

The present conflict between the workers and capitalists for Marx was basically ensconced in the fact that capitalists exploited workers at work via the extraction of surplus-value, indeed the factor responsible for the making of the capitalist class as distinct from the working class. This process of exploitation was based on the truism that human labor and wealth were intertwined, that the first was needed to create the second. Since, for Marx, every economic relation was also a social one, the encounter between capitalist and worker was not between equals. Thus, there emerged the resultant, of capital extracting from labor a surplus-value constantly added to an increasing formation of capital, which enlarged the socioeconomic gulf between the two principals. In fact, since labor was only a commodity in the value/ethical system of capitalism, the entrepreneur was simply being efficient to continually drive down his labor costs or number of workers, those not needed being thrown into the industrial reserve army (the unemployed), which allowed for an inexpensive pool of available labor. The unemployed themselves were usually pictured in bourgeois society as either being unfit or as parasites if on public relief.

Let us more fully delve into Marx's reasoning on surplus-value. Marx began with the simple commodity, "an object outside us, a thing that by its properties satisfies human wants of some sort or another," and thus had a use-value through "use or consumption." These use-values "constitute the substance of all wealth, whatever may be the social form of that wealth." In a capitalist society commodities were exchanged for the accumulation of more use-values or capital. For Marx, only labor-power created these commodities or use-values. In following classical political economy (from Locke to Smith to Ricardo—especially as refined by the last), Marx saw labor-power as the ultimate source of all value, as creating the existing technological structure. In a capitalist society the accumulation of wealth or capital was expressed in terms of money: "Money...as capital has lost its rigidity and from a tangible thing has become a process." Thus, money for Marx was a "measure of value which is immanent in commodities, labour-time." Or,

> *Like every individual subject within circulation, the worker is the owner of a use value; he exchanges this for money, for the general form of wealth, but only in order to exchange this for commodities, considered as the objects of his immediate consumption, as the means of satisfying his needs.*

The worker's use-value was necessarily consumed, any savings being for the worker's old age, to prevent his becoming a public burden. Thus, although the proletariat's labor-power was used only to furnish its basic needs, for capitalists, workers' use-values were used to create more use-values to expand existing capital.

For Marx, in the circulation of money with respect to commodity production, capitalism had profit at its very heart. Where M = money, C = commodity, and M^1 = money after a commodity is manufactured and sold, M^1 for capitalism to be capitalism must be more than M. For him, this increase over labor-power's "original value" (wage) was called "surplus-value" or exploitation of labor power. Specifically: "This surplus-value is the difference between the value of the product and the value of the elements consumed in the formation of that product, in other words, of the means of production and the labour-power." Jerold Seigel's *Marx's Fate* expressed this cogently: "The value of the surplus labor that arose from the difference between the concrete labor the worker sold and the abstract labor power the capitalist bought Marx called 'surplus-value'."

It may superficially appear that capitalist profit came only when selling products, and not from the surplus labor-time and the use-values of workers, but for Marx, it was first extracted from them in the productive process itself. Related to the concept of surplus-value was Marx's "relative surplus-value" (*"the reduction of necessary labour time relative to the working day, and as the reduction of the necessary labour population relative to the population"*), itself linked to the "development of the workers' productive power," indicating ever-increasing exploitation of the workingclass by capitalists. Ultimately, for Marx: "Capital is dead labour, that vampire-like, only lives by sucking living labour, and lives the more, the more labour it sucks." As for the rate of surplus-value or the profit that capitalists make from the labor-power of workers, there were many variables that govern it, the principal one being the strength of the workingclass vis-à-vis the capitalists.

That Marx and Engels were revolutionaries cannot be denied; they participated in the 1848 Revolution in Germany. Both expected a working-class revolution at this time and even afterward, which of course did not materialize. But certainly by the 1860s, they became reformists also, advocating the formation of working-class parties in nations where democracy, usually of a limited sort, was practiced. Their aim was to achieve piecemeal reform. Thus it was that they foresaw that socialism could be achieved gradually in such nations as Britain and the United States.

Marx's commitment to democracy and civil liberties is second to none. This is best illustrated in *The Civil War in France* (1871). In this detailed blueprint for a future socialist society, emulating the governmental model of the 1871 Paris Commune, Marx assigned to democracy the primary role to ensure orderly social progress as well as to prevent the evils of excessive bureaucracy from deforming socialism. Democracy was the pervasive instrument in choosing representatives: Those elected at the local communes would choose delegates to the district level, who, in turn, elected deputies to a national assembly, still bound by the specific instructions of the voters. The democratic power of the people was also manifested in their being able to recall before the expiration of their terms all judges and representatives. He also applauded these undeniably democratic features of the Commune's government: That its council included workers and that councilors be remunerated at average workers' wages. He then commended the Commune's proposed handling of most governmental functions in local and district communes under the watchful eyes of the people, and the Commune's desire to establish a "national militia" to forestall the formation of a military caste. Marx, then, importantly indicated his approval of linking political democracy to economic democracy when he characterized the Commune's economic formulation as "united co-operative societies" that would "regulate production upon a common plan." As may be readily observed here, Marx was for workers' control of industry. To be sure, Marx was not an anarchist, but his economic and political views were not far from basic anarchist conceptions. Later in this work, we shall observe Lenin's amplifying Marx's democratic ideas in *State and Revolution*.[33]

NOTES

1. Lewis Mumford, *The Myth of the Machine*, Vol. I: *Technics and Human Development*, Vol. II, *The Techniques of Power* (New York: Harcourt, Brace, and World, 1967, 1970), I, 188-211 on the "mega-machine." Robert Morrison MacIver, *The Web of Government* (New York: Macmillan, 1947), pp. 42 ff.

2. My definition of socialism. On the Veblen quotation, see Thorstein Veblen, *Theory of Business Enterprise* (New York: Augustus M. Kelley, 1965), p. 337.

3. On the Judeo-Christian tradition, Buddhism, Pythagoreanism, and so forth, see, for instance, the classic by Martin A. Larson, *The Religion of the Occident or the Origin and Development of the Essene-Christian Faith* (Patterson, NJ: Littlefield, Adams, and Co., 1961), pp. 83-106, 126-176, 195-422. Also, see selected passages of the *Old* and *New Testaments*. Plato's *The Republic* is a key work on the utopianism of the Greco-Roman world. I like *The Republic of Plato*, translated, with an Introduction, by A.D. Lindsay (New York: E.P. Dutton, 1957).

4. On early socialism, see, for instance, George Lichtheim, *The Origins of Socialism* (New York: Frederick A. Praeger, 1969). On utopia, see especially the following: Marie Louise Berneri, *Journey Through Utopia* (Boston, Beacon Press, 1950); Martin Buber, *Paths in Utopia* (Boston: Beacon Press, 1960). On Winstanley, see Lewis H. Berens, *The Digger Movement in the Days of the Commonwealth: As Revealed in the Writings of Gerrard Winstanley, The Digger, Mystic, and Rationalist Communist and Social Reformer* (London: Holland and Merlin Press, 1961). On 18th century French Socialism, see André Lichtenberger, *Le Socialisme au XVIIe siècle* (Paris: Félix Alcan, 1895). Its general thesis is that socialist conceptions were widely discussed.

5. On Locke, see, for instance, Ruth W. Grant, *John Locke's Liberalism* (Chicago: University of Chicago Press, 1987). On the Enlightenment, Liberalism and American and French Revolutions, see Peter Gay, *The Enlightenment: An Interpretation*, 2 vols. (New York: Alfred A. Knopf, 1966, 1969). R.R. Palmer, *The Age of the Democratic Revolution: A Political History of Europe and America, 1760-1800*, Vol. I: *The Challenge* (Princeton: Princeton University Press, 1959), p. 15 on the fact that the term "democrat" was not used before the 1780s in America and France.

6. On Rousseau, see, for instance, Ernst Cassirer, *The Question of Jean-Jacques Rousseau* (New York: Columbia University Press, 1954),;Jean-Jacques Rousseau, *The Social Contract and Discourses*, translated and Introduction G.D.H. Cole (New York: E.P. Dutton, 1950); Lichtheim, *Origins of Socialism*, p. 13 opines that Rousseau's "general will operates only in a society with equal distribution of

property." Therefore, Rousseau is a "precursor of socialism." Istvan Mészáros, *Beyond Capital: Towards a Theory of Transition* (New York: Monthly Review Press, 1995), pp. 708-09 approves of Rousseau's rejection of parliamentary democracy for the direct variety and of his inextricably intertwining equality with liberty.

7. On Diderot, see Carol Blum, *Diderot: The Virtue of a Philosopher* (New York: The Viking Press, 1974); see, Denis Diderot, *Rameau's Nephew and other Works*, Introduction Ralph H. Bowen and translated by Jacques Barzun and Ralph H. Bowen (Garden City, NY: Doubleday Anchor Books, 1956), for some of Diderot's controversial views—his *Supplement to Bougainville's Voyage*, is on the goodness of natural, as opposed to civilized, man. On Robespierre, see R.R. Palmer, *Twelve Who Ruled: The Year of the Terror in the French Revolution* (Princeton, NJ: Princeton University Press, 1941). On Hébert, see Morris Slavin, *The Hébertists to the Guillotine: Anatomy of a "Conspiracy" in Revolutionary France* (Baton Rouge, LA: Louisiana State University Press, 1994). On Roux and the *Enragés*, see Morris Slavin, *The Making of an Insurrection: Parisian Sections and the Gironde* (Cambridge, MA: Harvard University Press, 1986), pp. 125-41. On Babeuf and Buonarroti, see J. L. Talmon, *The Origins of Totalitarianism* (London: Secker and Warburg, 1952), pp. 167-247.

8. On Jefferson, see Fawn M. Brodie, *Thomas Jefferson: An Intimate Biography* (New York: Bantam Books, 1975); and Noble E. Cunningham, Jr., *In Pursuit of Reason: The Life of Thomas Jefferson* (Baton Rouge, LA: Louisiana State University Press, 1987). Charles M. Wiltse, *The Jefferson Tradition in American Democracy* (New York: Hill and Wang, 1960), is a good account of the various aspects of Jefferson's economic, social, and political views; Vernon L. Parrington, *Main Currents in American Thought*, Vol. I: *The Colonial Mind: 1620-1800* (New York: Harvest Books, 1954), pp. 347-62 on Jefferson.

9. For the quotation, see the excellent biography of Franklin by Carl Van Doren (New York: Viking Press, 1938), p. 774.

10. On Paine, see Eric Foner, *Tom Paine and Revolutionary America* (New York: Oxford University Press, 1976); see Paine's *The Rights of Man*, which is published with Burke's *Reflections on the Revolution in France* (in paperback) (Garden City, N.Y.: Dolphin Books, 1961); Parrington, *Colonial Mind*, pp. 333-47, on Paine is excellent.

11. On American utopias, see Alice Felt Tyler, *Freedom's Ferment: Phases of American Social History from the Colonial Period to the Outbreak of the Civil War* (New York: Harper Torchbooks, 1962); Donald Drew Egbert and Stow Persons, eds., *Socialism and American Life*, 2 vols. (Princeton: Princeton University Press, 1952); Vernon Louis Parrington, *American Dreams: A Study of American Utopias* (New York: Russell and Russell, 1964); Charles Nordhoff, *The Communistic Societies of the United States* (New York: Schocken Books, 1970), this work was first published in 1875; Mark Holloway, *Heavens on Earth: Utopian Communities in America 1680-1880* (New York: Dover, 1966). On the various links between socialism and Christianity, see Karl Kautsky, *Foundations of Christianity: A Study in Christian Origins* (New York: Russell and Russell, 1953); and Egbert and Persons, *Socialism and American Life*, I, 99-123.

12. On Saint-Simon and the Saint-Simonians, see Frank E. Manuel, *The New World of Saint-Simon* (Cambridge, MA: Harvard University Press, 1956); and Frank E. Manuel, *The Prophets of Paris*

(Cambridge, MA: Harvard University Press, 1962), pp. 103-48 on Saint-Simon, pp. 149-93 on Saint-Simonians. On Owen and New Harmony, see William E. Wilson, *The Angel and the Serpent: The Story of New Harmony* (Bloomington, IN: Indiana University Press, 1964). On Owen's life, see G.D.H. Cole, *The Life of Robert Owen* (London: Macmillan, 1930).

13. On Cabet's life, *Voyage en Icarie*, and settlements in America, see Jules Prudhommeaux, *Icarie et son fondateur* (Philadelphia: Porcupine Press, 1972). First published in 1907.

14. On Fourier's life and ideas, see Nicholas Valentine Riasnovsky, *The Teaching of Charles Fourier* (Berkeley: University of California Press, 1969). On Fourierism in America, see Egbert and Persons, *Socialism and American Life*, I, 173-89.

15. On Brook Farm, see Edith Roelker Curtis, *A Season in Utopia: The Story of Brook Farm* (New York: Thomas Nelson, 1961); Henry W. Sams, *Autobiography of Brook Farm* (Englewood Cliffs, NJ: Prentice-Hall, 1958). On Ripley, see O.B. Frothingham, *George Ripley* (Boston: Houghton Mifflin, 1882). On Emerson's quote, see Sams, *Autobiography*, p. 225. On Hawthorne's quotation, see his *Blithedale Romance*, p. 584 in *The Complete Novels and Selected Tales of Nathaniel Hawthorne*, edited and Introduction by Norman H. Peterson (New York: Modern Library, 1937).

16. On Transcendentalism, see O.B. Frothingham, *Transcendentalism in New England: A History* (New York: 1876, reprinted 1972); and, Vernon L. Parrington, *Main Currents in American Thought*, Vol. II: *The Romantic Revolution in America* (New York: Harvest Books, 1954), Part Three, "The Transcendental Mind," pp. 371-426.

17. On Emerson, see Van Wyck Brooks, *The Life of Emerson* (New York: The Literary Guild, 1932). The quotations have been culled from various works of Emerson. See, for instance, *The Works of Ralph Waldo Emerson*, 4 vols. in 1 (New York: Tudor Publishing Co., n.d.), and Mark Van Doren, edited and Introduction, *The Portable Emerson* (New York: The Viking Press, 1946).

18. Emerson's Review of Albert Brisbane's *The Social Destiny of Man*, "Fourierism and the Socialists," *Dial*, July 1842. Unsigned article. In addition, see Emerson's "Man the Reformer," and "The Young American," on his political views.

19. On Thoreau, see Joseph Wood Krutch, *Henry David Thoreau* (New York: W. Sloane Associates, 1948); Henry S. Canby, *Thoreau* (Boston: Houghton-Mifflin, 1939).

20. Carl Bode, edited and Introduction, *The Portable Thoreau* (New York: Viking Press, 1964), pp. 258-334 on the various quotes, all under the "Economy" section.

21. *Ibid.*, pp. 109-37 on "Civil Obedience."

22. For a "Plea for Captain John Brown," a speech delivered by Thoreau to the citizens of Concord on October 30, 1859, see H.S. Salt, ed., *Anti-Slavery and Reform Papers by Henry David Thoreau* (London: Swan and Sonnenschein, 1890), pp. 51-81.

23. Daniel Aaron, *Men of Good Hope: A Story of American Progressives* (New York: Galaxy Books, 1961), pp. 21-51 on Parker.

24. For the respective figures, see Alan Brinkley *et. al*, *American History: A Survey*, 2 vols., (New York: McGraw-Hill, 1991), I, 321.

25. Henry Steele Commager, edited and Introduction, *Theodore Parker: An Anthology* (Boston: Beacon Press, 1960), p. 143.

26. Commager, *Parker: Anthology*, pp. 143-47; Aaron, *Men of Good Hope*, p. 42.

27. Aaron, *Men of Good Hope*, p. 42; Commager, *Parker: Anthology*, p. 147.

28. Henry Steele Commager, *Theodore Parker* (Boston: Beacon Press, 1947), pp. 183-85.

29. On Phillips, see, Irving H. Bartlett, *Wendell Phillips: Brahmin Radical* (Boston: Beacon Press, 1961); and Richard Hofstadter, *The American Political Tradition and the Men Who Made It* (New York: Vintage Books,1948), pp. 137-63.

30. On William Dean Howells, see Kenneth S. Lynn *William Dean Howells: An American Life* (New York: Harcourt, Brace, Jovanovich, 1971); William Dean Howells, *The Altrurian Romances in A Selected Edition of William Dean Howells* (Bloomington, IN: Indiana University Press, 1968), XX, for *Through the Eye of the Needle* (1907); *A Traveller from Altruria*, pp. 36 and 145-73 (1894); and the brief *Letters of an Altrurian Traveller*.

31. On the persistence of utopian thought, see Karl Mannheim, *Ideology and Utopia: An Introduction to the Sociology of Knowledge*, translated from German by Louis Wirth and Edward Shils (New York: Harvest Book, 1963). Herbert Marcuse, *Eros and Civilization: A Philosophical Enquiry into Freud* (New York: Vintage Books, n.d.), p. 130.

32. On anarchism in general, see George Woodcock, *Anarchism: A History of Libertarian Ideas and Movements* (Cleveland, OH: Meridian Books, 1962) and James Joll, *The Anarchists* (New York: Universal Library, 1966). On Proudhon, see Edward Hyams, *Pierre-Joseph Proudhon: His Revolutionary Mind, Life, and Works* (New York: Taplinger Publishing Co., 1979). On Bakunin, see Arthur P. Mendel, *Michael Bakunin* (New York; Praeger, 1981). On Kropotkin, Martin A. Miller, *Kropotkin* (Chicago: Chicago University Press, 1976). On Grave, Louis Patsouras, *Jean Grave and the Anarchist Tradition in France* (Middletown, NJ: Caslon, 1995). On French anarchism, see Jean Maitron, *Histoire du mouvement anarchiste en France, 1880-1914* (Paris; Société Universitaire, 1951).

33. On Marx's life and thought, see Francis Wheen, *Karl Marx: A Life* (New York: W.W. Norton, 2000). Jerrold Seigel, *Marx's Fate: The Shaping of a Life* (Princeton: Princeton University Press. 1978). Marx's two most notable works are: *Capital*, I, *A Critique of Political Economy* (New York: Modern Library, n.d.); *Grundrisse: An Introduction to the Critique of Political Economy*, translated and Foreword by Martin Nicolaus (New York: Vintage Books, 1973). On Marx and democracy, see his *The Civil War in France* (New York: International Publishers, 1933). For an excellent one-volume account of Marxism, see George Lichtheim, *Marxism: An Historical and Critical Study* (New York: Frederick A. Praeger, 1962). On Engels, see David McLellan, *Friedrich Engels* (New York: Penguin Books, 1978).

III   Early Writings on Socialism

TWO AMERICAN SOCIALIST CLASSICS—Henry George's *Progress and Poverty* (1879) and Edward Bellamy's *Looking Backward, 2000-1887* (1888)—deeply influenced Veblen: He defended the first at Carleton and after reading the second in 1891, akin to a revelatory experience, he returned to academia.

George, born into a relatively poor Philadelphia family, with only a scant formal education, became a newspaper reporter and democratic socialist. In *Progress and Poverty,* he formulated a novel solution to the social problem, the single tax to be levied on land: It allowed for individual ownership of land directly used, which could not be sold or leased for profit (reimbursement by the state for improvements was permitted), but rent would be taxed at a hundred-percent rate. The resultant, for him, would lead to higher wages, allowing workers to gain control of large industries that "would assume the cooperative form, since the more equal diffusion of wealth would unite capitalist and laborer in the same person"—as in Emerson's model. He would gradually also socialize large utilities, like railroads and gas works. "The ideal of socialism is grand and noble; and it is, I am convinced, possible of realization; but such a state of society cannot be manufactured—it must grow." Government itself would ultimately become the agency to administer broad economic development under democratic auspices.[1]

At first glance, the single tax on land to achieve socialism seemed too simplistic. After all, with the rise of industry, most of the productive wealth would be concentrated in industry and commerce, but if the principle were extended to tax their profits at the same rate as those on rent, then, socialism could be rapidly achieved, as capital would be socialized through taxation.

When Veblen defended *Progress and Poverty*, he rejected the conventional economic wisdom of his economics text at Carleton, *Elements of Political Economy* by Francis Weyland, a Baptist minister from the East (it was revised by another clergyman, A.L. Chapin), which, in following the guidelines of the classical economists, regarded private property as sacred, labor unions and strikes as anathemas, and socialism as a negation of God and natural rights.[2]

Bellamy, a shy and reclusive son of a New England Protestant minister, was a graduate of Union College and lawyer, but left a "compromising" profession to become a Christian socialist who never attended church, constantly obsessed with the social problem.[3] The influence of his *Looking Backward* might be measured thus: Both Mark Twain and Howells praised it and in 1935, Dewey and Charles Beard hailed it as the most influential book published in America since 1885. Its popularity was fundamental in the founding of Nationalist Clubs in twenty-seven states by 1890, with six thousand, mostly middle-class, members and at least a million sympathizers whose clear and simple objective was to establish a socialist society as envisaged in the novel.[4]

Looking Backward espoused a state socialism that pictured society as one great trust, the state being the sole owner and employer of production, planning to the smallest detail in a sophisticated scientific and technological setting, but there were many traditional features to satisfy social conservatives. For instance, it upheld the nuclear family, with a strict moralistic stance on sexual intimacy, only in marriage, and demanded that able-bodied workers labor, failure to do so inviting incarceration, with solitary confinement on a diet of bread and water.

In common with most other utopias, it focused on the organization of work, undergirded by universal education to age twenty-one. The first stage of a person's work life, from age twenty-one to twenty-four, was in the ranks of a work army, performing the "dirty work" of society, its aim being to inculcate such less-than-utopian attitudes as "obedience" and "subordination"—apparently, work at this stage should not be pleasurable or creative. After this trial period, there was intense competition for the various jobs, but no wage system existed, everyone sharing equally in consumption, the exception being writers receiving royalties from their works.

The industrial machine itself was guided by a large and complex bureaucracy led by a general-in-chief or president, while its bottom was occupied by third-grade workers. Promotion was obviously in the hands of the higher bureaucrats who closely evaluated subordinates.

One might well ask what motivation existed in this egalitarian society to encourage work, itself regarded as a form of drudgery? Apart from the element of social solidarity, of laboring for the good of everyone, there was a system of personal rewards, of promotion and honors, like the "red ribbon." There was, thus, a competitive work model in which the psychic satisfaction of social approval was dominant in controlling human behavior and performance.

In the political arena, democracy was somewhat ignored as the higher positions in the bureaucracy were only elected by the retirees. (Wisely, Bellamy was aware that top positions could not be filled by the "better" people, because of a surplus of them, thus the resort to the political process through the ballot.) Political parties themselves did not exist, for, since there was pervasive socioeconomic equality, political differences would be minimal.

From a larger perspective, this society was basically humane, based on the belief "that human nature in its essential qualities is good, not bad, that men by their natural inclinations and structures are generous...images of God indeed." Thus, the needs of the sick and infirm were generously supported since they shared equally with others in consumption.

Despite the factory discipline and attendant hierarchy, this society allowed for the changing of occupations and repeated examinations for entry into any particular position. As for the workday, it was flexible, more difficult work requiring less-than-normal hours; the number of workday hours was not given, but probably no longer than eight, for Bellamy was certainly aware of labor's battle cry for an eight-hour day in the last quarter of the 19th century. Retirement at full pay was at age forty-five and half-pay at thirty-three. There was, thus, ample opportunity to have necessary time to cultivate creativity and sense of beauty. Furthermore, since production was in conformity with personal tastes and habits, individuality was respected in these areas. Too, a vigorous free press acted as a watchdog for any irregularities. But there was a form of sexism in that women, because of their supposedly more fragile nature, had their own industrial army, but their wages equaled men's.

Veblen himself would ultimately approve of a planned general communism without formal political parties, but would not have sanctioned women having their own industrial army, a form of sexism, and he rejected the rigidly hierarchical technocratic structure for one of constant economic fluidity, in which macro- and micro-economics were interwoven through the device of constant interchange between local workers' councils and regional/national coordinating economic centers—more on this topic later.

Bellamy's last novel, *Equality*, however, was close to anarchism as it was based on a pervasive democracy on economic matters: In addition to voting for elective bodies, the initiative, referendum, and recall were employed—"the entire nation is...almost like one parliament if needful" and "we vote a hundred times perhaps a year."[5]

The works of three British socialists who flourished from the mid-to-late 19th century, John Stuart Mill, William Morris, and John Ruskin, also strongly influenced Veblen. Mill, perhaps one of the outstanding economics and sociopolitical theorists of the period, espoused a socialism in the Fourierist/Transcendentalist vein, fought for women's rights, and endorsed the Paris Commune of 1871. Morris, a craftsmen and novelist (his *News from Nowhere* is a classic of anarchism), collaborated for a time with Frederick Engels. Ruskin, an art critic and social reformer, proposed state aid for workers and government-owned factories and socialist cooperatives to exist alongside capitalist enterprises.

At times, Veblen disagreed with Morris and Ruskin, who wished to return to the making of handmade goods to restore dignity and honor to work, regarding this as antiquated as their products were invariably more expensive than those of the machine variety. Veblen unflinchingly favored mass consumption through an ever more sophisticated technology to both expand material abundance and knowledge of the cosmos.[6]

Before delving into Veblen's early works on socialism, why did Veblen, from a relatively affluent immigrant family, who then scaled the heights of academia, become a socialist? Some tentative answers: His rapid upward social mobility reinforced his outsider immigrant awareness, undoubtedly heightened by his encounter in academia with the Yankee upper-class academic elite, the contrast and attendant tensions between his life situation and theirs being more than obvious. To be sure, Veblen's severe psychological problems (authoritarian father/overprotective mother syndrome and consequent unresolved Oedipus complex—recall his seven-year psychosomatic illness while in academic exile) might also have exacerbated his alienation and subsequent intellectual rebellion.[7] Furthermore, farmer discontent, Populism, and socialism were not peripheral phenomena in America during Veblen's lifetime. Radical liberalism and socialism, then and now, occupy a strong place in the American intellectual and social traditions.

A brief background to situate Veblen's early articles on socialism: Veblen was well aware of writing them in the early period of mass socialism, when socialism entered the political stream in force during the last few decades of the 19th century, more than a century after the Industrial Revolution began in England, but soon after other industrializations, like those of the United States, Germany, and France, which engendered a large workingclass. The articles appeared about a generation after the founding of the First International (1864-76), primarily by Marxists and anarchists, and during the tenure of the Second International (1889-1914), dominated by Marxists whose revolutionary rhetoric existed alongside the politics of reformist democratic socialism. He himself taught a course, as early as 1892, entitled "Socialism," at the University of Chicago, probably the first in American academic circles, if not the world. At this time, he did not admit to being a socialist, fearing to lose his university position for being a "Red."[8]

From 1891 to 1898, Veblen wrote almost twenty articles and reviews on socialism, a majority appearing in the prestigious *Journal of Political Economy* (funded by the University of Chicago), for which he did much of the editing, without, however, receiving due recognition. A representative cross section of these early works follows.[9] As early as 1891, in a stimulating essay entitled "Some Neglected Points in the Theory of Socialism," Veblen defended socialism from the barbs of the conservative social Darwinist Herbert Spencer's *From Freedom to Bondage*. He rejected Spencer's position that capitalism was based on "voluntary cooperation," while socialism on "compulsory cooperation" or "subjection of man to his fellow-man," arguing that democracy was so well ensconced among the "English-speaking people" that political decisionmaking would not be impaired under socialist arrangements. He, then, proposed a rather extensive socialization of the means of production: Not only for a public need necessitating the mildest form of socialism, or its municipal variety, encompassing "elementary education, street-lighting, water supply. etc.," but also one involving the main theaters of economic activity in a national setting. In the latter vein, he advocated the "supervision of natural monopolies," or "great industries," ostensibly those "of a semi-public nature," because the "modern development of industry and of the industrial organization makes it increasingly necessary," entailing nothing less than the nationalization of most industry and banks. Furthermore he saw that socialism would reduce waste and attacked the natural rights theory of property: The former element affirmed that luxuries produced for the wealthy were a great drain on labor and resources, associating the social turmoil of the period to this, itself involved with capitalist control of large industry: "The injustice, the inequality of the existing system," one of "natural monopolies," resulted in a "more or less widely prevalent discontent" related with socialism. He justified these observations by rejecting a natural-rights defense of property for one regarding it as conventional, neither eternal nor beyond human control. Finally, in the spirit of Rousseau and Marx, he proposed that a society of equality be established, "perhaps nobler and socially more serviceable" than the present one.[10]

Veblen again upheld socialism in reviewing Thomas Kirkup's *A History of Socialism*, whose author was pictured as a "sympathetic critic and conservative advocate of socialism." Veblen's mastery of socialist theory was evident here, as he involved himself in its various controversies, including the relative importance of its leading thinkers and activists. For instance, he agreed with Kirkup that Owen and Saint-Simon were not very important in the formation of modern socialism, but Michael Harrington, for instance, argued in *Socialism Past and Future* that the two and Fourier—utopian socialists—should not be neglected. He, then, commented on Kirkup's considering Marx as the most important thinker of socialism, while others assigned that role to Karl Johann Rodbertus, a German economist who flourished in the mid-19th century. Veblen did not delve into all of the intricacies concerning this problem, but agreed with Kirkup that Rodbertus' socialism was cast in a rigid Prussian monarchic mold. (Today, Rodbertus is recognized as a minor socialist thinker.)

In the course of reviewing the article, Veblen further defined his socialism by basically concurring with Kirkup's definition of it as "simply a movement for uniting labor and capital…through the principle of association," specifically workers' "participation in the ownership and control of land and capital." But he faulted Kirkup for solely relying on the "cooperative movement" to bring socialism about, although agreeing with him that socialism's further growth was predicated on the expansion of democracy and continued industrial development.[11] (Veblen so highly regarded this work that he used it as a textbook in his course on socialism.)

In a review of Karl Kautsky's (he was the leading Marxist thinker of the Second Socialist International), *Der Parlementarismus*, Veblen examined a problem causing great controversy among socialists: Should socialism be based on direct or representative democracy? He well delineated Kautsky's favoring representative democracy on the basis of modern society's complexity, but did not refer to Marx's solution to this vexing problem, one very near the anarchist position, in *The Civil War in France*, to have delegates chosen by the electorate that were bound by their specific instructions. As between these two general conceptions, under the rubrics of "industrial republic," for representative democracy, and "industrial democracy," for direct or participatory democracy, he favored, in this instance, the first, although he later reversed this stance.[12]

In a review of Professor Robert Flint's *Socialism*, Veblen again indicated his preference for socialism in rejecting Flint's definition of it as authoritarian, as limiting the "legitimate liberties of individuals to the will or interests of the community." He was also puzzled by Flint's assertion that: "What is called Christian Socialism will always be found to be either unchristian in so far as it is socialistic, or unsocialistic in so far as it is truly and fully Christian." His general view of the work was negative, regarding it as antiquated.[13]

The basis for forming a socialist consciousness was also of interest to Veblen. In a review of Richard Calwer's *Einfuhrung in den Socialismus* (*Introduction to Socialisms*), he agreed with the author that the decisive element in the rise of socialism was the glaring socioeconomic inequality between proletariat and bourgeoisie, employing the term "invidious comparison" to characterize this, and he approvingly quoted from Calwer that:

> You may feed the laborer well, you may clothe him decently, you may provide him with modest dwelling, in short, you may keep him as a well-to-do man keeps his domestic animals—still the laborer will not be beguiled into overlooking the fact that his place in life is determined by accidents and circumstances which do not permit him to lead the life of a man.[14]

He also endorsed Calwer's contention that military preparation and war had a deleterious economic consequence on "industrial evolution." Although this might not always be the case, as in German and Japanese industrial development in the late 19th century attested to, it certainly proved to be true in the industrial renaissance of these two nations, with the corresponding relative decline of the United States, after World War II.[15]

In an extensive review, basically a synopsis of Enrico Ferri's (he was a well-known Italian criminologist) *Socialisme et Science Positive*, Veblen agreed with the author's views that Darwinian biology complemented Marxian dialectics and class struggle in the social sciences thus: (1) That "equality of opportunity" did not hinder, but, indeed, further advanced Darwinian "natural selection." (2) That the struggle for existence was primarily conducted among "groups and institutions," not individuals.[16]

Notes

1. On Henry George, see Charles Albro Barker, *Henry George* (New York: Oxford University Press, 1955); and Rhoda Hellman, *Henry George Reconsidered* (New York: Carleton Press, 1987). On Veblen's defense of George, see Dorfman, *Veblen*, p. 32. Henry George, *Progress and Poverty: An Inquiry into the Cause of Industrial Depression and of Increase of Want with Increase of Wealth, The Remedy* (New York: Robert Schalkenbach Foundation 1949), pp. 321, 405, 468, 456-57.

2. Dorfman, *Veblen*, pp. 22-26.

3. *Ibid.*, p. 68. On Bellamy's life and work, see, for instance, Sylvia Bowman, *The Year 2000: A Critical Biography of Edward Bellamy* (New York: Bookman Associates, 1958).

4. *Ibid.*, pp. 115 ff.

5. Edward Bellamy, *Looking Backward: 2000-1887*, Introduction Heywood Broun (Boston: Houghton-Mifflin, 1917), pp. ff. 287-88, 258. Edward Bellamy, *Equality* (Upper Saddle River, NJ: The Gregg Press, 1968), pp. 274-75.

6. Dorfman, *Veblen*, pp. 35, 70, and 119. Thorstein Veblen, *The Theory of the Leisure Class: An Economic Study of Institutions*, Introduction C. Wright Mills (New York: Mentor Book, 1953), pp. 159-60. First published in 1899.

7. On ethnic and religious tensions in America, see Oscar Handlin, *Race and Nationality in American Life* (Boston: Little, Brown, and Co., 1957). Joel Kovel, *White Racism: A Psychohistory* (New York: Vintage Books, 1970), pp. 177-289, for instance. Dorfman, *Veblen*, pp. 12-13, 43. On interaction between psychology and general environment in the making of a revolutionary, see E. Victor Wolfenstein, *The Revolutionary Personality: Lenin, Trotsky, Gandhi* (Princeton, NJ: Princeton University Press, 1971), pp. 13-97. Herbert Marcuse, *Eros and Civilization: A Philosophical Inquiry into Freud* (New York: Vintage Books, 1955), the eleven chapters.

8. Dorfman, *Veblen*, p. 96.

9. *Ibid.*, pp. 90-96.

10. Thorstein Veblen, *The Place of Science in Modern Civilization and Other Essays* (New York: Russell and Russell, 1961), pp. 387-408. Quotations unless otherwise indicated are from this article. This article was first published in 1891.

11. Thorstein Veblen, Review of Thomas Kirkup's *A History of Socialism*, *Journal of Political Economy*, March, 1893, pp. 300-02.

12. Thorstein Veblen, Review of Karl Kautsky's *Der Parlemantarisms and die Volksge setzgebung und die Socialdemokratie*, *Journal of Political Economy*, March, 1894, pp. 312-14; Marx, *The Civil War in France*, pp. 40-41ff.

13. Thorstein Veblen, Review of Robert Flint's *Socialism*, *Journal of Political Economy*, March, 1895, pp. 247-52.

14. Thorstein Veblen, Review of Richard Calwer's *Einfuhrung in den Socialismus*, *Journal of Political Economy*, March, 1897, p. 271.

15. *Ibid.*, p. 272.

16. Thorstein Veblen, Review of Enrico Ferri's *Socialisme et Science Positive*, *Journal of Political Economy*, December, 1896, pp. 98-103.

IV   THE AMERICAN PLUTOCRACY ANd THE THEORY of THE LEISURE CLASS

THE RobbER BARONS

FROM ITS VERY BEGINNING THE AMERICAN EXPERIENCE has been marked by socioeconomic inequality; this is not surprising for America was an appendage of a European world becoming increasingly capitalistic during the Commercial Revolution. Thus, despite the prevalence of the family farm in the North, with its middle-class republican spirit, the fortunes of American Civilization were always firmly led by a capitalist elite enriching itself from labor, natural resources, and technology. Indeed, as a former colonial outpost of an imperialist Western European capitalism, the United States was intertwined with slavery and its train of alienating socioeconomic relations, furthering inequality.

From its very founding, the American government was dominated by local, state, and national business elites that used it to enrich themselves. Alexander Hamilton's economic views, many in *Report on Manufactures* (1791), brilliantly outlined the future path of an American capitalism which favored the increase of socioeconomic inequality: They essentially consisted of a partnership between government and business to establish a National Bank in 1790, a protective tariff to aid industry, immigration to provide for inexpensive labor, a large national debt to establish a creditor class, and increasing labor division in industry—overwhelming Jeffersonian democratic republicanism within a century.

The immediate task now is to highlight the major developments leading to the rise of the first large group of American billionaires in today's terms, the "robber barons," in the late 19th and early 20th centuries under the reign of industrial capitalism. The corporation as an accumulator of capital was decisive here, beginning in earnest in the 1830s, in which capitalists simply paid state governments a fee to incorporate, which included limited liability; before this time state legislatures would pass specific acts for incorporation. At first, because of the lack of capital to finance costly transportation projects, like canals, early railroads, and turnpikes, state governments and private capitalists were often their co-owners.

But even before the rise of the robber barons, there were wealthy Americans that would be multimillionaires today. George Washington, reputedly the wealthiest person of his time, representing the top of the Southern slavocracy, was one. In the North, the commercial and industrial elites of New England, New York and Pennsylvania produced some multimillionaires. In 1831, Stephen Girard, a Philadelphia banker, left an eight-million-dollar estate, and in 1848, John Jacob Astor in New York City one of twenty-five million dollars, worth more than a billion dollars today.

To be sure, the Civil War was the launching pad for the rise of the great American fortunes as Northern capitalists consolidated their position with lucrative government contracts and favorable legislation. The 1863 Bank Act permitted bankers to purchase government bonds at six percent interest, and then to lend them for up to ninety percent interest of their value to the public at high interest rates. The 1864 Morrill Tariff raised tariffs to forty-seven percent *ad valorem* on average; the 1897 Dingley Tariff, the highest ever, at fifty-seven percent to protect industry. To be sure, large capital also benefited from generous immigration policies to provide for inexpensive labor and government subsidies for internal improvements favoring the North, including 280,000 square miles in giveaways of state and federal lands from 1850 to 1872 to railroad speculators.

Some of the leading robber barons were John D. Rockefeller in oil; J.P. Morgan in railroading and banking; Cornelius Vanderbilt in railroading; Jim Fisk in railroading; Jay Gould in stock manipulation pillaging companies; and Andrew Carnegie in steel. They were the big winners of the Gilded Age, basically the last quarter of the 19th century, named after the title of the work by Mark Twain and Charles Dudley Warner, lampooning the wealthy's frenetic pursuit of wealth and conspicuous consumption.

Some highlights of the business careers of Vanderbilt, Rockefeller, and Carnegie: Vanderbilt, who made the first great railroad fortune, came from a business family, his father transporting people and freight from Staten Island to New York City. A rugged and illiterate youth, his great passion was to make money. He followed in his father's footsteps in the steamboat business there, drove out competitors, achieved monopoly, and raised rates. Later, he controlled the New York Central Railroad. His contempt for the public was legendary: "Can't I do what I want with my own?" and "What do I care about the law? Hain't I got the power?" On his death in 1877, he left an estate of 105 million dollars, today easily worth more than ten billion dollars.

Rockefeller, a pious Baptist from a lower-middle-class family, was also possessed by the desire for wealth; one of his classmates at Central High School in Cleveland, Marcus A. Hanna, a well-known capitalist and politician who groomed William McKinley for President, exclaimed that "John D., sane in every way, but one—he was money-mad." Rockefeller, as other religious capitalists, sincerely believed that God made him rich. Of course, he aided God in this enterprise by being utterly ruthless in his quest for wealth: He employed industrial espionage, forced his salespeople to meet their quotas or be discharged, coerced railroads to grant him rebates for transporting his huge volume of oil—this included "drawbacks" to pay him part of what his oil competitors paid to ship their goods—and underpriced his competitors, either forced to join his team or go bankrupt. For further savings, he vertically integrated his business, making its own barrels, pipelines, and ship tankers. By 1880, his Standard Oil Co. of Ohio refined ninety percent of the nation's oil. In 1882, Rockefeller established the Standard Oil Trust, dissolved by the U.S. Supreme Court in 1911, but he retained much of the stock in the thirty or so newly formed companies. He retired in 1911, worth 900 million dollars, the equivalent today of approximately 212 billion dollars. In fairness to Rockefeller, he was a generous philanthropist, establishing the Rockefeller Foundation, founding the University of Chicago, Spelman College in Atlanta, a school for black women; he also gave away about twenty thousand dimes.

Carnegie, from a working-class immigrant Scot family, made his early sizeable money by using his position as a superintendent of the Pennsylvania Railroad. Without any investment on Carnegie's part, T.T. Woodruff granted him an eighth of his sleeping-car company and the Keystone Bridge Company gave him part ownership, both out of gratitude for promoting their businesses—is this extortion or an amicable business arrangement or both?

With this base of capital, Carnegie entered the steel business, ultimately forming the Carnegie Steel Co., employing the same business tactics and practices (rebates from railroads, lower prices to undercut competitors, unfriendly competition among his department heads, vertical integration-ownership of coal mines, ships and railroads) as Rockefeller. When he retired in 1904, his company produced a fourth of the nation's steel, and his personal fortune was estimated at 450 million dollars, now worth 110 billion dollars. He bestowed most of it to philanthropy, for libraries and foundations bearing his name.

That big business after its rise controlled the basic contours of American governmental policy is obvious. This was not only the view of socialists, many of whom were part of the muckraker assault on big business in the late 19th, early 20th-century period, but of some of our more prominent Presidents. In the bitter 1912 elections, Theodore Roosevelt, in attacking the Democratic and Republican Parties, declared in the Progressive Party Convention, that they represented a "government of the needy many by professional politicians in the interests of the rich few." Woodrow Wilson, not to be surpassed by Roosevelt's blast, averred in his *New Freedom* (1913) that "the masters of the government of the United States are the combined capitalists and manufacturers of the United States."

There were varying degrees of corruption among businessmen and politicians, the worst under the Presidencies of Ulysses S. Grant and Warren G. Harding. State legislators were also notoriously touched by Veblen's "seizing the main chance." One example of this: The Erie Railroad War of 1868 pitted two rival capitalist groups—one led by Vanderbilt, the other by Gould and Fisk—fighting for control, in which the issuance of new stock certificates having the approval of the New York State Legislature was needed. The two sides literally spent millions of dollars in bribing the entire legislature, the going price for legislators in dollars being about fifteen thousand and seventy-five thousand for committee chairpersons; Gould and Fisk won by raising the price for key legislators to a hundred thousand, this at a time when average workers earned less than five hundred dollars a year.[1]

The business immorality of the robber barons was so obvious that even their apologists did not deny it. Allen Nevins, a well-known historian, for instance, admitted that Rockefeller indulged in many unethical business practices, including industrial espionage and railroad rebates, but excused him on the basis that he was no more wicked than others, and that in the long run business bigness, accelerated by these practices, was inevitable.[2] To be sure, Nevins was opposed by the muckrakers/historians, carefully cataloguing and condemning robber-baron crimes, like Gustavus Meyers in *History of the Great American Fortunes*, a landmark work; Ida M. Tarbell in *History of the Standard Oil Company*; and Matthew Josephson in *The Robber Barons*. Veblen himself, while not listing specific robber-baron crimes, delved into their general predatory and parasitical life style.[3]

The robber barons themselves justified their economic success, a prime example being two works by Carnegie, *Triumphant Democracy* and *The Gospel of Wealth*. Carnegie himself was a radical republican youth, from a politicized Scottish working-class family, his grandfathers being working-class leaders. Theoretically, even as a capitalist,

Carnegie defended labor unions and their right to strike without facing strikebreakers, but when confronted by the Homestead Strike against his steel company, he abandoned these positions. He unequivocally praised economic competition, regarding the wealthy as the winners in Darwinian "survival of the fittest," and approved of economic concentration in industry, viewing it as impossible to prevent, being part of the iron law of competition. But he insisted that as chief economic planners, capitalists had a social responsibility toward workers, aiding them to improve themselves, like endowing libraries, the aim being to conciliate them to capital. Furthermore, to maintain the inviolability of individual economic competition a *sine qua non* of the capitalist ethic, he favored high inheritance taxes on wealth.[4]

The top rung of these capitalists were the "Four Hundred"—actually approximately six hundred of them.[5] Obviously, following Veblen's dictum that the capitalist elite merged with older ruling elites, the great American capitalist families quickly married into the European nobility; Myers estimated that by the 1910s, approximately five hundred American heiresses did so.[6]

The Theory of the Leisure Class and Today's American Plutocracy

The Theory of the Leisure Class (1899) represented the fruition of Veblen's early writings on socialism. Parts of it included former articles: "The Economic Theory of Woman's Dress" (1894); "The Beginning of Ownership" (1898); and "The Barbarian Status of Women" (1898). This broadside against the master classes of history, from barbarian chieftain to nobleman and to capitalist, is an enduring socialist classic. Indeed, it was the very first in social history to indicate in exquisite detail how the economic, social, and political rulership of the leisure class translated itself into a cultural and social-psychological hegemony over the subaltern classes, permeating every element of their consciousness and social existence.

In the first or "Introductory" chapter, Veblen invited us to the banquet of the leisure class whose roots were in the lower barbarian period, with the Agricultural Revolution leading to a class society. Quite normally, for him, these changes produced a new social psychology concerning work, the central human activity; one characterized by the divisions engendered between "exploit and drudgery," the former term denoting employments that were "worthy, honorable, noble," of a "predatory" nature; the latter signifying those "unworthy, debasing, ignoble," or "productive" work associated with slaves, farmers, and workers whose labor was "irksome."[7]

The leisure class itself had its various ranks and gradations, its apex composed of the higher positions or the "vested interests": under feudalism, higher nobility and leading clerics; under capitalism, wealthy capitalists and others, like top military, political, and clerical personages. The lower reaches of this class were those in dependent positions of authority, like informational or intellectual labor, but Veblen did not include in this category his beloved engineers or scientists, because of their usefulness in promoting economic progress.

Chapter two, "Pecuniary Emulation," maintained that the mindset of a society dominated by a leisure class of great power and large property normally involved "invidious distinction" between individuals based on "emulation." Society was, thus, normally competitive as individuals wished to gain as much wealth and power as possible.[8]

Chapter three, "Conspicuous Leisure," emphasized the utter importance of the leisure class in not doing any productive work as related to agriculture and the industrial arts to indicate their superiority over the *hoi polloi*. Furthermore, the employment of servants or slaves became all-important in indicating leisure class exemption from useful work.[9]

Chapter four, "Conspicuous Consumption," related to "conspicuous leisure," claimed that the wasteful consumption of commodities bestowed "reputability." Women were principally involved in this nexus for as men's chief servants, their spending reflected on their men's wealth and position in the community.[10]

"The Pecuniary Standard of Living," chapter five, posited that the average individual/family tried to emulate the consumption patterns of the higher classes, the aim being to secure as much dignity and honor as possible. Thus, for instance, Veblen insisted that déclassé academics, with their limited economic resources, were forced to have fewer children than others in their socioeconomic position because, in close proximity to the rich, they must constantly strive to indulge in a more-than-normal conspicuous consumption.[11]

"Pecuniary Canons of Taste," chapter six, primarily maintained that a leisure-class-infested society not only had a double standard for punishing crime, but also determined what was aesthetically pleasing. On the former element, Veblen noted that in filching large sums of money, presumably through financial swindles, leisure-class criminals generally received light sentences, while petty working-class offenders paid with harsh ones. On the latter subject, he opined that the chief reason why handmade products were more aesthetically pleasing than manufactured ones was higher cost. In religion, for instance, this beauty was observed in the costly edifices and clothing serving an omnipotent God-master.[12]

Chapter seven, "Dress as an Expression of the Pecuniary Culture," associated women's dress with leisure-class habits of superiority over the common herd. For details on this, see chapter on women.[13]

Chapter eight, "Industrial Exemption and Conservatism," began with a description of how human institutions were instrumental in allowing for the fittest individuals to survive, who invariably became more conservative since they were molded by institutions which reflected any given period. Thus, attitudes critical of the fittest or the leisure class were considered "vulgar." Veblen was following a Darwinian-Spencerian track here, but in ironic hyperbole.

A cardinal thesis of this chapter was that since there was only so much consumption and wealth at any given time in society, the "accumulation of wealth at the upper end of the pecuniary scale implies privation at the lower end of the scale," with its corollary that leisure-class waste resulted in less consumption for the "lower classes," reinforcing their poverty and dependence, and thus, conservative mindset, restricting "new habits of thought."[14] The similarity of these assertions was very similar to those of Thoreau in *Walden's* "Economy" section.[15]

The "Conservation of Archaic Traits," chapter nine, traced the changes in the primary qualities prized by the leisure class. In the lower barbarian period, they were "massiveness, ferocity, unscrupulousness, and tenacity of purpose"; in the higher barbarian one, "shrewd purpose and chicanery"; while in the capitalist one, "pecuniary" ones of the "captains of industry," of "providence, prudence, and chicanery," with their "callous disregard for the feelings and wishes of others." But in opposition to the capitalist value system, he observed a nascent one developing within the workingclass based on "industrial efficiency" and a "spiritual attitude toward work," as yet not fully developed.[16] Chapter ten, "Modem Survivals of Prowess," indicated that the war/sport temperament had its roots in the barbarian stage, which prized "force and fraud."[17]

Chapters eleven and twelve, "The Belief in Luck" and "Devout Observances," fell under the rubric of religion, usually regarding it as a conservative force serving the basic interests of the leisure class.[18] Chapter thirteen, "Survivals of the Non-Invidious Interest," asserted that there were still many islands of "non-invidious" cooperation; as in religion itself, with its emphasis on "human solidarity and sympathy," and the "Young Men's Christian Association...sewing circles, social clubs, art clubs."[19] Chapter fourteen, "The Higher Learning as an Expression of the Pecuniary Culture," delineated the threads tying higher education to the leisure class.[20]

In the raging intellectual controversy following the publication of *The Theory of the Leisure Class,* Lester Frank Ward, the principal father of sociology in America, ably defended Veblen. Even before Ward reviewed it in the May 1900 issue of the *American Journal of Sociology*, Veblen, informed him that:

I need to say that I appreciate the honor of such an invitation at your hands…As a matter of course, you will find evidence in the book of my indebtedness to you. The absence of acknowledgment is due to the fact that I am indebted to so many and various teachers as to preclude detailed acknowledgment.[21]

To be sure, Ward's critique of the work was complimentary, praising its "plain and unmistakable" language, "some of which is likely to become classic." Then, too, he defended Veblen against critics who believed that he was too harsh towards the leisure class, on the grounds that "any examination into cultural pedigree always offends."[22]

Veblen replied: "Your unqualified approval has given me more pleasure than anything that has occurred in connection with the book, and I can only hope that it will not end with giving me an intolerable conceit."[23]

Veblen's *Theory of the Leisure Class* influenced contemporary and later thinkers. An example, others later: In his monumental *Pure Sociology* (1903), Ward often quoted from it, agreeing with Veblen that the American business elite was "predatory" in nature, and that "pecuniary occupations," i.e., bankers, were partly "quasi-predatory," with "deception" being a key element in their business.[24] In discussing upper-class women, he again quoted Veblen to the effect that they represented "vicarious leisure" and "vicarious consumption."[25] He also approved of Veblen's emphasis on human creativity, the propensity to the "instinct of workmanship," with work not irksome if one's faculties were not overtaxed.[26]

To be sure, Veblen favorably reviewed *Pure Sociology* in the September 1903 issue of the *Journal of Political Economy*, as a "lucid and forcible presentation," with a "great range and command of information" written in an "engaging style." He specifically commended Ward's "genetic" method, "which deals with the forces and sequence of development and seeks to understand the outcome by finding out how and why it has come about," and applauded its basic "proposition" that "deception may almost be called the foundation of business," and contention on the increasing "collectivism" of industrialized nations.[27]

Veblen continued his attacks on the plutocracy in his later works, as in *Absentee Ownership and Business Enterprise in Recent Times*. In this critique, he, at times, noted the positive contributions of the early entrepreneurs of the Industrial Revolution to economic progress, observing their creative role in industrial development and accumulation of capital.[28] In fact, for him, in the 1760 to 1860 period, many large capitalists possessed the creative qualities of "industrial insight," and "of initiative and energy," supervising daily production and borrowing money to expand business.

But with the rise of Trusts, big capital maximized profit by limiting production/fixing prices, and utilizing the services and expertise of managers and inventors. Under these conditions, large capitalists were necessarily parasitical:

> It is only that by force of circumstances the captain of industry, or in more accurate words the captain of solvency, has in recent times come to be the effectual spokesman and type-form of the kept classes as well the keeper and dispenser of their keep; very much as the War Lord of the barbarian raids, or the Baron of the Middle Ages.[29]

And:

> For a hundred years or so he was, cumulatively, the dominant figure in civilized life, about whose deeds and interests law and custom have turned, the central and paramount personal agency in Occidental civilization. Indeed, his great vogue and compelling eminence are not past yet, so far as regards his place in popular superstition and in the make-believe of political strategy, but it is essentially a glory standing over out of the past, essentially a superstition.[30]

But despite this preeminence "in the folklore of Political Economy," the great capitalist was "no longer the central and directive force in that business traffic that governs the material fortunes of mankind; not much more so than the Crown, the Country Gentleman, or the Priesthood."[31]

Veblen here is not entirely correct. Although it is true that today American corporations throughout the world are in a bureaucratic and rationalist mode, capitalist buccaneers, as those who have conducted leveraged buyouts (LBOs) and helped cause the Savings and Loan (S&L) and Enron debacles in the United States, can still sabotage the economic structure of society. On the other hand, creative capitalists, establishing new industries, like William Gates, still exist, but are overrated as there is no reason to suppose that technological innovation cannot flourish under socialism; under proper socioeconomic conditions Veblen's elements of "curiosity" and "workmanship" should be just as efficacious as that of economic gain.

Veblen also referred to the "free income" derived by the leisure class that privatized through its "absentee ownership" the natural resources of the nation, like "gold, and other precious metals, timber, coal...petroleum, natural gas, water power, irrigation," and of their wasteful expenditure.[32]

In summary, Veblen held that those who possessed capital "rule the affairs of the nation, civil and political, and control the conditions of life."[33] Or:

Life and experience in these democratic communities is governed by the price system. Efficiency, practical capacity, popular confidence, in these communities are rateable only in terms of price. "Practical" means "businesslike." Driven by this all-pervading bias of business principles in all that touches their practical concerns, no such democratic community is capable of entrusting the duties of responsible office to any other than business men. Hence...the incumbents of office are necessarily persons of businesslike antecedents, dominated by the logic of ownership. Legislators, executives, and judiciary are of the same derivation in respect of the bias which their habits of life have engendered and in respect of the drift which their bias subjects them in their further conduct of affairs.[34]

The Theory of the Leisure Class, along with *The Higher Learning in America* (the latter work will be examined later) were involved in a well-known incident of leisure-class disregard of academic freedom, in March 1922, involving Scott Nearing. (He was an outspoken socialist and economist who lost two teaching positions, at the Wharton School of Commerce of the University of Pennsylvania and at the University of Toledo, for attacking leisure-class privilege and opposing American entry into World War I; he was also a member of the Communist Party for a period in the late 1920s.) While Nearing was speaking about Veblen's two works before the Liberal Club of Clark University in Worchester, Mass., the university's president, Wallace A. Atwood, was so incensed by the talk's radical content that he peremptorily disrupted it; he failed to dislodge Nearing from the platform, but the lights were turned off. After many years of fighting the power structure, Nearing and his wife Helen lived as farmers in Vermont and Maine, emulating Leo Tolstoy and Thoreau. Dedication to ecology, simplicity, and nonexploitative lifestyle led to their becoming celebrities to the counterculture in the 1970s and beyond.[35]

Veblen's "leisure-class" thesis reverberated in the works of many 20th century thinkers. Examples follow. In a neo-anarchist vein, Mumford deeply imbibed from Veblen and the anarchist Kropotkin. His concept of the "mega-machine," of large-scale organization in the social and economic arenas, which intermeshed with the political and military ones to crush individual autonomy, complemented Veblen's leisure-class thesis. He also followed Kropotkin, who called for an end to a pernicious labor division and differences between the rural and urban areas, with a society of free and equal individuals fully empowered at work and play through participatory democracy.[36] The sociologist C. Wright Mills also developed a view of social reality very similar to Veblen's. His respect for Veblen was evident: "His biases are the most fruitful that have appeared in the literature of American protest." But Mills was not always in agreement with Veblen. For instance, he disagreed with Veblen's conflating the traits of the nobility with those of the great capitalists, viewing the former as less socially useful and creative than the latter.

A defense of Veblen's melding, at times, of the mindsets of the nobility/military (I add the frontiersman-imperialist) with the capitalist one follows: The American military popularly embodies the warrior, an almost indispensable badge for the Presidency. There are, of course, exceptions to this rule, as when William Jefferson Clinton, who did not serve in the military and opposed American intervention in Vietnam, defeated the incumbent George H. Bush, serving in World War II, which, however, happened only because H. Ross Perot also ran. But the general scenario holds true: George Washington, Andrew Jackson, William Henry Harrison, Zachary Taylor, Ulysses S. Grant, Rutherford B. Hayes, James A. Garfield, Theodore Roosevelt (of "Rough Rider" fame), and Harry S. Truman come to mind. Since the Second World War, every President but one—Clinton—served in the military. In World War II itself these Presidents, were involved: Dwight D. Eisenhower of Victory-in-Europe fame, John F. Kennedy of P.T. Boat 109 renown, Lyndon B. Johnson, Richard M. Nixon, Gerald R. Ford, and the elder Bush. Jimmy Carter was a navy officer and George W. Bush an air force reservist. In 1996, General Colin C. Powell, the first African-American to become Chairperson of the Joint Chiefs of Staff, was urged to run for the Presidency as a Republican, but declined to do so. Furthermore, historically, the nobility has been intermeshed with rising capitalists in business ventures and in imperialism, as in England, Germany, France, and Japan. Mills himself acknowledged the power in American society since World War II of the military-industrial complex.

Mills also objected to Veblen's tying the conspicuous-consumption theme to the wealthy, claiming that old wealth toned it down, although admitting that the new rich still reveled in it. But he did not address the problem of the great waste of resources caused by conspicuous consumption, including that of the middle classes and even workers in aping the rich as much as possible. Furthermore, since the Reagan 80s, a particularly virulent form of conspicuous consumption among the wealthy is again common.

In the main, both Veblen and Mills emphasized the power and influence of elite groups over the general population, Mills' "power elite" being the equivalent of Veblen's "leisure class." For both, the elite's core was the large corporate leaders, their underlings being the political and military ones.[37]

Another depiction of Veblenian leisure-class rule was by Michael Barrington Jr., a leading post-World-War II Harvard sociologist. In *Injustice, The Social Bases of Obedience and Revolt*, he recognized that on the matter of conspicuous consumption, *The Theory of the Leisure Class* revealed "social waste of upper classes that apparently receive general approbation," and noted their excessive reliance on "pageantry and display," related to their supposed possession of "mysterious and unusual attributes."[38]

Examples of Veblen's influence on well-known American historians follow. Matthew Josephson on predatory capitalism in *The Robber Barons* from *Theory of the Leisure Class* on conspicuous consumption: The looting by the "captains of industry" of the castles of Europe to embellish theirs in America, "the paintings, the tapestry, the china."[39] Other topics: That the charitable contributions of the wealthy advertised their "successful predatory aggressions of warlike exploits"; that the religiosity of the wealthy partly rested on their belief of being superior to the common herd, thus next to God himself; that there was a dichotomy between the workmanship of workers and capitalist concern for money, and that large trusts at times impeded technological progress.[40] From *Absentee Ownership*: That the wealthy now owned a large part of the nation's natural resources. From *Theory of Business Enterprise*: That predatory capital was based on the "ruling principle...cunning," wrapped up in euphemisms like "business strategy and diplomacy."[41] The American history textbook authored by Virginia Bernhard, et al., *Firsthand America* (1991), began a section thus: "The Bradley Martin Ball: Conspicuous Consumption." This 1897 ball in New York City was attended by "eight hundred socialites" who "spent about $400,000"—one of the guests, Mrs. Astor, wearing $200,000 worth of jewelry—the wealthy, then and now, have a penchant for such balls. In today's money, this happening would cost in the tens of millions of dollars.[42]

Ernest Mandel, a leading post World War II Marxist, was also cognizant of the deleterious consequences flowing from leisure-class waste as part of the social dynamics of class society. In following Paul A. Baran, a Marxist economist, he deplored the economic plunder of the Third World by its ruling elites which also accepted payoffs from First World capitalists exploiting their nations, much of the surplus value extracted being spent on luxuries in their nations and First World, in addition to their investing capital in the First World for safekeeping.[43]

In a vein very similar to Veblen's leisure-class, Mills' power-elite, and Mumford's mega-machine theses, is the work of G. William Domhoff, a sociology and psychology professor. In *Who Rules America Now?*, he examined the contemporary American elite, its heart being the great capitalists and their ancillaries. He empirically demonstrated the reality of this upper class of 0.5 percent of the people owning a fourth of the nation's private wealth, one well aware of its wealth/power/social prestige through social indicators, like Registers or Blue Books, the most prestigious being the Social Register, exclusive boarding schools, social/country clubs, especially in the larger cities and elite universities. It was from this upper class and social layers just beneath it that its top ranks were mostly recruited. About half of the upper class intermarried with others, obviously of lower status, but usually not much. Not surprisingly, the typical occupations of this business elite were heavily skewed to business, finance, and corporate law.[44]

The apex of this leisure class was composed of the wealthiest fortunes, CEOs, and other prominent figures of the leading corporations in banking, insurance, manufacturing, media/entertainment, and those of the political, healthcare, educational, military, and religious complexes. According to the capitalist bible, *Forbes* magazine, the wealthiest 400 individuals alone grouped into 82 families, in the early 1980s, owned about 166 billion dollars in corporate assets. (To have basic control of a large corporation, any single person/group having only 5 percent of the stock is in a good position to do so.)

But the 400 alone possessed stock of at least 15 percent of corporate capital worth 2.2 trillion dollars, itself representing at least 40 percent of its non-residential variety. The stock of the 400 and their ancillaries was tied to interlocking ownership/directorship of large banks and insurance companies that administer about half the stocks and bonds. The leading 21 of them—Bank America, Bankers Trust, Chase Manhattan, Citicorp, Morgan Guaranty, Prudential, Metropolitan, and Equitable Life, among others—had substantial shares with each other, but also with the other largest 122 corporations and their 2259 subsidiaries. But let us broaden this list to include the Fortune 500 or the top 500 corporations. The several thousand or so leaders of these corporations, CEOs and members of the boards of directors, many sitting on two or more corporate boards—they include many former political and military leaders—now control the basic economic decision-making power of the nation, indicating the preeminence of business among the interlocking pyramids of power, others being the political and military.[45]

In this panoply of power, successful stars in one area transferred their charisma to others. For instance, the actor Reagan, with the aid of General Electric and other business, became Governor of California, then President. The billionaire Ross Perot was a perennial Presidential aspirant, as it now appears are Steve Forbes, the heir to *Forbes* magazine, and Pat Buchanan, the television personality.

Notes

1. On American industrialization and the role of leading capitalists in it, see, for instance, Jonathan Hughes, *American Economic History*, 3rd ed. (Glenview, IL: Scott, Foresman/Little, Brown, 1990), pp. 267-428. Some good general college history books are excellent on the robber barons and related problems. See, for instance, Arthur S. Link, *American Epoch: A History of the United States Since the 1890s* (New York: Alfred A. Knopf, 1958), pp. 3-135. On the individual robber barons observed, as well as the others, see Gusatvus Myers, *History of the Great American Fortunes* (New York: Modern Library, 1936), appropriate pages; on the Erie Railroad War, pp. 75-99. Another excellent work on the robber barons is by Matthew Josephson, *The Robber Barons: The Great American Capitalists, 1861-1901* (New York: Harvest Book, 1962). Mark Twain and Charles Dudley Moore, *The Gilded Age: A Tale of Today* (New York: Trident Press, 1964), pp. 141-297, for instance, in which the pursuit of money is everything, although helping friends is also meritorious. On Wilson's remarks, see Woodrow Wilson, *New Freedom* (New York: Doubleday, Page, and Co., 1913), pp. 57-58.

2. See, for instance, Allen Nevins, *Study in Power: John D. Rockefeller, Industrialist and Philanthropist* (New York: Charles Scribner's Sons, 1953), I, vii-ix, 105 ff., and 249.

3. See, for instance, Matthew Josephson and Allen Nevins, "Should American History Be Rewritten?" *Saturday Review of Literature*, Feb. 6, 1954, pp. 7-9. Hal Bridges, "The Robber Baron Concept in American History," *Business Review*, XXXII, 1958, 1-13, on the great amount of criticism against the robber barons in the 1865-1900 period.

4. Robert Green McCloskey, *American Conservatism in the Age of Enterprise* (New York: Harper Torchbooks, 1964), Chapter 7 on Carnegie.

5. Josephson, *Robber Barons*, p. 329.

6. Myers, *History of the Great American Fortunes*, p. 378.

7. Veblen, *Leisure Class*, pp. 21-33 and 154 ff.; Dorfman, *Veblen*, pp. 427-28, 431-32, and 472-73 on the "vested interests."

8. Veblen, *Leisure Class*, pp. 33-40.

9. *Ibid.*, pp. 41-60.

10. *Ibid.*, pp. 60-80.

11. *Ibid.*, pp. 80-87.

12. *Ibid.*, pp. 87-118.

13. *Ibid.*, pp. 118-31.

14. *Ibid.*, pp. 131-44.

15. Thoreau, *Walden*, Bode edition, pp. 258-334.

16. Veblen, *Leisure Class*, pp. 145-64.

17. *Ibid.*, pp. 164-82.

18. *Ibid.*, pp. 182-216.

19. *Ibid.*, pp. 216-34.

20. *Ibid.*, pp. 235-58.

21. Dorfman, *Veblen*, p. 194.

22. Lester Frank Ward, Review of Thorstein Veblen's *The Theory of the Leisure Class, American Journal of Sociology*, May 1900,

23. Dorfman, *Veblen*, p. 195.

24. Lester F. Ward, *Pure Sociology: A Treatise on The Origin and Spontaneous Development of Society* (New York: Macmillan Co., 1903), p. 485.

25. *Ibid.*, p. 363.

26. *Ibid.*, p. 245.

27. Thorstein Veblen, Review of Lester Frank Ward's *Pure Sociology: A Treatise Concerning The Origin and Spontaneous Development of Society, Journal of Political Economy*, September, 1903.

28. Thorstein Veblen, *Absentee Ownership and Business Enterprise in Recent Times: The Case of America* (New York: B.W. Huebsch, 1923), pp. 101-18.

29. *Ibid.*, p. 114.

30. *Ibid.*, p. 101.

31. *Ibid.*

32. Veblen's environmental concerns are recognized by John Bellamy Foster, *The Vulnerable Planet: A Short Economic History of the Environment* (New York: Monthly Review Press, 1994), pp. 71-72. On Veblen and leisure-class waste related to absentee ownership, see Veblen, *Absentee Ownership*, pp. 122-29, 168-71, 186-91; the quotations are on pp. 171 and 188.

33. Veblen, *Absentee Ownership*, p. 118.

34. *Ibid.*, p. 405.

35. Dorfman, *Veblen*, pp. 463-64. John A. Saltmarsh, *Scott Nearing: An Intellectual Biography* (Philadelphia: Temple University Press, 1991), pp. 169-71 and 245-64.

36. On Mumford, see Thomas P. Hughes and Agatha C. Hughes, *Lewis Mumford: Public Intellectual* (New York: Oxford University Press, 1990), pp. 22, 42, 127, 157-58, and 289, on his relationship with Veblen. Mumford likes Veblen's anarchist emphasis on workers' autonomy in industry. Mumford, *Myth of the Machine*, I, 188-211 on the "mega-machine"; II, 209 ff. on utopias which he generally dislikes with the exception of Morris' *News from Nowhere*; pp. 333-34, on his being for technological progress when related to individual autonomy and liberty. Lewis Mumford, *The City in History: Its Origins, Its Transformations, and Its Prospects* (New York: Harcourt, Brace, and World, 1961), pp. 514-15, on his liking Kropotkin's small-scale technology requiring more "human initiative and skill." Mumford rejects the technologism of Veblen and Marx as the basic undergirding of the historical process.

37. On Mills, see Rick Tilman, *C. Wright Mills: A Native Radical and His American Intellectual Roots* (University Park, PA: Pennsylvania State University Press, 1984), pp. 12 ff. and p. 36, that Veblen, Dewey, and Mills are the principal exponents of American radicalism, Mills' radicalism being most heavily indebted to "Veblen, Dewey, and Read"; pp. 90-106, on Mills' encounter with Veblen, espe-

cially over the economic functionality of the wealthy which Veblen discounts, but not Mills. C. Wright Mills, *The Power Elite* (New York: Galaxy Book, 1959), pp. 269-97, on the "power elite," very analogous to Veblen's "leisure class" with respect to its power. This work, heavily influenced by Marx, Weber, and Veblen, is not Veblenian when it maintains that the work of the wealthy is not parasitical. C. Wright Mills, *White Collar: The American Middle Class* (New York: Galaxy Book, 1956), pp. 28 ff. and pp. 189-354, holds that large sections of the middle class are becoming proletarianized; this is a Marxist, not Veblenian, theme.

38. Barrington Moore Jr., *Injustice: The Social Bases of Obedience and Revolt* (White Plains, NY: M.E. Sharpe, 1978), pp. 37-43; on p. 35: "Probably in all cultures the confirmed slacker who refuses to do his or her part of the common task and who lives off the labor of others, constitutes a negative social model, *if that person is poor.*"

39. Josephson, *Robber Barons*, pp. 31 and 330ff. Also, see Frederick Lewis Allen, *The Great Pierpont Morgan* (New York: Harper and Brothers, 1949), pp. 185-207 on Morgan's conspicuous consumption.

40. Josephson, *Robber Barons*, pp. 322, 319, 280, and 370.

41. *Ibid.*, pp. 123 and 180.

42. Virginia Bernhard et al., *Firsthand America: A History of the United States*, 1st ed. (Saint James, NY: Brandywine Press, 1991), pp. 549-50.

43. Ernest Mandel, *Marxist Economic Theory*, 2 vols. (New York: Monthly Review Press, 1968), II, 618-20.

44. G. William Domhoff, *Who Rules America Now? A View for the 80s* (New York: A Touchstone Book, 1983) pp. 20 ff., "The Social Register"; pp. 28 ff., "Social Clubs"; pp. 41-43, "The Wealth and Income of the Upper Class"; pp. 44 ff., "Upper-Class Indicators."

45. Lester Thurow, "The Leverage of the Wealthiest 400," *New York Times*, Oct. 11, 1984, p. A27. Domhoff, *Who Rules America Now?* pp. 59 ff., "Ownership and Control"; pp. 66-70, "The Board of Directors"; pp. 98 ff. "The Opinion-Shaping Process"; Chapter 5, "The Power Elite and Government."

V   CRITIQUE of MARX

AS A STUDENT OF SOCIALISM, IT WAS ONLY NORMAL that Veblen delved deeply into the though of Karl Marx, its most important thinker. That Veblen admired Marx was axiomatic: He once expressed to Harold J. Laski, a noted British socialist and scholar, when the taught at the New School for Social Research, his profound "admiration for Marx."[1]

Veblen's most sustained analysis of Marx was in 1906-07, in two closely related articles entitled "The Socialist Economics of Karl Marx," with the two subtitles being "The Theories of Karl Marx" and "The Later Marxism." The fist critiqued Marx's thought; the second is a commentary on the debates in the German Social Democratic Party between orthodox Marxists, like Kautsky, and the revisionists, like Edouard Bernstein, the former being heirs to Marx's revolutionary side, the latter his reformism. This analysis will focus on these articles, but not neglect others.[2] (Veblen footnotes were in German on Marx's *Capital*, *The Communist Manifesto*, *Critique of Political Economy*, and *Misery of Philosophy*, among others.)

To begin, Veblen was much impressed by Marx's philosophy, particularly by its "certain boldness of conceptions and great logical consistency," adding, that although "the constituent elements of the system are neither novel nor iconoclastic," it "has an air of originality and initiative such as is rarely met with among the sciences that deal with any phase of human culture."[3]

Veblen's presentation of Marxism was faithful to its principal focus, the class struggle in history between master and subaltern classes, the former economically exploiting the latter, ending with the victory of the proletariat over the bourgeoisie. He also sketched a rather detailed picture of Marxism's intellectual roots: Left Hegelian materialism, English natural rights theory propounded by the English classical economists, English Radicalism, especially William Thompson, and Jeremy Bentham's hedonistic utilitarianism, but neglected the French revolutionary tradition and utopian-socialist elements, which he was aware of anyway.

But Veblen disagreed with Marx in several areas. Importantly, by following in the wake of the Marxist revisionists led by Bernstein, he concurred with them that contrary to Marx's assertions that the workingclass under capitalism was progressively impoverished, the opposite was occurring, thus the class struggle was diminishing, not increasing.[4]

Another difference concerned Veblen's rejection of the Marxian theory of surplus-value and its relation to class struggle between labor and capital. He correctly asserted that Thompson well-anticipated Marx's theory of surplus-value in the tradition of English natural-rights theory in which labor was central to wealth creation, and that capitalist appropriation of workers' labor time was self-evident and not a startling discovery, relating it to capitalist accumulation of capital.[5] Still, Veblen rejected Marxian surplus-value for a Darwinian concept that dismissed labor's valid right to wealth. Thus, instead of associating surplus-value with Marxian class struggle, he justified socialism from a Darwinian ethical perspective of group survival, of socialism's providing a fairer distribution of the material means of life than capitalism, a variation of Jeremy Bentham's formula of "the greatest good for the greatest number."[6]

Veblen's attack on Marxian surplus-value was muddled. He claimed that it was a species of reasoning of the natural-rights variety. It was that, Marx simply stating that every unequal economic relationship was also an unequal social one. Furthermore, although Veblen disavowed "surplus-value," he accepted Bernstein's concept of "surplus product," that capitalism inherently had a tendency for overproduction resulting in depression. The two terms were related in that they were opposite sides of the same coin. Also, in rejecting Marxian "surplus-value" for Bernsteinian "surplus-product," he vitiated his attack on capitalism by removing the principal focus of the class struggle from the point of production to that of distribution.[7]

Some commentary follows on Veblen's view that Darwinian evolution is not consonant with Hegelian dialectical Marxian class struggle leading to socialism, because the former, with an open view of the future, is not teleological. It is impossible for social science not to have basic assumptions on the historical drift of humanity, and in this sense, Marxism is no more teleological than any other *Weltanschauung*, including Darwin's. Darwin's natural selection, for instance, postulated the elimination of "inferior" non-European groups and proposed the continuation of a society based on antagonistic economic and social relations, great sympathy residing only in the family or other intimates—see chapter on human nature. Marx himself simply extended Darwinian struggle from the individual/family to status groups and classes.[8]

In the area of the primacy of the proletarian class struggle for the achievement of socialism, Veblen conceptualized that as a self-proclaimed Darwinist, he regarded the historical future as open and indeterminate, with political change only coming about in a slow or evolutionary manner, rejecting Marx's Hegelian penchant for the certainty of rapid revolution and socialism. In this vein, he posited that the socialist revolution was "by no means inevitable," or "irrepressible," there being "no warrant in the Darwinian scheme of things for asserting *a priori* that the class interests of the workingclass will bring them to take a stand against the propertied class." This was so, for him, because workers were usually subservient to their bosses, and regularly followed the opiate of "patriotism" and its corollary of war fostered by ruling groups. Furthermore, he was skeptical of workers' "abject poverty" being able to overcome their "abject subjection." (He forgot to mention that Marx and Engels in various works were more than aware of status differences dividing workers and of the cultural hegemony of the bourgeoisie over them.) Nevertheless, Veblen believed that socialism might prevail over capitalism, thus doing away with "economic class discrepancies, no international animosity, no dynastic politics."[9]

Veblen here favored a reformist socialism, analogous to slow Darwinian changes in biological evolution, in which strong trade unions, in protecting workers' interests, precluded Marxist "violent class struggles." Indeed, with this pattern gaining ascendancy, he believed that this disproved Marx's thesis that increasing socioeconomic misery for workers was inevitable under capitalism. But he neglected to mention that Marx modified this concept for one of "relative misery."[10] Nevertheless, he conceded that although the class struggle was not foreordained, it was still "reasonable and logical," a valid element for change.[11]

Veblen himself was guilty of the many "sins" that he attributed to Marx, especially those involved in deepening the class struggle between workers and bourgeoisie. In categorizing the wealthy as a "leisure class" whose economic role was clearly one "of exploitation, not serviceability," and of a "parasitic nature," and in maintaining that a basic human nature favored a socialist equality, that wealth and inventiveness were inherently of a social nature, and that when workers compared themselves to the bourgeoisie, they could not but see themselves as inferiors, was he not employing standard class-struggle Marxist arguments? In fact, he postulated that before the working-class struggle against the bourgeoisie became more acute, it required a series of socioeconomic reforms to strengthen the workingclass sufficiently enough to do so: "That the socialist revolution must be carried through not by an anemic workingclass under the pressure of abject privation, but by a body of full-blooded workingmen gradually gaining strength from improved conditions of life."[12]

But Marx and Engels specifically advocated a strong reformist socialist vein especially after the 1848 revolutions misfired, envisaging the possibility of socialism coming gradually through the ballot box in democratic nations like the United States and England. Indeed, Marxists always supported democratic and reformist politics, viewing them as necessary steps for socialism. It was anarchism, during the First and Second Internationals, that rejected parliamentary politics and reform on the basis that they might co-opt most of the workingclass to a bourgeois view of life, thus lessening the possibility for revolutionary change.[13]

Of interest in Veblen's dialogue with Marx was that he never commented on the horrific socioeconomic conditions endured by the workingclass, including farm workers—long workdays, deplorable working conditions, unremitting tyranny at work, the small margin for economic survival, and child labor. Perhaps Veblen, having experienced the rigors of farm life in his early years, simply took it for granted that this was the way life is for most workers, so why mention it?

Notes

1. Dorfman, *Veblen*, p. 451.

2. Veblen, *Place of Science*, pp. 409-56, for the two articles.

3. *Ibid.*, p. 409.

4. *Ibid.*, pp. 410-11 ff.

5. *Ibid.* pp. 412 ff.

6. *Ibid.*, pp. 444-45.

7. *Ibid.*, pp. 419 ff. and p. 444.

8. Maximilien Rubel and Margaret Manale, *Marx Without Myth: A Chronological Study of His Life and Work* (New York: Harper Torchbooks, 1976), pp. 169, 179, and 291. For a superb one-volume account of Marxism, see George Lichtheim, *Marxism: An Historical and Critical Study* (New York: Frederick A. Praeger, 1962). It clearly indicates this indisputable fact: that tactically by the 1850s, Marx and Engels paid most of their attention to parliamentary politics and democracy to achieve socialism by piecemeal reform. For the best brief exposition of the Marxist view of the world; see Karl Marx and Frederick Engels, *Manifesto of the Communist Party* (New York: International Publishers, 1948). Marx, *Capital: A Critique of Political Economy*, Vol. I: *The Process of Capitalist Production* (New York: Modern Library Edition, n.d., 1st published in 1867), is Marx's single most important work. On Marx's view of history, see William H. Shaw, *Marx's Theory of History* (Palo Alto, CA: Stanford University Press, 1978).

9. Veblen, *Place of Science*, pp. 440 ff.

10. Karl Marx, *Wage-Labour and Capital* (New York: International Publishers, 1939), p. 39.

11. Veblen, *Place of Science*, pp. 434-41.

12. *Ibid.*, p. 450.

13. Lichtheim, *Marxism*, pp. 122-29.

VI THE AMERICAN WORKING CLASS, LAbOR UNIONS, AMERICAN ANARCHISM, ANd THE IWW

THE AMERICAN WORKING CLASS

AS AN ENGLISH COLONY, THEN NATION, with few people relative to its vast virgin lands, the United States before its Industrial Revolution was a nation of mostly small farmers, especially in the North, with a class structure of much economic equality and rapid socioeconomic mobility, at least to the large "middle class" comprising about half the people. But if one included the large slave population in the South and the poor white, rural and urban workers in both North and South, at least half the adult males were without real property at any given time in the early 19th century.

It was in the 1830s and 40s that a relatively large urban working class first arose in the Boston-area textile factories made up of "Yankee Girls," farm women and others who worked for several years to earn a dowry for marriage, but largely replaced by inexpensive Irish immigrant labor toward the end of this period.

It was only during the several decades following the Civil War that industrial capitalism became important, fueled by low-priced immigrant labor, rich natural resources, a savage capitalist entrepreneurial spirit as evidenced by the "robber barons," and foreign capital, especially British.

By 1910, the United States was by far the premier industrial power in the world, alone producing more than its leading competitors combined—Germany, Britain, and France—with two-fifths of its population in urban areas, a third of the work force in industry. From 1860 to 1900, thirteen million immigrants came to America and from 1901 to 1920, another 14.5 million, the first accounting for a third of the total increase in population, the second, half. In the twelve largest cities in 1900, two-fifths of the population was foreign born, and by 1914, a third of the American population was foreign born or had one parent so. The sharp class division here between labor and capital resulted in relatively low wages, yet a third higher than those in Western Europe and many times higher than those in Eastern and Southern Europe, which from the 1890s provided most of the immigrants.

What were the working and living conditions of the American working class during Veblen's adult years? We begin with the workweek, certainly a key index on the quality of life. In 1900, it was sixty hours in six days; in 1914, fifty-five hours (forty-nine hours in six unionized industries, fifty-eight hours in eight nonunion ones) in six days; and in the 1920s, a nine-hour day in five-and-a-half days.

As for child labor, there were laws in thirty-nine states by 1914 specifying that a child must be at least twelve years old to work in a factory, with an eight-hour-day norm, ten the maximum; this legislation did not apply to farming. Obviously, child labor (from age ten to sixteen) was extensive, encompassing a fifth of the males and a tenth of the females. Working conditions themselves were hellish with many industrial accidents. In 1913, for instance, 25,000 workers were killed on the job, with 750,000 having serious injury, workers receiving little or no compensation before state workingman's compensation laws that two-thirds of the states had by 1916. Also, there were only a few private pensions; this was before the Social Security Act of 1935 (operative in 1942), the old living with children or relatives. Furthermore, medical and unemployment insurance were nonexistent.

As for real annual average wages in 1914 in dollars, they were 457 dollars in 1860, 500 dollars in 1900, and 714 dollars in 1920. In 1900, the average urban family's budget was 45 percent for food, 25 percent for rent, 25 percent for fuel, light, clothing, and other expenses, and 5 percent for savings; it was about the same in the 1920s. Some prices in 1913 in pounds—bread, 6 cents; round steak, 22 cents; butter, 38 cents. A new Ford sold for 600 dollars.

As for urban housing, larger cities were vast immigrant slums (two-thirds of New York City and Chicago), most immigrants settling in cities as they were poor. In New York City in the 1890s, up to a third of its inhabitants lived in dire poverty. A typical slum building there in 1900 was from three to five stories high, having two-room apartments, one nine by fourteen feet, the other nine by sixteen feet, with no heat or plumbing and little sunlight or free circulating air. Common bathroom facilities were the norm, two or more families sharing them. A 1907 law there mandated a one-window minimum for a bedroom. Crime itself was endemic, streets unsafe at night, dead or abandoned infants were commonplace, and pollution was widespread. Other facts of interest: By 1912 a sixth of American homes had electricity, by 1929, almost three-fourths. By 1900, in cities, public water and sewage system were widespread, and in public transportation, electric street cars or trolleys had replaced the horse-drawn variety. But despite the introduction of the fruits of advancing technology, in 1929, at the end of the booming 1920s and the year of Veblen's death, 70 percent of the families still earned under $2,500 annually, the amount needed for a "decent living standard," this group being basically propertyless, thus perpetuating the earlier sharp class divisions.[1]

Labor Unions

As a close observer of American life, Veblen was well aware of the role of labor unions in defending the rights of workers against capital. Although American unions in the main usually supported capitalism, there were often strong socialist currents even in the more conservative ones, and, indeed, some were socialist. American labor itself was often militant, fighting capital in many bitter strikes, an underlying key factor in Veblen's hope for an American socialist revolution.

Organized labor in America scarcely existed before the 1830s, although craft guilds flourished long before, an example being the Carpenter's Company in Philadelphia founded in 1724. (Craft guilds, labor's aristocracy, trained workers—from apprentice, to journeyman, to master—and acted as Benevolent Societies, providing members benefits for illness, burial, and aid to surviving family members. When divisions erupted between masters and journeymen, the latter often prevented by the former to join their elite circles, formed clandestine unions.) But strikes by workers were not precluded, with at least a dozen local and spontaneous ones from 1780 to 1820, some successful.

It was in the 1830s that America had its first modern unions, a response to early industrialization and the growing cleavage between labor and capital. In 1834, Northern workers organized the National Trades Union, which by 1837 had a membership of 300,000, a third of the North's skilled workers. Although this union conducted a successful city-wide general strike in Philadelphia in 1835 to win a ten-hour day, the Panic of 1837, with its high unemployment and consequent deep wage cuts, quickly destroyed it. In the 1830s and 40s, women textile workers in Lowell, Massachusetts organized unions (the Factory Girls Association in 1834 and the Female Labor Association under Sarah Bagley in 1845), which led to unsuccessful strikes. In the 1850s, several groups of skilled workers, like machinists and printers, also, formed associations.

It was only after the Civil War that American labor once again organized in a milieu of rapid industrialization as the National Labor Union was founded in Baltimore in 1866. Under its president, William H. Silvis, it fought for the eight-hour day, was friendly to the aspirations of African-Americans and women, and entered the political arena, with one of its chief organizers, Charles O'Connor, being the Presidential candidate of the Labor Reform Party in 1872, receiving thirty thousand votes. By 1871, the union had about a hundred thousand members, but expired with the Panic of 1873.

The next union wave principally involved the Knights of Labor, founded in 1869, but which flourished under the leadership of Terrence V. Powderly after 1878. By 1886, its membership stood at three-quarters of a million, with almost ninety thousand African-Americans and women. It sought one big union for workers, skilled and unskilled, based on local assemblies (women in separate, but affiliated, ones), allowing even non-union workers to join. Local assemblies would send delegates to a General Assembly to determine general policy.

The socialist orientation of this union was unmistakable, for in addition to its opposition to child labor and advocacy of equal pay for men and women, the eight-hour day, and a graduated income tax, it favored the nationalization of railroads and telephone and telegraph systems, and, in a decidedly anarchist fashion founded more than a hundred industrial worker-owned cooperatives to abolish the hated wage system; they failed for lack of capital and internal bickering.

The union's decline was caused by differences between skilled and unskilled members and the resistance of capital. In the 1885 strike against the Missouri Pacific Railroad (part of the Gould system), the union restored a wage cut, but in the Texas and Pacific Railroad Car Strike (another part of the Gould network), marked by much violence and sabotage, the public turned against the union as factories closed because of reduced coal shipments. Furthermore, the rift between skilled and unskilled workers deepened, the former being more cautious, wishing to return to work. Powderly himself proposed arbitration, which the owners rejected. With the crushing of this strike, the fortunes of the union declined rapidly, there being only a hundred thousand members in 1890, and it soon expired.

There were other important strikes in the 19th century. The first was the Railroad Strike of 1877, which disrupted rail service from the east coast to the Mississippi River; it witnessed open warfare between workers and federal troops/state militias, with more than a hundred strikers killed. The second was the 1892 Homestead Strike near Pittsburgh, launched by the Amalgamated Association of Iron and Steel Workers against Carnegie's steel plant. To subdue the strikers, Carnegie's chief lieutenant, W. Henry

Clay Frick, the General Manager of the Homestead Works, employed three hundred Pinkertons (the Pinkerton Agency was a strike-breaking company) whom the strikers defeated in a pitched battle. But the state intervened with eight thousand militia to ultimately subdue the workers. The third was the Pullman Strike of 1894, which pitted the American Railway Union (ARU) led by Eugene V. Debs against the Pullman Palace Car Co. (it owned Pullman, a company town near Chicago) of George M. Pullman, the inventor of the sleeping car. After Governor John P. Altgeld of Illinois refused to send the state militia to help Pullman, President Grover Cleveland dispatched federal troops to Chicago against the wishes of Altgeld to protect mail service, preventing any normal strike activity. Debs and other unionists were imprisoned for disobeying the government's injunction to resume rail service. In every one of these strikes, the unreasonable party was management, basically initiating steep wage cuts.

Also of interest were the actions of the Ancient Order of Hibernians, an Irish-American Fraternal Society, nicknamed the Molly Maguires (from a legendary Irish woman fighting rich English landlords) against the anthracite coal operators in the Scranton, Pennsylvania region. The brutally exploited Irish miners went on strike against the mine owners in 1875, in the course of which open warfare broke out between the Mollies and Pinkerton mercenaries. After three bosses and a police officer were killed by the Mollies, twenty of them were charged with their murders (there were no Irish jurors in the trial), found guilty, and hanged.

With the eclipse of the Knights of Labor, the American Federation of Labor (AFL), founded in 1886, rapidly became the foremost American union. It was personified by Samuel Gompers, its president, except for a year, from its founding to his death in 1924. Although at first a socialist, Gompers ultimately endorsed capitalism, not favoring the formation of a labor party, but supporting prolabor political candidates. To be sure, he used the weaponry of the strike and the boycott against capital, favored the eight-hour working day, abolition of child labor, and safe working conditions, but paradoxically opposed the minimum wage and unemployment insurance for unorganized workers. But there was a significant socialist current in this union: Max Hayes, a well-known Cleveland labor leader and socialist, who ran against Gompers as president in 1912, garnered about a third of the delegates' vote.

Membership of unions during the 1900-1930 period was never more than a sixth of the work force. The AFL itself, the largest union whose membership was from half to two-thirds of organized labor, never exceeded the three-million attained in 1920; it was a federation of independent trade unions comprising skilled workers, each bargaining independently with capital.

Some socialists built an alternative model, of having workers, regardless of craft, belong to a single union, promoting working-class solidarity by removing the boundaries of craft parochialism and its obvious divisiveness undoubtedly reinforced by the rise of the large factory. A variation of this model also tied unions to particular socialist parties ("dual unionism") to sharpen the proletarian class struggle against the bourgeoisie.

Two notable examples of this were the Socialist Trade and Labor Alliance (STLA), which lasted from 1895 to 1905, and the IWW. The STLA was a union promoted by the Socialist Labor Party (SLP), founded in 1877, a basically Marxist party after anarchists left it in 1883. Under the leadership of Daniel De Leon, the leading spokesperson of the party after he joined it in 1890, it insisted that its union activity be closely related to the party. In this vein, it attempted to detach workers from other unions which it considered reformist, like the AFL. The STLA had about fifteen thousand members in 1895, but by 1905, when it merged with the IWW, it had less than fifteen hundred. De Leon himself, a founding member of the IWW, was soon expelled from it as his "dual unionism" views impinged on its independence.

There were three principle causes for low union membership: (1) Unions could not overturn court injunctions peremptorily declaring strikes illegal. (Even with the passage of the Clayton Anti-Trust Act of 1914, which specifically stated that labor was not a commodity as the 1890 Sherman Anti-Trust Act insisted, thus not a "restraint on trade," to allow for peaceful strikes, picketing and boycotts, local and other courts could end strikes on the grounds of public safety.) (2) There was savage employer resistance to unions, any union activity by workers leading to almost certain discharge.(3) Although at times successful, union organizing was usually hampered by religio-ethnic divisions among immigrants themselves, with their own pecking order, the older ones in a superior socioeconomic position. This was seized upon by capital to further divide labor. Furthermore, within the working class itself, reflected in factory and office jobs procurred by social networks, the older immigrant groups usually had the better-paying or more desirable ones.[2]

American Anarchism and the IWW

In America, as already observed, anarchism was nourished by the fertile soil of its radicalism: Although its most illustrious exponents were Thoreau and Emerson, there were a number of lesser-known but more focused anarchists. The most well-known of the early Individualist Anarchists was Josiah Warren who founded the Proudhonian Village of Equity in Ohio in 1834, of six or so families who cooperated on the basis of mutuality or "on a labor-for-labor exchange"; it soon foundered because of illness among members. But Warren's two other mutualist experiments, Utopia (1848-mid-1860s), of a hundred or so inhabitants, and Modern Times (1851-60) in Long Island were more successful.

In urban areas, the Proudhonian National Reform Association in the 1840s, largely inspired by George Henry Evans, an English immigrant, attracted some interest in New York City, advocating that public lands remain perpetually so, i.e., to be used only by those working them, not to be sold or inherited. Other anarchists, like Lysander Spooner, William B. Greene—members of the First International—and Benjamin Tucker, basically reworked the ideas of Warren and Proudhon.

Tucker was the most known of the three; his weekly *Liberty* in Boston (1881-1907) drew such eminent writers as George Bernard Shaw, Walt Whitman, and H.L. Mencken. Basically a Proudhonian, Tucker resisted Bakuninist propaganda-by-deed and collectivism as well as Anarcho-Communism. But he translated portions of Bakunin's and Proudhon's works into English and was also interested in the writings of Kropotkin.

With the rise of an urban industrialized America and large-scale immigration, American anarchism from the 1880s onward was almost exlusively made up of recent immigrants, first largely of Germans and Czechs, then Eastern European Jews and Italians, the most important group being Jewish. In the 1880s, American anarchism comprised about seven thousand activists in eighty or so clubs, the largest single concentration of two thousand being in Chicago, with great influence in its union movement, followed by New York City. There were also anarchist clubs in Buffalo, Cleveland, Paterson in New Jersey, Boston, Pittsburgh, Denver, Los Angeles, San Francisco, and Portland, among other places.

The immigrants supplanted the Individualist and Proudhonian Mutualist strains with that of Bakuninist propaganda-by-deed and collectivism in the 1880s to early 90s, which then gave way to the Anarcho-Communism of Kropotkin, eschewing propaganda-by-deed for that of speech and press to educate workers and others to overturn capitalism by revolution at an opportune time.[3]

A transitional figure between old Americans and new immigrants was Voltarine deCleyre, the great writer of American anarchism. Unlike many anarchists, she was born into an "American" family, her father of French descent, her mother a Presbyterian. She was forced by her father (a free thinker turned Catholic) to spend four years as a teenager in a Catholic convent, an experience that made her into a rebel, an anarchist. She was an accomplished poet and essayist, a contributor to many anarchist journals, including *Mother Earth*, writing on such topics as anarchism—a notable one being "Anarchism and American Traditions"—the Paris Commune and Mexican Revolution. She was a splendid public speaker and teacher of English to immigrants, also interested in education reform to be conducted in anarchist schools. A conciliator, she sought to reconcile the various schools of anarchism—Individualists, Mutualists, and Anarcho-Communists—calling for each one to actually implement their views. Goldman has her as an Anarcho-Communist, but she was more than that. To be sure, deCleyre met Kropotkin in London and was utterly charmed by him and she translated Grave's *La Société mourante et l'anarchie* into English as *The Moribund Society and Anarchy*.[4]

The importance of anarchism in the American left during this period was clearly indicated in the May 1886 Haymarket Square riot in Chicago and the saga of the IWW. On May 1 (May Day), 1886, half a million workers went on strike for an eight-hour day, Chicago being the epicenter with eighty thousand. On May 3, the large McCormick Reaper works in Chicago, anticipating a strike for an eight-hour day, locked out its union workers and employed strikebreakers and police to battle them, in the melee six workers being killed by gunfire.

Under anarchist auspices, to show solidarity for the McCormick workers, more than fifteen hundred workers assembled in Haymarket Square on May 4. Towards the end of an orderly meeting, just when the last speaker, Samuel Fielden, a former Methodist minister, had almost finished, the police decided to terminate his talk over his objections. Then suddenly, a bomb was thrown at the police, killing one. The police, in turn, fired on and clubbed the assembled workers who defended themselves, resulting in the deaths of six policemen and four workers, with many injuries on both sides.

The government's riposte was to punish anarchism's better-known militants: Nine were charged on the basis that they "conspired to…excite the people…to sedition, tumult, and riot" leading to the deaths enumerated. Only two of the nine were even at the meeting, Fielden and Rudolph Schnaubelt, the latter fleeing to Argentina. Thus only eight defendants faced the wrath of the courts.

The trial itself was a farce. The prosecution offered no credible evidence that any of the defendants threw the bomb. The eight defended themselves ably: Albert Parsons, for instance, from Alabama, whose ancestors fought in the American Revolution, presented an eight-hour speech defending anarchism and condemning a justice system that without evidence murdered its enemies. Five of the eight were sentenced to be hanged (Parsons; Adolphe Fischer, a printer; George Engel, a toymaker; and Louis Lingg, an officer of the Carpenters' Union who committed suicide before the hanging); two to life imprisonment (Fielden and Michael Schwab); and one to fifteen years' imprisonment, Oscar Neebe, an organizer for the Beer Wagon Drivers' Union.

To be sure, the three surviving anarchists belatedly received a modicum of justice. Illinois Governor Altgeld (a German immigrant who defend labor and the poor in general, a rarity for a public official) pardoned them in 1893 on the basis that evidence against them was flimsy, thereby wrecking his political career as he lost his bid for re-election in 1896.[5]

Leading immigrant anarchists who have a secure place in American history include Emma Goldman, a determined feminist and revolutionary; Alexander Berkman, a one-time lover of Emma's, best known for wounding Frick during the Homestead Strike; Johann Most, a brilliant journalist and follower of Bakunin; and, of course, Nicola Sacco and Bartolemeo Vanzetti of the Sacco-Vanzettti Case, the most celebrated criminal one in American history.

Goldman was born into a lower-middle class Lithuanian-Jewish family (her father, a small businessman) under Russian rule in 1869 and came to America in 1886, often working in clothing mills. The indomitable "Red Emma" indefatigably propagated her Anarcho-Communist ideas, sprinkled with a layer of the elitist ones of Nietzsche so dear to many Individualist Anarchists, in innumerable conferences in which her brilliant oratory literally would overcome an often hostile or lukewarm audience.

Furthermore, Goldman was instrumental in the publication of the monthly *Mother Earth* (March 1906-August 1917) in New York City, the principal anarchist magazine of the period. Although much of the magazine's editing and daily work was done by others, she was its driving force. Much of its reportage was quoting from her almost countless talks. The journal covered anarchist activity not only in the U.S. but in Europe, Latin America, Japan, and elsewhere. Anarchist theory and activity were also well explored by such stalwarts as Proudhon, Eliseé Reclus, Kropotkin, and the French syndicalists, Pelloutier and Emile Pouget, and the German-English syndicalist Rudolf Rocker. And in an educational-literary vein, the magazine published excerpts from the writings of such well-known anarchists as Mary Wollstonecraft, Thoreau, Morris (both Marxist and anarchist), Max Nettlau, and Tolstoy, and nonanarchists, often sympathetic to anarchist concerns, like Anatole France and Theodore Dreiser. Poetry itself was provided by Arturo Giovanitti and Ben Hecht, among others, while cover drawings were by such well-known artists as Man Ray and Grandjuan. In these endeavors, *Mother Earth* followed the pioneer work of Grave.

Goldman's anarchism included freeing women from their subordinate role in society, working at times with Margaret Sanger to promote contraception and birth control, and antiwar activity, principally as one of the organizers in the No-Conscription League in 1917.

On the question of propaganda-by-deed, Goldman with one exception, to be examined with Berkman, was opposed to individual or small-scale collective acts of violence (she was no pacifist), but defended anarchists who committed them, viewing their actions as responses to capitalist exploitation and brutality. For instance, she defended Leon Czolgosz who assassinated President William McKinley in 1901 on this basis. Most anarchists condemned this act, believing that Czolgosz was mentally ill. Czolgosz himself was involved only peripherally in anarchism, the police extracting a confession from him that a Goldman lecture inspired him "to do something heroic for the cause I loved." The anti-anarchist hysteria that followed this act led to Congressional legislation in 1903 barring anarchist aliens from coming to the U.S. and laws in New York, New Jersey, and Wisconsin made it illegal to espouse anarchist views or defend anarchist groups.

Goldman herself would be expelled from the U.S. as an alien. With American entry into World War I in 1917, she, Berkman, and others began the No-Conscription League, resulting in a two-year imprisonment for them, then expulsion to Communist Russia in December 1919, along with many others. Once there, the two became disillusioned, leaving after two years. She then lived in Canada working on behalf of Spanish anarchists in the 1936-39 civil war in Spain. She died in 1940.[6]

Like Goldman, Berkman was also born into a Lithuanian-Jewish family in Vilna in 1870, a wealthy merchant one that later moved to the Russian capital St. Petersburg. After the death of his parents, he came to New York City in 1888, almost immediately plunging into anarchist activity, already a radical, influenced greatly by his uncle Mark "Maxim" Natanson, a founding member of the revolutionary Chaikovsky Circle in Russia and one of the leaders in the Russian Socialist Revolutionary Party. Berkman, who already had finished the *Gymnasium*, worked in factories to support himself. In 1889, he met Goldman, the two becoming not only associates, but lovers, always remaining friends afterward, although romantically involved with others.

Berkman should be pictured as a dedicated idealist advocating social revolution, willing to give up his life for the liberation of the oppressed masses, viewing himself as a kindred spirit of the terrorist Rakhmetov in Nikolai G. Chernyshevsky's *What Is to Be Done?* This would be partially consummated thus: The 1892 Homestead strike, already observed, vehemently opposed by Frick, prompted Berkman and Goldman to plan for his assassination to avenge strikers killed by Pinkertons. This *attentat* ("outrage" in French) or propaganda-by-deed to arouse the lethargic masses from acceptance of the status quo was also used in Europe, as in France by Ravachol, Auguste Vaillant, Emile Henry, and Santo Ceasario at the time, the last resulting in the assassination of the French President Sadi Carnot.

Thus it was that Berkman went to Homestead, met Frick, shot him with a revolver and then stabbed him several times with a sharp steel file. But Frick survived. Berkman himself was promptly apprehended, thus preventing his planned suicide with a nitroglycerine capsule. For this act, he was sentenced to a twenty-two year imprisonment, serving fourteen years. Most American anarchists found Berkman's action distasteful, but Goldman defended him.

Upon his release from prison in 1906, Berkman resumed his anarchist activity through speech and writing. In the latter area, he proved to be an able theorist in *What Is Communist Anarchism?* After his antiwar activity and so forth, Berkman lived in various European cities, working as a translator. In 1936, he committed suicide in Nice.[7]

Even before coming to the U.S. from Germany in 1882 at age thirty-six, Most had a most tempestuous life. By trade a bookbinder, he was elected as a socialist candidate to the German Reichstag from 1874 to 1878 and served as an editor of various anarchist newspapers. He left Germany for France, then for England after repeated imprisoments for attacking the traditional verities of nationalism and religion.

Most's anarchist activity in America was of the utmost importance in tracing the fortunes of American anarchism in the 1880s. It was Most who, in ceaseless speeches and writing through his newspaper *Die Frieheit* in New York City, persuaded the Socialist Revolutionaries, who, after leaving the reformist Socialist Labor Party, then formed Socialist Revolutionary clubs in Chicago, New York, and other cities to join the anarchist cause. Most himself for many years was a proponent of propaganda-by-deed, writing articles in his newspaper on making nitroglycerine, but when Berkman wounded Frick, he condemned the act, perhap jealous of Goldman's close relationship with Berkman, among other reasons. At one time he asked Goldman to marry him; she refused.[8]

World War I itself was divisive to socialism and its anarchist contingent. Although most socialists and anarchists opposed war, once it began, most of the former rallied to the siren call of their respective nationalisms, but not most of the latter, although an influential minority of them, including Kropotkin and Grave, supported the Allies.

Government repression of anarchists during the war and rise of Soviet Communism led to the end of anarchism as a vibrant force in the U.S. and most of Europe with the exception of Spain, although anarchism still survived in the form of small groups and clubs. However, there was a renaissance of anarchism in selected nations in the 1960s, as with the advent of the Students for a Democratic Society in the U.S. and the French May Events of 1968, both movements/events having a strong anarchist flavor. Today, anarchism is prominent in the peace and anticapitalist globalization movements; it is particularly strong on college campuses.

On April 15, 1920, in South Braintree, Massachusetts, five men, while robbing a shoe company of sixteen thousand dollars, killed a paymaster and a guard. On May 5, two immigrant Italian anarchists, Nicola Sacco, a shoemaker, and Bartolomeo Vanzetti, a fish peddler at that time, were arrested for the crime. They were tried in nearby Dedham (May 31 to July 14, 1921), found guilty of first degree murder and sentenced to death.

Doubts about the guilt of the two were quickly expressed as the money was never found and witnesses who placed them at or near the murder scene were disputed by others who placed them many miles away. Indeed, the jury accepted unconvincing eyewitness evidence of the former but discounted that of the latter. The judge himself was heavily biased against immigrants and anarchists. In fact, the case took place in the poisoned atmosphere of the Red Scare, of fear and hatred toward recent immigrants and radical ideas which some of them expressed.

The Sacco-Vanzetti Case and the execution of Sacco and Vanzetti on August 23, 1927, aroused great interest not only in the U.S., but worldwide. In the former, a Sacco-Vanzetti Defense Committee was organized by Joseph Ettor and Arturo Giovannitti, soon joined by many noted writers, like Mencken, Dos Passos (he mentioned them in a "Camera Eye" in *USA*), Upton Sinclair (his *Boston* concluded that Sacco was probably guilty), Dorothy Parker, Edna St. Vincent Millay ("Justice Denied in Massachusetts" and "Fear"—the former, a poem; the latter, a poetic essay), and Maxwell Anderson (he wrote two plays, *God of the Lightning* about it and *Winterset* reflecting on it, its main character being Sacco's son, Dante).

Letters and commentary to save the lives of Sacco and Vanzetti came from many sources. From rightists, no less a person than Benito Mussolini, the fascist chief of the Italian government, asked that their lives be spared, while the Royalist *Action Française* attacked American justice. Even the apolitical Alfred Dreyfus, of Dreyfus-Case fame in France, offered to come to America to plead for them. On the left, newspapers in France, like the Communist *L'Humanité* and *Pravda* in the Soviet Union railed against American justice. Also, President William Green of the AFL, the American Civil Liberties Union, and thousands of professors and college students signed petitions asking for a commutation of the death sentence or for a new trial, as did half-a-million signatures worldwide.

On the day before and after the execution of Sacco and Vanzetti, demonstrations and riots occurred, including the stoning of American embassies in Europe, Latin America, and elsewhere, particularly intense in Paris, Geneva, Bremen, Hamburg, Stuttgart, Sidney, and Mexico City, with Diego Rivera speaking at a mass meeting there. But in the U.S., nothing of note happened.[9]

The IWW was a quasi-anarchist Revolutionary Syndicalist union founded in 1905 in Chicago by such socialists stalwarts as Debs, De Leon, the ever indomitable "Big Bill" Haywood, and the irrepressible Mary Harris (Mother) Jones. Its greatest appeal was in the West, among unskilled farm workers, miners, lumberjacks, longshoremen, and seamen—usually young men without families, drifters—membership never reaching more than a hundred thousand, this in 1917; but brief membership, given the nature of the work, allowed for a million to pass through its ranks.

The IWW's aim was to be "a labor organization builded as the structure of socialist society, embracing within itself the working class in appoximately the same groups and departments and industries that the workers would assume in the working-class administration of the Co-operative Commonwealth," to be headed by a general administration headed by a president. The IWW was more centralized than the CGT in that its "one big industrial union" concept held that each IWW local union, which itself would erase any craft-union narrowness, was part of the one larger one, locals to be aided by others during strikes. This concept was related to the unskilled and semiskilled workers composing the IWW. The CGT, on the other hand, made up of skilled workers, lent itself more readily to a looser organizational structure, each union closely guarding its independence.

To be sure, the IWW was only partly anarchist; Anarcho-Syndicalists were against the notion of one big union, wishing for a decentralized society, where unions, for instance, would federate, each union maintaining its independence. Furthermore, there were Marxist elements in this union. But in calling for the quick abolition of the wage system and craft unionism, which inevitably divided the working class, emphasis on direct action or daily struggle against capital at the point of work, including sabotage during strikes, disdain of political activity, stress on local working-class initiative and democracy, and opting for a series of strikes culminating in the general one to overthrow capitalism, the IWW was clearly in the Anarcho-Syndicalist tradition. (There was one union, however, that was purely Anarcho-Syndicalist in America, the Union of Russian Workers with nine thousand members.)

A revolutionary union under Haywood and others, the IWW soon rejected political activity for direct action against factory and mine owners in the form of daily organizing workers, always prepared to strike and commit sabotage to intensify the class struggle. Direct-action sabotage prompted Debs and De Leon to leave.

The IWW was involved in many notable strikes, the two most celebrated in the East were the January 1912 Lawrence, Massachusetts strike of unskilled immigrant textile workers, led by Giovannitti, and the 1913 Paterson, New Jersey Silk Strike, again by unskilled immigrants, led by Big Bill Haywood, Elizabeth Gurley Flynn, and Carlo Tresca.[10]

Veblen himself commented on various aspects of anarchism, especially its Revolutionary-Syndicalist facet. He was indeed on solid grounds in locating much of the anarchist and socialist critique of capitalism in 18th century "natural rights" theory of the "unalienable freedom and equality of the individual," which rejected "prescriptive ownership," i.e., wealth acquired from employing the labor of others. But he neglected to mention that anarchism was influenced by other socialist currents, as the 19th century layers of the Romantic revolt and Darwinian mutual aid.

Because anarchism followed a natural-rights perspective in justifying its egalitarianism, Veblen characterized it as "senselessly extreme."[11] But if one closely observed Veblen's ultimate view of humanity, with its propensities for "idle curiosity," "workmanship," and "care of children," (examined in a later chapter), was it not also based on "natural" human attributes? Furthermore, he supported a general strike to establish socialism, the Soviets, and New England town meetings, all decidedly in the anarchist tradition. In this respect, key elements of the anarchist spirit were not antithetical to the Bolsheviks in the early phases of their revolution, of which Veblen thoroughly approved. Especially was this so in the Soviets, in which workers were in charge of the shop floor in factories and of local government affairs.

Veblen himself wrote a report on the IWW while working for the federal government as a statistician and trouble-shooter in the Food Administration in 1918. This came about when farmers demanded additional workers because of the war. Veblen was to have visited Missouri, Iowa, Illinois, Minnesota, and North and South Dakota to examine farmer wishes, but felled by a cold, he could not make the trip. His assistant Isador Lubin did. He, then, reworked, Lubin's findings into a finished paper, "Farm Labor and the IWW," most sympathetic to the IWW.

This work first mentioned that a large portion of the "transient farm labor" were IWW members who wished to be adequately paid, properly boarded and lodged, and to have their civil rights respected, the last demand being listed under the phrase of "freedom from illegal restraint." He, then, defended members charged with being prone to violence, acknowledging that if wronged, they would resort to "non-resistant sabotage," which they called "deliberate withdrawal of efficiency," or "malingering." He also commented on the anarchist nature of the IWW, holding that its leadership had only an "advisory" relationship with local farm chapters. Thus, for him, if IWW farm workers ever felt cheated by employers, general contracts between farmers and the IWW were meaningless. Then, too, he was impressed by the strong spirit of solidarity among members, an injustice to one being an injustice to all. He, furthermore, supported members under attack from government and local conservative business, urging government to deal with some 150 of them arrested for disloyalty to the government as "leniently" as possible, and not to interfere with IWW activity. But he admitted that although members "may not be in the right," since their services were so critical to the war effort, "generosity is the best policy." Finally, he proposed that IWW farm workers be allowed to set up their own work units under elected officers, i.e., to work in the democratic work environment of anarchist collectives. (If Veblen's recommendation had been accepted—it wasn't—it would have intensified social conflict between farm workers and owner-farmers, many of the latter being members of the Nonpartisan League in South Dakota, advocating such socialist measures as state ownership of grain elevators and warehouses and state control over banks and railroads to prevent big business from manipulating prices.)

In an appendix to this report, there was a letter to Veblen from Maurice G. Bresnan, the secretary-treasurer of the Agricultural Workers Union (the farm branch of the IWW), that described brutalities inflicted on IWW members by business and police, as in being railroaded to jail and taken for rides in the countryside for methodical beatings.[12]

Veblen was also involved in aiding IWW militants against government persecution in 1918. In viewing World War I as a capitalist war, thus opposing military service (but most IWW members signed up for the draft), and refusing a no-strike pledge (unlike the AFL), the IWW initiated a series of strikes against copper companies. The federal government's response was to indict 101 IWW leaders for hindering the war effort. In the hysteria surrounding the trial in Chicago, Veblen, along with the social philosopher and educator, John Dewey, the historians James Harvey Robinson and Carleton J.H. Hayes, and others, signed a petition that not only asked for monies to defend the Wobblies, but also pleaded for a fair trial. It did little to stop the government juggernaut which found the defendants guilty, with unusually stiff sentences, the average being eight years of imprisonment, later commuted by President Warren G. Harding. It was this event that marked the demise of the IWW as a viable organization.[13]

As an almost anarchist, Veblen regarded unions as a normal workers' response to industrial capitalism, although a time lag was involved:

> An interval of discipline in the ways of the mechanically standardized industry, more or less protracted and severe, seems necessary to bring such a proportion of the workmen into line as will give a consensus of sentiment and opinion favorable to trade-union action.[14]

This movement was a step toward socialism, a "compromise between received notions of what 'naturally' ought to be in matters of industrial business…and what the new exigencies of industry demand," an attack on bourgeois natural-rights conceptions because it "denies individual freedom of contract to the workman, as well as free discretion to the employer to carry out his business as may suit his own ends." These remarks were related to unions protecting labor against capital over matters of wages, hours of work, and welfare programs. But only when unions attacked the "natural-rights institutions of property and free contract," the "latest, maturest" form of trade unionism, would they come to "socialism."

Only the IWW, for Veblen, could meet the test of mature unionism, but it was hampered by its low membership and largely unskilled workers. As for the AFL, he viewed it as "one of the Vested Interests, as ready as any other to do battle for its own margin of privilege and profit." Indeed, for him, its craft unions, engaging in nepotism and limiting their numbers through apprenticeships to better bargain with employers, were chiefly interested in simply defeating rival unions and utilizing the strike only to achieve higher wages and better working conditions for themselves only. This analysis, similar to Lenin's *What Is To Be Done?*, claimed that working-class consciousness seldom transcended parochial bread-and-butter issues.[15]

NOTES

1. On the statistics presented, see, for instance, Robert H. Bremner, *The Discovery of Poverty in the United States* (New Brunswick, NJ: Transaction Publishers, 1992), pp. 164-268. On wages, see Robert C. Puth, *American Economic History* (Chicago: Dryden Press, 1982), p. 296. Another gold mine on social and economic statistics is in Link, *American Epoch*, pp. 296-317.

2. On American labor, see Bruce Levine, Stephen Brier, David Brundage *et al.*, *Who Built America?: Working People and the Nation's Economy, Politics, Culture and Society*, Vol. I: *From Conquest and Colonization Through Reconstruction and the Great Uprising of 1877*; Joshua Freeman, Nelson Lichtenstein, Stephen Brier *et al.*, *From the Gilded Age to the Present*, Vol. II (Nev York: Pantheon Books, 1989 and 1992). (Under the direction of Herbert G. Gutman.) Philip S. Foner, *History of the Labor Movement of the United States*, 4 vols. (New York: International Publishers, 1947-65). On Gompers, see his autobiography, *Seventy Years of Life and Labor* (New York: E.P. Dutton, 1948). On De Leon, see Carl Reeve, *The Life and Times of Daniel De Leon* (New York: Humanities Press, 1972), pp. 43-78 on his union activity and views on unions.

3. On American anarchism, see James J. Martin, *Men Against the State: The Expositors of Individualist Anarchism in America, 1827-1908* (New York: Libertarian Book Club, 1957), a third of the work is on Tucker; William O. Reichert, "The Anarchist as Socialist via the Mutualist Connection," in Louis Patsouras, ed. *The Crucible of Socialism* (Atlantic Highlands, NJ: Humanities Press International,

1987), pp. 161-80; and Terry M. Perlin, *Anarchist-Communism in America, 1890-1914* (Ph.D. Dissertation, Brandies, 1970; University Microfilms, Ann Arbor, MI).

4. On deCleyre, see Perlin, *Anarchist-Communism*, pp. 146-73.

5. On the Haymarket events, see Paul Avrich, *The Haymarket Tragedy* (Princeton, NJ: Princeton University Press, 1984).

6. On Goldman, see Alice Wexler, *Emma Goldman in America* (Boston: Beacon Press, 1984), for instance, pp. 100-12 on Czolgosz; p. 53 on her Anarcho-Communism. Emma Goldman, *Living My Life*, 2 vols. (New York: Dover Publications, 1970), is a superb work. On *Mother Earth*, see Perlin, *Anarchist-Communism*, pp. 174-237.

7. On Berkman, see Perlin, *Anarchist-Communism*, pp. 91-118, for instance.

8. On Most, see Perlin, *Anarchist-Communism*, pp. 60-75, 105-08, 132-34.

9. On Sacco-Vanzetti, see Francis Russell, *Tragedy in Dedham: The Story of the Sacco-Vanzetti Case* (New York: McGraw-Hill, 1962), p. 466, that Sacco may have been guilty of murder. William Young and David E. Kaiser, *Postmortem: New Evidence in the Case of Sacco and Vanzetti* (Amherst, MA: University of MA. Press, 1985), pp. 158-64, that Sacco and Vanzetti were innocent of murder.

10. On the IWW, see John S. Gambs, *The Decline of the IWW* (New York: Russell and Russell, 1966). Joyce L. Kornbluh, *Rebel Voices: A IWW Anthology* (Ann Arbor, MI: University of Michigan Press, 1964).

11. Thorstein Veblen, *The Theory of Business Enterprise* (New York: Scribner's, 1904), pp. 338-39.

12. Thorstein Veblen, "Farm Labor and the IWW," in Leon Ardzrooni, ed., *Essays in Our Changing Order* (New York: Augustus M. Kelley, 1964).

13. On the petition defending the IWW, see Gambs, *IWW*, p. 22.

14. Veblen, *Business Enterprise*, p. 328.

15. *Ibid.*, pp. 329 ff.

VII Populism, Progressive Movement, and American Socialism, 1892-1917

Populism and Progressivism

THERE WERE THREE STRONG MOVEMENTS for reform in America during Veblen's lifetime: Populism, the Progressive Movement, and socialism. As an enthusiast for socialism by the early 1890s, Veblen could not but welcome reforms, especially those that would empower workers and farmers. Of the three, Populism and socialism, in particular, attempted to maintain small business, principally the family farm. Indeed, socialism itself wished for a political alliance between the workers and lower-middle class against the upper-middle class and wealthy. The workers, in owning the factories in varying degree would join the lower-middle class in sharing the American dream of economic abundance and general equality.

The first national people's movement to reform American society was Populism, largely composed of small independent and tenant farmers, its leaders coming from the rural middle class—small office holders, editors of newspapers and lawyers. Dorfman did not inform us whether Veblen was sympathetic to Populism, but given his defense of the Greenbackers and Henry George, we can safely assume that he approved of its general political orientation. In fact, Commager, in the *American Mind*, as previously observed, saw Veblen as being basically influenced by a homegrown "agrarian radicalism."[1]

In their Omaha Convention in June 1892, Populists enunciated a platform whose primary aim was to strengthen the interests of workers and farmers against big business. It included the secret or Australian ballot, a graduated income tax, the free coinage of silver to encourage inflation, direct election of senators, briefer workday, prohibiting strikebreakers, government ownership of railroads, the initiative (voters to directly legis-late for new laws), the referendum (voters to repeal laws passed by special interest groups), two-percent government loans to farmers, government- operated postal savings banks, and immigration restriction.

The class-struggle conceptions of Populists greatly resembled those of Veblen, en-visaging conflict between the average farmers and workers, along with small business, on the one hand, and big business (large banks and other corporations), on the other—between the producers and the leisure class. Sockless Jerry Simpson, a Populist spokesperson, exclaimed: "It is a struggle between the robbers and the robbed," while James B. Weaver, the Populist presidential candidate for the 1892 general elections pro-claimed that "it is a fight between labor and capital, and labor is in the vast majority."

A Populist manifesto declared (note the similarity to Veblen's pronouncements):

There are but two sides in the conflict...On the one side are the allied hosts of monopolies, the money power, great trusts, and railroad corporations, who seek the enactment of laws to benefit them and impoverish the people. On the other side are the farmers, laborers, merchants, and all other people who produce wealth and bear the burden of taxation...Between these two sides there is no middle ground.

The high tide of Populism as an independent force was reflected in the 1892 elections when it garnered 8.5 percent of the vote.[2]

The Populist revolt was succeeded by the Progressive movement whose greatest vibrancy was from 1900 to 1917, although elements of it continued to the early 1920s. Its agenda was greatly aided by a rising socialist tide spearheaded by a band of journalists, the Muckrakers who exposed the ties between big business and political corruption and publicized such evils as hellish working conditions, child labor, contamination of food, and poor housing.

Many of the Muckrakers were socialists, like Upton Sinclair and Lincoln Steffens. Examples of their works: Sinclair's *The Jungle* (1906), in not only recounting the horrid working conditions of meat workers, but even the lack of elementary sanitation in the processing of meat, led to a torrent of public protest, resulting in the passage in 1906 of the Pure Food and Drug Act and Meat Inspection Act. Steffens' articles in *McClure's Magazine* in 1904 (*The Shame of the Cities*) tellingly probed the connection between business money and venal politicians.

The muckraking spirit undoubtedly contributed to the rise of socialism during this period, especially its gas-and-water variety (municipal ownership of public utilities and transportation), and to social legislation, as in child labor laws in most states by 1914, forbidding work under age twelve in factories; federal attempts to suppress child labor, as the Keating-Owen Act of 1916, were struck down by the United States Supreme Court, as was the 1920 federal Minimum Wage Law for women in the District of Columbia.

The Progressive movement was also instrumental in the enactment of constitutional amendments and in other manifestations to further democratize politics: The 16th Amendment in 1913 allowed for the levying of an income tax; the 17th, also in 1913, called for the direct election of senators; the 18th in 1919 prohibited liquor; and the 19th in 1920 granted women the general suffrage. Then there was passage in almost all states by 1915 of the direct primary, in which voters directly voted for candidates, weakening bossism; the initiative in thirteen states by 1918; the referendum in twenty-one by 1918; and the recall, a special election procedure to remove public officials, in ten states by 1915. In the realm of preventing monopoly, the Clayton Anti-Trust Act of 1914 strengthened the Sherman Anti-Trust Act. Although these acts dealt fatal blows to monopoly, they did not prevent oligopoly.[3]

On balance, these reforms, especially in the social arena, were not insignificant. Other reforms, proposed by President Theodore Roosevelt in the 1907-09 period and in his run for the Presidency in 1912, like the eight-hour day, graduated income and inheritance taxes, more compensation for victims of industrial accidents, were not enacted. Indeed, a system of national social security, as in Germany by the 1880s—old age pensions and medical and accident insurance—would not be even partially enacted until the New Deal and Great Society programs of Franklin Delano Roosevelt and Johnson.

American Socialism, 1892-1917

The reform impulses of Populism and Progressivism were deepened by American socialism whose heyday was in the 1900-1920 period, the work of De Leon's Socialist Labor Party (SLP) in the 1890s being a key preparatory step. De Leon, born into a middle-class Jewish family in the island of Curacao, came to the U. S. in 1872. After graduating from the Columbia Univ. Law School, he lectured there from 1883 to 1889, losing further appointments because of his socialist activity. In 1890, after membership in the Knights of Labor and Bellamy's Nationalist Clubs, he joined the SLP and soon emerged as its leading spokesperson. An indefatigable revolutionary Marxist, he edited the weekly party journal, *The People*, which became *The Daily People* in 1900, the first English socialist daily.

The American Socialist Party (SP), representing the principal thrust of socialist success, was founded in 1901 by socialist groups and individuals desiring unity, like Debs' Social Democratic Party, Morris Hillquit from the SLP, Bellamyists, Christian Socialists, and Populists. The SLP and Fabian socialists did not join.[4]

The SP had Debs as its inspirational leader who ran as its Presidential candidate in 1904, 1908, 1912, and 1920. He came to socialism from industrial unionism, founding the ARU in 1893. His leading the Pullman Strike in 1894 resulted in a six-month prison term, permitting his reading of Marxist literature, decisively influencing his becoming a socialist by 1895. He was at once a political democrat, a revolutionary socialist who accepted Marxian class struggle, and an advocate of industrial unionism with its corollary of workers' control of industry. Debs was influenced by both the American and European radical traditions: From his Alsatian immigrant father, he became aware of both the European Enlightenment and Romanticism, to which he added a Marxism interpreted by Karl Kautsky; from his readings of American history, he was especially influenced by Paine, Jeffersonian democracy, the socialism of Phillips, Bellamy's *Looking Backward*, and Laurence Gronlund's *The Co-operative Commonwealth*. His vision was to update and extend the democratic egalitarianism and individualism of the frontier to fit the new urban/industrial reality in a democratic and cooperative socialism that included women and African-Americans as equal participants.

There was also in Debs an anarchist streak commented on by Goldman. When she conversed with him in 1898, she was so struck by the similarity of their ideas that she declared him to be an anarchist. But there remained this critical difference between them: He was for reformist electoral politics to reach workers, which she rejected, but it should be pointed out that as leader of the socialist party for more than two decades, he neither became a member of its National Executive Committee before 1922, nor engaged in its hair-splitting debates and bureaucratic infighting. Furthermore, his anarchism, consonant with Marx's views, stressed "industrial democracy," or what is currently termed as "participatory democracy." Ever fearful of bureaucrats and officials, he called for "*ruling* from the bottom up instead of *being ruled* from the *top down*." More specifically:

> Socialism proposes that the people—all the people—shall socially own the sources of wealth and social means with which wealth is produced; that the people, in other words, shall be the joint proprietors upon equal terms of the industries of the nation, that these shall be cooperatively operated and democratically managed.

These views were related to his affinity for Revolutionary Syndicalism, being one of the founders of the IWW. Although he left this union, it was not because of its advocacy of workers' control of industry, but because of its employing sabotage during strikes.[5]

In addition to Debs, the socialists had many other well-known activists, especially Hillquit and Berger. Hillquit was an immigrant from Latvia who came to New York City when he was still in his teens. Born into lower-middle-class Jewish family—his father a teacher—Hillquit excelled in school, graduating from the Law School of New York University. Even before becoming a lawyer, he was a member of De Leon's SLP, but left because De Leon could not brook a serious rival to his leadership. A Marxist, he stressed reform before a revolutionary overturn of capitalism. The main aim of the party, therefore, was to succeed politically to reform capitalism, which, at a critical point would lead to socialism, either through the ballot box or through revolution by the majority.[6]

Victor Berger was another immigrant, from Austria, already well educated. A Marxist, he plunged into socialist activity in Milwaukee, editing two newspapers, one in English, the other in German, and building an effective political machine intimately tied to AFL unions that in 1910 elected a socialist mayor and him as the first-ever socialist congressperson, representing the Milwaukee area in Congress until 1928.[7]

The SP rapidly made its presence known in the political scene. With an expanding membership, twenty thousand by 1904 and one hundred and twenty thousand by 1912, it quickly increased its electoral and officeholder strength. Soon afterward the membership was swollen by immigrants organized into Foreign-Language Federations, which in 1917 numbered thirty-three thousand of the eighty-thousand total membership—the German, Italian, Finnish, Jewish, Lithuanian, Polish, Russian, South Slavic, and Ukrainian.

In the 1912 elections, as Debs garnered over 900,000 votes or 6 percent of the total for the Presidency, socialists re-elected Congressperson Berger, and captured fifty-six mayorships, including those of Milwaukee; Berkeley, California; Butte, Montana; Flint and Jackson, Michigan; and, St. Mary's, Ohio; and elected twenty-one state representatives, and about 160 city councilors, and more than one thousand local and state officers.

A large and vigorous press also testified to socialism's success: Eight foreign-language dailies, the most important being the Milwaukee *Leader*, the New York *Call*, and the Jewish *Daily Forward*, and two national magazines, the weekly *Appeal to Reason* and the monthly *Wilshire's Magazine*. The first periodical, founded in 1895 by J.A. Wayland, from Girard, Kansas, had a circulation of half a million; the second, founded by Gaylord Wilshire, a millionaire socialist involved in many financial endeavors in publishing and mining (Los Angeles' Wilshire Boulevard is named after him), had a circulation of 400,000. Both featured many socialist writers, like the novelists Jack London and Sinclair.

Not only was socialism important in the 1910s in the political arena, but even more so in the artistic/literary/intellectual spheres. In 1905, the irrepressible Sinclair founded the Intercollegiate Socialist Society (ISS), renamed the League for Industrial Democracy (LID) after World War I, with London, who spread the gospel of socialism far and wide, as its first president. This organization was closely identified with a democratic socialist view of society: Socialism, evolving democratically, would nationalize large industries in manufacturing, transportation, utilities, and banks, but allow for small private business.

Among the more prominent members of the ISS and LID were Dewey; Walter Lippmann, a distinguished political commentator; Charles P. Steinmetz, a noted inventor; Florence Kelley, a champion of women's and children's rights, one of the founders of the Women's Trade Union League, director of the National Consumer League which advocated industrial reform through consumer activism, and an associate of Jane Addams in Chicago's Hull House; Roger Baldwin, a leading founder of the American Civil Liberties Union; Randolph Bourne, a mordant social critic who uncompromisingly upheld socialist ideals; the novelist Ernest Poole; Walter Weyl, political and cultural commentator whose *The New Democracy* was a powerful cry for social justice; the economist Paul H. Douglas, who later became a Democratic senator from Illinois; Vida Scudder, a well known Christian Socialist; Stuart Chase, an economist who was basically a Veblenian; A.J. Muste, a leading pacifist and civil libertarian; and Max Eastman, a prolific journalist and commentator. Socialist literary and visual-arts journals also flourished with the *Masses* 1911-17), and its successor, the *Liberator* (1918-23), both published in New York City, with a circulation fluctuating from ten to twenty thousand.

The *Masses* was begun by such notables as the poet Louis Untermeyer, the artist John Sloan, the cartoonist Art Young, and its first editors, Piet Vlag (a Dutchman) and Thomas Seltzer. It was a journal firmly in the democratic socialist camp, but after 1912, it turned leftward under its editor Max Eastman and Floyd Dell, a novelist and literary critic, declaring its independence from capitalism and reformist socialism thus:

> This magazine is owned and published cooperatively by its editors. It has no
> dividends to pay, and nobody is trying to make money out of it. A revolutionary
> and not a reform magazine; a magazine with a sense of humor and not re-
> spect for the respectable: frank, arrogant, and impertinent.

As a revolutionary socialist journal, it sympathized with the IWW's direct-action orientation to achieve socialism. When it opposed American entrance into World War I, Eastman, Dell, John Reed, a well-known journalist, and Young were indicted under the wartime Espionage Act, but their cases were dropped by the government. The journal then resumed operations under its new name, tThe *Liberator*, under Eastman as editor.

Some of the more important contributors to these journals (all were socialists, but some were not of the revolutionary variety) included the novelists Sinclair, Dos Passos, Poole, the Russian Maxim Gorky; the philosopher, mathematician, and historian, Bertrand Russell; the poets Giovannitti, Amy Lowell, Vachel Lindsay, and Carl Sandburg; the playwright George Bernard Shaw; Edmund Wilson, one of the most versatile men of letters in the American experience, novelist, critic, essayist, and historian; the indomitable Bourne; Baldwin; and Chase; and the cartoonists/painters Young, George Bellows, and Sloan.

Mention should also be made of *The Seven Arts,* a short lived literary socialist journal which lasted from 1916 to 1917. Its editors were the poet James Oppenheim, Bourne, and the outstanding literary critic and writer, Van Wyck Brooks.[8]

NOTES

1. Commager, *American Mind*, p. 238.

2. John D. Hicks, *The Populist Revolt* (Lincoln, NE: University of Nebraska Press, 1959) is the classic work on Populism. It was first published in 1931. Richard Hofstadter, *The Age of Reform: From Bryan to F.D.R.* (New York: Vintage Books, 1960), pp. 3-130 are on the farmers and Populism; Theodore Saloutos, *Farmer Movements in the South: 1865-1933* (Lincoln, NE: University of Nebraska Press, 1964).

3. On various aspects of the Progressive movement, see Hofstadter, *Age of Reform*, pp. 131-328; Arthur S. Link and Richard L. McCormick, *Progressivism* (Arlington Heights, IL: Harlan Davidson, 1983); Gabriel Kolko, *The Triumph of Conservatism: A Reinterpretation of American History, 1900-1916* (New York: Free Press of Glencoe, 1963); James Weinstein, *The Corporate Ideal in the Corporate State, 1900-1918* (Boston: Beacon Press, 1968); Noble, *Progressive Mind*; Louis Filler, *Crusaders for American Liberalism: The Story of the Muckrakers* (New York: Collier Books, 1961); White, *Social Thought in America*; Harvey Swados, edited and Introduction, *Years of Conscience: The Muckrakers* (Cleveland, OH: Meridian Books, 1962). On perhaps the best-known of the Muckrakers, Lincoln Steffens, see Justin Kaplan, *Lincoln Steffens: A Biography* (New York: A Touchstone Book, 1974), pp. 97-98. He quotes Steffens that "politics is a business." In this context, Steffens "allied himself with other American moralists, from Emerson and Henry Demarest Lloyd to Veblen, who decried a business society...which was corrupt and corruptive."

4. On American Socialism, see: Ira Kipnis, *The American Socialist Movement: 1897-1912* (New York: Columbia University Press, 1952); Howard H. Quint, *The Forging of American Socialism: Origins of the Modern Movement* (Columbia, SC: University of South Carolina Press, 1953); David A. Shannon, *The Socialist Party of America* (Chicago: Quadrangle Paperback, 1967); James Weinstein, *The Decline of Socialism in America: 1912-1925* (New York: Monthly Review Press, 1967); Egbert and Persons, *Socialism and American Life*; Theodore Draper, *The Roots of American Communism* (New York: Viking Press, 1957); Howard Zinn, *People's History of the United States: 1492-Present* (New York: HarperPerrennial, 1995), pp. 314-49, entitled "The Socialist Challenge."

5. On De Leon, see Reeve, *De Leon*, pp. 1-41, for instance. On Debs, see Nick Salvatore, *Eugene V. Debs: Citizen and Socialist* (Urbana, IL: University of Illinois Press, 1982); Ray Ginger, *The Bending Cross: A Biography of Eugene Victor Debs* (New Brunswick, NJ: Rutgers University Press, 1949); Jean Y. Tussey, ed., *Eugene V. Debs Speaks* (New York: Pathfinder Press, 1970), p. 236 on the long quotation.

6. On Hillquit, see Morris Hillquit, *Loose Leaves from a Busy Life* (New York: Macmillan, 1934).

7. On Berger, see Victor Berger, *Voice and Pen of Victor Berger: Congressional Speeches and Editorials* (Milwaukee, WI: *The Milwaukee Leader*, 1929).

8. On American Socialism/Communism in the literary/artistic scene, see Daniel Aaron, *Writers on the Left* (New York: Avon Books, 1961). Walter B. Rideout, *The Radical Novel in the United States: Some Interrelations of Literature and Society* (New York: Hill and Wang, 1956). Egbert and Persons, *Socialism and American Life*, I, 599-751. Richard Hofstadter, *Anti-Intellectualism American Life* (New York: Vintage Books, 1966), pp. 288 ff., claimed that socialism attracted many American intellectuals during the decade or so before World War I.

VIII   Veblen, Communist Revolution, and American Socialism's Demise

Communist Success in Russia and Failure of American Socialism

BEFORE OBSERVING VEBLEN'S DEFENSE of Bolshevism, we present a brief background of the views of Marx and V.I. Lenin (the leader of the Bolshevik Revolution) on the importance of a pervasive democracy to forestall authoritarian bureaucratic tendencies to ensure a proper socialism. Indeed, it should be noted that these elements of Marxism are closely related to anarchism. Early Bolshevism itself in practice and theory during the Bolshevik Revolution had a distinct anarchist flavor, which explains most of its popularity among workers and farmers. Then, we delve into how the Bolshevik Revolution influenced the American scene, especially its socialism.

An important quality of any totalitarian/authoritarian society was its reliance on bureaucracy, an excrescence that Marx abhorred. In *Critique of Hegel's Philosophy of the State*, he rigorously criticized Hegel's pronouncements that the Prussian bureaucracy under a hereditary king represented the universal interests of the people. For Marx, this was patently untrue, because "bureaucracy possesses the state's essence, the spiritual essence of society, as its *private property*." Thus, bureaucracy presented a false consciousness, because it signified two intentions to everything, a "real and a bureaucratic meaning," which bifurcated "knowledge" and "will." Furthermore, bureaucracy encouraged a pervasive secretiveness and accompanying "subordination and passive obedience" to survive in its labyrinth. Indeed, a repressive bureaucracy was a normal malformation of a society characterized by sharp individual and social antagonisms:

In bureaucracy the identity of the state's interest and particular private purpose is established in such a way that the *state's interest* becomes a *particular* private purpose opposed to other private purposes.

Bureaucratic oppression was also pervasive in industry, for Marx and Engels, who in *The Communist Manifesto*, for instance, viewed workers as being condemned to be the "privates of the industrial army...under the command of a perfect hierarchy of officers and sergeants," in reality "slaves of the bourgeois class and state." Ultimately, for Marx, bureaucracy would only cease to exist as a chimera when "the *particular* interest becomes *universal*."[1] Marx's commitment to democracy and equality, already observed, was best illustrated by the specificity given it in *The Civil War in France*.[2]

Although Lenin himself distrusted democracy to usher in socialism, as in *What Is to Be Done?*, which viewed workers as not rising far above trade-union consciousness, *State and Revolution*, written just before the successful Bolshevik Revolution, called for a democratic and egalitarian socialism. Although this vision was largely contingent on the Western European workingclass also launching a socialist revolution begun by Russian workers, it optimistically believed that Russian workers could quickly be "educated" not only to perform their work democratically, but also to participate in democratically running the government. Lenin envisaged a socialist democratic and egalitarian society, presumably with full civil liberties for all except a thin slice comprising the Russian elite, nobility and bourgeoisie, particularly the *haute bourgeoisie*.

In a Marxist manner, Lenin pictured the state as "an organ of class domination, an organ of oppression of one class by another." Thus, the new socialist state, an alliance of peasants and workers, would first destroy the old police forces, military, and bureaucracy by a "dictatorship of the proletariat," composed of the "armed people," to bring about new and democratic institutions to reflect its pervasively democratic quality. He also rejected parliamentary democracy, equated with the rule of the bourgeoisie, quoting from Marx's *The Civil War in France* that the Paris Commune of 1871 established a government that was "a working, not a parliamentary body, executive and legislative at the same time." For him, this specifically signified that all officials were to be "elected and subject to recall *at any time*, their salaries reduced to 'workingmen's wages'."

In insisting on a general wage equality and recall of officials, Lenin's aim was clear—to prevent the rise of a bureaucratic socialist class thrusting itself above workers and farmers. As for the fear among many socialists that inequality of functions based on prevailing labor division might catapult mental labor over the manual one, and thus establish a bureaucratic socialist elite, Lenin, like Marx, thought that a pervasive democracy, a direct one for all practical purposes, would prevent this.[3] (Marx, in *The Critique of the Gotha Program*, did assign higher salaries to mental over manual labor, but never stated its extent; not too steep. Until 1931, the Soviet Communist Party's Partmax [Party Maximum] forbade members to earn more than skilled workers.)

Furthermore, Lenin, again echoing Marx's (*The Civil War in France*) "united co-operative societies," had the "united workers themselves who hire their own technicians, managers, bookkeepers, and pay them *all*, as indeed, every 'state' official, with the usual workers' wage."[4] He, of course, qualified this socialist democracy and egalitarianism with the caveat that "with human nature as it is now," "subordination, control," and "managers," were still needed under the umbrella of participatory democracy. These views prompted George Lichtheim, a leading 20th-century commentator on socialism to label Lenin's *State and Revolution* as "quasi-anarchist."[5]

The March to November period of 1917 was momentous. In March, revolution in Russia toppled the Czar. In April, the United States declared war on Germany to preserve the balance of power and to protect its large loans to the Allies, principally Great Britain and France. In November, the Red Guard of twenty thousand armed workers, with the assistance of the Kronstadt sailors, launched the first successful socialist revolution in history, in Petrograd, toppling the government of Alexander F. Kerensky, himself a moderate socialist who ruled with the support of the middle class. The Bolsheviks, left-wing socialists who launched this revolution, were determined to take advantage of the chaotic economic and military conditions that followed the end of Czarism. In quick order, they enacted a sweeping socialist program that confiscated the land of the wealthy and nationalized the factories under the control of workers' committees, but the land of the small peasantry (those who tilled their own land) was left undisturbed.

The question normally arises as to the extent of popular support enjoyed by the Bolsheviks in the former Russian Empire? In the November 25, 1917 Constituent Assembly elections, which most observers held to have been relatively open and honest, the Bolsheviks received 25 percent of the vote and the deeply divided Social Revolutionary Party (SRP), basically the party of the peasantry, 58 percent, but its left wing, from about a third to half of it, allied itself with the Bolsheviks. The Bolsheviks themselves prorogued the Assembly, and with good reason: SRP representatives had been picked before the radicalization of the peasantry, thus, not accurately representing their constituents. There was no doubt that the Bolshevik-Left SR alliance had majority support at this time.

Despite the antidemocratic nature of Soviet Communism, to be examined later, its sweeping economic and social changes, nationalization of industry, laws to protect women, promise of extensive social insurance, and stress on equality and class struggle against the bourgeoisie, won it many supporters among workers and intellectuals throughout the world.

The Bolshevik success in the former Russian Empire, coupled with the defeat of Germany and Austria-Hungary, opened the possibility of communist revolution in Europe. In Germany, the Marxist Social Democratic Party (most of which was reformist) and the Independent Socialists (who urged an immediate nationalization of industry), held the reins of government, and the latter with the Sparticists (the German communists) demanded a left-wing government not dissimilar to the one in Russia. In Italy, during the summer of 1920, hundreds of thousands of workers seized six hundred factories. And, in France, in 1919-1920, the CGT launched a series of strikes that involved hundreds of thousands of workers, and the French Socialists veered leftward as the majority of them voted to join the new French Communist Party. It was also at this time that the Bolsheviks successfully overcame their internal and foreign opposition, and resumed a military counteroffensive whose aim was to spread the revolution to the rest of Europe. For a brief period, it seemed that Germany, and even France and Italy, might become part of the red tide. But the old order withstood these revolutionary assaults, isolating a governing communism to what became the Soviet Union.[6]

The 1917-21 period in America, of war and postwar reconversion, was a tempestuous one for socialists. When America entered the war in April of 1917, socialists were divided between those supporting it and those insisting that international working-class solidarity demanded neutrality because of its capitalist origin.[7] At this time, a spate of pro-war intellectuals left the party, including London and Sinclair.[8]

During periods of war, governments normally want everyone to fall into line, the American being no different. In June 1917, the Espionage Act made it a federal crime to commit espionage or sabotage or hinder the war effort, including to "willfully cause or attempt to cause insubordination, mutiny, or refusal of duty or willfully obstruct the recruiting or enlisting service." A guilty party could pay up to twenty thousand dollars and serve up to twenty years in prison. Any ambiguity regarding the thought control of this act was swept away by the Sedition Act of May 1918, which outlawed "disloyal, profane, scurrilous, or abusive remarks about the form of government, flag, or uniform of the United States, or any language intended to obstruct the war effort," in print and speech. Furthermore, the government could deny mail service to suspects.

About fifteen hundred socialists were prosecuted under these acts (more than three hundred from the IWW), nine hundred of whom were incarcerated. Debs, for instance, was sentenced to a ten-year term for uttering a few antiwar remarks during a summer 1918 speech in Canton, Ohio. (President Warren G. Harding in 1921 pardoned Debs and most of the others incarcerated under the two wartime acts.) The government also barred the socialist press from using the mails.

These laws also helped to fan anger against German-Americans, who, although opposing America's entry into war, supported the government. Fear against German-Americans was so great that with the war's commencement, German books were removed from the libraries, German language courses in public schools were terminated, performances of music composed by German composers were often banned, sauerkraut became "liberty cabbage," and German names of cities were often changed.

The American Protective League, a vigilante group of a quarter-of-a-million "super patriots," enforced the acts by tapping telephones, opening mail, and prying into the opinions of neighbors, to ensure conformity. President Wilson's first Attorney General, Thomas W. Gregory, called them a "patriotic organization." Irish- and Jewish-Americans were, also, to a lesser degree, suspected of disloyalty, since they disliked the British and Russian allies.[9]

The end of World War I on November 11, 1918, did not spell the end of government repression of socialists because among the capitalist elite there undoubtedly was some fear that the Bolshevik Revolution would spread to America. A basis for this was the social and economic turmoil experienced in America following the war.

Social tensions were exacerbated by the massive strike wave of 1919, of more than 2,500 strikes involving four million workers. It commenced with the Amalgamated Clothing Workers striking successfully for a shorter workday and higher wages in November 1918. This was soon followed in February 1919 by the Seattle General Strike, in which many thousands of workers shut the city down for several days, the city's mayor, Olé Hanson, informing the nation that the strike was the beginning of a working-class revolution. In the same month, a sixteen-week strike of textile workers erupted in Lawrence, Massachusetts, while simultaneously the metal miners of Butte, Montana struck, and in Portland, Oregon, workers formed a "Council of Workers, Soldiers, and Sailors," emulating the Russian example. The summer itself witnessed the Great Steel Strike led by William Z. Foster (a syndicalist who later became the secretary of the American Communist Party), when 350,000 workers struck United States Steel and Bethlehem Steel. It failed. Other significant strikes involved the United Mine Workers under John L. Lewis, who defied an injunction to strike, telephone workers, longshoremen, and railroad switchmen, and when Boston police officers tried to affiliate with the AFL and warned of a strike, Massachusetts Governor Calvin Coolidge backed the police commissioner who fired their nineteen leaders.[10]

It was in the midst of this strike wave, in April of 1919, that a plot to assassinate prominent government officials and wealthy men was discovered. The Post Office found sixteen bombs in the mail destined for Rockefeller, Morgan, Attorney General A. Mitchell Palmer, and Justice Oliver Wendell Holmes, among others. Within a brief period,

Palmer's and two other homes of judges were damaged by bombs. In September 1920, the most successful of these attacks struck the offices of J.P. Morgan and Co., killing thirty-eight people and injuring more than two hundred.

On May Day 1919, fights broke out in Boston, Cleveland, and New York between parading socialists and police aided by military personnel, while in the last city, more than four hundred soldiers and sailors invaded the offices of the socialist daily, the *Call*, injuring a number of its employees. In the same year, on November 11 (Armistice Day, now Veterans' Day), in Centralia, Washington, after IWW members, in defending an IWW building, killed four attacking American Legionnaires, a mob lynched one of them. The courts retaliated by finding IWW members guilty for the crime of defending themselves, sentencing eleven of them to long prison sentences.[11]

The press, as usual, reported these events in a sensationalist manner, suggesting a possible Red revolution. Thirty-four state legislatures in 1918 and two in 1920 responded by passing laws specifically directed against socialists, these in addition to the sabotage and sedition acts already on the statute books. The new sedition laws specifically forbade the red flag from being shown, of belonging to organizations that advocated the overthrow of government through violent means, and employing seditious speech.[12]

The Red Scare reached its climax with the infamous Palmer Raids (of Attorney General Palmer) on January 2, 1920, when buildings of the new Communist parties were raided by local constabulary and federal agents, arresting approximately six thousand aliens and citizens, many of whom were not Communists. Even visitors of prisoners were jailed on the suspicion of being Communists. Alien Communists were deported, 556 of them, while citizen Communists were tried under state sedition laws.

These egregious attacks on civil liberty were the most serious in peacetime since the Alien and Sedition Acts of 1799. Palmer himself had set up a spy network to infiltrate and destroy the Communist movement through fear and intimidation; his actions, which had the full support of President Wilson, should be understood in the light of his wishing to be the next Democratic nominee for president.[13]

A possible socialist revolution itself in America had to overcome the deep ethnic/"racial" and religious divisions within the American workingclass. We begin with the black and white division. During the war hundreds of thousands of blacks streamed North to find employment and 400,000 served in the armed forces, many going to France. These happenings led to increased social tensions in the Northern urban areas between blacks and whites. Returning black servicemen could not but become more assertive in a society where the legacy of slavery continued in the form of severe discrimination, in which voting and other basic human rights were denied them in many states. This explosive mixture in the South led to an increase in black lynchings, thirty-four in

1917, sixty in 1918, and about seventy in 1919, ten being members of the armed forces or just being discharged.

The social tensions between working-class whites and blacks resulted in a series of riots in 1919, some twenty-five in all, including in Washington, D.C., Chicago, Knoxville, Tulsa, and Omaha. The worst, in Chicago, witnessed thirteen days of terror as working-class mobs fought one another, the National Guard being powerless to prevent the horror as hundreds were killed and injured.[14] (This was repeated from 1965 to 1968 as blacks rioted in hundreds of urban ghettos [Detroit, the Watts area of Los Angeles, Chicago, Newark, Cincinnati, Tampa, and Atlanta, among many other] as hundreds were killed and thousands injured.)

In addition to the social cleavage posed by the legacy of slavery, the fact that America is a nation of immigrants has also played a significant role in dividing the workingclass along ethnic and religious lines, the older immigrants being in the higher socioeconomic positions. In this diagram, the degree of "Americanization" is a given involving divisions between the older immigrants, mostly Western European and Protestant, and the newcomers from Eastern and Southern Europe, mostly Catholic, but also Jewish and Eastern Orthodox, subjected to intense prejudice. The Catholic Irish may be viewed as a bridge between them. Since World War II, the large influx of Hispanics and Asians has been added to the previous mixture.

As already observed, the new immigrants constituted a significant part of the American people in the early decades of the twentieth century: By and large, like most Americans, they were poor with little or no education, from traditional rural settings where throne and altar dominated the cultural horizon. Understandably, they lived in their ethnic/religious ghettos, apart from the older immigrants, having their own socioeconomic, political, and religio-cultural networks, which at times, however, did intersect with the larger society, especially with publicschools, and in the political arena, especially with Bossism that provided them with some social welfare for their votes. Socioeconomic mobility for these immigrants, as others before them, was based on Americanizing themselves, i.e., to learn American English and accept the dominant conservative business culture as propagated by education and the popular media.[15]

It should not be forgotten that religion itself was intermixed in the animosity against the new immigrants, mostly Catholic and Jewish. White Protestants, reflecting the religious wars between them and Catholics in Europe, regarding themselves—as the others did so also—as God's chosen people, saw Catholics, Jews, and others as being both in debased religions and un-American, Protestantism itself being equated with Americanism. Protestants, for instance, burned Catholic churches and convents, rioted against Catholics, and published lurid anti-Catholic literature.

Recent immigrants also quickly perceived that not only were they members of inferior/un-American religions, but also of inferior ethnicity. In academia, this racism was related to a reactionary social Darwinism.[16] An example of this was *The Immigration Commission Report* of 1910, a massive forty-two volume exposition sponsored by Senator William P. Dillingham, Republican of Vermont. The study concluded that there were unmistakably innate differences among the various ethnic groups, with the new immigrants from Eastern and Southern Europe having brains and physiques inferior to the Germanic and Celtic groups (by this time the Irish were no longer considered too inferior by older immigrants). The poverty and crime—slum life—of the new immigrants was simply explained on the grounds of genetic inferiority.[17]

There was also much opposition to the new immigrants from organized labor (the AFL understandably rejected the policy of almost unrestricted immigration) and from many Northern European Protestants from the working and lower-middle classes who formed the mass membership of the powerful Ku Klux Klan in the 1920s, which was not only against blacks, but also Jewish, Catholic, and other immigrants. It was very strong politically in twenty states—in the South, but also Midwest, as in Ohio and Indiana; the Southwest, as in Texas and Oklahoma; and West, as in California and Oregon.

Other broad socioeconomic elements should be considered in delineating the class alignments and conflicts of the period: When Veblen was born in 1857, more than half the people lived on farms; when he died in 1929, 30 percent still did. Thus, during his lifetime, the capitalist spirit of small farm and other small business, reinforced by ethnic and religious divisions, in a milieu of general economic scarcity and related economic individualism/alienation, made broad-based reform difficult to achieve.

These elements were part of this tripartite class structure of the period: The wealthiest 2 percent possessed three-fifths of the private wealth; they were followed by a middle class—from lower to upper middle—of independent farmers and urban small business, office workers, and various professionals, like physicians and lawyers, of a third of the people with 35 percent of it; and finally by the bottom two-thirds, tenant and poor farmers and workers, many recent immigrants, and blacks, with 5 percent of it.[18]

The Bolshevik Revolution was greeted with great enthusiasm by American socialism, Veblen being no exception. The leading liberal and socialist journals of the period—the *Dial*, the *Nation*, and the *New Republic* heartily endorsed it. In the SP, for instance, it was supported by all factions—from the right, by the reformist Marxists, Berger and Hillquit, to the left, by Debs, Charles Ruthenberg, and the rising young stars, Louis C. Fraina and John Reed. Even De Leon's SLP, anarchists, like Berkman and Goldman (both went to Russia in 1919 only to be soon disappointed), and the syndicalist IWW were favorable towards it. Debs expressed this sentiment best: "From the crown of my head to the soles of my feet, I am a Bolshevik and proud of it." (But Debs opposed a Bolshevik-like solution for America on the basis of a different history.)[19] The American connection to the revolution itself was through Reed's *Ten Days That Shook the World, a stirring eye-witness account.*[20]

In February 1919, the young rebels led by Fraina, with the help of some old militants, like Ruthenberg and Alfred Wagenknecht, published a left-wing "Manifesto" which urged the SP to follow the Bolshevik example, i.e., to establish workers' councils to usher in a Communist America. They were able to persuade the majority, including much of the center, to join them. But the departing left and center fractured into two Communist parties, squabbling over matters of tactics and divided by sociocultural differences between the "Americans" and foreign-language federations. These disputes were ultimately resolved, and by 1921 there emerged a united Communist Party of America (CP), distinct from the SP, basically a democratic-reformist party.[21]

Was a socialist revolution possible in the America of 1919-20, when the Red Scare was at its height? Did socialists have the numbers to effect revolution? Were socioeconomic conditions ripe for it (this included the 1920-22 recession which at its height in 1921 had five million unemployed)? Obviously not! Furthermore, even during the Great Depression of the 1930s, the left did not do well in elections. Overall, the socioeconomic, political, and cultural hegemony of the bourgeoisie—at least a third of the people—was simply too great for a divided working-class, not far from the traditions of rural conservatism and parochialism, to overcome.

To be sure, the SP had some political clout and socialism was important in the labor movement and in vogue in the world of art and among intellectuals and it is also undeniable that in the 1917 municipal elections, the antiwar platform of the party attracted many hyphenated Americans, principally German, Jewish, and Irish: In New York City Hillquit garnered 22 percent of the vote in his bid for mayor, and socialists did well in a number of other cities, with 25 percent in Buffalo, 44 in Dayton, 35 in Toledo, 20 in Cleveland, and 12 in Cincinnati. But in the 1920 presidential election, Debs slipped to 3 percent of the vote.

Among the left, only the two Communist parties, with a combined membership of less than forty thousand, the IWW with about fifty thousand members, De Leon's SLP, a sect of about a thousand, and a thousand or so anarchists, were for revolution. Even if this less than a hundred thousand number were multiplied many times for sympathizers, it would still be a minuscule part of the population: the SP of about forty thousand members and the AFL of 3.3 million "labor aristocrats" were certainly overwhelmingly against revolution.[22]

But the moderate left was still strong. In the 1924 presidential elections, the Progressive Party under Robert M. La Follette received almost five million votes or 17 percent of the total on a platform which included public ownership of railroads and public utilities (gas, water, electricity), congressional power to override Supreme Court decisions, and outlawing court injunctions to prevent strikes.

In retrospect, the Red Scare, greatly abetted by the yellow journalism of the press (its mindset reflected that of the middle class and wealthy who regarded the bottom two-thirds of the people with fear and loathing), was predicated for Arthur S. Link, a noted American historian, on baseless fear: "Never was a great nation so afraid of the phantom invaders and so agitated by groundless fears."[23] Objectively, this is true, but not subjectively for the two classes just mentioned.

Although socialism as an organized political movement was destroyed by the superpatriotism of World War I and the subsequent Red Scare, the two main parties of the American left continued to exist, the CP and the SP. Both had some influence during the decade of the Great Depression, the CP playing an important role in organizing the Congress of Industrial Organization (CIO), and the SP in forming the Tenant Farmers Union in the South, an association of blacks and whites.

Then, too, some of the intelligentsia and artistic community greatly supported the left. In the League for Independent Political Action, founded in 1928, Dewey, Douglas, Norman Thomas (he ran as the SP presidential candidate many times), Chase, Mumford, and Reinhold Neibuhr, a leading Protestant theologian, called for a democratic socialist America. In a well-known pamphlet, *Culture and the Crises*, issued in October 1932, the writers Dreiser, Dos Passos, Erskine Caldwell, Steffens, Wilson, and Sherwood Anderson advocated a Communist solution to end the Great Depression; this was again advanced in the American Writers Congress of 1935, by the first three and Richard Wright, James T. Farrell, and Mumford (the last obviously moving further left). But despite the vogue of socialism among artists and intellectuals, in the critical 1932 presidential race, Thomas, the SP candidate, garnered about 900,000 votes (2.2 percent of the total), while Foster, the CP one, a hundred thousand. But some quasisocialist movements, like Huey Long's Share-the-Wealth-Plan and Father Charles Coughlin's National Union for Social Justice had millions of followers.[24]

Bolshevik

From the inception of the Bolshevik Revolution in 1917 to his death in 1929, Veblen was its avid defender, especially during the tempestuous 1918-21 period when it rose from near defeat to challenge the old order in Europe. The means employed were through the pen in the *Dial*, a fortnightly, whose circulation at this time was about ten thousand.

The *Dial* was a descendant of the original one, located in Cambridge, Massachusetts (1840-44), identified with Transcendentalism, its two original editors being Emerson and Margaret Fuller. In 1880, it was resurrected in Chicago by Francis E. Browne, and in 1918 transferred to New York. There, under its new owner and president, Martyn Johnson, and its chief editor, George Bernard Donlin, it became a leading liberal/socialist voice with such contributing editors as Veblen and Dewey and scholar/activists as Laski and Charles Beard.

From July 1918, to November 1919, Veblen wrote nineteen articles, including editorials, in the *Dial,* which indicated his true color, that he was a "Red," by not only supporting the IWW, but the Bolshevik Revolution in Russia, although he never joined any American Communist party.[25]

There could be no doubt that Veblen was a champion of Bolshevism for he castigated mere reformist socialists:

> But neither the Bolshevists nor the Socialists will admit that the two are alike in any substantial way. Indeed, the certified Socialists are among the staunchest enemies of Bolshevism, as is quite intelligible.

Ultimately, for him, the Bolshevik specter menaced the present capitalist order because it nationalized larger property:

> Bolshevism is a menace to absentee ownership. That is its unpardonable sin. But it is also a sufficiently mortal offense, inasmuch as it is the sin against the Holy Ghost of established Law and Order.[26]

On the irrational fear of the Bolshevik Revolution exhibited by the press and government (the Red Scare), Veblen was not only amused by it, but, at times, even perhaps believed that this fear was based on a modicum of reality, and that, yes, an American Bolshevik revolution was not outside the realm of possibility. Some of Veblen's comments of wild merriment on this:

> The commercialized press all see Red. So do the official and quasi-official conspiracies, such as the Lusk Commission, the Union League Club, the Security League, and the Civic Confederation, as well as the Publicity Police, the Workday Politicians, the Clerics of the Philistine Confession, and the Wild Asses of the Devil generally.

And:

> All persons who refuse to be stampeded by the Red Alarm are open to suspicion—unless they are visibly identified with the Vested Interests—and any person who falls under the suspicion of the official and quasi-official alarmists is, in effect, assumed to be guilty of sedition.[27]

He perceptively traced this "Red Scare" to the "Vested Interests," or businessmen, who, aware of their privileged position relative to workers, acted hysterically to a perceived threat.[28]

Veblen warned the ruling class and the victorious Allies at the Paris Peace Conference following World War I, that the Bolshevik Revolution is a social phenomenon of vast and serious scope that would not easily be suppressed:

> The colossal proportions of the movement as a whole have to do not only with its extent but with its character. It is a movement in which people know what they want and, as they are opposed, will arm and fight to get it.

He also appealed to capitalist profit motive as a reason for not interfering with the new Soviet power:

> Meantime Soviet Russia offers an attractive market for such American products as machine tools and factory equipment, railway material and rolling stock, electrical supplies, farm implements and tools, textiles, wrought leather goods, certain foodstuffs and certain metals.[29]

Veblen's support of Soviet Communism included two key ideas which he thought represented its heart, democracy and equality:

> It aims to carry democracy and majority rule over into the domain of industry. Therefore it is a menace to the established order. It is charged with being a menace to private property, to business, to industry, to state and church, to law and morals, to the world's peace, to civilization, and to mankind at large.[30]

But Veblen realistically saw that a red revolution was, at best, only remotely possible in America. To begin, he was cognizant of the web of power—economic, social, political, and cultural—which accustomed most people to accept a conservative political position. This was politically and culturally expressed in favoring a "representative government," which reflected the supremacy of "business interests," that controlled a "commercialized press" representing their views.[31]

These factors, for Veblen, greatly contributed toward making a largely conservative workingclass that scarcely dared to question the status quo, reflected in the American trade union movement whose largest and most successful organization, the AFL, acted like a business in its apprenticeship programs which sought to make labor more expensive.

To be sure, Veblen noted that a minority of American workers were imbued with "socialistic" and "anarchist" ideas, and although viewing the IWW as the "vanguard of dissent," he dismissed it as unimportant because of its small number and inability, most members being unskilled and semiskilled workers, to assume "the highly technical duties involved in the administration of the industrial system."[32]

Veblen's scenario for the tentative American revolution bore a striking similarity to the events characterizing the March and November 1917 Russian Revolutions, in which the demands of war on an industrially backward nation brought about food and fuel shortages in the cities when the transportation system was severely crippled. In a revealing article in the September 1919 issue, Veblen presented an apocalyptic scenario featuring "riotous discontent," arising from a partial collapse of the transportation system in the coming winter, which would lead to a "fuel famine," resulting in hardship among the people and perhaps revolution. Indeed his refrain of "not yet" expected the revolution at any moment.[33] Of the two revolutions, Veblen's model would more closely follow the spontaneity of March, based on a general strike, rather than the November seizure of power made by armed workers and friendly military units.

Veblen's schema for a successful socialist revolution was predicated on an alliance between workers, the potentially most revolutionary class, and the engineers who would lead it not only on the basis of their "instinct of workmanship, increasing class consciousness," and utilitarian rejection of "waste and confusion in the management of industry by the financial agents of the owners,"[34] but belief of being indispensable in production.[35] The workers themselves, for Veblen, becoming ever more skilled with the passage of time, would have a greater role in management.[36] This class alliance would thus be based as much as on shared cultural values as on broad socioeconomic interests.

In *The Communist Manifesto*, Marx and Engels averred "that a small section of the ruling class cuts itself adrift, and joins the revolutionary class"—"of the bourgeois ideologists, who have raised themselves to the level of comprehending theoretically the historical movement as a whole."[37] For Veblen, this not only included academics as himself, but the critical group of engineers who are the key players in running the industrial system. But his analysis disregarded the sharp class dichotomy at this time between manual and mental labor in a society of general economic scarcity basically devoid of a broad socialist culture.

But there were a few liberal and even socialist engineers who either worked with labor or had dreams of a socialist commonwealth under their aegis. Two, whom Veblen never met, were Morris L. Cooke and Harvey L. Gantt, both leading disciples of Frederick W. Taylor, the father of scientific management—indeed they were two of only four who had Taylor's official blessing to propagate his system. Cooke, as early as 1919, was friendly to organized labor, favoring collective bargaining between capital and labor and co-authoring a book with Phillip Murray (later president of the CIO).[38] Gantt himself, deeply influenced by Veblen and his socialism, was associated with the New Machine movement, which lasted from 1916 to 1919, that proposed the replacement of an inefficient capitalism with a socialism headed by managers who would substitute public service for immediate profit,[39] engineers being the leading group.[40]

Veblen's conception for revolution stressed its realization through the general strike, obviously influenced in this not only by the March 1917 events in Russia, but by extensive socialist literature which emphasized it as the leading vehicle for revolution:

> The obvious and simple means of doing it is a conscientious withdrawal of efficiency; that is to say the general strike, to include so much of the country's staff of technicians as will suffice to incapacitate the industrial system at large by their withdrawal, for such time as may be required to enforce their argument.

The time frame for this would be in weeks. But before revolution occurred, the engineers would have to take the lead in organizing it:

> So soon—but only so soon—as the engineers draw together, take common counsel, work out a plan of action, and decide to disallow absentee ownership out of hand, that move will have been made.

This would include the engineers working out an alliance with the workers to seize power based on two broad points:

> (a) An extensive campaign of inquiry and publicity, such as will bring the underlying population to a reasonable understanding of what it is all about; and
> (b) the working-out of a common understanding and a solidarity of sentiment between the technicians and the working force engaged in transportation and in the greater underlying industries of the system: to which is to be added as being nearly indispensable from the outset, an active adherence to this plan on the part of the trained workmen in the great generality of the mechanical industries. Until these prerequisites are taken care of, any project for the overturn of the established order of absentee ownership will be nugatory.[41]

But, then, Veblen calculated that the chances of this revolutionary scenario happening were not too propitious for reasons already presented although he still held out a modicum of hope—"just yet."[42]

There was in Veblen, at times, a patronizing tone towards workers when he asserted that the technocrats "must consistently and effectually take care of the underlying population,"[43] thus acknowledging, the continuing dichotomy between manual and mental labor. He also did not discuss any of the average wage differentials among the various occupations, but even in the early days of an egalitarian Soviet Union, they were on the order of eight to one.

Undoubtedly, Veblen's revolutionary scenario is more compatible with present class relations than with those during his lifetime because contemporary technology, in demanding an almost universal mass of educated labor, has largely proletarianized lower-middle class mental labor, which includes engineers, facilitating more coopera- tion between them and blue-collar workers. Patterns of such a model were clearly evi- dent in the 1968 French May Events when blue- and white-collar workers cooperated to occupy offices and factories in a general strike that almost toppled Charles de Gaulle's government.[44]

Once revolution began, Veblen would have us believe that the capitalist elite would not resist it, but given the extensive industrial warfare in the United States during his lifetime, his pacific rulers appeared unreal, unless this was another of his ruses.[45]

After the socialist revolution, Veblen would rapidly expropriate large private prop- erty or "absentee ownership," prohibiting "title to property not in use by the owner," and remove the old managers from their positions "to avoid persistent confusion and pro- spective defeat." It should, however, be emphasized that he would permit small private property or small business directly owned.[46]

Veblen's most extensive account of the main socialist parameters of the new soci- ety, including its technological organization, was in "A Memorandum of a Practicable Soviet of Technicians," one of a planned economy directed by a "central directorate":

> Evidently the most immediate and most urgent work to be taken over by the
> incoming directorate is…the due allocation of available resources, in power,
> equipment, and materials, among the primary industries. For this necessary
> work of allocation there has been substantially no provision under the old or-
> der.

This body, composed of a "tripartite executive council," was involved with "productive industry, transportation, and distributive traffic," or the distribution of goods to the pub- lic. The technical aspect was uppermost for Veblen here, i.e., the best way to produce something at the lowest possible cost, which is handled by "resource engineers." The central directorate in turn not only coordinated its activities with "consulting econo- mists" and "production economists," but closely cooperated with "subcenters and local councils," or local workers' councils, the Soviet councils being its models, thus ensuring economic democracy.[47]

This model, for him, would infinitely deepen the one of a mere political participa- tory democracy inherent in the New England town meeting:

> In American usage "democracy" denotes a particular form of political organi-
> zation, without reference to the underlying economic organization; whereas

"bolshevism" has primarily no political signification, being a form of economic organization, with incidental consequences—mostly negative—in the field of politics.[48]

This insistence on economic democracy, as might be readily observed, was very similar to that of Lenin's *State and Revolution*, Marx's *The Civil War in France*, and analogous to the views of two well-known English 20th century socialists of the syndicalist variety, Sir Herbert Read and G.D.H. Cole who proposed worker control of the means of production, or industrial democracy, and a parliament, representing both unions and consumer groups, to decide the broad outlines of society.[49] This political schema was infinitely more democratic than representative democracy under bourgeois hegemony, malformed by sharp socioeconomic (including extensive labor division marked by the dichotomy between manual and mental labor), and cultural inequalities.

There were, of course, many problems that Veblen, in his brief view of how a future socialism was to be run, did not address. For instance, he neither considered how technological innovation affected worker unemployment in particular industries and how this would be handled, nor confronted the issues of the continuing tensions between manual and mental labor at work and between the productive base and coordinating/planning commissions over sharing the economic pie in societies still under the rule of general economic scarcity, related to power relationships between workers' councils and economic coordinating centers of higher bureaucrats. Nor did he discuss the problem of efficiently allocating resources for economic development and consumer spending; some form of pricing system, an actual or shadow one, would be needed in these areas. (But in Veblen's lifetime, mass consumerism was scarcely developed.) Nor did he mention critical problems like length of workday and overcoming the dichotomy between manual and mental labor. No matter, Veblen presented a socialism of economic democracy which was dynamic and vibrant, details to be worked out by its practitioners; in this sense he was not a utopian sketching preordained pictures.

Veblen himself supported the Bolshevik Revolution, although more than likely aware that it did not enjoy majority support of the people, especially when the Left SRs broke their alliance with the Bolshevik in March 1918, opposing the treaty of Brest-Litovsk when the Bolsheviks made peace with the Germans. Then, too, the Bolsheviks by 1921 defeated the sizeable anarchist movement of Nestor Makhno in the Ukraine which had seven million people in its area of control, with an army of fifteen thousand. Makhno importantly advocated independent workers' committees to run and own the factories and the peasantry to own the land singly or in communes. There were also a number of anarchist groups, such as the Federation of Anarchist Groups in Moscow and the Union for Anarcho-Syndicalist Propaganda in Petrograd. They were to be outlawed by the Bolsheviks. The Left SRs, a relatively large group, also had a program close to that of classic anarchism, advocating a communal socialism in the countryside centered on the mir, with workers to run the factories in urban areas, and the seizure of land and factories from the bourgeoisie and nobility with no compensation. Of course, Kropotkin was the most known anarchist in Russia at the time; he lived in a village near Moscow. The Bolsheviks wisely let him alone.

Inexorably, the Communist Party eroded working-class power and democracy. With the advent of civil war in 1918, the Party expelled the other socialist parties (SRs and Mensheviks) from the Soviets after they won many elections within them, and by 1922 outlawed all parties. As for worker control in nationalized factories, as early as 1918, workers' committees in running the factories were replaced by one-man management to be responsible to the Party. In the fateful 10th Party Congress in 1921, the Workers' Opposition, which desired all economic power to be in the hands of unions and which was against the Party's economic bureaucracy, was defeated. In 1927, strikes and slow-downs by workers were forbidden. In 1934, collective bargaining was terminated and workers' councils abolished. In short order, the workers were reduced to becoming serfs of the state. A key event of Bolshevik repression of popular forces was the crushing of the Kronstadt Mutiny of soldiers and sailors of March 1921. Among the principal demands of the mutineers were the reinstitution of free speech and assembly and secret and open elections in the Soviets. These events clearly indicated that the Bolsheviks had seized power from the majority of the people, relegating the democratic parts of Marxism and Lenin's *State and Revolution* to the dustbin of history. Communist justification for holding on to power was their winning the civil war.

In light of these developments, why did Veblen support the Communists? I would think that he did so because the Communist experiment, the first successful socialist revolution in history, had triumphed against great odds—the British, French, Americans, and Japanese had landed troops to support the conservative and reactionary "Whites," in addition to supplying them with large amounts of arms and ammunition. Perhaps Veblen thought that the antidemocratic and anticivil libertarian measures of the Bolsheviks were temporary aberrations caused by civil war and economic backwardness, more than counterbalanced by Bolshevik stress on general equality and nationalization of industry. (Nationalization of industry itself is not socialist, but it is against private capitalism; it is state capitalism. For anarchists and classical Marxists, socialism demands that factories be under the direction of workers' committees.) Then, too, the New Economic Policy period of 1921-28 indicated the reasonableness of the Party in allowing for the existence of small private property, basically in agriculture. Furthermore, when Veblen died in 1929, the policies of Stalinism, collectivization of agriculture, the brutal elimination of the kulaks (richer farmers), and five-year plans to industrialize rapidly were in their infancy. Stalin himself did not gain full power within the Party until the late 1920s and the bloody purges in the Party would occur in the mid-1930s.[50]

Veblen's views on the state and political change in history were germane here. For Veblen, the state itself was inextricably involved with the rule of the leisure class from the lower barbarian period to the present one under capitalism and the ruling bourgeoisie. Only under socialism would it come under the sway of the workingclass. But once this happened, contrary to Marx and anarchists in general, Veblen did not discuss the disappearance of the state. Instead, he took it for granted that the new institutions, those of a basically syndicalist state, would be of a noncoercive nature.

A basic question arises here: Under what circumstances can the workers defeat the bourgeoisie for state control? For the anarchists and Leninists, working-class control of the state would not come about through voting but through a revolutionary overturn during a period of economic crisis and social turmoil; this view was partly shared by Marx, who also believed that an electoral working-class majority might also be efficacious for this end. Veblen himself favored the former position because he thought that in a representative democracy, democratic means could not effectively bring about socialism because working-class divisions, with the many status groups that they were enclosed in, in addition to bourgeois economic, social, political, and cultural hegemony, were sufficient to prevent the divided masses from achieving socialism.

NOTES

1. On the *Critique of Hegel's Philosophy of the State*, see Loyd D. Easton and Kurt H. Guddat, eds. and translators, *Writings of the Young Marx on Philosophy and Society* (Garden City, N.Y.: Doubleday, 1967), pp. 186-87: Karl Marx and Friedrich Engels, *Manifesto of the Communist Party*, p. 16.

2. Karl Marx, *The Civil War in France* (New York: International Publishers, 1933), pp. 40-44.

3. V.I. Lenin, *The State and Revolution* (New York: International Publishers, 1932), pp. 26 ff.

4. *Ibid.*, p. 43.

5. Lichtheim, *Marxism*, p. 351.

6. On the Bolshevik Revolution, see, for instance, E. H. Carr, *The Bolshevik Revolution: 1917-1923*, 3 vols. (Baltimore, MD: Penguin Books, 1966). On the possible spread of Communism after the revolution, see, for instance, Eric Hobsbawm, *The Age of Extremes: A History of the World*, 1914-1991 (New York: Pantheon Books, 1994) , pp. 65-71.

7. Theodore Draper, *The Roots of American Communism* (New York: Vintage Press, 1957), pp. 50-57.

8. Daniel Bell, "The Background and Development of Marxian Socialism in the United States," in *Socialism and American Life*, eds., Egbert and Stow Persons, I, 312.

9. On the two laws, of sabotage and sedition, and their effects on Socialists and German-Americans, see Shannon, *The Socialist Party of America*, pp. 99-125; Draper, *The Roots of American Communism*, pp. 92-96; Link, *American Epoch*, pp. 92-96 and 241-44; Zinn, *People's History*, pp. 356-62.

10. Link, *American Epoch*, pp. 238-41; Zinn, *People's History*, pp. 368-72.

11. Link, *American Epoch*, pp. 241-44; Zinn, *People's History*, p. 370.

12. Link, *American Epoch*, pp. 242-43; Shannon, *The Socialist Party of America*, pp. 109-25.

13. Link, *American Epoch*, pp. 243-44; Shannon, *The Socialist Party of America*, pp. 123-24; Draper, *The Roots of American Communism*, pp. 202-09.

14. Link, *American Epoch*, pp. 244-46. An excellent work on the pervasiveness of American racism is by Joel Kovel, *White Racism: A Psychohistory* (New York: Vintage Books, 1971), pp. 13-92, for instance. Also, see Glenn C. Altschuler, *Race, Ethnicity, and Class in American Life: 1865-1919* (Arlington Heights, IL: Harlan Davidson, 1982), pp. 1-39.

15. Altschuler, *Race*, pp. 40-75, has much material on ethnic divisions in the process of Americanization, of a working class that could not basically overcome its ethnic/religious, let alone "racial" divisions, in this stage of the class struggle, vitiating the socialist project. Also, on this, see Daniel Bell, "Marxian Socialism," in Egbert and Persons, *Socialism and American Life*, I, pp. 215-17.

16. Oscar Handlin, *The Uprooted* (New York: Grosset's Universal Library, 1951), pp. 195-97.

17. Oscar Handlin, *Race and Nationality in American Life* (Boston: Little, Brown and Co., 1957), pp. 93-138.

18. Link, *American Epoch*, p. 23, has the richest, one percent of the families owning 47 percent of the private wealth in 1910.

19. Draper, *Roots of American Communism*, pp. 110-13 and 325. Bell in Stow and Persons, *Socialism and American Life*, I, 319-29.

20. John Reed, Foreword V.I. Lenin, Introduction Granville Hicks, *Ten Days That Shook the World* (New York: Modern Library, 1935).

21. Draper, *Roots of American Communism*, pp. 197-281.

22. *Ibid.*, pp. 188-93 on the membership of the two communist parties.

23. Link, *American Epoch*, p. 242.

24. See Aaron, *Writers on the Left*; Rideout, *Radical Novel*; Egbert and Persons, *Socialism and American Life*, I, 599-751; Hofstadter, *Anti-Intellectualism*, pp. 292-96.

25. Veblen's articles in the *Dial* were reprinted in his *Engineers and the Price System* and *Essays in Our Changing Order*. Frederick J. Hoffman, Charles Allen, Carolyn F. Ulrich, *The Little Magazine: A History and Bibliography* (Princeton, N.J.: Princeton University Press, 1946), pp. 196-206 on the *Dial*.

26. For the two quotations, see Thorstein Veblen, "Between Bolshevism and War," in Ardzrooni, *Essays in Our Changing Order*, pp. 342-43.

27. For the two rather lengthy quotations, see Thorstein Veblen, "The Red Terror At Last Has Come to America," *Dial*, Sept. 6, 1919, pp. 5-6.

28. *Ibid.*

29. Thorstein Veblen, editorial in *Dial*, April 5, 1919, pp. 362-63, for the two long quotations.

30. Thorstein Veblen, "Bolshevism Is a Menace—To Whom?" *Dial*, Feb. 22, 1919, p. 174.

31. Thorstein Veblen, *Business Enterprise*, pp. 286-88; Lerner, *Portable Veblen*, p.164.

32. Thorstein Veblen, *The Engineers and the Price System*, Introduction Daniel Bell (New York: Harcourt, Brace, and World, 1963), pp. 97-98.

33. *Ibid.*, pp. 94-107; the quotations are from p.106.

34. Thorstein Veblen, *The Engineers and the Price System* (New York: B.W. Huebsch, 1921), pp. 52 ff.

35. *Ibid.*, p. 84.

36. *Ibid.*, p. 137.

37. Marx and Engels, *Communist Manifesto*, p. 19.

38. On Cooke, see Kenneth E. Trombley, *The Life and Times of a Happy Liberal: A Biography of Morris Llewellyn Cooke* (New York: Harper and Brothers, 1954).

39. On Gantt, see Milton J. Nadworny, *Scientific Management and the Unions, 1920-1932: A Historical Analysis* (Cambridge, MA: Harvard University Press, 1955), pp. 12, 14-15, 107.

40. Henry L. Gantt, "Wake Up Engineers," *Industrial Management*, April, 1919, Vol. 57, No. 332.

41. Thorstein, Veblen, "Bolshevism and the Vested Interests in America," *Dial*, Nov. 1, 1919, p. 380, on the last three quotations.

42. "A Memorandum on a Practicable Soviet of Technicians" in Veblen, *Engineers and the Price System* (1963), p. 151 on the long quotation followed by the "just yet."

43. *Ibid.*, p. 149.

44. On the 1968 French May Events, see Adrien Dansette, *Mai 1968* (Paris: Plon, 1971).

45. Veblen, *Engineers and the Price System* (1921), p. 141.

46. Veblen, "A Memorandum on a Practicable Soviet of Technicians," in Veblen, *Engineers and the Price System* (1963), pp. 34 ff.

47. *Ibid.*, pp. 134-35 and p. 137 for quotations in this paragraph. Reisman, *Veblen*, pp. 32-33.

48. Veblen, "Bolshevism is A Menace—To Whom?" *Dial*, Feb. 22, 1919, p. 174.

49. See Sir Herbert Read, *The Philosophy of Anarchism* (London Freedom Press, 1940), pp. 28-29, and G.D.H. Cole, *Guild Socialism Re-Stated* (London: Leonard Parsons, 1920).

50. On the destruction of democracy in the Soviets and unions, see Samuel Farber, *Before Stalinism: The Rise and Fall of Soviet Democracy* (London: Verso, 1990), pp. 19-89. On Bellamy's rejection of political parties, see *Looking Backward*, pp. 191 ff.

PART II   VEBLEN AND PROBLEMS of SOCIALISM

IX   Capitalist Versus
Veblen's Socialist Economics

Capitalist Economics

THE PRINCIPAL THINKERS OF CAPITALIST ECONOMICS were the British classical economists, their father being Smith, followed by Malthus, Ricardo, and Mill who became a socialist. With the exception of Mill, reflecting the hegemony of the bourgeoisie, they regarded entrepreneurs as the mainspring of economic activity, workers as mere ciphers. This could not be otherwise in a deeply divided British class society, when even in 1900, only 1 percent of the people owned 75 percent of the wealth.

The shibboleths of the first three economists and their epigones, with the partial exception of the first, extolled the sacrosanctity of private property, the beneficence of free trade, with legislation to only aid entrepreneurs, like enforcing individual liberty to make contracts, including children with their employers, but prohibiting workers to form unions and to employ the boycott and strike against capital. They had scant concern for the plight of workers, seen only as vehicles to enrich the bourgeoisie, indeed to live at a precarious subsistence level, doomed to everlasting poverty because of their supposed individual improvidence.[1]

Smith, a professor of moral philosophy at the University of Edinburgh, authored *The Wealth of Nations* (1776), which is to capitalism what Marx's *Capital* is to socialism for intellectual justification. He principally observed that economic activity was distinctly related to social class—workers with labor, capitalists with profit, and landlords with rent, viewing the last as parasites, having a monopoly price on food: "They love to reap where they never sowed," and, he regarded the monarchy, army, church, and bureaucracy as part of the unproductive sector. But he glorified the industrialist/entrepreneur as the great accumulator of wealth.

To achieve maximum results for capital accumulation and economic efficiency, Smith employed the model of the self-regulating market, in which competition (the invisible hand of the marketplace) determined wages, prices of goods, and profits.[2] Capital itself, from profit, invited ever more investment to produce more goods leading to higher wages and lower prices for commodities.

The state itself, for Smith, had a positive role: It maintained the military, the justice system, and public education, subsidized some industry—that of shipping to aid national defense—and regulated the price and quality of bread because of its importance as a commodity for only private markets to control. He would also impose steep taxes on luxury goods to fund welfare laws for the poor and even advocated progressive income taxes. Furthermore, in contradistinction to many of his followers, he displayed a deep sympathy for workers, demanding that they be "tolerably well fed, clothed and lodged."

On the economic relations between labor and capital, Smith drew an antagonistic model between them, workers fighting for higher wages, capitalists, for lower, but capitalists being fewer in number and economically stronger than workers, who without employment were soon penniless, had the advantage. Furthermore, he pointed out that the law favored capitalists because it deemed strikes illegal for higher wages and shorter workdays. (In England, there were conspiracy laws, which did not allow for labor unions until 1825, and forbade workers to strike for higher wages or shorter workdays until 1871 and 1906).[3] Also, in a vein similar to Marx and Veblen, he maintained that "civil government...is in reality instituted for the defense of the rich against the poor, or those who have some property against those who have none at all."[4]

On the question of differences in human intelligence, with obvious implications concerning the possibility for at least a future socioeconomic equality, Smith was an egalitarian: "The difference of natural talents in different men is, in reality, much less than we are aware of," being "not so much from nature, as from habit, custom, and education." He was also aware that labor division was basically responsible for the intellectual degradation of workers.[5]

A free trader, Smith not only opposed tariffs and guilds (unions), but business combinations (monopoly was a tax on consumers), particularly suspicious of business: "People of the same profession or trade meet together but the conversation ends in a conspiracy against the public or in some diversion to raise prices."

But despite all of the misgivings that Smith had about capitalists, he assigned to them the central role in accumulating capital, taking for granted an economically motivated individual with a "predisposition to barter and exchange,"[6] never economically satisfied, who in pursuing private ends to make more money also benefitted the general community by employing labor. As for the technology to create wealth, although aware of machinery, he did not dwell on its importance to increase output, but concentrated on labor division's key role in doing so.

On commodity value, Smith was a proponent of the labor theory of value, holding that "labor…is the real measure of the exchangeable value of commodities," although this fact "is not altogether so natural and obvious."[7] (The principal intellectual source of the modern labor theory of value was John Locke's Chapter V in the second of the *Two Treatises of Government*, which proposed that human labor, intermixing with nature common to all, created property. It was elaborated on by Smith, Malthus, and especially Ricardo, which Marx built upon to justify his socialism. But there was ambiguity in Locke's labor theory of value. On the one hand: "One can have as much property as he can make use of to any advantage of life before it spoils. Whatever is beyond this is more than his share and belongs to others." On the other hand: "The turfs my servant has cut become my property without consent of anybody." In the first statement, Locke undoubtedly referred to humanity in the state of nature, in the second, in civilization, in which a worker's time and production are owned by the employer.)[8]

All in all, Smith was a progressive political economist as indicated by his favorable views on social welfare, sympathy for workers, and advocacy of progressive income taxation.

An influential conservative whose views are still in vogue was Thomas Robert Malthus, an upper-middle class Anglican parson, whose *An Essay on the Principle of Population* wrestled with the still perplexing problem for capitalists, the need for inexpensive labor, but fear that overpopulation might lead to social catastrophe. He began with two basic postulates, that humanity required food to exist, and that male/female passion resulted in having children.[9] In this relationship, population tended to increase more rapidly than the available food supply—food at an arithmetic rate, population at a geometric one. But the dire consequences of this were mitigated by two checks—positive, like sickness, starvation, and war, and preventive, like continence and late marriage.[10]

By using this conflict-ridden model, which supposed a struggle among individuals for food, Malthus, at once, justified the wealth of capitalists and the accompanying poverty of the workers thus: A proponent of economic progress, represented by capital, which needed inexpensive labor for profit, he related this to the especially sinful nature of English workers who, by begetting too many children, kept wages low and profits high. But if workers became more "virtuous" by having less children, higher wages and lower profits followed, causing economic downturn and more unemployment. In this scenario, the working class was doomed to poverty no matter what. Malthus, of course, opposed birth control through contraceptives (the traditional Christian view), favored by Owen and others.

Malthus' model of wealth and poverty pleased the wealthy who could exploit workers with the clear conscience that God himself ordained it. Being a good parson, Malthus admonished workers to have less sin/sex, but since most of them were evil, reformation was not possible.[11] He neglected some of the obvious causes for high working-class birth rates: High infant mortality rates, the necessity for child labor to provide for basic family needs, and reliance on children to care for old or incapacitated parents, there being no social security at that time.

Aware of economic downturns and the social instability caused by high unemployment, Malthus resisted an overly rapid industrialization and urbanization of England, preferring the continuance of a stable gentry landowner class to employ agricultural laborers. In rejecting Smithian free trade, he preferred tariffs on food despite their impeding industrialization by increasing the price of labor and decreasing profit/investment.[12]

The deep conservatism of Malthus was also exhibited by his opposition to the Speenhamland System of 1795, with its basic assumptions that the indigent and working poor had the right to live with the aid of government subsidies while keeping their families intact, and by his advocacy of the Poor Law of 1834 criminalizing poverty, forcing the unemployed to labor in workhouses, leading to the breakup of their families, consonant with his views that it was useless to help the poor.[13]

The social views of Malthus also feared a working-class revolution; he lived during the period of the French Revolution. Indeed, to better control workers, he recommended they be taught to accept their lowly position in life and that attempting to change the status quo was foolhardy.[14]

In the genealogy of Malthus' views, we should consider Joseph Townsend, an upper-middle class reactionary Anglican minister, who espoused an embryonic Social Darwinian doctrine that condemned the poor, always multiplying, to poverty and early death. His *A Tract of the Poor Laws by a Well-Wisher of Mankind* rejected poor relief because it aided the hungry which "tends to destroy the harmony and beauty, the symmetry and order, of that system which God and nature have established in the world." Indeed, workers should not be too far from hunger for "hunger is not only a peaceful, silent, unremitting pressure, but, as the most natural motive of industry and labour, it calls forth the most powerful exertions." And, he recommended that "the poor should be to a certain degree improvident...to fulfill the most servile, the most sordid, the most ignoble offices in the community." This, in turn, allowed the nobility and bourgeoisie, "the more delicate…to procure those callings which are suited to their various dispositions."[15]

The Malthusian economic picture accurately portrayed the mind-set of a triumphant conservatism during the early stages of industrialization, reflecting the relatively low level of production and accompanying sharp class divisions which subjected the majority of the people to the mutilations of poverty.[16]

From a wealthy Sephardic Jewish family (his father, a banker), David Ricardo made money by playing the stock market, became a Quaker (his wife was one) and a member of the House of Commons, and extensively corresponded with Malthus. In *On the Principles of Political Economy and Taxation*, following Smith, he divided the socio-economic pie into three parts: Wages/workers, profits/capitalists, rents/landowners. Wages, representing labor, remained at a subsistence level, which, however, varied according to society's economic development. Wages themselves revolved around the natural price of labor (the Malthusian one where births and deaths were at equilibrium), contrasted to the market price fluctuating to reflect disparities in the birth/death ratio of available labor. Profits were related to wages inversely, higher wages lowered profits, lower wages raised them.

As for rents, they were the prerogatives of gentry landowners, whom Ricardo, following Smith, pictured as parasites: Contrary to creative entrepreneurs, they simply leased land to tenants who hired agricultural laborers, and with the increase in population and demand for more food, simply elevated rents, making food more costly and consequently labor more expensive, thus lowering profit margins of industrialists. The end result was the tendency toward zero profit or economic stagnation for industry. He obviously underestimated technology's ability to raise crop yield even with the employment of more marginal or less fertile land.[17]

In the area of how value was determined, Ricardo refined Smith:

The real values of commodities vary inversely with the productivity of labor in the making of them. The trend in the natural exchange values of commodities corresponds roughly to the relative amount of labor embodied in their production.[18]

Marx would especially employ Ricardo's (and Thompson's) insights to formulate his labor theory of value. To be sure, both Malthus and Ricardo, contrary to the more optimistic Smith who lived earlier, did not fail to observe that workers' wages and quality of life were abysmal, not significantly rising with the progression of capitalism.

The battle between the classical economists and radical liberals/socialists was already in earnest by the first quarter of the 19th century. For instance, Malthus, in *An Es-*

say on the Principle of Population, attacked the egalitarian notions of Paine, Godwin, and Owen on the basis that humans, being naturally lazy and selfish, must be literally forced to work by the fear of starvation (the "original sin" argument). Any leveling, for him, inexorably resulted in overpopulation and consequent social disaster.[19] Furthermore, present inequality was just and normal, for him, as it was the resultant of the efforts of past and present generations, a view which he shared with Edmund Burke, the most noted conservative thinker of the 18th century.

Malthus' chief acolyte was Spencer. To indicate the superiority of capitalism to socialism, he principally identified socialism with primitive cultures, past civilizations, and economically underdeveloped areas of his time, calling Native American cultures north of the Rio Grande River, as well as Native American civilizations, socialist, while in his contemporary period he identified the Montenegrins as such. He reproached the collectivistic aspects of these societies, or their strong sense of social solidarity, which, contrary to his economically calculating bourgeois family (he endorsed the differences between the "ethics of family life and the ethics outside the family") did not make as great an ethical distinction between the private and public spheres. And he solemnly declared that the socialist principle of loving all children impartially was "biologically fatal" and "psychologically absurd."[20]

Socialism itself, for him, ensured "an industrial subordination parallel to the military subordination," in which "obedience is requisite for the maintenance of order, as well as for efficiency, and must be enforced with whatever rigour is found needful." Thus, it would be organized hierarchically, with "multitudinous officers, grade over grade, having in their hands all authority and all means of coercion." This "bureaucracy," would run roughshod over all other social formations, including elected representatives of the populace, forming themselves into a "new ruling class" that "would wield a power far beyond that of any past aristocracy."[21]

In the economic realm, the followers of the classical economists were ensconced in the neo-classical school whose leading thinkers included William Stanley Jevons and Alfred Marshall, and today, one as well-known as Milton Friedman, the leading exponent of the Chicago School. Their economics focused on the concepts of "equilibrium" and "marginal analysis": The first referred to the economy at average levels of production and consumption at any given time, which might be affected by forces of disequilibrium (like shortages and new industries with their influence on prices); the second, the attaining of maximum efficiency in allocating capital for profit under the guise of "free competition." These concepts are now applied to capital in search of profit to roam the world for inexpensive labor, savagely lowering wages and the social safety net.[22]

Friedman, the leading Republican economics guru from the 1970s to the present, formulated the theoretical basis for "Supply-Side" economics or "Reaganomics," which slashed taxes for the wealthy and corporations more so than for the working and lower-middle classes to stimulate investment and consumer spending. A believer in laissez-faire economics and the inviolability of private property, which he equated with liberty, he held that big government was its mortal enemy, the *sine qua non* for the possible rise of socialism. An ardent proponent of individual freedom and responsibility, or "rugged individualism," which glorified a murderously competitive society and the authoritarian ethos of the corporation, he pictured himself as a traditional liberal of the 19th-century variety whose constant refrain was to cut federal social welfare programs perpetuating individual dependence on government and to increase economic incentives of the more resourceful and successful, i.e., the wealthy.

Although Friedman often quoted Smith, his fear of government or collective effort to solve socioeconomic problems made him a Spencerite, although a moderate one. He himself claimed that he "is not an anarchist" (there was a quasianarchist strain in Spencer), as government, indeed, had a proper role in protecting property and citizens from internal and external enemies, intervening to "enforce contracts," safeguard consumers against "technical monopolies," and aid the mentally ill and children. But he was against government subsidies to farmers and other business in the form of tariffs and collusion with business to raise prices, like the Texas Railroad Commission which limited oil prices by reducing output. As a corollary to this, he rejected any close regulation of industry, as by the Interstate Commerce Commission. He also opposed public housing, minimum wage laws, social security programs as now constituted, rent controls, and other present social welfare programs for the poor and unemployed. In their stead, he proposed a system of cash subsidies supplemented with a negative income tax. As for taxes, he called for a federal flat-rate income one, steeply regressive, falling most heavily on the working and lower-middle classes, now favored by Republicans.

In his analysis of economics, Friedman blithely overlooked the free gifts to capital from workers and government: From the former, extraction of surplus-value; from the latter, public education to cheapen labor relatively, fire and police protection, tax abatements, community revenue bonds, laws and supreme court decisions protecting corporations—they are simply seen as persons, despite their immense economic power—research and development assistance, and low taxes. He also seemed to be oblivious to increasing corporate mergers and tendency to ever more oligopoly, or to the truism that American capitalists demanded and received high tariffs not too long ago to allow infant American industry to survive, or to the high costs of militarism/imperialism intimately related to the bourgeois ethic, or to the interference of the IMF in the internal affairs of poor nations, or to the waste of scarce economic resources by the affluent in conspicuous consumption. Ultimately, is not Friedman's "free trade" mantra simply an apology for Western and Japanese capital to rule the world?[23]

Veblen's Socialist Economics

Veblen was the principal father of American institutional economics which insisted that economic practices and ideas reflected the views of those dominating the process, i.e., capitalists whose principal goal was to make profit. By institutions, Veblen meant the property system and its accompanying social structure, like production and credit facilities, corporations and banks, government, education, and religion. In "Why Is Economics Not an Evolutionary Science?" (The title of an 1898 article in the *Quarterly Journal of Economics*), he categorically challenged the beliefs/assumptions of the classical economists and their followers with his socialism.

To begin, Veblen questioned the hedonistic and selfish individual representing the "natural" superiority of private over communally-owned property. He did this not only through the "instinct-of-workmanship" argument, but by duly noting the contradictions arising between a hedonistic-acquisitive individual and the actual workings of a capitalist economy:

> The substitution of investment in the place of industry as the central and substantial fact in the process of production is due not to the acceptance of hedonism simply, but rather to the conjunction of hedonism with an economic situation of which the investment of capital and its management for gain was the most obvious feature.

But, for him, mechanical will of the individual working rationally for hedonistic gain did not explain why one's resources eroded in periods of economic downturn: "The course of market events takes its passionless way without traceable relation or deference to anyone's convenience and without traceable guidance towards an ulterior end."[24] Thus, hedonism in a capitalist context was often wasteful in that depressions left in their wake the tragedy of unused labor and capital.

Veblen also questioned the cherished beliefs of classical economics on the natural character of private property, insisting that large private property originated in military conquest,[25] and challenged the accepted truth that capital formation was only possible through private means. Instead, for him, the actual accumulators of capital were the workers and engineers who produced the goods and designed the technology, not capitalists, whose functions of managing and coordinating capital could easily be handled by economists and statisticians.[26]

Veblen, then, focused on the various elements making for waste in the normal course of capitalist economic activity, like the cost of often "spurious goods" and "salesmanship," which included the:

> multiplication of merchants and shops, wholesale and retail, newspaper advertising and billboards, sales-exhibits, sales agents, fancy packages and labels, adulteration of bands and proprietary articles.

This "salesmanship alone, for him, accounted for approximately half of the price of commodities." (In this particular instance, Veblen was undoubtedly exaggerating, but we do not underestimate the cost of advertising alone—in 1999, 215 billion dollars was spent on it from a GDP of 7.577 trillion dollars—a socialist society can largely dispense with this.) He also factored in the waste of unemployed labor and idle equipment, both associated with the "monopolization of resources, withholding information from business rivals," and of market relations which required limiting output to increase profit, resulting in "a habitual shortage of production." His charge against monopoly and price fixing are still valid, corroborated by an investigation conducted by Senator Philip Hart, Democrat from Michigan in the 1960s, estimating that between 30 and 40 percent of personal consumption is an overcharge, and by the recent fleecing of Californian consumers by electric companies limiting output to raise prices.

But this is not all, for following Veblen, a leisure-class-dominated society, based on the ethos of "invidious distinction" and conflict and its alienating features could not but indulge in conspicuous consumption, resulting in a misallocation of resources. Some examples: The worldwide tourist industry in 1990 was in the 232 billion dollar range and by 2000, easily double this figure. (Eight percent of the world's population—the wealthier—annually travel to other nations.) A 1987 survey found that the average price of a home in fifty American exclusive suburbs was approximately 1.2 million dollars and in forty other wealthy suburbs, approximately half a million dollars (in 2000, these figures are again easily doubled). The behemoth mansion (it includes a theater, spas, arcade, library, and guest house, among other amenities) of Bill Gates, Chairperson of Microsoft, valued at fifty-three million dollars, is certainly one of the standards that other rich now wish to emulate. Even a modest diminution of resources for housing the wealthiest 10 percent of the people should easily solve the problem of substandard or no housing for the bottom third or so of the people. The automobile itself, a key component of the American dream machine, invariably propels most families to purchase the latest, costliest, and most tasteful models possible. The housing, automobile, and leisure-time complex are now the holy trinity of the consumption-status/class nexus, the last composed of vacations and entertainment (movies, plays, concerts, and dining out), along with stylish clothing. Leisure-class-dominated capitalism today, following Veblen, with monopoly pricing, salesmanship waste, and conspicuous consumption distortions, in addition to the effects of alienation, unemployment, militarism and pollution, consumes a third of the GDP.[27]

Apologists of capitalism may protest that without venture capitalists, akin to magicians, like Gates, the wonders of modern technology and related progress would come to a halt; that socialist committees, lacking the economic incentives of capitalism would not be boldly innovative. There may be a modicum of truth here, given the inherited cultural horizon, but modern science and technology and capital formation, today are of a collaborative nature. It would have been impossible for Gates to accumulate a seventy-billion-dollar fortune without the aid of his many lieutenants, science (and its past accomplishments), unequal economic and social relations between labor and capital, early government development of computers and the internet, government infrastructure and policies—education, favorable tax laws, and protection of private property.

In a vein similar to Marx, Veblen emphasized the increasing primacy of the machine since the Industrial Revolution and its decisive influence under capitalism in the growth of the corporation. The machine itself, for him, from its simplest to its most complex forms, permitted humanity to gain ever more mastery over nature, and in the process to progressively change economic, social, and political organizations, with concomitant patterns of culture. To be sure, it was only with the Industrial Revolution in England in the mid-18th century that machinery became so much more sophisticated and widespread than previously, allowing ultimately for an economic structure in which industry took precedence over agriculture.

In *Theory of Business Enterprise*, Veblen insisted that "the material framework of modern civilization is the industrial system," associated with the "machine process," whose "mechanical standardization" signified "economy at nearly all points of the process of supplying goods," with the "standardization of services as well as goods" and of labor. This process, ensconced in the factory/corporation, for him, progressively increased interdependence and cooperation among peoples and nations (despite barbarian leisure-class nationalism/war), and also struck a blow at conventional bourgeois natural property rights as it made them more impersonal. His key players in this scenario were capitalists whose aim was "pecuniary gain" through "purchase and sale," for the "accumulation of capital."[28]

Some background on the corporation, the dominant form of capitalist property in the 20th century. Its forebears were the joint-stock companies of the early 17th century,

allowing many investors to combine their capital in a common enterprise, but whose unlimited liability forced them to disgorge money above what they invested in bankruptcy.
But by the late 17th century, law permitted for a limited liability, confining losses to only
those directly invested in an enterprise.

The corporation, itself a legal entity, having the same rights as an individual in the
American legal system, was organized to promote various activities, usually of an economic nature for profit (there are also charitable and religious corporations), by issuing
stock and profit and loss associated with shares owned. Although the federal government grants corporate charters, most are issued by the states, the most lenient include
Delaware, Maryland, New Jersey, and Maine.

The first large corporations were in the railroad industry, quickly spreading to oil
and steel. Veblen himself located the rise of the corporation in the second half of the 19th
century, becoming the main engine of American economic development. The corporation, for him, "is a means of making money, not of making goods," to maximize profit.[29]
To this end, the corporation, especially the large one, continuously attempted to keep
prices and demand up, including colluding with competitors.[30]

One of the earlier commentators of the business cycle, the periodic occurrence of
vigorous economic activity followed by slumping production and mass unemployment,
Veblen regarded economic downturns as normal in a capitalism "under the consum-
mate regime of the machine, so long as competition is unchecked and no *deus ex machine* interposes," i.e., the state.[31] Thus, in good times, prices, profits, production and
employment were high and credit easily secured, but in a prolonged economic downturn, these indices became negative, capital itself being liquidated as stock and bond
prices fell. In this pattern, he associated business or the pecuniary with the industrial
arena—"industrial depression is primarily a depression in business." More explicitly:

> Industrial depression means that the businessmen engaged do not see their
> way to derive a satisfactory profit from letting the industrial process go for-
> ward on the lines and in the volume for which the material equipment of in-
> dustry is designed.[32]

Veblen, then, examined "overproduction"—a "state of affairs that prevails when business cannot make a good profit from goods sold at a particular price," there being "too
many competitive producers and too much industrial apparatus to supply the market at
reasonable prices" relative to investment.[33] Thus, "new investments are made on the
basis of current rates of interest and with a view to securing the differential gain prom-
ised by the excess of prospective profits over interest rates." But in a depression, industry did not perform at its maximum rate to make a "reasonable" profit, dynamic machine

technology exacerbating this: Machines, "ever increasing in efficiency, turn out the mechanical appliances and materials…at an ever decreasing cost."[34] This, in a normally competitive market, resulted in lower prices, but only the newer plants with the latest technology could reap cost advantages allowing them to underprice their less technologically advanced competitors forced out of business.[35]

Another cause for depression, according to Veblen, were periodic battles between competing business groups to acquire particular companies through "pecuniary coercion," inflicting "pecuniary damage" and "a set-back to the industrial plants concerned and a derangement, more or less extensive, of the industrial system at large."[36]

Was it possible, then, for Veblen, for capitalism to prevent depression by not overproducing, through wasteful private leisure-class expenditures ("conspicuous consumption") and increased government spending in "armaments, public edifices"—the last anticipated by Keynesianism?[37] The only way out for capitalism, he first claimed, was to have business combinations become near monopolies or preferably "trusts"—monopolies which could effectively regulate output, thus prices and profit, in addition to effecting "considerable economies in the cost of production" to further increase profit. Or:

> But when the coalition comes effectually to cover its special field of operation, it is able, not only to fix the prices which it will accept (on the basis of what the traffic will bear) , but also in a considerable measure to fix the prices or rates which it will pay for materials, labor, and other services (such as transportation) on a similar basis—unless it should necessarily have to deal with another coalition that is in a similar position of monopoly.[38]

This formation of monopoly to obviate depression by Veblen was theorized as a means of overcoming the ravages of deflation which intense competition contributed to: In 1866, the wholesale price index stood at 174, in 1880 at 100, and in 1890 at 82. The depressions of 1873-76 and 1893-97 were partly caused by larger firms successfully driving smaller ones into bankruptcy or simply acquiring them.

Monopoly itself was legalized by the Trust, first used by Samuel Dodd, a Standard Oil Company lawyer, in the 1880s. This legal arrangement had competing companies assign their stock to a group of trustees, who, in turn, issued new stock certificates, enabling them to exercise control over the various companies, the aim being to regulate production and prices. By 1902, there were 232 Trusts the most notable being Rockefeller's in oil, founded in 1882, which by 1904 controlled 85 percent of oil refining and 90 percent of the oil pipelines. Another was Morgan's Steel Trust in the U.S. Steel Corporation (the Morgan interests bought out Carnegie's steel empire in 1901), which by 1904 produced two-thirds of the steel output. These Trusts involved "horizontal" integration (combining firms into a single corporation) and the "vertical" variety, as in U.S. Steel's ownership of mines and railroads. As early as 1900, 1 percent of manufacturing firms in America produced a third of the goods in this area.

But there is more. The Pujo House Subcommittee of 1911-12 revealed the close ties among American big business: They principally included the House of Morgan whose two major banks through holding companies and interlocking directorates controlled three large insurance companies, U.S. Steel, General Electric, and various large railroads. They were opposed by the Rockefeller group in control of Standard Oil Co., two large banks, and nine railroads. By the 1907-13 period, the two combinations penetrated one another, resulting in command of 112 banks, insurance, manufacturing, public utility, and transporation companies in a grand economic design.

Adolphe Berle Jr. and Gardiner C. Means, in *The Private Corporation and Private Property* (1932), established that the 200 largest manufacturing corporations controlled about half of industrial corporate wealth, with a split between owners and managers of corporations. But recently, Domhoff has shown top management itself as a significant holder of corporate stock, upholding the traditional Marxist view of wealth and power being intertwined.

To be sure, there was great public outcry to destroy these corporate giants. The Sherman Anti-Trust Act of 1890, specifically enacted to eliminate Trusts, was employed in the first two decades of the 20th century to do so in celebrated cases, like those of the Standard Oil Company in 1907, settled in 1911, and the National Packing Company in 1907, settled in 1921.

The Clayton Anti-Trust Act of 1914, which extended the power of Sherman Anti-Trust, established a Federal Trade Commission in 1914 which could issue "cease and desist" orders against "unfair trade practices" and employ the court system for non-compliance. Furthermore, it outlawed rebates, local pricing cuts for a one-price nationwide system, and interlocking directorates if they lessened competition (almost impossible to prove).[39] But bigness in business continued in the form of oligopoly in which several producers with interlocking directorates agreed to limit both output and price competition.

Another way out of depression, for Veblen, was for business to engage in the consumption of military goods or war preparedness under the rubric of "patriotism," which also inculcated a sense of servility among the general population, reflecting the rise of the military, in the process stifling an overt class struggle against the bourgeoisie by unemployed/impoverished workers.[40] (This happened in Nazi Germany, for instance, in the 1930s, which embarked on a war economy in preparation for war.) But Veblen warned business that patriotic fervor might undermine its prerogatives or "sacrifice the profits of the businessman to the exigencies of the higher politics," or to government control under the aegis of the military.[41]

Of course, the military/war complex froze class positions, the working class checked all the more, dissent being equated with treason. But with the advent of total war and its mass destruction and many sacrifices, socialism gained greatly. Indeed, without World Wars I and II, Soviet and Chinese Communism would not have triumphed and the rise of labor and socialist parties in the West and other places would not have been as rapid.

In his later works, especially *Absentee Ownership and Business Enterprise in Recent Times: The Case of America* (1923), Veblen now exclaimed that even business mergers/concentration could not prevent depression, emphasizing that oligopoly/monopoly for the sake of higher prices and profits had this contradiction: It resulted in a "prudent measure of unemployment," causing an imbalance between production and consumption, deleterious to the economic process.[42] Or:

> Unemployment, in other words sabotage, to use a word of later date, was becoming an everyday care of the business management in the mechanical industries, and was already on the way to become, what it is today, the most engrossing care that habitually engages the vigilance of the business executive.[43]

The views of Veblen on depression were very similar to Marx's. For Marx, more capital not only resulted in more workers, but linked to a dynamic technology whose aim was to constantly lower per-unit cost of production to maximize profit, the larger firms would drive the smaller ones into bankruptcy or acquire them. Unemployment itself was always a permanent problem since new technologies constantly downgraded existing labor skills, while intense competition for jobs among workers relatively depressed wages. In this scenario, wages lagged behind industrial and other productivity, leading to periodic depressions caused by the imbalance between overproduction and underconsumption of goods that exacerbated unemployment.[44] Thus, I disagree with Paul Sweezy's assertion that Veblen, contrary to Marx, did not "solve" the "relation between the monopolization process and the tendency to chronic depression."[45]

From an overarching perspective, the crisis of modern 20th-century capitalism, for Veblen, was in the contradiction between "twentieth century technology," which has "outgrown the eighteenth century system of vested rights" or private property, which in the corporation is seen by the division between "business management," representing profit, and the "technological experts" or engineers and workers representing technicity and production.[46]

For Veblen, the following conditions exacerbated this: (1) the tendency to depression and concentration of production and credit facilities; (2) the widening wealth and power gap between capitalists and workers ("the workmen do not and cannot own or direct the industrial equipment"), subverting "the exercise of free contract, and the other powers inhering in the natural right of ownership," their being "incompatible with the modern machine technology." These elements were related to the modern capitalist corporation, the heart of modern capitalism.[47]

Some observations are now in order on the causes of the Great Depression in the United States, confirming the views discussed: In 1919-1929, while real wages increased 26 percent, productivity rose 40 percent, an imbalance reflected in huge corporate profits—730 million dollars on average in the 1916-25 period, as opposed to 1.4 billion dollars in the 1926-29 one. Corporate cash surpluses in billions of dollars also mounted—in 1921, 3.5; in 1929, 9.0. There were large amounts of money in the hands of speculators (the wealthiest 1 percent played the stock market the most heavily), who put down only 5 percent of a stock's price to purchase it, rapidly driving up the market to unparalleled heights, the Dow Jones Stock Average stood at 50 in 1922 and 200 just before the 1929 crash. Banks themselves used depositors' money for this frenzied speculation. These developments transpired in an economy dominated by big business. Oligopoly reigned—in terms of respective market percentages—three auto companies had 82; four meat packers, 70; Aluminum Company of America, 100; nine steel companies, 86. The free market was a myth here, as "administered prices" of the large corporations were designed to hold prices of commodities up, disregarding fluctuations of demand. In oligopoly—for instance, in the early 1930s—although iron and steel production dropped by 80 percent, its price fell only 6 percent (inelastic pricing); but where there was intense competition among many producers, as in agriculture, the price plummeted precipitously, although not production—a bushel of wheat was $1.05 in 1929, 39 cents in 1931 (elastic pricing). Internationally, just as the Germans defaulted on war reparations to the Allies for damages in World War I, so did the Allies default on U.S. loans during the war, signifying the collapse of the international credit market. These economic events/conditions adversely impacted an American capitalism whose richest 2 percent owned three-fifths of the wealth.

In October 1929, when British investors left the American market in droves because British interest rates were raised to 6.5 percent, the market declined 30 percent. Although, from November 1929 to April 1930, the market rose by 50 percent, it, then, inexorably fell to its nadir in 1933, losing about three-fourths of its highest value in 1929.

In the 1930-1933 period, 5000 banks failed, with depositors losing all of their savings, deflation struck as the price index fell by a fourth, private investment dipped in billions of dollars from 15 to less than 1, interest rates dropped slowly from 5 percent to 3.8 percent (their low in 1936 at 1.7 percent), and unemployment sharply increased from 3 percent in 1929 to 25 percent in 1933, its high in the 1930s.

The federal government itself acted, although not too promptly or efficaciously, to prevent the horrendous socioeconomic misery of unemployment. President Herbert Hoover in the 1930-32 period engaged in government pump priming, averaging 2.5 billion dollars a year; with the New Deal under President Franklin Delano Roosevelt in the remainder of the 1930s, it was rapidly increased, reaching 15 billion dollars by 1936, itself aiding private investment which reached 10 billion dollars by 1936.

The New Deal enacted legislation to prevent mass starvation, initiated relief programs and restarted the economy by providing jobs through measures like the Federal Emergency Relief Administration, Public Works Administration, Works Progress Administration, and the National Industrial Recovery Act whose section 7a gave labor the green light, preventing employer coercion to form unions, which once having the majority of workers in a plant could bargain collectively. It also helped business through the Reconstruction Finance Corporation (RFC), begun by Hoover in 1932, lending money usually to big business, totaling 15 billion dollars from 1932 to 1941, most being repaid; in fact this agency realized a half-billion-dollar profit.

Furthermore, the federal government became involved in various other areas in this period, like protecting savings accounts by the Federal Deposit Insurance Corporation, divorcing speculative from commercial banking in the Glass-Steagall Act, providing pensions for the elderly and assisting families with the Social Security Act, and promoting regional economic development as in the Tennesee Valley Authority.

But these and other measures did not end high unemployment, which fluctuated from 14 percent in 1937, to 19 percent in 1938, and to 10 percent in 1940. Only World War II solved the unemployment problem. Indeed, without massive government regulation and assistance and/or war, capitalism is neither viable economically nor able to end large-scale working-class misery.[48]

The foremost capitalist economist of the 20th century who examined the nightmare of depression and devised a way to preserve a modified capitalism was John Maynard Keynes in his *General Theory of Employment, Interest, and Money* (1936). His central tenet denied the validity of Say's Law, that production or supply automatically created its own demand; money demand was needed and without it the unemployed/underemployed simply could not purchase available goods in a depression period. His remedy was massive government intervention to restart the economy by implementing lower interest rates, monetary expansion or inflation, and public investment in public works, to be partly financed by higher taxes on the wealthy. This scenario, which candidly admitted that capitalism could not survive without extensive government assistance, was ultimately based on promoting large-scale government deficit spending, inviting in the back door an increasing group of government bond holders as key economic players.[49]

But this was not all, for with the continuing economic stagnation of the 1930s, Keynes in "Democracy and Efficiency," in 1939, formulated an economic model to ensure prosperity, which he termed "Liberal Socialism."

> A system where we can act as an organized community for economic purpose
> and to promote social and economic justice, while respecting and protecting
> the individual—his freedom of choice, his faith, his mind and its expression,
> his enterprise and his property.

This new paradigm was simply an amalgam of capitalism and some state socialism in the form of many quasipublic corporations run by a managerial elite, the chief architects of his new society, preserving the power of a now supposedly chastened and public-spirited bourgeoisie, a pious, but unrealistic view of them.[50]

This mixed-economy model was partly adhered to in Western Europe after World War II, with extensive nationalization of industry and banking and rising social welfarism, but bourgeois hegemony over the working class continued unabatedly in the form of a dominant "free market" economy, despite periodic economic crises in Japan, East Asia, Russia, much of Eastern Europe, the European Union, Latin America, and U.S.

The last problem in this section involves the division between the management and stockholders of large corporations—a normal feature of mature capitalism—which some capitalist economists, like Keynes, hoped would soften capitalist desire for profit for community good because of public pressure. From the hindsight of the 1980s and 90s, with Friedmanite economics in the ascendancy, Veblen, who denied that this split would soften managerial concern for profit, has proven to be correct. Managers in the U.S., are in this profit-maximization cage: They own large blocks of stock in their companies and receive large bonuses—part of their perquisites—but must also please the managers of mutual funds and their vision of short-term maximization of profit, failure to do so resulting in their companies losing market value.[51]

Capitalism after World War II to the Present

Veblen's principal theses that capitalism would not only lead to ever more economic concentration but to continual economic crises, always prone to economic stagnation, unless working-class action would force some balance between production and consumption, and that its "chicane" would proceed as usual has been borne out in the last half century.

Prompted by fear of Soviet Communism, the need to rebuild after the devastation of World War II, and increased working-class activity, capitalism, in a Keynesian mode in the U.S., a mixed economy one (part capitalist and socialist) in Western Europe, and a *Kiretsu* (large capitalist conglomerates, cooperating with government) one in Japan, ushered in a period of rapid economic growth to the mid-1970s.

Thereafter, economic growth markedly diminished in a setting characterized by the rise of large transnational corporations (TNCs), trading blocs, like the European Union (EU) and North American Free Trade Agreement (NAFTA); they are coupled to largely international free trade, mostly carried out by the TNCs, sanctioned by the World Trade Organization (WTO), aided by the International Monetary Fund (IMF) and World Bank (WB), all promoting privatization, indicating the power of capital over labor.

Today, the largest 600 American corporations generate at least 80 percent of sales revenue, the other 22 million businesses (a third part-time and a third of one person), the remainder. As for the market value of publicly traded companies today, the Standard and Poor's 500 (the top 500 corporations), has 85 percent of it. In manufacturing, for instance, the top 200 corporations had 48 percent of sales value in 1950 and 60 percent in 1980 and of total assets in manufacturing, 53 percent in 1955 and 61 percent in 1983.

This concentration of capital is based on the inexorable drive of capital to expand, in addition to greater amounts of it needed for research and development, as well as savings related to economies of scale. During the Reagan and Bush Presidencies, a plethora of mergers and acquisitions, including leveraged buyouts (LBOs) numbered 44,518 at 2.17 trillion dollars, and for the Clinton one to June 2000, 78,811 at 6.66 trillion dollars, 80 percent among American corporations, the remainder between them and foreign ones.

Large mergers/acquisitions from 1998 to 2000 in billions of dollars (some involving foreign corporations) included (the acquired company comes second): Vodafone AirTouch with Mannesmann, 203; America Online with Time Warner, 111; Pfizer and Warner Lambert, 90; Exxon with Mobil, 86; GlaxoWellcome with Smith Kline Beecham, 78. In the auto industry, as an example, in billions of dollars, there is Daimler-Benz with Chrysler at 40; others, including partial acquisitions, include Renault, 5.4 for control of Nissan Motors; Ford purchasing the automobile-making part of Volvo for 6.5; General

Motors acquiring a fifth of Subaru for 1.4; and Daimler Chrysler purchasing 34 percent of Mitsubishi motors for 2. In banking, in billions of dollars, they included First Union with CoreStates; Chase Manhattan with Chemical Bank; NationsBank with Bank of America; Bank One with First Chicago; Citicorps with the Travelers Group (the latter comprised Travelers Insurance and the investement firm of Salomon Smith Barney—this merger has made the Glass-Steagall Act of 1933, separating commercial from investment banking, obsolete); and J.P. Morgan with Chase Manhattan. Capital concentration was abetted by federal deregulation of corporations in the last twenty years supposedly to foster more competition. (For economists, monopoly competition, of administered pricing in which price competition is minimal, results when four companies have at least 50 percent of the sales domestically and five do so with at least 50 percent globally.)

In the domestic market today, concentration usually in fractions or as percentage of sales revenue by number of companies: seven telephone ones, with most; four airlines, two-thirds; four appliance makers, more than 90; three computer software firms, half; twenty in insurance, half; three in mass merchandising (one alone with half), three-fourths; four drugstore chains, almost half; ten in pharmaceuticals, including foreign, with most; two grain exporters, half; in food processing, three in beef, almost 80, four cereal ones, 85, and four milling in flour, 60; for farms, one percent with 38; in hospitals, one chain alone with 10. In assets, the top ten to fifteen companies in banking have half in 2000, and by 2005, it should be 90 percent; for gas and electric firms, there were 150 in 1995, a hundred in 2000, and by 2010, "a couple of dozen"—this horror in the midst of deregulation.

Small business is now becoming ever less viable by the growth of the capital/technology nexus. In the sphere of auto dealerships, although there are now twenty thousand, consolidation in the form of superdealerships is now on the scene and automakers are attempting to abolish dealer franchise laws making it illegal for automakers to sell directly to the public through the internet and company-owned dealers. Sales commissions of independent insurance agents have been halved by insurance companies, their number falling by 37 percent between 1987 and 1999, and travel agencies have had their commissions cut by half as travelers contact airlines and hotels directly through the internet. In the grocery business, there were 530,000 outlets in 1950, but 126,000 in 1998, with five companies now controlling 30 percent of the market. In the restaurant business, national fast-food chains, like MacDonald's, and regional ones, like Bob Evans, now dominate.

This economic concentration masks even a greater one with interlocking directorates; inside directors carry on daily business, while outside ones represent larger perspectives, as of business in general and numerous relationships with others in the elite business community: Thus it is that in the larger corporations, common broad policies are formulated through the latter directors serving on many corporate boards simultaneously. Not surprisingly, banks and insurance companies are key players here. Holding companies, which control other companies, especially common in the public utilities area, also heighten this concentration.[52]

Globally, increasing capital concentration is primarily by TNCs and international lending institutions like the IMF. TNCs are the unifying productive element here, having plants in two or more nations, with a fourth to a third of their profits coming from outside the parent location. The largest 500 TNCs in 1998, for instance, conduct 70 percent—40 percent of it intra-firm—of the 3.2 trillion-dollar world trade. Indeed, the leading 350 alone have more than a fourth of the world's productive assets and comprise a third of the GDP of economically advanced nations. Of the top 500 in 1999, 244 are from the U.S., 173 from the EU, and 46 from Japan, and of the top hundred, 70 are from the U.S., 26 from the EU, and 4 from Japan. Three-fourths of TNC investment is in the First World, the remainder in developing nations, but in the late 1990s, new capital flows to the latter are 40 percent of foreign direct investment; worldwide, their cumulative total was 3.5 trillion dollars in 1997. Imports and exports today are a large part of many national GDPs—a fourth for the U.S. and half for France, Germany, and the UK.

With the now large international stock and bond flows, nations are ever more economically intertwined. In the U.S., for instance, in early 2000, foreigners purchased 30 percent of the stock and 40 percent of bonds, including federal ones. Another instance of this is France, where American and British investors through their pension funds own between 30 and 40 percent of its stock-market. In the realm of industry, foreigners own a fourth of the French and up to two-fifths of the British. In factories and other installations, American and EU TNCs have invested about a trillion dollars in each others' markets.

The TNCs are so huge that the largest ones have sales exceeding the GDPs of many nations: the leading 25 alone had annual sales topping 25 billion dollars or more by the early 90s. The largest five in percent of sales now have a monopoly advantage in consumer durables (70), automobiles and trucks (60), airlines (55), aerospace (55), electrical/electronics and components (more than 50), and steel (50); and not far from it in oil (more than 40), personal computers (more than 40), the media (more than 40), chemicals (35), and insurance (25).

The power of the TNCs and large banks is so pronounced over national governments that the last shred of national sovereignty over TNCs is now proposed by the Organization for Economic Cooperation and Development (OECD), made up of the leading twenty-nine nations, with the cooperation of the IMF. Its economic package, the

Multilateral Agreement on Investment (MAI), offers a *carte blanche* to TNCs in purchasing, selling, and moving companies without regard to national laws. Furthermore, under MAI rules, nations would neither subsidize their domestic industries nor demand that foreign corporations abide by national guidelines for economic development. Capital now would be truly globalized, making national boundaries largely superfluous. Near-term consequences of this would include weakening of labor laws and environmental protection. Because of socialist and other opposition, MAI talks have stalled, but for how long? Even without the MAI, the economic phenomena of TNCs, globalization of stock, bond, and currency markets, larger economic integration, and increasing percentages of imports/exports relative to GDP, is reinforcing the power of the international bourgeoisie.

In 2000, more than three trillion dollars daily circled the globe, of which 15 percent was in the form of capital funds and commodity trading, the remainder in currency and other complex forms of speculation, like hedge funds. Trading is conducted through giant computer networks, the largest being the New York Clearing House Interbank Payment System (CHIPS), made up of eleven private banks that offer their services to 142 other banks globally; it interacts with smaller similar networks, like Society of Worldwide Interbank Financial Communications (SWIFT) in Belgium, linking a thousand or so banks, and a few other smaller computer complexes.

This almost uncontrolled computer/electronic system has encouraged tax havens in the Bahamas, Cayman Islands, Bermuda, Hong Kong, Isle of Man, and elsewhere; in the Grand Cayman Island alone there are 575 banks and trust companies handling 500 billion dollars in assets. But, of course, laws permit this squirreling away of money. It is estimated by Merrill Lynch that in 1998, six trillion dollars was deposited by the world's wealthy (two-fifths held by U.S. citizens) in these off-shore tax havens, with an annual 70 billion-dollar loss for U.S. taxpayers alone. Indeed, one expert on money movement, Anthony Ginsberg, estimated, that about half the stock of the industrialized world was associated with tax havens. William Mulholland, the CEO of the Bank of Montreal, informed Canadian parliamentary committee that "I can hide money in the twinkling of an eye from all the bloodhounds that could be put on the case." (About 400 billion dollars annually made from illegal drugs is an integral part of this money laundering.) The Securities and Exchange Commission, in a well-known finding, itself allowed that "off-the-books transactions, bogus transfers, and double sets of accounts"—all standard routines of New York's Citibank—were consistent with "reasonable and standard business judgment" that circumvent "currency regulation" and "tax laws." Obviously, the line between the legal and illegal is so blurred here that normal law is almost inoperative as it has been transcended by secrecy and speed; as in recent revelations of Russian money laundering in the many billions of dollars by government insiders and their accomplices. In the meantime, there was a partial U.S. deindustrialization as manufactured goods were produced in low-wage nations like Mexico, China, and Indonesia: For instance, the percentage of manufactured goods produced in the U.S. for domestic consumption was 86 percent in 1969 and 62 percent in the 1980s. Furthermore, since 1990, foreign direct investment in the U.S. exceeded that of the U.S. abroad, much of this being related to massive U.S. trade deficits since 1976, 369 billion dollars in 2000 alone, and climbing. By 2000, foreigners hold 6.7 trillion dollars of gross U.S. assets, equaling two-thirds of U.S. GDP; but in net assets held by foreigners (subtracting what U.S. residents own abroad and debts owed them), it is 1.4 trillion dollars.

Some perspective on globalization of capital: In the 1860s and 70s, the world witnessed much free trade, high tariffs coming later. Too, capital movements abroad as percentage of GDP were in the 1990s lower than those in the late 19th century when the wealthy of England and France heavily invested in Australia, Canada, New Zealand, and the U.S. After World War I and during the Great Depression, international investment and trade dropped drastically as autarky reigned, but after World War II they rose again. But while international investment before was of the long-range variety, as in railroads and manufacturing, today much of it is in international assembly lines making manufactured goods and in short-term stock, bond, and currency funds, highly leveraged and speculative. Indeed, with the instant electronic technology of today, the herd mentality easily leads to economic crises. Worldwide, in the last twenty years, there were ninety major bank crises, while from 1870 to 1913, only five, with only one leading to a crisis in currency exchange rates.

With the increasing importance of global mutual funds in stocks and bonds, in conjunction with the new powers of the GATT/WTO complex, any democratic socialist success, as in France, is hostage to international capital and to regional economic integration requirements, like those of the EU. Indeed, global monopolization of the TNCs, and their attendant economic and political power, is forcing nations and various states in the U.S. to grant them favorable subsidies and tax breaks simply to operate there. This development compels smaller companies beholden to them economically to ruthlessly compete with one another for their contracts, in the process either lowering wages and benefits for workers or causing higher unemployment, thus the race to the economic bottom for workers, including the savaging of unions.

These economic phenomena, of an ever more internationalized capitalism, have reduced trade wars among nations, although they still persist, as the U.S. recently forced Russia, Japan, and Brazil to curtail steel exports to it, and the EU prevented U.S. TNCs from being subsidized with off-shore tax havens.[53]

Veblen's near-predatory leisure class, the large capitalists, have inherited all of the negative qualities of the older master classes, especially "chicane" or duplicity, involving outright cheating and swindling, and when need be, employ brutal overt force, as in the rival armies of the American robber barons and in imperialistic ventures. Several leading contemporary examples follow.

A most important one was the Savings and Loan debacle under the Reagan and Bush Presidencies, which, with the assistance of a Democratic Congress, will cost taxpayers more than 500 billion dollars in twenty or so years. It commenced with the deregulation of the S&Ls in 1982, which instead of only lending money for homes, were also allowed to do so for office buildings, junk bonds, and so forth to increase their earnings, interest rate ceilings being removed. This caused a wild, speculative frenzy leading to fraud in appraising real estate (Reagan drastically reduced the number of auditors), outside auditors permitting questionable practices, with S&L officials awarding tainted loans to family members and associates, often receiving kickbacks in return. According to legal experts, fraud cases are difficult to prove, requiring mountains of evidence to distinguish between poor management and fraud. The crash happened in the late 1980s and by 1991, two thousand S&Ls were declared insolvent. William Seideman, the former chairperson of the FDIC, estimated that fraud was involved in three-fifths of the bankruptcies, indeed, being the primary cause in half of them. In the 1990s, the Justice Department tried 21,000 fraud cases, 1,300 of major proportion. Many S&L failures were preordained as S&Ls were not able to overcome the high inflation of the 1970s, their former fixed-rate mortgage loans inevitably forcing them into speculative frenzies and illegalities to survive.

LBOs are another scheme to make money quickly, a typical example follows. About 70 percent of the capital to acquire a company by corporate raiders—like Carl Ichan and Boone Pickens—is borrowed from lending institutions at high-interest rates which are tax write-offs. This amount is, then, converted into "junk bonds," added to the debt of the captive company as the raiders sell off various divisions at high profit. These and other financial maneuvers, like repurchasing company stock to increase its value (the salary package of CEOs includes purchase of stock options, higher stock prices leading to more remuneration) have increased the corporate debt of the S&P 500 relative to their equity from 84 percent in the 1980s to 116 percent in 1999. But from 80 to 90 or so percent of new plant and equipment from 1980 to 2001 has been financed from profit and tax-depreciation allowances. Needless to say, these corporate developments indicate the parasitical nature of leisure-class machinations.

Another example are the financial maneuverings of George Soros, an international speculator, chief of the Quantum Fund, based in the Netherlands Antilles, which deals in the risky and arcane areas of highly leveraged hedge funds in options, futures, and derivatives, sheltering profits in various tax avoidance maneuvers. In a particularly brazen and successful venture, the Soros investment group drove down the English pound in September of 1992, in the course of which they made a two-billion dollar profit, while the British government lost six billion dollars. Soros blithely admitted to this economic rape causing some of his wealthy cohorts some embarrassment. He, of course, is hailed as a philanthropist and courted for advice by heads of state, including President Clinton.

Finally, there are the exotic and deadly hedge funds, highly leveraged capital pools (approximately three thousand of them existed in the U.S. in 2000) operating secretly and unregulated. The typical one has a leverage of about thirty to one as opposed to twenty-seven to one for the five largest investment banks and fourteen to one for the five largest commercial banks—the last two are regulated by federal agencies. The "hedge" applies to the practice of betting that two forms of investments will similarly rise and fall. To participate in these funds, minimum amounts may range from a hundred thousand to millions of dollars.

One such fund was Long Term Capital Management, a limited partnership which demanded a minimum of ten million dollars from each investor, private or institutional, to join its privileged circle. Its leading operatives were John M. Meriwether, a Wall Street wunderkind, and two Nobel Prize laureates in economics, Myron S. Scholes and Robert C. Merton.

Specifically, this fund invested in government bonds—of the U.S. Treasury, European nations, including Russia (which defaults), and developing nations, many of which in 1998 were in an economic free fall—and in bonds for mortgages. It wagered, for instance, that the interest rates between corporate and U. S. Treasury bonds would narrow to a less than 1 percent difference (is this productive?), which did not happen in a given time. In fact, the fund's prophecy that U.S. Treasury Bonds would fall in price proved to be incorrect as the 1998 economic crash in Asia and Russia, invited investors to them.

This fund leveraged its initial 2.2 billion-dollar capital to about 125 billion dollars through borrowing on it, then, employed the latter amount as collateral to purchase 1.25 trillion dollars worth of various exotic investments in many complex derivatives. When one of its already stated plans misfired, it was faced with running out of capital to pay short-term obligations, thus facing bankruptcy. At this juncture, the Federal Reserve Bank of New York intervened to save this fund from bankruptcy by arranging for leading banks and brokerage houses, some of which had lent it money in addition to being its partners, like J. P. Morgan and Co., Merrill Lynch, and Morgan Stanley Dean Witter, to purchase most of it for 3.5 billion dollars. If this bail out would not have succeeded, knowledgeable opinion held that it might have triggered large bank failures in the U.S., which, in turn, would have spread worldwide.

To be sure, in any given year, many corporations are hauled before the courts for overcharging customers and other fraud. Some of the more egregious examples of this in fines in dollars are now presented: Marc Rich's corporations (Rich is an international trader living in Switzerland who often shaves legality; he was pardoned in 2001 by President Clinton before leaving office), 200 million; Prudential, 35 million and it agreed to pay 1.7 billion to policyholders because of deceptive practices; SmithKline Beecham, 325 million for false billings to Medicare; Archer Daniels Midland, 100 million for price fixing; Michael Miliken, the "junk-bond king," 1.1 billion (he will still be worth 125 million) for financial fraud; one of his cohorts, Ivan Boesky, only 100 million; Blue Cross and Blue Shield of Illinois, 144 million in civil and criminal fines. The government has charged Columbia/HCFA Healthcare and Quorum Health Group with 1.1 billion dollars in fraudulent expense claims. In 2001, Walter A. Forbes, former chairperson of Cedant is charged for causing its investors a loss of 19 billion dollars by declaring "phony profits." Cedant itself has compensated shareholders at 2.8 billion dollars.

An energy shortage has gripped the U.S., which for part of 2001 was of crisis proportion for consumers. In oil, the international oil monopoly, Organization of the Petroleum Export Countries (OPEC), was reducing oil output; in electric power, relative over-supply and relatively low prices again discouraged investment. Thus, low investment, lack of government oversight to ensure conservation (low-mileage sports utility vehicles now proliferate as the auto lobby is triumphant), and government failure to force regulated companies, like electric utilities, to increase investment to keep up with demand, conspired to set the stage for the energy crisis.

Now, it was within this backdrop that deregulation occurred in natural gas and recently in electric power—in the latter, twenty-four states by 2001 supposedly to foster more competition and lower prices. But these utilities are natural monopolies, or become oligoplies, like natural gas with attendant monopolistic competition. (Utilities themselves, because they are natural monopolies, were regulated by the states by the early 20th century to allow them a fair profit and consumer price stability.)

In California, in which there were rolling blackouts, deregulation was supported by both major political parties, the utilities, and large business on the basis that it would lower their energy costs—some electric companies had lower prices as they mainly did not rely on expensive nuclear energy. But for deregulation to proceed, consumers also will have to pay "stranded costs" or fixed costs incurred by poor electric company investments mostly in nuclear energy.

But these simultaneous developments have brought about steeply rising prices: (1) the building of fewer plants because regulatory profits, although more than fair, were not high enough to attract sufficient investment; (2) market manipulation by rival companies which may somewhat lower the price until a few dominate, setting up capitalist regulation or monopolistic competition, then under-investing; (3) short-term power manipulation by electric companies through convenient power outages because of "repairs"—almost quintupling since deregulation.

The plan to deregulate involves this "shell game." Electric power companies would sell their power plants to energy companies furnishing the power, the electric companies simply becoming the transmission belts retailing to the public. The producers are not limited to any one geographical area, thus allowing them to further manipulate the market for highest possible returns. Not suprisingly, profits are up for the producers, but the carrriers are going bankrupt as they are still somewhat regulated. To be sure, the transmission and energy companies themselves are part of large conglomerates.

In the electric power area alone, prices are so very high in California, that its Democratic governor Gray Davis is now proposing the establishment of a state energy board to reimpose price regulation, including state purchase of generating plants from private companies and to even build new state-owned ones.

Ultimately, the lack of planning in this economic scenario fleeced California consumers in the 2000-02 period of many billions of dollars in higher rates. For maximum consumer protection state ownership of utilities is a must.

In connection with the gross overcharging of rates in California and other Western states, poetic justice occurred when a mayor culprit of this outrage, Enron, a large energy and trading company, imploded by late 2001. Once a company whose stock value in 2000 reached ninety billion dollars, making it the seventh largest corporation in the S&P 500, by December of 2001 its stock sold for pennies. Its demise was because of its being plundered by principal officers who created a web of intricate financial arrangements, such as partnerships based offshore in the Cayman Islands, that allowed the hiding of company debt, while netting enormous profits for themselves. To be sure, Enron is now being investigated by many Congressional committees and the Justice Department. Enron itself made enormous profits from the deregulation of energy, especially in the electricity segment in California, controlling a significant share of that market, being exempt from any oversight by the Commodity Futures Trading Commission. The consequences of the Enron implosion included huge losses for its employee retirement accounts, for banks, like J P Morgan Chase, and for the stock market. Its CEO, Kenneth Lay, alone earned 205 million dollars in stock options in the last four years of his office.

Since the implosion of Enron, a plethora of American companies were soon exposed as being involved with fraudulent practices which led to overstating profits, thus keeping their stock prices artificially up: When fraud was discovered, it quickly led to their bankruptcy. They included WorldCom, Adelphia Communications, Global Crossing, and Tyco. For instance, WorldCom overestimated its profits at 3.85 billion dollars in a little more than a year in the 2001-2002 period. It employed a simple accounting trick in this deception: Instead of deducting current expenses as a cost of doing business, it listed them as "capital expenditures," allowing their cost to be spread over a number of years. Its CEO Bernie Ebbers borrowed 366 million dollars in the last three years of his reign and was compensated 183 million dollars, 163 million of which was in stock options. As for Adelphia, it was looted by its founder John Rigas and his family who borrowed 2.3 billion dollars from it. In the case of Global Crossing, its CEO, Gary Winnick enriched himself with 735 million dollars in stock options as the company was imploding. With respect to Tyco, Dennis Kozlowski received 345 million dollars in stock options in the last three years of being its CEO, again personally contributing to its demise.

Corporate fraud itself was abetted by laws permitting CEOs and other executives to gain income through stock options, themselves tied to stock prices—they were not regarded as a company expense—thus raising company profits from 20 to 30 percent, which inflated stock prices. To make stock options more lucrative, companies would lend money to top executives who, in turn, would purchase more of them; this device again was not listed as an expense. Furthermore, companies would go into more debt to banks in repurchasing their stock in the market, the aim here being to again raise stock prices, thus also the value of stock options. In short, while these companies were going bankrupt, but hiding their losses through illegal accounting practices, their top executives as insiders would sell their stocks at high prices, knowing that they would soon fall, enriching themselves by billions of dollars.

The enormity of these economic disasters cannot be overestimated. For instance, WorldCom's demise saw its stock fall from a high of 64.5 dollars a share to less than a dollar within three years, costing investors more than 175 billion dollars. To be sure, tens of thousands of employees have lost their jobs because of these scandals.

In some of these fraud cases, the Arthur Andersen accounting firm was involved in "cooking" their books: Although serving as auditors of these companies, it was also involved in devising accounting practices to manufacture higher profits. This company that paid a 110 million dollar civil-settlement fine for accounting malpractice in the collapse of Sunbeam, also audited the books of Enron and WorldCom. It is now fined again by the government for the Enron scandal and is currently going out of business.[54]

In an American society blaming those on welfare for living off the public's largesse, the huge amounts of money spent on "corporate welfare," are largely ignored. In the matter of taxes alone, corporate contribution has decreased substantially from the 1950s to 2000. Corporations paid 39 percent of all federal income taxes in the former date, but only 12 percent in the latter; although the corporate tax is 35 percent in the 1990s, various deductions, as on interest payments on "junk bonds," "special dividends" for their CEOs and stockholders, and on half of social-security ones, as well as on fringe benefits, like medical insurance, resulted in low taxes.

In the mid-90s, annual federal corporate welfare costs in the billions of dollars run from 53 for Common Cause; 167 for the liberal Nader's Center for the Study of Responsive Law; and 87 for the conservative libertarian Cato Institute (Spencerites). (These statistics do not include, another 50 or so billion dollars granted annually to business by local and state governments in the form of industrial revenue bonds, tax abatements, and tax-increment financing, the last reimbursing business for taxes collected from them to aid in their building costs.) Some of the larger annual dollar costs, in billions, include: 18.3 for the S&L debacle; 9 lost in taxes from mergers and acquisitions; from 8 to 29 in agriculture, much of it to the larger farmers and food corporations—half of farm income in 2000 is in government subsidies; 12 to oil companies as write-offs for royalties to other nations; 30 in excessively high depreciation allowances for corporate plant and equipment; a minimum of 25 (it may be double this amount) for TNCs shifting expenses and revenues to other nations through "creative" accounting; 29 for business meals and entertainment; half a billion for the non-payment of royalties for mining on public land; 60 in research and development by public and private universities; 70 to the media giants in the Telecommunications Act of 1996 for the digital spectrum; and 4.1 in tax beaks for TNCs doing business abroad to establish offshore tax havens—terminated in 2000 because of EU and WTO objections. Also much of research and development by public and private universities, much of its tax-exempt, has greatly aided business. The federal government through the Department of Defense (as the Pentagon's Manufacturing Technology Program that is instrumental in modernizing manufacturing, combining the latest techniques of automation and computer technology) and other agencies developed atomic energy and the internet with its hardware and software. As for the transistor, although invented by Bell Telephone, government purchases of it and high tariffs on less expensive and superior Japanese computers allowed the domestic variety to flourish. Government subsidies in these areas must be in the tens of billions of dollars. In these giveaways the role of big-business lobbyists and political action committees was critical.[55]

Notes

1. Leo Rogin, *The Meaning and Validity of Economic Theory: A Historical Approach* (New York: Harper and Brothers, 1956), pp. 51-231 on Smith, Ricardo, Malthus, and J.B. Say—all viewed from a socialist perspective. Also, see Robert L. Heilbroner, *The Worldly Philosophers: The Lives, Times, and Ideas of the Great Economic Thinkers* (New York: Simon and Schuster, 1953), pp. 33-66 on Smith; pp. 67-95 on Malthus and Ricardo.

2. Bruce Mazlish, ed., *The Wealth of Nations: Representative Selections*, Adam Smith (Indianapolis, IN: Bobbs-Merrill, 1978), pp. 162 ff.

3. *Ibid.*, pp. 65-66.

4. *Ibid.*, p. 257.

5. *Ibid.*, p. xvii and pp. 16-17.

6. *Ibid.*, p. 17.

7. *Ibid.*, pp. 31 and 33.

8. Edwin A. Burtt, *The English Philosophers from Bacon to Mill* (New York: Modern Library, 1967), pp. 413-23 is Chapter 5 of Locke's *Concerning Civil Government*.

9. Thomas Robert Malthus, *An Essay on the Principle of Population* Introduction T.M. Hollingsworth (London: Dent, 1892), pp. 5-11, on food tending to increase arithmetically, while population increases geometrically. This work was first published in 1798. The fifth edition (1817) was against birth-control measures.

10. *Ibid.*, Books I and II are entitled "The Checks to Population."

11. *Ibid.*, Book III, p. 25: Malthus is against the egalitarianism of Robert Owen. Equality, for Malthus, would perpetuate a "natural indolence," inimical to progress; for him the poverty of the workers is because of their having too many children, a moral evil.

12. *Ibid.*, Book, III, pp. 97-125.

13. *Ibid.*, Book IV, pp. 200-44.

14. *Ibid.*, Book IV, pp. 200-15.

15. R.R. Popper, *The Open Society and Its Enemies*, Vol. I: *The Sell of Plato*; Vol. II, *The High Tide of Prophecy: Hegel Marx, and the Aftermath* (New York: Harper Torchbooks, 1963), II, 710.

16. My view of Malthus' *Essay on the Principle of Population* is similar to Marx in *Capital*, I, p. 675, "this work in its first form is nothing more than a schoolboyish, superficial plagiary of De Foe" and others.

17. On Ricardo, see Rogin, *Meaning and Validity*, pp. 110-56. Heilbroner, *Worldly Philosophers*, pp. 67-95.

18. Rogin, *Meaning and Validity*, p. 118.

19. Malthus, *Essay on the Principle of Population*, Book III, p. 1-29.

20. J.D.Y. Peel, edited and Introduction, *Herbert Spencer on Social Evolution: Selected Writings* (Chicago: University of Chicago Press, 1972), pp. 244 ff.

21. *Ibid.*, pp. 246-49 for the quotations.

22. On the neo-classical economists, see, Rogin, *Meaning and Validity of Economic Theory*, pp. 454-80 on Jevons, pp. 554-616, on Marshall. On Friedman and "Supply-side economics," see Charles K. Wilber and Kenneth P. Jameson, *Beyond Reaganomics: A Further Inquiry into the Poverty of Economics* (Notre Dame: University of Notre Dame Press, 1990), pp. 64-67, 92-121.

23. On Milton Friedman, see his (with the assistance of Rose D. Friedman), *Capitalism and Freedom* (Chicago: University of Chicago Press, 1962), pp. 22-55, 177-89, for instance. Milton and Rose Friedman, *Free To Chose: A Personal Statement* (New York: Harcourt, Brace, Jovanvich, 1980), pp. 38-149, for instance. Milton and Rose Friedman, *Tyranny of the Status Quo* (San Diego, CA: Harcourt, Brace, Jovanovich, 1984), pp. 1-67, 105-31, for instance.

24. For quotations, see Thorstein Veblen, *Place of Science*, pp. 139-41.

25. Veblen, *Leisure Class*, pp. 33-40.

26. Veblen, *Place of Science*, pp. 324-51.

27. On tourism, see Richard J. Barnet and John Cavanaugh, *Global Dreams: Imperial Corporations and the New World Order* (New York: Touchstone Books, 1995), p. 29. On wealthy suburbs, see *Akron Beacon Journal*, Sept. 9, 1987, p. A2. On Gates' castle, see *USA Today*, Sept. 26, 1997, p. 1B. On Veblen material, see Veblen, *Engineers and the Price System*, pp. 108 ff. On other information, see Ralph Estes, "Public Cost of Private Corporations," (Abstract) (JAI Press, 1995), pp. 329-ff.

28. Veblen, *Absentee Ownership and Business Enterprise*, pp. 1-20.

29. *Ibid.*, p. 85.

30. *Ibid.*, pp. 82-118, entitled "The Corporation."

31. Veblen, *Theory of Business Enterprise*, p. 255.

32. *Ibid.*, p. 213.

33. *Ibid.*, p. 217.

34. *Ibid.*, p. 218.

35. *Ibid.*, pp. 218-29.

36. *Ibid.*, p. 32.

37. *Ibid.*, pp. 255 ff.

38. *Ibid.*, pp. 241-61; the long quotation is on p. 261.

39. Link, *American Epoch*, pp. 51-52. Hughes, *American Economic History*, pp. 320-57. Adolf A. Berle Jr. and Gardiner C. Means, *The Modern Corporation and Private Property*, rev. ed (New York: Harcourt, Brace, and World, 1968), pp. ix-x and 18-46. First published in 1933.

40. Veblen, *Business Enterprise*, p. 391.

41. *Ibid.*, p. 395.

42. Veblen, *Absentee Ownership*, p. 97.

43. *Ibid.*, p. 112.

44. *Capital*, I, 671-711.

45. Paul Sweezy, "The Theory of Business Enterprise and Absentee Ownership," *Monthly Review*, IX (July-August, 1957), 110.

46. Thorstein Veblen, *Engineers and the Price System,* pp. 56 ff. and 100.

47. Veblen, *Business Enterprise*, pp. 264-67.

48. On the causes leading to the Great Depression, see, for instance, John Kenneth Galbraith, *The Great Crash, 1929* (Boston: Houghton Mifflin, 1961), pp. 1-199. On the New Deal, see, for instance, William E. Leuchtenburg, *Franklin Roosevelt and the New Deal* (New York: Harper Torchbooks, 1963), pp. 41-196. Also, see Rogin, *Meaning and Validity*, pp. 617-684 on Keynes and the problem of economic depression.

49. John Maynard Keynes, *General Theory of Employment, Interest, and Money* (New York: Harcourt, Brace, and Co. 1936), p. 378 on the fact that the "somewhat comprehensive socialisation of investment will prove the only means of securing an approximation to full employment."

50. John Maynard Keynes, "Democracy and Efficiency," *New Statesman* and *Nation*, Jan. 28, 1931, p. 131.

51. Veblen, *Business Enterprise*, pp. 265-66. Paddy Ireland, "Corporations and Citizenship," *Monthly Review*, May 1997, pp. 10-27. Veblen is mentioned on p. 13.

52. On ever more economic concentration in the U.S., see: Steven Brouwer, *Sharing the Pie: A Disturbing Picture of the U.S. Economy* (Carlisle, PA: Big Picture Books, 1991), pp. 14-16. Walter Adams and James B. Brock, *Dangerous Pursuits: Mergers and Acquisitions in the Age of Wall Street* (New York: Pantheon Books, 1989), pp. 12-15 ff. Davi Korten, *When Corporations Rule the World* (West Hartford, CT: Kumarian Press, 1995), pp. 221-22 ff. On concentration in banking, see *Consumer Reports*, March 1996, pp. 10-15. On concentration in public utilities, see *New York Times*, Dec. 18, 2000, p. C6. On interlocking directorates, see Domhoff, *Who Rules America?* pp. 33-49. On recent mergers, see, for instance, *New York Times*, Jan. 19, 1998, pp. A1 and A10 and *Akron Beacon Journal*, Jan. 2, 2000, p. C10. On consolidation in various industries, see *Akron Beacon Journal*, Jan. 11, 1998, pp. E1 and E3. On big business overrunning small business, see *New York Times*, Sept. 14, 2000. On concentration in retail trade, see *Akron Beacon Journal*, July 16, 2000, pp. A1 and A10.

53. On TNCs, see Korten, *Corporations*, pp. 163-77 and 187. William Greider, *One World Ready or Not: The Manic Logic of Global Capitalism* (New York: Simon and Schuster, 1997), pp. 211-22. Edward S. Herman, "Globalization in Question," *Z Magazine*, April, 1997, pp. 8-11, affirms that any single national attempt to control capital movements is now impossible as it exposes it to international capital flight. William K. Tabb, "Are New Trade Wars Looming?" *Monthly Review*, Nov., 1999, pp. 23-24, avers that international capital is too strong to permit trade wars among nations/trade blocs. On the six-trillion dollars worldwide in tax havens, see Alan Cowell and Edmund L. Andrews, "Undercurrents at a Safe Harbor," *New York Times*, Sept. 24, 1999, pp. C1 and C4. On foreign stock ownership in France, see Craig R. Whitney, "Anxious French Mutter as U.S. Envoy Tries to Sell Globalism," *New York Times*, Dec. 2, 1999, p. A 10. On U.S. stocks and bonds owned by foreigners in early 2000, see Robert Brenner, "The Boom and the Bubble," *New Left Review*, Nov./Dec., 2000, pp. 28-29.

54. On the S&L debacle see Mary Fricker and Stephen Pizzo, *Inside Job: The Looting of America's Savings and Loans* (New York: McGraw-Hill, 1989) and articles in the *New York Times*, as in June 6 and July 31, 1990. On Soros, see Connie Bruck, "The World According to Soros," *New Yorker*, Jan. 23, 1995. On hedge funds, see, John Cassidy, *New Yorker*, July 5, 1999, pp. 28-32. On the fleecing of California's public by the electric industry and the other corporate crimes/implosions, see, for instance: Larry Everest, "California's Energy Crisis," *Z Magazine*, April 2001, pp. 33-39; Daniel Kaldec, "WORLDCON," *Time*, July 8, 2002, pp. 26-51; and John Cassidy, "The Greed Cycle," *New Yorker*, Sept. 23, 2002, pp. 64-77. The *New York Times* has covered these events in great detail.

55. On government giveaways to corporations, see *Common Cause Newsletter*, March, 1996. Robert L. Borosage, "The Politics of Austerity," *Nation*, May 27, 1996, pp. 22-24. Noam Chomsky, "Power in the Global Arena," *New Left Review*, No. 230, July/August, 1998, pp. 13-18. Neil deMause, "To the Highest Bidder," *In These Times*, May 31, 1998, pp. 11-13.

X Human Nature, Intelligence, and Class Struggle

THE DEBATE OVER HUMAN NATURE AND ITS relationship to good and evil, itself related to either justifying or condemning the prevalent status quo of socioeconomic oppression/inequality, tied to supposedly large differences in human beings in intelligence and so forth, seems to be endless. To be sure, liberal and socialist social and biological scientists posit that there is a basic human nature, invariably good, which, however, is malleable, the product of the various technological/historical periods, while conservatives insist that while human nature is usually cooperative and solicitous for family and friends, it is selfish and competitive in the wider community, including the acceptance of war. (This subject is also examined in other chapters, being germane, for instance, in relationship to religion, and alienation.)

The main battle lines of the nature-of-human-nature arguments after the middle of the 19th century primarily revolved around the formulations of Charles Darwin who revolutionized the subject through two major works: *Origin of Species* (1859), on evolution in general, and the *Descent of Man* (1871), which focused on its impact on humanity.

In theorizing about the development of human nature, Darwin postulated, following Malthus' *An Essay on the Principle of Population*, that:

> Many more individuals of each species are born than can possibly survive...there is a frequently recurring struggle for existence...[which] follows that any being, if it vary slightly in any matter profitable to itself, under the complex and sometimes varying conditions of life, will have a better chance of

surviving and thus be *naturally* selected. From the strong principle of inheritance, any selected variety will tend to propagate its new and modified form.[1]

Thus it was that this upper-middle-class Englishman reaffirmed the bourgeois shibboleth that individual competition in the economic arena was sanctioned by nature itself, replacing, a theistic god as final arbiter.

In the *Descent of Man*, Darwin extolled the importance of "struggle for existence" for bringing humanity to its present high allowing level of development, "the more gifted men...[to] be more successful in the battle for life than the less gifted." In "open competition...the most able [men] should not be prevented by laws or customs from succeeding best and rearing the largest number of offspring."[2] But, then, Darwin qualified this line of thought:

> Important as the struggle for existence has been and even still is, yet as far as the highest part of man's nature is concerned there are other agencies more important. For the moral qualities are advanced either directly or indirectly, much more through the effects of habit, the reasoning powers, instruction, religion, and the like, than through natural selection; though to the latter agency may be safely attributed the social instincts which afforded the basis for the development of the moral sense.[3]

This "moral sense" or "conscience," for him, was an integral part of humanity's "well-marked social instincts," including "parental and filial affections," being "in the society of [one's] fellows," and having "a certain amount of sympathy with them, and to perform various services for them." This "sociability" was not only evident among humans, but also among animals. Indeed, sociability and accompanying sympathy were "increased through natural selection" and "those communities which included the greatest number of the most sympathetic members, would flourish best and rear the greatest number of offspring."[4]

There was, thus, a deep ambivalence in Darwin on competition as against cooperation among humans, which reflected the socioeconomic contours of bourgeois society. His model was one of intense mutual aid in the family and among other intimates as opposed to a lesser one for the general community. Thus, he rejected legislation to aid indigents and to permit birth control on the grounds that they subverted natural selection. Furthermore, he was a typical 19th-century racist in affirming that the "biologically inferior races" would soon be eliminated.[5]

Darwin's biological/social/political perspective was continued by two of his major disciples, Spencer in Britain and Sumner in the United States. One of the founders of sociology, the conservative Spencer enunciated a view of human nature that closely followed Darwin's. It held that, yes, individuals possessed such good qualities as curiosity, taking care of the young, and working, but that in the present, they were basically proper only to buttress competing families, not pity the economically unsuccessful, i.e., the workingclass and the unfit, deficient in Darwinian natural selection. Thus there was the paradox of "good" human qualities co-existing alongside negative ones, like economic aggression and general unconcern for the community, needed to weed out the unfit, a prerequisite for human progress.[6]

Spencer reinforced this outlook by also being a disciple of Jean-Baptiste de Lamrack, a French naturalist preceding Darwin, whose theory of "acquired characteristics" posited that offspring inherited the good and bad qualities of parents. In this model, biological fitness, including intelligence, became the decisive factor for success/goodness in a bourgeois-dominated competitive society. Thus, as the poor/unfit were progressively eliminated, the wealthier groups would become the majority. Thus, through the aegis of biological and economic competition, altruism, in the end, would prevail in some form of socialism, which somehow would overcome the Marxian law that capitalism, left to its own devices, inexorably resulted in ever increasing concentration of capital, ever deeper class polarity, and relative poverty.[7]

The Darwinian-based laissez-faire economics of Spencer decreed an end to all trade unions and any social legislation to aid the workingclass, fearing, for instance, that any working-class combination simply contravened natural law in asking for higher wages and allowed union leaders to abrogate the individual rights of workers. But business trusts were permitted on the basis of survival of the fittest.[8] He also rejected any state laws for minimum-age requirements for employment, to inspect and regulate working conditions in factories, provide workers with unemployment insurance, initiate compulsory vaccination programs, and establish compulsory and publicly-financed primary education and accompanying academic standards.[9] (He did, however, allow for private charity to aid the poor.) He even opposed public regulation of city "drainage systems" on the grounds that government normally bungled any economic undertaking.[10] In fact, for him, any state legislation was an attack on "voluntary cooperation."[11] Not surprisingly, he hoped that increasing state interference in the socioeconomic realm would be reversed by the Tory-dominated Liberty and Defense League whose shibboleth was "Individualism versus Socialism."[12]

A fierce economic individualist, who believed in the necessity of individual antagonistic relations, Spencer also subscribed readily to the realities of status groups, class, and class struggle. For instance, "barbarous and civilized communities are alike characterized by separation into classes, as well as by separation of each class into more and less important units." And: "So long as men are constituted to act on one another, either by physical force or by force of character, the struggles for supremacy must finally be decided in favor of some class or some one."[13] In this class progression, he considered the bourgeoisie as more genetically fit than workers and employed workers more so than the unemployed.[14]

It was claimed by some of Veblen's students that in using concepts as "idle curiosity," and "opaque cause and effect," Veblen was indebted to Spencer. But he employed these as well as other elements of Spencerian evolution against Spencer himself and other conservatives.[15]

Darwinian-Spencerian human nature reflected a Britain of great socioeconomic and political inequality in which working-class social misery was endemic: It was the one of Benjamin Disraeli's *Sybil*, of "The Rich and the Poor," of Charles Dickens' *Nicholas Nickleby* and *Hard Times*, of hellish working conditions, of twelve-to-fifteen-hour workdays, six or seven days a week, of food taking more than 50 percent of family income. Politically, workers had scant political rights: It was only in 1867 that skilled workers won the right to vote, bringing the male electorate to 30 percent, with the 1884 electoral reform assuring almost full male suffrage—women did not vote until the second decade of the 20th century. The House of Lords itself until the second decade of the 20th century could veto indefinitely any legislation passed by the House of Commons. Finally, it was one in which a small minority owned most of the wealth; in the first fourth of the 20th century, for instance, the top 1 percent had 68 percent of it.

The leading academic Spencerian conservative of late 19th-century America was Sumner, the son of an immigrant English worker. After Sumner graduated from Yale to become an Episcopalian minister, Spencer's unknowable God overwhelmed his theism, prompting his leaving the ministry and returning to Yale as a professor of economics and sociology to expound the Spencerian creed.[16]

To be sure, Sumner's conservatism was not always consistent: It went awry when he opposed American imperialism in the Spanish-American War on the grounds that it was inimical to democracy and when he defended labor unions and their right to strike and boycott goods to test the market, a collectivistic aberration. But, apart from these follies, he followed the Spencerian track.[17]

Like Spencer, in the name of the iron law of Lamarckian and Darwinian genetics, Sumner portrayed a mercilessly competitive world of self-interest and vanity outside the individual's immediate circle. Government here was not to be involved as an arbiter between different socioeconomic classes or in developing social programs to aid the poor, any attempt to do so being useless, simply wasting resources on them.

The class progression in Sumner's social diagram, based on different levels of intelligence and competence, was of a tripartite nature: The wealthy few at the apex possessed the "genius and talent" to attain this lofty position, followed by the "masses" or "middle class," the majority of the populace, described as "mediocrities," and the dregs/defectives of society, the unskilled workers and illiterates, usually in a state of criminality and dependency, there being no deserving poor. But it was comforting to note that the bottom group was now only a minority of the people.[18]

Sumner also readily admitted to the reality of class conflict. Indeed, for him, since American democracy permitted the "many and the poor"—their cupidity wishing to despoil the rich of their property—to organize and contest the rulership of the rich, the end of the American frontier, with its largesse of inexpensive land and corollary of high wages, would intensify the class struggle between them. But Sumner's "natural" competitive-evolutionary struggle, curiously did not extend to the realm of natural human rights, discarding Locke for Burke.[19]

In contradistinction to the conservative social Darwinism of Spencer and Sumner, there was the reform-minded one of Thomas Henry Huxley in England and Ward in America. After examining this current (Ward's views are not too far from Veblen's), we observe the socialist "Darwinists," Marx, Veblen, and Kropotkin.

A physician, biologist, and naturalist, Huxley was instrumental in popularizing Darwin. Although he agreed with Darwin that evolution, in the main, was involved with struggle for existence in which the strongest or those with the most cunning survive, or the existence of "animal man," he saw that with the advent of human progress, it was perfectly possible to control the struggle for existence through the intervention of a community-based ethics resting on the lofty concepts of loving others, the rule of law, and of impartial justice. Thus, it was feasible for "ethical man" to effect social reform to help the poor. This social reformism, however, adamantly opposed any socialist solution on the basis that natural selection was not to be fully impeded, the assumption, again, being that biological inequality was linked to the socioeconomic sphere.[20]

The principal father of American sociology, Ward was one of the intellectual giants of 19th-century thought. Born into a frontier family in Joliet, Illinois in the 1840s of a worker and farmer father and a clergyman's daughter, he labored on farms and in factories to further his studies to become a secondary school teacher. After being severely wounded in the Northern Army in the Civil War, he worked as a clerk in the Treasury Department in Washington, D.C. while attending night college, earning degrees in law, medicine, and the liberal arts by 1872, then becoming a paleontologist for the government. Only toward the end of his life did he become an academic, a sociology professor at Brown University, authoring many works, the best remembered being *Dynamic Sociology* and *Pure Sociology*.

A radical liberal not far from socialism (an intellectual ally of Veblen) and an acerbic critic of conservatism, Ward castigated, Malthus, Ricardo, and Spencer for being watchdogs of a brutal capitalism exploiting rural and urban labor. Along these lines, although accepting Darwinian natural selection/evolution, he asserted that it represented the "genetic" phase of the past, paralleled by a competitive and unsavory "animal economics," to be replaced by the new phase of human development, the "psychic" one, representing an emerging and purposeful human intelligence to consciously order human progress with planned economics to largely replace the present wasteful and competitive one. Thus, humanity would consciously control the blind forces of a supposed free competition only benefitting the wealthy.

A believer in the importance of a quasisocialist environment to change human destiny, Ward fought for universal public education, which, in conjunction with high income and inheritance taxes, mitigated the advantages of privilege based on inherited wealth. Thus, although some socioeconomic inequality would continue to exist, opportunity for individual socioeconomic mobility would be enhanced, bringing about a form of meritocracy. This social model obviously included numerous governmental social services for the citizenry.[21]

In *Pure Sociology*, Ward observed that collectivism, equated with public ownership of the means of production and exchange, was further advanced on the Continent than in England, and, in an opening to a possible future socialism, stated in a 1906 American Sociological Society conference that: "Every step in the direction of a true collectivism has been and must be a step in the direction of true individualism."[22]

That Marx had a theory of human nature is axiomatic, amply reflected in works like *The Holy Family, Economic and Philosophical Manuscripts, Theses on Feuerbach, The German Ideology*, and *Capital*. In the sixth thesis in *Theses on Feuerbach*, for instance, he wrote that "the essence of man is no abstraction inherent in each single individual. In its reality it is the ensemble of the social relations," whose "essence, therefore, can be regarded as many individuals in a *natural way*."[23] In the *Economic and Philosophical Manuscripts*, he again revealed that "man is not merely a natural being; he is a *human* natural being."[24] In *Capital*, in criticizing Jeremy Bentham's views of utilitarianism, he pointed out that there was a "human nature in general," which is "modified in each historical epoch."[25] For instance, although the desire for money, representing security, wealth, and power, was understandable under capitalism, it was not an eternal human attribute.[26]

To be sure, Marx was aware of primitive cultures with their generally cooperative and peaceable individuals living in egalitarian and democratic constructs, but he held that with the increase of labor division and greater productivity in technology and related formation of classes and warfare to bring about civilization, a "human nature" accepting social oppression and war in which individual and class competition played a critical role, also existed.[27]

Marx himself explicitly described the ideal communist person in many of his works, as in *Capital*, I, of the "fully developed individual" who was "fit for a variety of labours, ready to face any change of production, and to whom the different social functions he performs, are but so many modes of giving free scope to his own natural and acquired powers."[28] In *The German Ideology*, he and Engels called for an individual who can "do one thing today and another tomorrow."[29] In *The Economic and Philosophical Manuscripts,* he postulated that under "communism" it was possible to conceive of "the return of man himself as a social, i.e., really human being, a complete and conscious return which assimilates all the wealth of previous development."[30]

In 1902, the most influential work of socialist quasi-Darwinism appeared, Kropotkin's *Mutual Aid: A Factor in Evolution*, viewing mutual aid as even more basic than "love, performing sympathy and self-sacrifice," playing "an immense part in the progressive development of our moral feelings." Broadly:

> It is the conscience—be it only at the stage of instinct—of human solidarity.
> It is the unconscious recognition of the force that is borrowed by each man
> from the practice of mutual aid; of the close dependence of every one's happi-
> ness upon the happiness of all; and of the sense of justice, or equity, which
> brings the individual to consider the rights of every other individual as equal
> to his own. Upon this broad and necessary foundation, the still higher moral
> feelings are developed.[31]

Kropotkin was well aware that his thesis of mutual aid was antithetical to Spencer's and Huxley's social Darwinism which he portrayed as Hobbesian. Specifically, he disagreed with their position that primitive humans, outside of their immediate group, were involved, as Huxley put it, in a "Hobbesian war of each against all."[32] He did not deny a struggle for existence among "individuals of the same species for the means of subsistence," but insisted that it was of a "limited extent," not of the same magnitude as the spirit of cooperation or mutual aid which was paramount.[33]

This close kinship between mutual aid and ethics was further amplified in Kropotkin's last work, *Ethics: Origin and Modern Development*, which emphasized Darwin's positive assertions on human sociability and sympathy in the *Descent of Man* as a starting point for an outline of ethics among various religious and moral philosophers. In his synthesis of what forms ethics, Kropotkin combined the biological with the sociological and psychological to present a grand design for human survival, whose basic thesis was "that the prosperity and happiness of no nation or class could ever be based, even temporarily, upon the degradation of others classes, nations, or races."[34] In this picture, modern science would play its proper role to free humanity "from superstition, religious dogmatism, and metaphysical mythology,"[35] as the "I" is replaced by the "We."[36]

But Kropotkin did not have a pollyanish view of humanity's fate. He acknowledged that oppressive societies since the rise of classes, with their antagonistic socioeconomic relations glorifying force/power and wealth, and the accompanying institutions which upheld them—"parasitic growths"—might further misshape human nature to the extent that humanity would destroy itself. This view was analogous to Veblen's "leisure-class" thesis.[37]

Veblen himself necessarily regarded humans as a product of Darwinian evolution, as having a relatively fixed nature, one that was eminently purposeful and active:

> Man's great advantage of other species in the struggle for survival has been his superior facility in turning the forces of the environment to account. It is to this proclivity for turning the material means of life to account that he owes his position as lord of creation. It is not a proclivity to effort, but to achievement—to the compassing of an end. His primacy is in the last resort an industrial or economic primacy. In his economic life man is an agent, not an absorbent; he is an agent seeking in every act the accomplishment of some concrete, objective, impersonal end.[38]

And, to sum up:

> He [man] is not simply a bundle of desires that are to be saturated by being placed in the path of the forces of the environment, but rather a coherent structure of propensities and habits which seek realization in an unfolding activity.[39]

These passages, among others, unmistakably related Veblen to an activist American psychology whose leading figure was William James, a philosopher and psychologist (a contemporary of Veblen), the principal exponent of Pragmatism, which discarded final and fixed ends for the truth of solving immediate problems. Thus, for James, humanity was not preordained to be merely passive to any given environment, but to change it. This openness and plasticity themselves assured that tradition was continually challenged to meet the new demands of the present.[40]

Veblen pictured historical change as itself related to the substream of a basic human nature formed by natural selection over hundreds of thousands of years when humanity in its "savage" state conditioned the individual to closely cooperate with the group, for in comparison to many other animals, humans were weak and not swift, formidable only by virtue of their intelligence, social organization, and technology. In this schema, group solidarity overrode individual "self-interest."

Veblen also contended that "savage groups" lived in an economy in which "differentiation of employments is still less elaborate and the invidious distinction between classes and employments is less consistent and rigorous" than that of barbarian groups. Thus, contrary to the barbarians of the late Neolithic Age, savages did not possess a "leisure class," with its train of deleterious habits and attitudes. Indeed, he emphatically remarked that savage cultures (his examples being the Andamans, Todas, and Eskimos, among others), had no "hierarchy of economic classes," living in a general equality that did not have a "defined system of individual ownership." Furthermore, they were "peaceable," having "a certain amiable inefficiency when confronted with force or fraud."[41]

It was in the seed or "savage" period, for Veblen, that humanity developed, in its struggle to survive, three basic "instincts" (he employed the terms "propensity" and "instinct," the latter indicating a stronger and more elementary element than the former): (1) The "parental bent," which did not merely signify care for the young, but concern for or sympathy with other human beings in varying degree, of humanity in general. (2) "Workmanship," the complex of elements related to manipulation and alteration of the environment through technology, which also involved the qualities inherent in doing this, like skill and perseverance. (3) "Idle curiosity," or the desire to know as much as possible of the cosmos, irrespective of material gain, or what might be termed as abstract thought with all of its ramifications.

These "instincts," for him, were not to be considered in the ordinary sense of the term, like the hand-grasp of infants when presented with an object, or as "drives," like the sexual one and avoidance of thirst or hunger, but as deep sociobiological qualities or attributes of the human condition, which its expanding brain developed over hundreds of thousands of years of social life. (Anthropologists, like Ashley Montagu, also asserted that natural selection over the course of time conspired to replace instinctual behavior in humans; the threefold increase of the brain in the first three years of life reflected this.)[42]

Furthermore these human "instincts," for Veblen, were malleable. With the advent of civilization and its corollaries of war and socioeconomic oppression, these primary attributes became deformed—today, the "parental bent" by throwaway children, and workmanship and curiosity by long hours of exhaustive and/or routine labor (of the heavy physical type or of the assembly-line variety) in authoritarian settings. Despite deformities, these primary "instincts," which Veblen related to socialism, would hopefully overwhelm leisure-class predatory traits.[43]

The question of whether Veblen was a racist, which some commentators claimed, is now addressed.[44] In *The Theory of the Leisure Class* and in articles, like "The Mutation Theory and the Blond Race," and "The Blond Race and the Aryan Culture," some of his remarks might be construed as racist, as when he stated that "dolicho-blonds" or Nordics, whom he correctly believed were an offshoot of the Mediterranean type, were more prone to "barbarism" and of being more "predatory" than Mediterraneans, and that they liked green lawns because of their pastoral ancestors. Furthermore, he opined that Mediterraneans were not suited to the "cold and damp" of Northern Europe. Obviously, these statements were of a playful and mirthful nature.[45]

Since Veblen's death, the controversy over the nature of human nature, including the matter of the correlation between ethnicity/class and intelligence, has continued. The conservative side included the ethologist Konrad Lorenz; Robert Ardrey, one of his popularizers; the zoologist Edward O. Wilson; the psychologist Richard J. Herrnstein; and the political scientist/sociologist Charles Murray. The left liberal and socialist camps included anthropologist Montagu; the geologist, biologist, and science historian Stephen J. Gould; the evolutionary geneticist Richard Lewontin; the neurobiologist Steven Rose; the psychologist Leon J. Kamin; the biologist Richard Levins; and the sociologist Jeffrey M. Blum.

Konrad Lorenz was an eminent scientist, one of the founders of ethology, a Nobel Prize laureate in 1973 for his work in this field. In *On Aggression*, he argued that early hominids employed pebble tools to not only kill game, but also one another. Thus, since human beings came from warlike ancestors, essentially competitive and selfish, it was only normal that they established large-scale institutions, like the state, promoting war and economic exploitation. Thus biology was the root cause of human evil.[46]

A popularizer of Lorenz was Robert Ardrey whose *Territorial Imperative* again alleged that human beings, descendants of a "killer-ape," were innately aggressive with a well-developed instinct of territoriality. These precedents inevitably would lead to the rise of private property and consequent social inequality, hierarchy, and war. A society of equality, therefore, was simply utter nonsense.[47]

A distinguished present-day zoologist at Harvard, Wilson is widely known for his *Sociobiology: The New Synthesis* whose general outlook is Spencerian. Sociobiology itself, for him, is "the systematic study of the biological basis of all social behavior." In his study of it, he concentrated on "animal societies," but also covered "early man" and the "more primitive contemporary societies," and by extension contemporary civilized humanity.[48]

With many qualifications, Wilson postulated that human destiny rested with its genes; he was a biological determinist. Although he admitted that human beings "sometimes cooperate closely," as insects do, they often "compete for the limited resources allocated to their role-sector," winners securing a disproportionate share of the rewards, while the least successful are displaced to other less desirable positions." Those with the better genes would move up the socioeconomic ladder, while those not as well endowed would not. Competition also involved "competition between classes," which "in great moments of history...has proved to be a determinant of societal change."[49]

Wilson's biological determinism was of a "polygenic" nature. "Hereditary factors in intelligence," thus not only encompassed the IQ, but, also, qualities of "creativity, entrepreneurship, drive, and mental stamina," which genetically may be "uncorrelated or even negatively correlated."[50] Nevertheless, these genetic qualities or traits as a whole explained why some individuals succeeded, while others failed. Social and economic advantages that some individuals enjoyed over others were ignored, not recognized as playing a role.

Again, with many qualifications, Wilson utilized his sociobiology to explain such social phenomena as (1) tribalism (now nationalism) and fear of the stranger, associated with territoriality; (2) why men, physically stronger than women, were socioeconomically superior to them; and (3) why the higher-ranking males had more children through polygyny than the lower-ranking ones.[51] But he neglected to point out that the upper bourgeoisie of today have less children per capita than farmers or workers. Are the wealthy committing class suicide for their own benefit?

The biological determinism of Wilson was so ubiquitous that it even explained why human "ethical standards" were "innately pluralistic": Because "the genetic foundation of which any such normative system is built can be expected to shift continuously." But he was also fearful that the increased "gene flow around the world" could lead to "an eventual lessening of altruistic behavior through the maladaptation and loss of group-selected genes." But to indicate the complexity of the genetic nightmare, he then asserted that "we do not know how the most valued qualities are linked genetically to more obsolete destructive ones." Thus, for instance, "cooperativeness toward groupmates might be coupled to aggressivity toward strangers, creativeness with a desire to dominate," and so forth.[52]

To be sure, Wilson was afraid of a future and perfect communist society run by the acolytes of B.F. Skinner, a leading educational psychologist, novelist, and social philosopher, whose *Walden II* socially planned all aspects of society. But, of course, Wilson also believed that neurobiology would have to be employed to alter the genetic makeup to make this possible. ("Only when the machinery can be torn down on paper at the level of the cell and put together again will the properties of emotion and ethical judgment come out clear.")[53] Regrettably, this form of society, for him, might have to come, "to fit the requirements of the ecological steady state." But he consoled himself by projecting this communist society at least one hundred years into the future.[54] But he does have a way out of his nightmare, to follow Aldous Huxley's *Brave New World*, in which biological and social engineering are consciously employed to maintain social inequality.

A leading 20th century anthropologist, Montagu, acknowledged a deep debt to Kropotkin's views on evolution and human nature. In numerous works (*Man: His First Million Years*; *On Being Human*; *The Nature of Human Aggression*; *Darwin: Competition and Cooperation*), like Kropotkin, Ward, and Veblen, he theorized that Darwin overemphasized competition and undervalued cooperation in the make-up of human nature. He believed that the primary factors ensuring early human survival were "cooperation and mutual aid." Thus, *Australopithecines*, for him, were "amiable and sociable," and humanity probably inherited these predispositions, related to the maintenance of individual and group survival, so very necessary to hunter-gatherer cultures.

For Montagu, the close cooperation needed for human survival was undergirded by the very act of reproduction itself and the consequent necessity to nurture progeny, central to human activity and purpose. Along with the increasing size of the human brain, linked to a more complex technological and cultural levels, the necessity for learning and communicating became central for survival, speech increasingly related with learning: "Speech is by nature a cooperative venture; it is designed to put one into touch with others; without someone to talk to, talking is meaningless. Without someone to answer, talking is profitless." Speech itself made people "increasingly interdependent; they needed each other more." Indeed, without some form of love, speech and human intelligence were unimaginable—a child to survive and flourish simply required a proper support system. Thus, not surprisingly, for him, "cooperation" and "amiability," central elements of the human condition, were imperative for human survival. Biologically, then, an individual was born with the capacity to love and cooperate, but if the environment denied them, in varying degree, corresponding aggressive behavior manifested itself.

Montagu presented many examples of contemporary behavior in hunter-gatherer cultures, like the Eskimo and !Kung, to bolster his generalization that primitive societies exhibited only a minimal aggression within and outside their groups, of their intensely cooperative bent. In this vein, he asked if this was not because "any undue aggressiveness might fatally upset the delicate balance" for group survival. Thus, it was likely that "the highest premium is placed by natural selection on cooperative behavior, and a negative premium on aggressive traits," there being no evidence of "hostility between neighboring prehistoric populations," and if any, infrequent.[55] Along with Veblen, Montagu claimed that "during almost the whole of man's evolutionary history he lived in peace and cooperation with his fellow man,"[56] and that the primary human drives were basically of a cooperative and peaceful nature.

To be sure, along with Veblen, Marx, and Kropotkin, Montagu averred that the evils of war and class society were of recent vintage in human development, coming about from technological factors, and that the partially selfish and competitive individual who emerged since then was socially, not biologically, conditioned to act so.[57] This learned behavior could be unlearned by altering present institutions, presumably along radical republican or socialist lines. In conjunction with this, he categorically affirmed that humans did not have instincts to dominate others.[58]

In the nature-of-human-nature arguments, the problem of differences in intelligence invariably arise. It, too, is approached along divisions between conservatives opposing radical liberals and socialists.

In classist societies with extensive labor division, like the 20th-century bourgeois-dominated and communist varieties, formal education increasingly was universally employed to train and steer students into occupations with different incomes and socialpower, related to status and class, those with more schooling generally having more than others. Thus, in contemporary America, a physician and lawyer command more power and respect than a nurse, engineer, and teacher, who, in turn, are higher in the pecking order than blue-collar workers.

Not surprisingly, conservative social Darwinists, like Spencer and Sumner, were among the first to assign a higher intelligence to the bourgeoisie, especially of the *haute* variety, over that of workers. Indeed, Spencer and Sir Frances Galton, a cousin of Darwin, were the first to examine closely intelligence as part of a eugenics movement to improve the English stock, to eliminate those of low intelligence or the very poor. Galton, for instance, in many scientifically flawed studies, insisted that intelligence was inherited from parents, although conceding that environment played a secondary role. He even convinced Darwin that inherited intelligence was the key to intellectual and material success.

Alfred Binet, the principal father of "intelligence" tests, circa 1910, devised tests in France to determine how successfully school children could adapt to the demands of formal education, but did not believe, like Spencer and Glaton, that he was literally measuring some definite or known quantity as intelligence. In the United States, conservative psychologists like H.H. Goddard and Lewis Terman accepted the views of Spencer and Galton, but influenced by Binet, formulated tests to prove it. (In the American educational system, the Stanford-Binet IQ test was used to steer students into "appropriate" occupations.[59])

A recent conservative work on intelligence and ethnicity and class will serve as a prime example of continuing conservative insistence on stressing the importance of heredity over environment: *The Bell Curve* (1994), by two Harvard Professors, the psychologist Richard Herrnstein and political scientist and sociologist Charles Murray. With a plethora of studies on IQ as proof, they claimed that from 40 to 70 percent of intelligence is hereditary. The two, then, pictured an American society formed by three distinct classes: Two diametrically opposed—a college-educated "cognitive elite" and slow learners (disproportionately black) mired in the world of poverty and welfare, of out-of-wedlock children, and criminality—between them being the average workers. Thus, the resurrection of Spencer and Sumner![60]

Intelligence tests in the 20th century have yielded these results: In the United States Army Alpha Test during World War I, Eastern and Southern-European immigrants, including Jews, scored lower than the older immigrants from Northern and Western Europe, but Northern blacks did better than Southern whites. In standardized IQ tests in America after World War II, whites in general had about the same average scores, with Jewish-Americans being somewhat higher. IQ tests in the 20th century also revealed that in Northern Ireland, Protestants (the dominant socioeconomic group) averaged ten points higher than Catholics—both are Celts; that the average student in Japan had an IQ of 110 as opposed to about 100 in the United States; that American blacks, with an average IQ of 85 had fifteen points lower on average than whites; that the children of` American professionals, like lawyers, physicians, and engineers, were fifteen points higher than those of manual workers; and that in Japan, the *Buraku-min*, an ethnically Japanese group of about two million, traditionally in ghettos because of their ancestors' lowly occupations, performed fifteen points lower than average among Japanese, but did just as well as other Japanese-Americans who scored higher than the white average. It should also be pointed out that adverse environmental influences, like castelike relations in the United States with respect to African-Americans, produced great anxiety or "situational pressure" related to "stereotypic threat" or "negative stereotyping" of their intelligence. In attempting to overcome this hurdle in tests, blacks worked under greater tension, thus with less efficiency than others, the resultant leading to more errors, thus lower scores.[61]

The response of progressives and socialists to conservatives concerning intelligence was that its formation was determined by a complex interaction occurring simultaneously between genetic and environmental factors, that there were many forms of intelligence itself, and that the criteria involved in intelligence testing were obviously less than perfect.

For Montagu, the genetic or hereditary component of intelligence testing could not be measured in any great degree for it was inevitably intertwined with the social environment, thus incumbent on society to enrich the lives of all children.[62]

Gould, a Harvard professor and Marxist, followed in *The Mismeasure of Man*. In a detailed critique of 19th-century craniometry and 20th-century intelligence tests, whose methods and data are meticulously examined, he saw that American IQ testers like Goddard and Terman, and the British psychologist Sir Cyril Burt—all of whom emphasized the importance of heredity and scarcely noticed the role of the environment in the making of academic intelligence—were guilty of reifying intelligence, of trying to make concrete a complex phenomenon composed of many qualities.

Gould himself, like Montagu, rejected a biological determinism for general intelligence among humans:

> Our large brain is the biological foundation of intelligence; intelligence is the ground of culture; and cultural transmission builds a new mode of evolution more effective than Darwinian processes in its limited realm—the "inheritance" and modification of learned behavior.[63]

In *Not in Our Genes*, Lewotin, Rose, and Kamin continued in the footsteps of Montagu and Gould to attack the biological determinists whose ardent champion, Burt, was exposed as producing fraudulent studies favoring heredity over environment in forming intelligence. (Burt influenced American scientists, like Arthur Jensen, viewing whites and the middle class as being innately more intelligent than blacks and workers.) To be sure, IQ tests also measured the environment, critical in the formation of academic intelligence. Indeed, the authors claimed that in careful but limited studies, there was good evidence to support the thesis that a proper environment decisively improved performance on intelligence testing and decreased academic failure. For instance, in a French study of working-class infants adopted by bourgeois parents, the children in question averaged sixteen points higher than their siblings raised in a working-class environment. In similar studies in the United States of adopted infant children, including African-American by white parents, which compared the adopted to the biological children, the general consensus was that the "children reared by the same mother resembled her in IQ to the same degree, whether or not they shared her genes."[64] This being the case, the authors saw that IQ can be increased "as much as social organization will allow,"[65]and that "our biology" allows us the flexibility of "recreating our own psychic and material environments"; that ultimately "our biology makes us free."[66] Gardner, a Harvard psychologist, also, disagreed with the view that there was only one kind of intelligence, that assigned by IQ. In addition to "linguistic" and "logical-mathematical" intelligence stressed by IQ tests, he affirmed others, like "musical," "bodily-kinesthetic," "spatial," and various "personal."[67]

There is another interesting phenomenon to consider: IQ scores are rising throughout the world; for instance, "27 points in Britain since 1942 and 24 points in the United States since 1918…with comparable gains throughout Western Europe, Canada, Japan, Israel, urban Brazil, China, Australia, and New Zealand." This, again, indicates the importance of various environmental factors (including test preparation) in determining "intelligence," as against a supposedly relatively fixed hereditary one that environment cannot change much in short periods of time for the genetic pool changes only slowly.[68]

Recent studies support the views of Montagu, Lewontin, Rose, Kamin, and others on the decisive importance of environment interacting with heredity in affecting intelligence and personality. In fact, a special edition of *Newsweek* in 1997, entitled *Your Child*, has a series of articles based on studies by psychiatrists, psychologists, pediatricians, neurobiologists, and others that indicate that early environmental factors are critical in determining intelligence and personality, that the plasticity of the human brain is indeed great, formed by experiences after birth.

Thus it is that children raised in intellectually enriched and more psychologically secure environments do better on intelligence testing and are more stable emotionally than those without these advantages. Abused and traumatized children, for instance, under great stress from fears and anxieties and resultant hyperactivity, have elevated stress hormones and invariably suffer from learning and emotional problems; their hippocampus and frontal lobes, for instance (the first involves memory, the second, higher cognitive abilities, like speech and logic controlling emotions), are either smaller or have less neural activity than those of normal children. Positron-emission tomography (PET) scans, for instance, indicate less neural activity in the temporal lobes of children suffering extreme deprivation than for those of normal ones. This, in turn, impinges on learning ability for "some percentage of capacity is lost. A piece of the child is lost forever," according to Doctor Bruce Perry of the Baylor College of Medicine. There is now even some evidence that severe trauma experienced by parents has some genetic transference influencing children's mental health, again demonstrating the interplay of genetics and the environment.[69]

Socioeconomic status and mental illness and their relationship to rearing children, thus, on average, have a bearing on the good life, including intelligence. In this vein, the multiple stresses of poverty and recent reductions of social welfare for the poor do not bode well for their children.

From the perspective of human intelligence, there is no reason to suppose that the "average" individual is incapable of fully participating as a general equal in an egalitarian and democratic socialist society. In Japan, the average IQ of 110 allows, even by the standards of traditional intelligence testers, for the successful completion of a university education.

Veblen himself, undoubtedly aware of the controversy surrounding intelligence—he did have an encyclopedic mind—commented on it briefly. He was aware that certain occupations requiring more education than average, like engineering, were critically necessary to running a complex technological society. But in the tradition of Marx and Proudhon, and contrary to Plato, with his obsession on educational testing to determine employment and leadership, Veblen's socialism, in focusing on workers' education and participation in running industry, insisted on the development of the all-around individual performing many tasks, not fixated on who was more intelligent or more creative than others, a preoccupation of status and class-ridden societies.

Some closing comments on intelligence and "race." Recent studies employing mitochondrial DNA passed on from mother to daughter indicate that Africans have a greater genetic diversity than other populations strongly suggesting an African ancestry for modern humanity, coming from a gene pool of 20,000 or so people approximately 100,000 years ago. The recently completed genome project also attests to the fact that all human beings are 99.9 percent alike genetically, again indicating humanity's newness, while chimpanzees, the closest animal to humans, have much larger genetic differences among themselves, indicating a direct remote ancestry stretching back millions of years.[70]

Recent advances in genetics, coupled with the rise of socioeconomic inequality under present capitalist arrangements, pose a danger to the radical republican/socialist view of society being composed of more or less equal individuals in general ability when a proper environment is given in childhood. Indeed, Wilson may be comforted by the scenario drawn by Lee M. Silver, a molecular biologist at Princeton University, who, in *Remaking Eden*, warns that an upper-bourgeoisie of about 10 percent of the population, through free choice and economic superiority, will be able to enrich their children through new gene-addition methods that can be passed on to succeeding generations, eventually dividing the population into two castes, the "GenRich," or synthetically "gene enriched" individuals, and the "Naturals," or average people conceived under normal natural selection.

Although admitting to the key role of environment in determining personality and general achievement, Silver underscores the obvious genetic advantages of the "GenRich" over the "Naturals," further exacerbating existing socioeconomic inequalities between them. But this is not all, for he predicts that within three centuries, any mating between the "GenRich" and "Naturals" will not usually produce offspring, and in a thousand years the two will have "no ability to cross-breed," forming two distinct species. "Human nature" in this future society will reflect this division.[71] Silver's views on genetic enrichment—much of it through generically engineered "gene-packs" influencing particular skills as proficiency in music or athletic ability and even general intelligence—are not necessarily antithetical to those of Gould and others, in the sense that they may provide the necessary means to create a group of super humans. To be sure, if need be, a socialist society can genetically enrich all children, the resources for this easily coming from savings eliminating conspicuous consumption.

Final remarks on the nature of humanity: For socialists and radical liberals, the basic problem is not whether human beings are cooperative or intelligent enough to participate as equals in society, most are, if given the proper environment. Even in the most class-ridden societies, forced cooperation is *de rigeur* in everyday life or in conducting war. That humanity is basically sociable and cooperative has been verified by history. The main point of contention concerning human nature is whether humanity can construct societies in which the cooperative and sociable spirit is established along egalitarian and non-exploitative arrangements, the critical issue dividing left and right, which, if not resolved, may lead to humanity's either destroying itself through atomic and biological warfare or pollution, or dividing itself into two different species.

NOTES

1. Charles Darwin, *The Origin of Species*, (London: John Murray, 1859), pp. 4-5.

2. Charles Darwin, *The Descent of Man*, (London: John Murray, 1874), pp. 145-46.

3. *Ibid.*

4. Charles Darwin, *The Descent of Man and Selection in Relation to Sex* (New York: D. Appleton, 1897), pp. 97ff.

5. On Darwin's conservative social policies and his justification of imperialism on the basis of racial superiority, see Ashley Montagu, *Darwin: Competition and Cooperation* (New York: Henry Schuman, 1952), pp. 89-95.

6. For an excellent overview of Spencer's influence and views, see Robert L. Carneiro, edited and Introduction, *The Evolution of Society: Selections from Herbert Spencer's Principles of Sociology* (Chicago:

University of Chicago Press, 1967); Hofstadter, *Social Darwinism in American Thought* (New York: Harper Torchbooks, 1955), pp. 31-50,

7. See Hofstadter, *Social Darwinism*; Commager, *American Mind*; and Carneiro, *Evolution of Society*, pp. ix-xvii.

8. Herbert Spencer, *The Man Versus the State* (Calwell, ID: Caxton Printers, 1969), pp. 74-75 ff.

9. *Ibid.*, pp. 10-16.

10. *Ibid.*, pp. 96-97.

11. *Ibid.*, p. 59.

12. *Ibid.*, p. 21.

13. Herbert Spencer, *First Principles* (New York: D. Appleton and Co., 1903), p. 391 for the two quotations.

14. Herbert Spencer, *Social Studies* (New York: D. Appleton and Co., 1896), pp. 149ff. on an economic survival of the fittest that is biologically determined—the unemployed/unfit would not be aided by the state.

15. Dorfman, *Veblen*, p. 30 and pp. 274-75.

16. On Sumner, see the excellent biography by Harris E. Star, *William Graham Sumner* (New York: Henry Holt and Co., 1925); Robert Green McCloskey, *American Conservatism in the Age of Enterprise: A Study of William Graham Sumner, Stephen J Field and Andrew Carnegie* (New York: Harper Torchbooks, 1964).

17. On labor unions, see Hofstadter, *Social Darwinism*, pp. 62-63; on stand against imperialism, see Starr, *Sumner*, pp. 262 ff.

18. On Sumner's views in this paragraph—economic man, class, and so forth—see William Graham Sumner, *Folkways: A Study of the Sociological Importance of Usages, Manners, Customs, Mores, and Morals* (Boston: Ginn and Co., 1906), pp. 40 ff., and Starr, *Sumner*, p. 400 and pp. 463-76.

19. Starr, *Sumner*, pp. 432-36 and 448-59; Hofstadter, *Social Darwinism*, p. 60.

20. Thomas Henry Huxley, *Evolution and Ethics and Other Essays* (New York: D. Appleton and Co., 1896); Thomas Henry Huxley, "The Struggle for Existence," *The Nineteenth Century* (London), Vol. 23, February, 1888, pp. 161-80; on p. 165: From a moral perspective, "the animal world is on about the same level as a gladiator's show."

21. On Ward, see the splendid study of his life and thought by Samuel Chugerman, *Lester F. Ward: The American Aristotle* (Durham, N.C.: Duke University Press, 1939); Hofstadter, *Social Darwinism*, pp. 67-84, Chapter Four, is entitled "Lester Ward: Critic"; Commager, *American Mind,* pp. 199-226, Chapter Ten, is entitled "Lester Ward and the Science of Society." I have incorporated many of their insights.

22. Ward, *Pure Sociology*, p. 561. The quotation is from Commager, *American Mind*, p. 208.

23. See Norman Geras, *Marx and Human Nature: Refutation of a Legend* (London: Verso Editions and NLB, 1983), p. 29 on the quotations of Marx's 6th thesis.

24. Erich Fromm, *Marx's Concept of Man*, with a translation from *Marx's Economic and Philosophical Manuscripts* by T.B. Bottomore (New York: Frederick Ungar, 1966), p. 183.

25. Marx, *Capital*, I, 668.

26. Fromm, *Marx's Concept of Man*, pp. 25-26.

27. Karl Marx and Friedrich Engels, *The German Ideology*, Parts I and III (New York: International Publishers, 1947), pp. 16-24, for instance.

28. Marx, *Capital*, I, 534.

29. Marx and Engels, *The German Ideology*, p. 22.

30. Fromm, *Marx's Concept of Man*, p. 127. See, also, Adam Schaff, *Marxism and the Human Individual* (New York: McGraw-Hill, 1970), pp. 49-102; and John Plamenatz, *Karl Marx's Philosophy of Man* (Oxford: Clarendon Press, 1975), pp. 36-85.

31. On Kropotkin, see, for instance, Martin A. Miller, *Kropotkin* (Chicago: University of Chicago Press, 1976) and Stephen Osofsky, *Peter Kropotkin* (Boston: Twayne Publishers, 1979). Peter Kropotkin, *Mutual Aid: A Factor in Evolution* (New York: Alfred A. Knopf, 1919), pp. 5-6 on the quotations.

32. Kropotkin, *Mutual Aid*, pp. 6-7.

33. *Ibid.*, p. 2.

34. Peter Kropotkin, *Ethics: Origin and Development* (New York: The Dial Press, 1924), p. 4.

35. *Ibid.*, p. 5.

36. *Ibid.*, p. 64.

37. Kropotkin, *Mutual Aid*, p. 9.

38. Thorstein Veblen, "The Instinct of Workmanship," in Ardzrooni, *Essays in Our Changing Order*, pp. 80-81. Veblen, *Leisure Class*, p. 259. "The leisure class canon demands strict and comprehensive futility; the instinct of workmanship demands purposeful action."

39. Thorstein Veblen, "Why is Economics Not an Evolutionary Science?" in *The Place of Science in Modern Civilization and Other Essays* (New York: B.W. Heubsch, 1919), p. 74.

40. On James, see R.B. Perry, *The Thought and Character of William James* (Cambridge, MA: Harvard University Press, 1948).

41. Veblen, *Leisure Class*, pp. 22 ff.

42. Ashley Montagu, *The Nature of Human Aggression* (New York: Oxford University Press, 1976), pp. 64-65 and 78 ff. Thorstein Veblen, *The Instinct of Workmanship and the State of the Industrial Arts* (New York: Augustus M. Kelley, 1964), pp. 25-26 ff.; Riesman, *Veblen*, pp. 51 ff.

43. Veblen, *Leisure Class*, pp. 41-46; Tilman, *Thorstein Veblen and His Critics*, p. 174.

44. Tilman, *Veblen*, p. 207.

45. Veblen, *Leisure Class*, pp. 98, 136, 152. The two articles are in Veblen, *Place of Science*, pp. 457-96.

46. Konrad Lorenz, *On Aggression* (New York: Harcourt, Brace, and World, 1966), p. 231, for instance, on the hominid Australopithecus Africanus—not a direct ancestor of modern man—as a killer.

47. Robert Ardrey, *The Territorial Imperative* (New York: Atheneum, 1966), pp. 269-319.

48. Edward O. Wilson, *Sociobiology: The New Synthesis* (Cambridge, MA: Harvard University Press, 1975), p. 4.

49. *Ibid.*, p. 554 for the quotations in this paragraph.

50. *Ibid.*, pp. 554-55.

51. *Ibid.*, pp. 286-87.

52. *Ibid.*, p. 575.

53. *Ibid.*

54. *Ibid.*

55. Montagu, *Human Aggression*, pp. 135-85 on the last four paragraphs of the text.

56. *Ibid.*, p. 301.

57. Ashley Montagu, *Man: His First Million Years* (New York: Mentor Books, 1957), pp. 105-06. Montagu, *Human Aggression*, pp. 301-02.

58. Montagu, *Human Aggression*, pp. 233 ff.

59. On salaries, see, for instance, *U.S. News and World Report*, Oct. 31, 1994, pp. 110 ff., on salaries of professionals, per year in 1993/1994: for midlevel engineers, about $60,000; for lawyers, between $70,000 to $80,000 in law firms; for physicians, median incomes for those in group practice with 8 to 17 years, internists, $142,00, psychiatrists, $153,00, obstetricians/gynecologists, $218,00; while median earnings per year for drill press operators is $14,700; lathe operators, $27,700, and machine repairers, $30,300.

60. Herrnstein and Murray, *Bell Curve*, pp. 535-52.

61. On IQ testing, heredity versus environment, and so forth, the radical republican/socialist view is upheld in these representative works: Ashley Montagu, *Statement on Race*, 3rd ed. (New York: Oxford University Press, 1972), pp. 115-16. Ashley Montagu, *Man's Most Dangerous Myth: The Fallacy of Race*, 5th ed. (New York: Oxford University Press, 1974), pp. 241 ff. Stephen J. Gould, *The Mismeasure of Man* (New York: W.W. Norton, 1983), pp. 192-223. R.C. Lewontin, Steven Rose, and Leon J. Kamin, *Not in Our Genes* (New York: Pantheon Books, 1984), pp. 83-129. Richard Levins and Richard Lewontin, *The Dialectical Biologist* (Cambridge, MA: Harvard University Press, 1985), pp. 120-27 ff. and 159. Jeffrey M. Blum, *Psuedoscience and Mental Ability* (New York: Monthly Review Press, 1978), pp. 25-112 and 145-95. For the conservative position, reminiscent of Spencer and Sumner, see Richard Herrnstein and Charles Murray, *The Bell Curve: Intelligence and Class Structure in American Life* (New York: Free Press, 1994), pp. 269-340, for instance, on ethnic differences in IQ. For an excellent critique of this work, see Adolph Reed Jr., "Looking Backward," *Nation*, Nov. 28, 1994, pp. 654-62. On black anxiety in testing, see Claude M. Steele and Joshua Aronson, "Stereotype Threat and the Intellectual Test Performance of African Americans," *Journal of Personality and Social Psychology*, Nov. 1995, pp. 797-811.

62. Montagu, *Man's Most Dangerous Myth*, pp. 241 ff.

63. Gould, *Mismeasure of Man*, pp. 15 ff.; the lengthy quotation is on p. 325.

64. Lewontin *et al.*, *Not in Our Genes*, pp. 127-29.

65. *Ibid.*, p. 129.

66. *Ibid.*, p. 290.

67. Howard Gardner, *Frames of Mind: The Theory of Multiple Intelligences* (New York: Basic Books, 1993), pp. 3-70 and 331 ff. Steven Fraser, ed., *The Bell Curve Wars: Race, Intelligence, and the Future of America* (New York: Basic Books, 1995), particularly articles by Stephen Jay Gould, Howard Gardner, Richard Nisbett, Jacqueline Jones, Andrew Hacker, and Orlando Patterson.

68. On the recent upsurge of IQ scores (the Flynn effect, after James R. Flynn, professor of political philosophy, University of Otago in New Zealand), see Sharon Begley, "The IQ Puzzle," *Newsweek*, May 6, 1996, pp. 70-72.

69. See, for instance, articles in *Newsweek* (Special Edition), *Your Child*, Spring/Summer, 1997: Sharon Begley, "How to Build a Baby's Brain," pp. 28-32 and p. 32 on the quotation by Dr. Perry; Marc Peyser and Anne Underwood, "Shyness, Sadness, Curiosity, Joy: Is It Nature or Nurture?" pp. 60-63; Debra Rosenberg, "Raising a Moral Child," pp. 92-93.

70. On the African connection of modern Homo sapiens, see Brian M. Fagan, *World Prehistory: A Brief Introduction* (New York: HarperCollins, 1996), pp. 81-85. Luigi Luca Cavalli-Sforza and Francesco Cavalli-Sforza, *The Great Diasporas* (Reading, MAI: Addison-Wesley, 1996), pp. 66-125. William A. Turnbaugh *et al.*, *Understanding Physical Anthropology and Archeology*, 6th ed. (Minneapolis/St. Paul: West Publishing Co., 1996), pp. 112-17. John H. Relethford, *The Human Species: An Introduction to Biological Anthropology* (Mountain View, CA: Mayfield Publishing Co., 1996), pp. 334-47.

71. Lee M. Silver, *Remaking Eden: Cloning and Beyond in a Brave New World* (New York: Avon Books, 1997), pp. 1-11, 91-125, 240-50. Also, see Jeremy Rifkin, *The Biotech Century: Harnessing the Gene and Remaking the World* (New York: Jeremy P. Tarcher/Putnam, 1998), pp. 2-4, 10-31, 117-74, 222-23.

XI Alienation/Oppression and Economics

THE SOCIO-PHILOSOPHICAL CONCEPT OF ALIENATION is important in socialist theory because of its centrality to explain social misery and oppression. After presenting an appropriate background of it, we will examine the Marxian contribution, contrasting it with that of Veblen, then bring it to the present, relating it to class and economics.

The concept of alienation holds that although human beings are social animals living in a milieu of mutual aid, as separate individuals, they are divided from one another in varying degree. For instance, while others may empathize with an individual, only he/she experiences first hand, joy and sorrow, futility and rage, life and death. This obviously supposes a human nature already described.

Alienation, however, is largely magnified in class-exploitative societies, with their inordinate competitive features, pitting, in varying degree, individuals, status groups, classes, nations, and religions against one another in a milieu of general economic insecurity and poverty for most amidst affluence and power for elites. That the individual, since the dawn of civilization, has been psychologically and ethically deformed by these antagonistic and exploitative socioeconomic and other relations is a truism.

To be sure, although there was less alienation in primitive cultures than in civilization because of intense mutual aid and social equality, it was still not negligible as economic scarcity, and its corollary of limited needs, was omnipresent, as was the brevity of life. But with the advent of the Agricultural Revolution and subsequent rise of civilization, alienation increased geometrically. In the *Old Testament*, God banished Adam and Eve from the Garden of Eden because the serpent (the personification of evil) tempted

Eve to induce Adam to eat the apple of knowledge, representing the Agricultural Revolution and rise of subsequent civilization, with their attendant evils of class, war, and oppression, condemning most of humanity to hard and unrelenting toil, but sparing the leisure class of this indignity.

In the modern period alienation was well explored by Marx, influenced by Rousseau, but particularly Georg Hegel. In *Discourse on the Origins of Inequality*, Rousseau contrasted the troubled civilized individual at war with others with the happy and noble savage. In *The Phenomenology of the Spirit*, Hegel amply described tragic human fate: Normally, despite alienation, human beings desired not only to fulfill themselves, but to aid and respect others (the mutual-aid aspect). But since human existence was confronted by the perennial problem of economic scarcity—there not being enough to fully satisfy essential material and social needs—conflict erupted, in the course of which the winners became the masters, the losers, slaves, part of whose labor was appropriated by the former. In this nexus, the two groups feared and hated one another. Furthermore, the masters were not creative, but parasitical, while the slaves, the productive and creative classes through their understanding of the technology, would ultimately realize their importance to win independence.[1]

Marx expanded upon Hegel's views on the individual, class and labor. He proposed that everything made by the individual was at the expense of his time and energy. Thus,

> enslaving him instead of being controlled by him—as long as man remains in
> natural society, as long as a split exists between the particular and general in-
> terest, and as long as the activity is not voluntarily but naturally divided.[2]

This underlying condition, for Marx, led to the emergence of private property, proliferation of labor division, and subsequent formation of antagonistic individual, status, class, and tribal/national relations, each entity viewing itself in varying degree as being apart or different from the others. Thus for him, under capitalism, in which commodities were bought and sold to accumulate more profit/capital, labor itself became one, forced to sell its labor-power to capital, only to be mercilessly exploited and degraded at work, failing to do so inviting either the workhouse or petty crime to simply survive, or death by illness for lack of food and shelter.

For Marx in *Capital*:

> All means for the development of production transform themselves into
> means of domination over and exploitation of the producers; they mutilate
> the laborer into a fragment of a man, degrade him to the level of an appendage
> of a machine, destroy every remnant of charm in his work and turn it into a

hated toil; they estrange from him the intellectual potentialities of the labor-process in the same proportion as science is incorporated in it as an independent power; they distort the conditions under which he works, subject him during the labor process to a despotism the more hateful for its meanness; they transform his lifetime into working-time, and drag his wife and child beneath the wheels of the Juggernaut of capital.

All in all, for Marx, workers were simply slaves of the bourgeoisie, "enslaved by the machine, by the overlooker; and above all by the individual bourgeois manufacturer himself," and eternally damned by debt to "the landlord, the shopkeeper, the pawnbroker, etc."[3]

But in this world of "self-alienation," the bourgeoisie, for Marx, at least, found the "confirmation and its good, its own power: it has in it a semblance of human existence."[4] To be sure, this may be observed today when comparing, for instance, the lives of bankers, doctors, and lawyers with those of blue-collar and lower white-collar workers.

Thus it was that Marx intertwined alienation/oppression to class and work, including its bureaucratic component, themselves related to labor division along the lines of manual versus intellectual and administrative labor.

Capitalist apologists overlooked the devastating results of alienation/oppression, perfectly willing to relegate the workingclass to perform horrific and meaningless work or even be unemployed, thus severed from the economic loop. Indeed, from a narrow and one-dimensional perspective, they condemned individuals in the lower positions of the class/labor-division chain on the grounds of either biological inferiority, including mental illness, or moral improvidence, like having too many children, and of previous generations failing to provide sufficient capital for their progeny.

That the workplace made workers simple automatons was also expressed in the writings of Frederick W. Taylor, the father of scientific management, and practices of Henry Ford, the automobile magnate, who emulated the moving assembly line of the meat-packing industry, calling for a continuous synchronization between the mobile human body and the material handled, reducing work to a few bodily movements. Taylor, the principal father of work-time studies, had no less an object in mind than to reduce manual labor to simply a series of mindless motions for he specifically removed any intellectual element from the factory floor, the end being a deskilled and inexpensive blue-collar work force. Before Taylorism took hold in the early 1900s, skilled blue-collar workers had much autonomy in the workplace. Taylorism itself was symptomatic of the fact that the power of capital led to a technology and organization which in the end reduced blue-collar workers to a generalized mass of poor and dependent retainers in an increasing labor division, itself spawning more bureaucracy, signifying the growing so-cioeconomic distance between capital and labor.[5] Smith himself in *Wealth of Nations* praised increasing labor division in the Lombe Brothers factory employing children, but admitted that labor division in the main made workers "as stupid and ignorant as it is possible for a human creature to become."[6]

Veblen shared many of Marx's views on alienation/oppression and its deleterious consequences because his leisure-class thesis was predicated on deep class polarity and on the almost absolute power of the master classes in history over their subaltern ones, a hegemony encompassing every element of life, socioeconomic, political, and cultural. It is no exaggeration to affirm that this is the primary concern in Veblen's thought. Indeed, it was the overcoming of leisure-class hegemony, related to alienation, which illuminated Veblen's work with ethically-laden and generally interrelated terms like "emulation," "in-vidious distinction," "conspicuous consumption," and "chicane." For instance, does not "conspicuous consumption" involve antagonistic "emulation" and "invidious distinc-tion," in which the alienated labor of the masses is appropriated by the master classes, a condition magnified by the masses themselves in technologically advanced capitalist so-cieties who wish to emulate bourgeois profligacy, thus doubling chaining themselves to wasteful labor? Then, does not "chicane" characterize much of life now under bourgeois auspices, another wall separating individuals? Today, for instance, half of working-class repairmen overcharge their clients.

Like Marx, who condemned the alienating work in the capitalist factory, Veblen, too, was concerned how it affected workers, especially their general intelligence:

> For more than a hundred years past, this change in the habits of thought of the workman has been commonly spoken of as a deterioration or numbing of his intelligence. But that seems too sweeping a characterization of the change brought on by habituation to machine work. It is safe to say that such habitua-tion brings a change in the workman's habits of thought—in the direction, methods, and content of his thinking—heightening his intelligence for some purposes and lowering it for certain others. No doubt, on the whole, the ma-chine's discipline lowers the intelligence...but it appears likewise to heighten his intelligence for such purposes as have been brought to the front by the machine. If he is by nature scantily endowed with the aptitudes that would make him think effectively in terms of the machine process, if he has intellectual capacity for other things and not for this, then the training of the machine may fairly be said to lower his intelligence, since it hinders the full development of the only capacities of which he is possessed. The resulting

differences in intellectual training is a difference in kind and direction, not necessarily in degree.[7]

Importantly, Veblen stated here that mechanical aptitude should not be seen as inferior to that employed in the liberal arts. Indeed, he believed that despite the deleterious effects of the machine, modern industrial workers were much more aware of the general culture than farmers and the handicraft workers of the past. He, thus, implied that the culture of the city, which complemented industrialism, compensated for the monotony and mindlessness of labor involved in industry. But he was mindful of the differences between manual and mental labor in industry, contrasting average workers to skilled workers and engineers: For the former, the machine process "falls upon them blindly and enforces an uncritical acceptance of opaque results;" for the latter, those who "comprehend and guide the process," there is "theoretical insight into the casual sequences which make up the machine process."[8] Thus, the more skilled manual workers, "skilled mechanics," and the engineers, were more receptive to the machine process than the unskilled.

The new machine technology and its work rhythms, although having alienating features, were observed by Veblen as not only very important for the realization of socialism—he regarded skilled workers and petty-bourgeois engineers as its principal standard bearers—but also in the long-run as the antidote to alienating features, like business dishonesty, as the patterns of social life became permeated by the sameness of standardization and "matter-of-fact" business transactions. But this has not yet happened. (An aside on Veblen's engineers: Most have not embraced socialism, but as they become more numerous, and as their wage differentials to skilled workers lessen, they may become more open to socialist ideas. Today in the United States, engineers are now second only in number to teachers among mental labor—of a total work force of about a hundred million full-time workers, four million are teachers, and more than 1.8 million are engineers).[9]

The basic problem, for Veblen, superseding the new mechanical intelligence as a requisite for the new technological/socialist civilization, was not how boring or repetitive a job is, but the class dimensions assigned to it:

> The irksomeness of labor is a spiritual fact; it lies in the indignity of the thing…Indeed, it is all the more substantial and irremediable on that account. Physical irksomeness and distastefulness can be borne, if only the spiritual incentive is present. Witness the attractiveness of warfare, both to the barbarian and to the civilized youth. The most commonplace recital of a campaigner's experience carries a sweeping suggestion of privation, exposure, fatigue, vermin, squalor, sickness, and loathsome death…yet warfare is

an attractive employment if one only is gifted with a suitable habit of mind. Most sports, and many other polite employments that are distressful but creditable, are evidence to the same effect.

These observations by Veblen indicated his appreciation of how leisure-class psychology was decisive in influencing the desirability of an occupation. Furthermore, although Veblen, as already indicated, was acutely aware of the dichotomy between manual and mental labor with its class relationship, he did not believe that resolving it was as important to realizing socialism as Marx did. He himself read much on labor and the modern factory, citing works, like Sidney and Beatrice Webb's *Industrial Democracy*.[10]

An examination now on Veblen's views on the rise of capitalist oligopolistic mass marketing and the economic waste engendered by it. These insights were acknowledged by Harry Braverman in *Labor and Monopoly Capital*, ("marketing organization becomes second in size only to the production organization in manufacturing corporations"), who quoted extensively from Veblen's *Absentee Ownership and Business Enterprise*: That mass production in manufacturing demanded "a quantity-production of customers" or "the upkeep of customers already in use by the given concern...at a stated production-cost per unit; and its operation lends itself to quantity production," in "the fabrication of customers," which "can now be carried on as a routine operation, quite in the spirit of the mechanical industries and with much the same degree of assurance as regards the quality, rate and volume of output," under the aegis of "publicity engineers." Ultimately, for Veblen, capitalist "rationality" of "salesmanship" led to the "multiplication of merchants and shops, wholesale and retail, newspaper advertising and billboards, sales-exhibits, sales agents, fancy packages and labels."

To be sure, the resultant multiplication of wants was intimately related to status groups and class whose apex was the leisure class, itself receiving the best of the commodity crop of conspicuous consumption, with the remainder of the population chasing them for less expensive facsimiles, thus intertwining capitalist consumerism with class, a key Veblenian insight. This progression might be related to Marx's concept of commodity fetishism (the "definite social relations between men, that assumes, in their eyes the fantastic form of relations between things"), which under capitalist relations further alienated and dehumanized labor, making it principally an end to acquire goods for social prestige.[11]

Since Marx and Veblen, a bevy of socialist and others, have commented on the consequences of alienation/oppression at work and in society. But before continuing on this track, a brief aside is needed to understand the socialization process of the individual because it is axiomatic that an alienated society is composed of alienated families and children. It is in the family that most children first are socialized in the primary human patterns, trust and love, fear and hate. In Erik Erickson's eight stages of human psychological development, five critical ones (three from birth to age five—"trust versus mistrust," "autonomy versus shame and doubt," and "initiative versus guilt"—and two from age six to eighteen) transpired when the individual was closely associated with the immediate family.

Thus it is that for the neo-Marxists Eric Fromm, as in *Escape from Freedom* and *The Sane Society*, and Theodore W. Adorno and others in *The Authoritarian Personality*, children socialized in an "exploitative child-parent relationship," itself reflecting a society deeply riven by inequality and conflict, become sadomasochistic and obsessive-compulsive adults attempting to mitigate their insecurities through incessant work and submission to the prevailing religious, socioeconomic, and political authorities, basically intolerant of others who are of different ethnic and religious groups and lower on the socioeconomic scale. It is these individuals who are prone to follow Nazism and other authoritarianisms.[12]

Manifestations of the consequences of alienation/oppression in the American family recently included the following: Shepard, in *Sociology*, presented a series of surveys in the 1970s with these results:

> Almost seven of ten parents had used some form of violence on their children…Nearly eight percent admitted to kicking, biting, or punching their children; four percent had beaten up their children; and three percent had threatened their children with weapons.

The following horrors of alienation encompassed the 1980s and 90s: Perhaps as many as a fifth of men and a third of women were sexually abused in childhood, usually by father, mother, or near relative (this according to the American Psychological Association and others), with an essentially compulsive personality, addicted in varying degree to work, religion, power, and sex; this pattern of the Adornian male abuser may also be applied to females. Is it any wonder, then, that one of ten teenagers attempted suicide according to the Centers for Disease Control and Prevention in a survey conducted in 1997. This child abuse is related to violence among spouses in about a third of the marriages. To be sure, there is also sibling rivalry and violence, and abuse of the elderly, especially the "weak, disabled or female." It is now estimated that between half-a-million to 2.5 million elderly parents are annually battered by their children.

The harried, insecure, competitive existence of modern life obviously contributes to sexual dysfunction. A recent extensive study of 1,750 women and 1,410 men—the most thorough since the discredited Kinsey Report of the 1940s, which lacked representative examples of interviewees—co-authored by University of Chicago Sociology Professor, Edward O. Laumann, and Dr. Raymond C. Rosen of the Center for Sexual and Marital Health at the Robert Wood Johnson Medical School in New Jersey—reveals the significant following: A fourth of women fail to achieve orgasm and a third between eighteen and thirty-nine lack any interest in sex; and 30 percent of men have problems with premature ejaculation and 15 percent lack sexual interest. Not surprisingly, the study concludes that poverty, various stresses, early traumatic sexual experiences, like child molestation, or later ones, like rape, lead to the greater possibility of sexual dysfunction. Economic problems play an important role here; women whose incomes decline by more than 20 percent in the last three years before being interviewed have a 60 percent greater likelihood for lower sexual desire than those whose incomes increase. Furthermore, more education and wealth translate into a healthier sexual life, the truism being that the bourgeoisie are less alienated than the working-class.

Then, according to Dr. Judith Lewis Herman, in *Trauma and Recovery*, from 50 to 60 percent of psychiatric patients requiring hospitalization and from 40 to 60 percent of those who are outpatients are physically or mentally abused in childhood. To be sure, genetic predisposition may be present in mental illness, especially in psychosis, but it is certainly exacerbated by environmental factors. More than a fifth of the population in the U.S. today suffers annually from diagnostically recognizable neurotic symptoms, like excessive anxiety and depression, pronounced phobias, obsessive-compulsive disorders, manic depression, and major depression, and a little more than 1 percent are psychotic or paranoid schizophrenic. Indeed, over a lifetime, perhaps as many as 70 percent of the people have some form of mental illness.[13]

In alienated capitalist societies riven by deep socioeconomic inequalities and competitive norms, replicated by authoritarian and fear-driven work relations in which individuals can lose their lobs at any time, individuals and families are increasingly isolated from one another in a meaningful manner. Thus, able sociopaths or psychopaths, the "aggressive egocentrics" and those exhibiting "paranoid, hysterical and obsessional patterns," obviously well-endowed to survive in the Machiavellian labyrinths of the higher economic and political complexes, flourish. In this respect, Hitler and Stalin come readily to mind, both psychopaths able to function and succeed in their political milieux, undoubtedly terrifying those about them to further consolidate and maintain their power. Furthermore, for Dr. Alex Comfort, a neo-anarchist critic of culture, in *Authority and Delinquency in the Modern State*, paranoiacs in difficult times have a powerful hold over people as they are able through projection to identify common hatreds, thus able to find scapegoats, like ethnic/religious minorities. His views were reinforced by Harold Greenwald, a well-known psychologist:

> The reasons why we generally do not discuss the successful psychopath is because we would then have to discuss many of the rulers of the world…Many of the symptoms…as lack of morals and apparent lack of guilt, exist widely among people of power and influence.

An earlier commentary on elite psychopathology was the well-regarded work by the political scientist Harold D. Laswell, *Psychopathology and Politics*, presenting detailed descriptions of personages caught in the web of neurosis and power.[14]

In observing alienation under capitalism in which the focus is generally on the United States, there is also awareness of the intense alienation in former "socialist" societies, like the former Soviet Union, whose top layers rejected civil liberties and workers' control of the workplace and participation in economic planning, decisive elements indicating their intensely antagonistic socioeconomic and political relations, resurrecting capitalism.

The delineation between work and alienation/oppression continues in other studies. A key one was by Braverman in *Labor and Monopoly Capital* whose principal Marxist thesis held that the wondrous technological advances since the 1950s intensified worker dissatisfaction in the workplace because the technology was designed to magnify workers' powerlessness, condemning most workers to doing work requiring little or no intellectual challenge, as well as chaining them to a "round of servile duties." Indeed, as the technology advanced, most workers who labored on it would become ever more inconsequential because they did not "own the machine and the labor power."[15] Another by the Marxist Bertell Ollman in *Alienation: Marx's Concepts of Man in Capitalist Society*, saw that Marx's theory of alienation represented "the devastating effect of capitalist production on human beings, on their physical and mental states and on the social processes of which they are a part."[16]

These views were similar to those of two socialist academics who spent time in factories as workers—Simone Weil, the noted French anarchist (*La Condition ouvière*), in the 1930s in the Paris area; and Richard M. Pfeffer, a Harvard Ph.D. in government, and member of the Johns Hopkins faculty (*Working for Capitalism*), in the 1970s in greater Baltimore. Both unsparingly indicted the capitalist factory system for its viewing workers as things or objects to be used, rigidly caging them in a social milieu of strict bureaucracy and inhumanity, with almost endless job gradations, rules and regulations whose aim was to exploit, divide and disempower them as much as possible. But workers might also at any moment be dismissed, either singly or in groups, thrown into the whirlwind of more helplessness and despair. Furthermore, foremen treated workers like children, using harsh language and other devices to discipline them, further eroding their human dignity. The work itself was abominable—repetitive and utterly boring, at maximum speed in hellish working environments, with long workdays and low wages. These realities confirmed to workers of their belonging to the inferior and humiliated class, not surprising, since they neither owned the workplace nor were consulted in the organization of work. Furthermore, since workers had limited education, the mechanical and other principles of science would remain a mystery to them, further increasing their alienation.[17]

That work basically defines a person's life, associated with status and class divisions and all they entail, was poignantly described by Studs Terkel (an icon in left journalism) in *Working*, a magnificent tome of oral history in which more than a hundred Americans recounted how work affected their lives. Mumford, one of Veblen's admirers, on the book's jacket, pictured this study as "powerful, original, incredible." In covering the continuum of work-class, this study affirmed the obvious, that there were more losers than winners in the race for success: For most workers, jobs were usually physically exhausting and psychologically stressful, caught in a hierarchic cage characterized by humdrum work routines. But for the fortunate ones—the happy few—work was creative and often accompanied with great financial rewards. To be sure, there were a few socialists who questioned the status quo.[18]

Terkel's observations were confirmed by Barbara Garson, a well-known social activist, in two works: in *All the Livelong Day*, a brilliant reportage of the work lives of blue- and white-collar workers, stripped of all dignity and autonomy as labor division increasingly multiplies, ever more fragmenting work and accelerating its pace. In *The Electronic Sweatshop*, she indicted the new and spreading computer technology for subjecting white-collar workers to a new work slavery, the aim being to de-skill them, "restrict their autonomy," and "to make people cheap and disposable." She also observed the deleterious consequences of electronic surveillance at work recording and evaluating every second in the office assembly line, white-collars being effectively proletarianized, with "Big Brother" watching them. In this critique, she followed Braverman's objections to Taylorism. In 2001, 80 percent of American companies employed some form of electronic surveillance of employees.[19]

Another major study on capitalist work relations in America was by two well-known left writers, Richard Sennett and Jonathan Cobb, *The Hidden Injuries of Class*. In addition to recounting the wasteland of work for most workers, they described the underlying social psychology of a society that was ferociously competitive, dividing people between the successful and the failures, the latter usually blaming themselves for their shortcomings. The tack of this study was Veblenian, as it intertwined work with class, with a built-in cultural/value system favoring the dominant bourgeoisie over the proletariat.[20]

Yet another well-regarded study on the workplace by Chris Argyris, Beach Professor of Administrative Sciences, Yale University, *Personality and Organization*, relied on a number of detailed studies on work to indicate that workers at the lower end of the work-class progression experienced infinitely more feelings of powerlessness and frustration than those performing mental labor. Thus, for instance, assembly-line workers faced with the rapid pace and repetitive nature of their work, along with long work hours, often succumbed to psychosomatic and related illnesses, like "high blood pressure and heart disease, and were more prone to accidents."[21]

The problems caused by unremittingly boring and repetitive work at high speed, now often electronically monitored, have been recently examined by three studies: A United Nations International Labor Organization report, "Job Stress: The 20th Century Disease" (1993); Mitchell Marks' *From Turmoil to Triumph* (1994); and Jeremy Rifkin's *The End of Work* (1995). The first insisted that the annual economic costs of alienation at work on the American economy in the form of illness, absenteeism, lower productivity, and job turnover is in the 200 billion-dollar range, while in Britain, as much as 10 percent of its GDP. It also finds that as many as 40 percent of Japanese workers fear death by overwork or "karoshi."[22] The second, by a psychologist on organization and consultant to business, examines worker anger at management in the wake of recent mergers and downsizing, increasing unemployment and work time (the latter resulting in "burnout"), and decreasing real median wages. The third, by a labor economist, reiterates in great detail the problems posed by the first and second and recommends a thirty-hour workweek.[23]

Before proceeding to measure annual human casualties and economic costs of class alienation in the U.S., these general statistics are in order for the late 90s—there are 2.3 million annual deaths, 100 million full-time workers, and a GDP of 8 trillion dollars.

The American work place is invariably riven by violence, reflecting the classist, sexist, and racist (including ethnic and religious divisions) nature of society: For instance, a 1996 report by the National Institute for occupational Safety and Health reports a million crimes annually in it (11 percent of the total), including 1100 murders (4 percent of the total), and 8 million robberies. A survey conducted by the Northwestern National Life Insurance Co. of 600 workers in 1993 obtained similar results to those of the Justice Department—a sixth physically attacked and a fifth threatened by physical harm. The "workplace avenger" who kills fellow workers and supervisors in a fit of rage is not un-known. Then, there is the specter of "covert," "passive" or "hidden aggression," di-rected against workplace competitors, including malicious gossip, dirty looks, rudeness, and hostile criticism, impinging on efficiency and profits, whose high costs are difficult to quantify. In a recent study of these aggressions conducted by three university profes-sors of psychology and/or management, Robert A. Baron, Joel H. Neuman, and Deanna Geddes, of 452 anonymous employees surveyed in six states, in a period of a month or less, more than a quarter reported experiencing them, while a sixth saw themselves at times as recipients of discourtesies, as not being informed of meetings.

Workplace aggression is undoubtedly related to the earlier bullying of children by parents, which in turn manifests itself in children bullying one another on the street and in school, including for ethnic and religious differences, especially virulent in a racist and multi-ethnic and religious U.S., where the "strong" (usually the majority or the stronger) prey on the "weak" or minority by speech (teasing or name calling), shunning and physical attack. At times, those picked on may resort to indiscriminate murder—the all-are-guilty syndrome—as in the recent Columbine High School case in Colorado. A recent study of bullying in school, for instance, reveals that a third of children from the sixth to tenth grades indicate verbal or physical bullying concerning race, ethnicity, reli-gion, and disabilities, like speech.

There are also high human costs related to an unhealthy and hazardous workplace environment, like toxic air, dangerous machinery, unsafe work procedures, and speedups. According to the National Safety Council, 250,000 workers died on the job from 1970 to 1995, many from employer negligence; in this time, only four people, ac-cording to the Occupational Safety and Health Administration (OSHA)—a federal agency monitoring the workplace—served a prison sentence for subjecting workers to an unsafe work environment. But the average number of annual deaths by accidents in the 1990s has dropped by 40 percent or to 6,000. Nevertheless, there are still from 50,000 to 70,000 annual deaths from occupationally related illnesses, like lung cancer, and 6 million are injured, of whom 1.4 million leave the workplace for varying periods of time, 50,000 permanently. OSHA itself in 1987 had less than 800 inspectors to cover 6 million work sites; in 1998 the number is 2,000.

These workplace disasters are related to an increasingly helpless work force, with ever less union protection and job security, constantly driven to perform ever more in less time. A 2001 report issued by the Families And Work Institute, "Overworked: When Work Becomes Too Much," claims that almost a third of the American work force be-lieves that it is chronically overworked—the "karoshi" syndrome—up to a half at times.

Not surprisingly, the study concludes that this alienation results in "physical and emotional health problems," like "loss of sleep" and resentment towards bosses.

These statistics are part of two larger pictures: In Indiana, for instance—this is probably so nationwide—construction workers, most of whom are males, live ten years less than the national average for men, and in a study of two Lordstown automobile plants near Youngstown Ohio, the respective mortality rates from cancer are 40 to 50 percent higher than the average. From an overarching perspective on life longevity, a *New York Times* article ("For Good Health, It Pays to be Rich and Important") reported that wealthy white men live 6.6 years longer than their poor counterparts and whites live longer than blacks, at age sixty-five, 7.4 years for men, and 3.7 years for women.

Tensions and conflicts at work are now exacerbated by downsizing as permanent lifetime jobs are becoming ever more scarce. Since most workers identify themselves closely with their work, intimately related as it is with socioeconomic self-worth, unemployment often results in feelings of shame and worthlessness. When debts cannot be repaid and family possessions dwindle, the psychological health of all family members is imperiled. Not surprisingly, the long-term unemployed have a 30 percent higher rate of divorce than average and abuse their children and spouses more often and more severely than others. From a general perspective, a 1 percent increase in unemployment in America results in a rise of 4 percent for suicide, almost 6 percent for murder, and 4 percent for men and 2 percent for women in admittance to state psychiatric hospitals.

Another ever more costly phenomenon not to be overlooked, now affecting most businesses, which regard workers as disposable garbage in this era of downsizing, is active resistance against them by alienated workers through sabotage to damage their operations. Especially is this sabotage effective in the highly complex area of computer technology, in which a solitary individual can create havoc. A pending case of this involves a computer programmer charged with obliterating the sales records of a company, inflicting ten million dollars in losses. Thus, although restricting worker autonomy, new technologies also allow workers to inflict more damage on capital, an element of the ongoing class struggle, costing many billions of dollars annually.[24]

Middle and higher management, although at or near the top of the work chain, also cannot escape the competitive and alienating parts of oppression/alienation. Workers are to some degree protected by unions, although in the 1990s, only a tenth of the private work force. But in middle and upper management, there is a high-stakes game of money and power where competition for them is intense as it consumes both their working and social lives, the latter in networking and politicking for promotion and job protection. In this labyrinth, uncertainty usually reigns. Furthermore, middle management is now be-

ing savaged by recent trends in corporate downsizing and introduction of new technologies, leading not only to mass layoffs and corresponding lower salaries, but to increased
workloads, inexorably to greater job stress and burnout. This group is also losing its favored status in the work force because mass higher education has increased its numbers.

In the contemporary Darwinian jungle of middle and upper management, the supposed rationality and efficiency of merit in the business world is largely mythical. For instance, in promotions, more than half of middle managers readily admit that they are
made on a "largely subjective evaluation or arbitrary decision." Even top executives have
been concerned with recent downsizing and increased work loads accompanying them.
In a 1991 survey of senior executives in the largest thousand American companies, 54
percent fear losing their jobs and 26 percent of "burnout," the two leading anxieties. (Of
course, senior executives usually have clauses in their contracts protecting them for a
number of years in case of dismissal, but workers do not.)

Along with the many irrationalities in promotion, there is the specter of inherent
economic waste in the American corporation as organizational structure, which David
Gordon, an economist, in *Fat and Mean*, contrasts with the more cooperative German
and Japanese ones, necessitating that American corporations have three times as many
managers and supervisors as their Japanese and German counterparts, this despite recent downsizing also involving management. Whereas Germany had 3.9 percent and Japan had 4.2 percent of their work forces as managers and supervisors, the U.S. had 13
percent in the early 1990s.[25]

There are many other consequences of alienation/oppression, including obesity,
bulimarexia, compulsive gambling and buying, extensive use of injurious drugs, legal
and illegal, and crime in its various manifestations: The psychic costs of these manifestations are incalculable, but the annual costs (human and economic) in the late 90s are
largely measurable. The first two involving eating disorders cause 300,000 deaths and
their economic cost in illness, work missed, and early death is more than 200 billion dollars. The third, or compulsive gambling, heavily engages about 5 percent of the population, who bet much of the more than 500 billion dollars legally wagered, and many tens of
billions in illegal betting, profits at 50 billion dollars. Although legal gambling pays taxes,
the social costs of gambling—robbery to pay debts, child and spousal abuse, divorce, and
job loss—are 90 billion dollars in 1988 and well above 200 billion dollars in 2000. The female counterpart to male compulsive gambling is compulsive shopping (90 percent of
compulsive shoppers are women), which afflicts approximately 8 percent of the populations annual costs of this malady run into the tens of billions of dollars.

In the realm of psychoactive drugs, legal and illegal (often used by people with deep
psychological pain seeking relief at any price), the two most harmful are smoking to-

bacco and alcoholic drinks. Now annually, the first, with 50 to 60 million regular users, has an economic cost of 100 billion dollars and results in more than 430,000 deaths; the second with 100 million habitual users, results in the deaths of 65,000 to 150,000 and costs 185 billion dollars, including treatment of 14 million alcoholics, and 30 percent of 37,000 automobile deaths from accidents. In the area of illegal drugs, like marijuana, cocaine, and heroin, they inflict 16,000 annual deaths among 12 to 15 million addicts, 3 million being hard core, with 200 billion dollars in costs for purchasing the drugs, treatment, property stolen, and incarceration.[26]

Crime itself in its various manifestations denotes the lack of human solidarity in a society riven by deep individual and social antagonisms in which economic insecurity and Veblenian invidious distinction drive people to be endlessly acquisitive. Crime may be divided into three parts, within the family (already examined), street, and business. The second or street crime, of burglary and robbery (motor vehicles, jewelry, currency, and household goods), consumes annually 16 billion dollars. This does not include the loss of priceless human life and the psychological and monetary damages of 4,000 street murders in 1999.

A detailed Justice Department report released in 1996, "Victim Costs and Consequences: A New Look," asserts that the total annual toll for family and street crimes—it includes rape, injury and murder, factoring in physical injury and psychological trauma and attendant hospitalization, time lost from work, and police and legal costs—is 450 billion dollars. This amount neither includes the 40 billion dollars expended by prisons and related parole and probation systems nor the 210 billion dollars for private business and individual security with anti-theft devices and 1.5 million private guards.

The third or business crime is all pervasive, its annual cost to the public in the 90s at 300 billion dollars. Corporations employing kickbacks, bribery, fraud, extortion, violating federal regulations and tax evasion take the greater part of it, while employee embezzlement is from 20 to 40 billion dollars. In any given decade, about a fifth of the largest 500 corporations are penalized by the federal government. Among the more costly frauds of the last decade in annual dollar terms: The Savings and Loan (S&L) debacle in the 20 billion range; military procurement wasted, 25 billion; and healthcare, 100 billion. Some of the more egregious examples of this in fines and restitution in dollars for the 1990-2000 period are now presented: Marc Rich's corporations (Rich is an international trader living in Switzerland who often shaves legality—he was pardoned in 2001 by President Clinton before leaving office—paid 200 million. Prudential agreed to pay 1.7 billion to policyholders because of deceptive practices. SmithKline Beecham paid 325 million in fines for false billings to Medicare. Archer Daniels Midland, paid a

100 million fine for price fixing. Michael Miliken, the "junk-bond king," paid a 1.1 billion fine (he will still be worth 125 million) for financial fraud. One of his cohorts, Ivan Boesky, was only fined a hundred million. Martin A. Frankel, another financial wizard, who fled the country to Germany, will return in 2001 to face financial fraud charges of many hundreds of millions of dollars. Blue Cross and Blue Shield of Illinois paid 144 million in civil and criminal fines. Columbia/HCFA Healthcare and Quorum Health Group paid a 1.1 billion fine for fraudulent expense claims. In 2001, Walter A. Forbes, former chairperson of Cedant was charged for causing its investors a loss of 19 billion by declaring "phony profits." Cedant itself has compensated shareholders at 2.8 billion. Furthermore, employers withheld from workers 20 billion dollars annually according to an employer-sponsored think tank. Lawyers and their ancillaries, of course, in a litigious society command 124 billion dollars annually.

A recent United States Judiciary Committee report affirms that America is the "most violent and destructive nation on earth," with the highest homicide and robbery per capita rate among the economically advanced nations. This is reflected in these statistics: In 2000, prisoners number 2 million (a third in city and county jails, two thirds in state and federal prisons; a fifth incarcerated for drug-related offences) of whom 46 percent are black, 34 percent white, 17 percent Hispanic, and 3 percent other, four-fifths having illegal drug and alcohol problems, suggesting high stress levels and mental illness. Especially involved in this social catastrophe are black males: Almost a third of them in their twenties today are either in prison, on parole, or on probation, 7 percent of them in prison at any given time (many being repeat offenders), and of 17,000 murders a year, over half committed by them. (Five percent of Americans are imprisoned during their lifetime.) Illegal drugs, especially crack cocaine and its higher penalties for possession than regular cocaine, contribute to this. These problems should be viewed from this economic alienation: half of black men, from ages twenty-five to thirty-four, are either unemployed or earn wages below the poverty line for a family of four.

It should be added that white-collar criminals involved in financial crime face less imprisonment than blue-collar ones with a gun for usually not much money and those committing nonviolent drug offences facing stiff minimum sentencing—for selling two ounces of cocaine in New York as a first-time offender, it is fifteen years to life. For instance, in cases of fraud, insider trading, and tax evasion of a million or more dollars, there is a maximum of three years imprisonment (often not any). These sentences, however, have now been increased significantly.

To be sure, under the rubric of crime, these elements of it should not be neglected. According to the Internal Revenue Service (IRS), under-reporting of income is

20 percent for professionals, 30 percent for farmers, and 50 percent for small business. In any given year many of the top 500 corporations and individuals in the Forbes 400, do not pay any income taxes, and in cases involving more than ten million dollars owed between them and the IRS, its recovery rate is 17 percent, as it is faced by a multitude of lawyers. It also includes 3 trillion dollars in illegal offshore tax-free bank accounts and various domestic phony trusts that siphon 300 billion dollars annually from the IRS. The IRS itself has lost 19,000 employees or a third of its staff, further vitiating enforcement.[27]

Is anyone surprised that alienation/oppression with its train of drugs and crime takes such a heavy toll in lives and economic resources, especially savaging minority youth in the nation's inner cities, murder and crime zones of hellish intensity? When Louis Chevalier, a French social scientist, observes that 10 percent of Parisians in the 1850s are criminals, poverty being the basic cause, is it unreasonable to claim that this also applies for street crime in American cities in the 1990s?[28]

A substantial part of the costs related to pollution, including human illness and attempts to mitigate it, are also the resultant of class-alienated capitalism, with its particular technological structures and consumerist demands with their inherent waste. Certainly, a cooperative world socialism is more likely to solve these problems than the present order. The following statistics are generally annual ones for the early 1990s in the U.S.: Cancer rates (cancer accounts for a quarter of deaths), according to the National Cancer Institute in 1989, climb rapidly from 1950 to 1986, increasing by 21.5 percent for children under age fourteen and 22.6 percent for adults. It may be argued that the rising adult cancer rate may be partly explained by an aging population, but this does not hold true for children. The workplace itself, according to the National Safety Council, accounts for 23 to 38 percent of cancer deaths, or 150,000, which alone cost 275 billion dollars. As for air pollution from industry and transportation, the health costs are 226 billion dollars, while for water pollution, more than a billion dollars. Other annual pollution dollar costs in billions: to remove hazardous wastes from earth and water from 32,000 sites, 20; air pollution damage to residential and industrial buildings and other structures, 30; water pollution effects on recreational activity, swimming and boating, 11. These costs do not include the loss of irreplaceable natural resources in the many tens of billions of dollars.[29]

Other wasteful annual costs for the early 1990s in billions of dollars in which class-alienation is prominent: Better vehicle safety can save the public 136 according to Murray Weidenbaum, Chairperson of President Reagan's Council of Economic Advisors; 138 for advertising; 165 for racial discrimination against African-Americans; 300 for the military.[30]

That the very costs enumerated create tens of millions of jobs and great profits, and consequent special interest groups fearful of change lest they lose their jobs/profits, is also obvious. But if class alienation can be overcome by socialism, the savings effected—some, like pollution, may take generations to correct, others, as those involved with social injustice, may be solved relatively rapidly—can, within the context of contemporary technology, allow for a six-hour day without loss of jobs and present living standards in the United States and other developed nations within the near future.

In *The Culture of Narcissism*, Christopher Lasch (a history professor best known as a culture critic) traced the American character in its successive stages, from the 17th century Puritan centered on work as a "calling," to the 18th century "Yankee" personified by Franklin, more materialistic and individualistic, but still related to some virtue and community, to the 19th century one of unbridled individualistic success and self-improvement, to the late 20th century one of the narcissistic "Happy Hooker," materialistic and acquisitive, living for the moment, consumerism being nirvana, but forced to fit in within the bureaucratic cage of monopoly capitalism, devoid of any sense of self-entitlement and power. His way out of this alienating impasse had a Veblenian ring to it:

> The struggle against bureaucracy therefore requires a struggle against capitalism itself. Ordinary citizens cannot resist professional dominance without also asserting control over production and over the technical knowledge on which modern production rests...They [citizens] will have to create their own "communities of competence." Only then will the productive capacities of modern capitalism together with the scientific knowledge that now serves it, come to serve the interests of humanity instead.[31]

Lasch's consumerist Nirvana was, of course, related to the alienation or meaninglessness of work for most of the work force whose basic compensation now is to frequent the new temples and pleasures of capitalism, the retail outlets, and to indulge in frequent vacations, promoted by the new priests dispensing meaning to life, the advertisers and salespersons.

Notes

1. Carl J. Friedrich, edited and Introduction, *The Philosophy of Hegel* (New York: Modern Library, 1954), pp. 399-410.

2. Loyd D. Easton and K. Guddat, editors and translators, *Writings of the Young Marx on Philosophy and Society* (New York: Doubleday Anchor, 1969), p. 424—from Marx and Engels, *The German Ideology*.

3. On the quotations and other pertinent material, see Marx, *Capital,* I, 708. Erich Fromm, *Marx's Concept of Man*, with a translation by T.B. Bottomore from Marx's *Economic and Philosophical Manuscripts* (New York: Frederick Ungar, 1969), pp. 93-219. Marx and Engels, *Communist Manifesto*, p. 16.

4. K. Marx and F. Engels, *The Holy Family or Critique of Critical Critique* (Moscow: Foreign Languages Publishing House, 1956), p. 51.

5. On Taylorism, labor division, worker control of the work place, and so forth, see Sudhir Kakar, *Frederick Taylor: A Study in Personality and Innovation* (Cambridge, MA: MIT, 1970); and Dan Clawson, *Bureaucracy and the Labor Process: The Transformation of U.S. Industry: 1860-1920* (New York: Monthly Review Press, 1980), pp. 38 ff., 71 ff., 126 ff., 202-67.

6. On Smith, see *The Wealth of Nations: Representative Selections*, ed. Bruce Mazlish (Indianapolis, IN: Bobbs-Merrill, 1961), pp. xvii, 3-5.

7. Veblen, *Theory of Business Enterprise*, p. 313.

8. *Ibid.*, p. 312.

9. *Statistical Abstracts of the United States, U.S. Dept. of Commerce, Bureau of the Census*, 1991, p. 395. In 1989, there were 1.823 million engineers, 3.936 million teachers in primary and secondary education, and 709,000 college teachers. In the 1990s, there were about 36.4 million full-time blue-collar workers.

10. Veblen, *Essays in our Changing Order*, p. 95, on the long quotation: Veblen, *Business Enterprise*, p. 313.

11. Veblen, *Engineers and the Price System*, pp. 108 ff.; Veblen, *Absentee Ownership*, pp. 305-06; Harry Braverman, *Labor and Monopoly Capital: The Degradation of Work in the Twentieth Century* (New York: Monthly Review Press, 1974), pp. 265-66; Marx, *Capital*, I, 83.

12. Erik H. Erikson, *Identity: Youth and Crisis* (New York: W.W. Norton, 1968), pp. 91-141. Erich Fromm, *Escape from Freedom* (New York: Farrar and Rinehart, 1941), pp. 141-206. Erich Fromm, *The Sane Society* (New York: Holt and Rinehart, 1955), pp. 12-52. T.W. Adorno *et al.*, *The Authoritarian Personality* (New York: Harper and Brothers, 1950), pp. 759 ff.

13. On the family and its discontents, see John M. Shepard, *Sociology*, 5th ed., (Minneapolis/St. Paul, MN: West Publishing Co., 1993), p. 344. John Bradshaw, *The Family: A Revolutionary Way of Self-Discovery* (Deerfield, FL: Health Communications, 1988), pp. 16-126 ff. Dennis Coon, *Introduction to Psychology: Exploration and Application* (St. Paul, MN: West Publishing Co., 1980), pp. 42-84. Judith Lewis Herman, *Trauma and Recovery* (New York: Basic Books, 1992), pp. 96-135. Anne Sappington and Mike Paquette, "Family Violence," *Akron Beacon Journal*, Aug. 24, 1996, p. A8 on sexually abused children. On attempted suicide by teenagers, see *Akron Beacon Journal*, Aug. 14, 1998, p. A4. "Body-bag journalism" as daily reported on television and radio and in the press usually presents the tragic alienation of the lowest economic third of the people. On sexual dysfunctions, see Peter J. Howe (*Boston Globe*), "Study finds not everyone enjoying sex," *Akron Beacon Journal*, Feb. 10, 1999, pp. Al and A4.

14. Alex Comfort, *Authority and Delinquency in the Modern State* (London: Routledge and Kegan Paul, 1950), pp. 31-65. Harold Greenwald, "Treatment of the Psychopath," p. 364, in Harold Greenwald, ed., *Active Psychotherapy* (New York: Atherton Press, 1967). Harold D. Lasswell, *Psychopathology and Politics* (New York: Viking Press, 1960), pp. 1-77. This work is first published in 1930.

15. Braverman, *Labor and Monopoly Capital*, pp. 95, 194, and 241.

16. Bertell Ollman, *Alienation: Marx's Concept of Man in a Capitalist Society* (London: Cambridge University Press. 1976) p. 131.

17. Simone Weil, *La Condition Ouvrière* (Paris: Gallimard, 1951), pp. 15 ff. Richard M. Pfeffer, *Working for Capitalism* (New York: Columbia University Press, 1979), pp. 47-102, for instance.

18. Studs Terkel, *Working: People Talk About What They Do All Day and How The Feel About Their Work* (New York: Pantheon Books, 1974), cf.; for instance, Mike Lefevre, factory worker, pp. xxxi-xxxviii, with David Bender, factory owner, pp. 393-97.

19. Barbara Garson, *All the Livelong Day: The Meaning and Demeaning of Routine Work* (Garden City, NY: Doubleday, 1975), pp. 38-58 ff. and 90 ff. Barbara Garson, *The Electronic Sweatshop: How Computers Are Transforming the Office of the Future into the Factory of the Past* (New York: Simon and Schuster, 1988), pp. 40-114, 166-263. On the 80 percent figure, see Christian Parenti, "Big Brother's Corporate Cousin," *Nation*, Aug. 6/13, 2001, p. 26.

20. Richard Sennett and Jonathan Cobb, *The Hidden Injuries of Class* (New York: Alfred A. Knopf, 1972), pp. 30-55 ff., 72-92 ff., 147-62 ff.

21. Chris Argyris, *Personality and Organization: The Conflict Between System and the Individual* (New York: Harper Torchbooks, 1970), pp. 76-122.

22. On the ILO report, see David Briscoe, "Labor Force Reluctant Lot, Report Says," *Akron Beacon Journal*, March 23, 1993, p. D6; and Frank Swoboda, "Employers Recognizing What Stress Costs Them, U.N. Report Suggests," *Washington Post*, March 23, 1993, p. H2.

23. On recent downsizing and megers of corporations, with resultant widespread layoffs of workers, coupled to overwork and higher stress for them, see Mitchell Lee Marks, *From Turmoil To Triumph: New Life after Mergers, Acquisitions, and Downsizing* (New York: Maxwell Macmillan International, 1994), pp. 3-28. Jeremy Rifkin, *The End of Work: The Decline of the Global Work Force and the Dawn of the Post-Market Era* (New York: G.P. Putnam's, 1995), pp. 182-90.

24. On increasing alienation in the family and workplace, manifested by higher levels of violence, continued unsafe working conditions, greater job insecurity, higher medical costs, and lower longevity of life for workers relative to the rich, see Rifkin, *End of Work*, pp. 194 ff. Blair Justice and Rita Justice, *The Abusing Family* (New York: Plenum Press, 1990), pp. 191-93; William Greider, *Who Will Tell the People: The Betrayal of American Democracy* (New York: Simon and Schuster, 1992), pp. 111-22; Ralph Estes, *Tyranny of the Bottom line: Why Corporations Make Good People Do Bad Things* (San Francisco: Berrett-Koehler, 1996), pp. 180-82. *In These Times*, Nov. 14-20, 1990, p. 16. For the daily press—a good source for the consequences of alienation at work and elsewhere. For instance, at work, see *Akron Beacon Journal*, Aug. 13, 1990, p. A4; Jan. 28, 1996, pp. Al and A4; July 9, 1996, p. A3. On sabotage at work, see Mary Curtius, (*Los Angeles Times*), "Employee Vandalism Gouging Companies," *Akron Beacon Journal*, Nov. 8, 1998, pp. G1 and G8. On "passive aggression," see Micheal Lopez (*Al-*

bany Times Union), "Aggression on the Job: Gossip, Dirty Looks," *Akron Beacon Journal*, Jan 25, 1999, p. D4. Lisa Cornwell, "Workplace Violence on the Rise," *Akron Beacon Journal*, Sept. 4, 1995, pp. D1 and D4. On workers competing with one another at work and its deleterious effects, see Sherwood Ross, "Competition on Job Is Internal Strife," *Akron Beacon Journal*, March 11, 1996, p. D3. On bullying at school, see Lindsey Tanner, "Bullying Affects One in Three, Study Says," *Akron Beacon Journal*, April, 25, 2001, pp. A1 and A2. On longevity of life, see "For Good Health, it Helps to Be Rich and Important," *New York Times*, June 1, 1999, pp. D1 and D9. On overworked Americans, see Diane Stafford, "Workers Complain They Are Swamped," *Akron Beacon Journal*, May 20, 2001, p. F3.

25. On job stress and higher unemployment rates for managers (approximately 8 percent of the work force), see Marks, *From Turmoil to Triumph*, pp. 6-14; Dennis Weintraub, "Office Politics: A Deadly Game for Losers," *Akron Beacon Journal*, March 22, 1974. Earl Shorris, *The Oppressed Middle: Politics of Middle Management* (Garden City, NY: Anchor Doubleday, 1981), Chapters 6 and 7. Carl Hecksher, *White-Collar Blues: Management Loyalties in the Age of Restructuring* (New York: Basic Books, 1995), pp. 3-94. On corporate waste involving too many managers in the U.S., see David Gordon, *Fat and Mean: The Corporate Squeeze of Working Americans and the Myth of Managerial "Downsizing"* (New York: Free Press, 1996), pp. 33-60.

26. On drugs, see Steven B. Duke and Albert C. Gross, *America's Longest War: Rethinking Our Tragic Crusade Against Drugs* (New York: Jeremy P. Tarcher/Putnam Book, 1993), pp. 23-32 on tobacco, 33-42 on alcohol, pp. 54 ff. on heroin. On gambling, see Marc Cooper, "America's House of Cards," *Nation*, Feb. 19, 1996, pp. 11-19.

27. On the Senate Judiciary Report, see *Akron Beacon Journal*, March 13, 1991, p. A6. On murder and suicide, see *Mother Jones*, Jan.-Feb., 1994, p. 40. On the "Victim Costs and Consequences," see *Akron Beacon Journal*, April 22, 1996, p. A4. On black males, see *U.S. News and World Report*, Oct. 16, 1995, pp. 53-54. David Remnick, "Dr. Wilson's Neighborhood," *New Yorker* (Black in America issue), April 29/May 8, 1996, p. 54. On street murders and costs of white-collar and street crimes, see Russell Mokhiber, "Underworld U.S.A.," *In These Times*, April 1-13, 1996, pp. 14-16; Ralph Estes, "The Public Cost of Private Corporations," *Advances in Public Interest Accounting*, VI (1995), 339-45; Robert Sherrill, "A Year in Corporate Crime," *Nation*, April 7, 1997, pp. 11-20. On the costs of private anti-theft measures and the legal industry, see George Winslow, "Capital Crimes: The Political Economy of Crime in America," *Monthly Review*, Nov., 2000, pp. 38 and 51. On individual income-tax cheating, see *Akron Beacon Journal*, May 14, 1978; on the 300 billion dollars lost by the IRS to tax cheaters and so forth, see NBC Evening News with Tom Brokaw, April 5, 2001; and Curt Anderson (Associated Press), "Tax Evasion Scams Explode on Internet," *Akron Beacon Journal*, April 9, 2001, p. D5.

28. Louis Chevalier, *Laboring Classes and Dangerous Classes in Paris During the First Half of the Nineteenth Century* (New York: Howard Fertig, 1973), pp. 275 ff.

29. Estes, *Tyranny of the Bottom Line*, pp. 171-89; Estes, "The Public Cost of Private Corporations," pp. 337-43.

30. Estes, *Tyranny of the Bottom Line*, pp 183-84 on unsafe vehicles; pp. 179-80 on racial discrimination; p. 95 on advertising.

31. Christopher Lasch, *The Culture of Narcissism: American Life in an Age of Diminishing Expectations* (New York: Warner Books, 1979), p. 396 on the quotation.

XII   The Second Sex

SINCE MEN AND WOMEN ARE HUMANITY, relations between them are of primary importance in understanding the human condition. Indeed, in the socialization process of human beings, gender relations within the crucible of the nuclear/extended family are interwoven with those of status and class to form the individual's social horizon. In this light, gender relations, as part of the class struggle, not only reflect its progress for socialism, but are a reliable general index in measuring the level of technological development.

To what degree have men and women throughout history been equal? The following according to contemporary anthropology: Throughout most of human history, which stretches back to many hundreds of thousands of years and beyond, most of it in the Paleolithic Age or "savage" period of hunting-gathering, in which humanity lived in small groups or bands numbering less than a hundred, the sexes were more than likely equal or almost so. But certainly in the Neolithic Age or "barbarian" period with the advent of the Agricultural Revolution, including domestication of animals, with general organized warfare and beginning of class society, the position of men over women over time became well established, as men being larger and stronger than women made better warriors, women themselves because of child-bearing being more vulnerable than men in social relations. (But in the early stages of the Neolithic Age, with women's discovery of agriculture, women actually enhanced their already high position relative to men as is evidenced by many female goddesses, only to rapidly lose it.) But this inequality is relative, for in many Neolithic groups, women had a high position in society, more so among sedentary agriculturalists than herders, as determined by matrilocal/patrilocal and matrilineal/patrilineal proportions. It was during the later Neolithic Age that polygyny definitely came about.

By the time of early civilizations women were in a subordinate position to men, but, again, in Egypt and with the Minoans, they occupied a high social position, and among the latter were probably men's equals. Polygyny among the wealthier men was now common in some societies, like the Hebrew, with Solomon, for instance, having seven hundred wives and three hundred concubines. The earlier Hebrew herder patriarchs, like Abraham, were also polygynous. And, in the *Iliad*, the Greek conquerors enslaved Trojan women not only to satisfy their sexual appetites, but also to enrich themselves.

In the classic Greco-Roman world, women continued to be subservient to men. Among the Greeks, with the exception of Sparta whose girls trained alongside boys, women were secluded in the home. But the position of Roman women was much higher for, although unable to hold political office, they could join their husbands in outside-of-home activities, as in "respectable parties, games, shows, and even political gatherings," and have "access to money and power."

The general oppression of women in civilized societies was invariably intertwined with religion, the traditional unifying institution. Notable examples: Among Hindus, polygyny was widespread and women were excluded from the sacred learning, strictly subject to fathers and husbands, taught to regard them as veritable gods, and encouraged to commit *suttee* upon a husband's death; among Christians, they were commanded to obey their fathers and husbands and be silent in church (they could not be priests) because of a supposed excessive carnality, thus tendency to evil; among Moslems, they were relegated to polygyny and concomitant subordination, the *Koran* allowing men four legal wives who can be divorced.

More historical background on women's oppression, complementing the traditional religious one, follows. In China, for instance, women's inferiority was indicated by polygyny, with brides being forced to live with their husbands' families. In this patrilineal/patrilocal arrangement, women usually were regarded as being—especially without sons—as not much higher than servants. For wealthy Chinese men, there was access to many women, their sensual pleasures being fulfilled by concubines and prostitutes, like the "singsong" girls (geishas in Japan). Furthermore, footbinding, the crippling of women making them more fully dependent on men (erotic playthings), was common. Where Islam was dominant, the custom of *purdah*, usually prevailed, the sequestering of women at home and veiling them. In sub-Sahara Africa, polygyny was still widespread in the late 20th century, with its usual patrilineal/patrilocal arrangements. The exceptions here were among the Igbo and Yoruba in West Africa, women being equal to men, both genders having parallel power structures, capped by a dual monarchy for the Igbo. Female infanticide, still prevalent in India and other parts of the world, was yet another expression of women's inferiority. And, of course, the double standard of sexual behavior still often continues, infidelity being an egregious sin for wives, but not for husbands, women to be chaste before marriage, but not men.

In the West, patrilineality and patrilocality have also been the norms. There was women's subordination, for instance, in the early 19th century Napoleonic Code, in which, unless special arrangements were made, a wife's property belonged to her husband, and in the English practice, from about 1750 to 1850, of selling unfaithful wives in the marketplace, usually purchased by lovers. For most of the 19th century in the United States, women neither voted nor owned property if married, nor protected themselves legally if beaten by their husbands, nor easily initiated divorce proceedings, nor spoke before mixed gatherings, nor received a good education. (The first woman to be admitted to higher education was in 1837, at Oberlin College in Ohio.)

But women's equality or near equality is not a new idea: Socialist utopians have championed it throughout the ages: In Plato's *The Republic* women were generally equal to men in the guardian class, with the exception of the top generalship. In More's *Utopia*, women did not enjoy absolute equality, but had the vote and generally equal education. In Campanella's *City of the Sun*, the family was abolished and universal suffrage and co-education existed, although women could not be magistrates.

In 19th-century utopian socialism, gender equality, for instance, was of major concern. The Shakers, founded by Anne Lee Stanley who believed that God was both male and female, practiced a celibacy and communism based on sexual equality. Owen's New Harmony in the mid-1820s also proclaimed sexual equality, as did Brook Farm and the religious Oneida Community (1848 to 1880) whose Bible Communism emphasized complex marriage, allowing men and women to love and procreate with other members of the community. Even the Icarians of Cabet in the 1850s and later, although regarding the father as the head of the family, urged gender equality for work and education.[1]

Two significant works on women's liberation by socialists, Mary Wollstonecraft's *Vindication of the Rights of Women* (1792) and John Stuart Mill's (one of the fathers of British socialism) *Subjection of Women* (1869), have also played a leading cultural/intellectual role in its achievement. The first, a landmark work, presented a detailed exposition for women's emancipation, insisting that gender equality be realized in all avenues of activity (economic, social, political, and cultural), present inferiority being based on oppressive institutions, not nature. In her far-ranging criticism of present society, Wollstonecraft was well aware of the pernicious influence of private property and the resultant unequal social divisions that made for a corrupt leisure class, which, among its other failings, had contributed to the enslavement of women: "Destructive, however, as riches and inherited honours are to the human character, women are more debased and cramped…than men" because of their yet lowlier position in society. She also boldly opposed the "legal prostitution" of marriage that condemned many supposedly happy women to intense alienation ("the most respectable women are the most oppressed") and favored women "who can enter any profession and industry, from which would flow a more loving relationship between the genders," for "the state of war which subsists between the sexes should end to the advantage of all concerned."[2]

The second, a most eloquent work, argued for gender equality in marriage, education, employment, suffrage, in all aspects of life. Mill, acutely aware of the unequal power relations between men and women throughout the ages, held that to undo this mistakenly "natural" condition would be difficult, but not impossible. In this contention, he contrasted Aristotle, who proclaimed the normality of the few ruling the many, including women, with Plato, who was impressed by the high social status of Spartan women.[3]

As for marriage, Mill maintained that wives silently endured the harshness of their husbands sanctioned by law and custom and added that the unequal relations between the genders had men wishing "the woman most nearly connected with them" to be "not a forced slave but a willing one, not a slave merely, but a favorite." For him, that this state was accepted by most women indicated the power of traditional social conditioning. He would replace this nightmare by the "justice" of equality.[4]

The enormity of women's oppression was so great for Mill that he compared it to that of "unenlightened societies," in which "colour, race, religion, or in the case of a conquered country, nationality, are to some men, sex is to all women; a peremptory exclusion from all honourable occupations," so deep that:

> Sufferings arise from cause of this nature usually meet with so little sympathy, that few persons are aware of the great amount of unhappiness even now produced by the feelings of a wasted life.[5]

The great reputation of Mill in intellectual circles was an important catalyst to the women's movement, not only in England, but also in the United States. Among the many prominent individuals whom Mill influenced to champion women's rights was the outstanding English socialist (a brilliant mathematician, philosopher, and historian), Bertrand Russell.[6]

Two significant events signaled the rise of the women's movement in the United States. The first was the women's rights convention, organized by Elizabeth Cady Stanton and Lucretia Mott, at Seneca Falls, New York in 1848, which drafted a "Declaration of Sentiments and Resolutions," that unequivocally called for equality with men in all spheres of life. The second, in 1890, organized by Susan B. Anthony, Stanton, Mott, and others, was the founding of the American Woman Suffrage Association, which was instrumental in the passage of the 19th amendment to the Constitution in 1920, federally granting women the right to vote, the decisive political happening for gender equality.

Modern socialism itself has continued to play a proper role in the women's movement throughout the world. In the United States, for instance, Florence Kelley was a prime example of an activist in both socialism and feminism in the early 20th century. American feminists themselves often employed the threat of becoming socialists if their demands for equality were not promptly heeded, as by Stanton at the International Council of Women in 1888.

In the Second Socialist International, socialist women forcefully fought for gender equality and the suffrage. Socialist feminism during this period was especially strong in the United States, Germany, and Austria. Although many socialist women, like Clara Zetkin and Rosa Luxemburg, urged postponing the women's right issue until after the revolution, many, like Emma Goldman and Alexandra Kolantai, fused it with the struggle to achieve socialism itself.[7]

The first nations to grant women the general suffrage were New Zealand in 1893 and Australia in 1902; between 1918 and 1920, Great Britain, Germany, and the United States adopted it, and by 1945 and 1946, France and Italy did so, as did Switzerland later. It is safe to assert that today women have formal legal equality with men, including the vote, in the economically advanced nations, as well as in many of the poorer ones, although, because of the oppressive past, women, have yet to achieve full economic and other equalities with men.

Veblen's concern for the plight of women occupied a sizable part of *The Theory of the Leisure Class*. In his analysis of this oppression, Veblen constructed an intricate mosaic linking the economic to the social and cultural in the context of a historical background covering thousands of years. Although he never proposed a strategy for women's liberation, his support for the Communist Revolution in Russia indicated his approval of its revolutionary changes on behalf of women. Its 1918 Family Law, for instance, favored gender equality, permitting "divorce at will for either party, awarding alimony to either party based on need rather than gender," and ending the concept of illegitimacy."[8]

In delineating the broad divisions between men and women, Veblen employed the operative concepts of "exploit" and "drudgery," the first term being associated with men, the second with women. Men under the first were "stouter, more massive, better capable of a violent and sudden strain, and more inclined to self-assertion, active emulation, and aggression," possessing the "qualities of massiveness, agility and ferocity." Women, under the second, were the smaller and more pacific gender. These differences arose because of a "selective adaptation to the new distribution of employments," which in the late Paleolithic presumably involved male large-game hunting, while women were occupied not only with childbearing and caring for the young, the earliest labor division, but with butchering, cooking meat and gathering food. But gender inequality in the late Paleolithic was not of sufficient magnitude, for him, to destroy general male equality. But Harris, *Culture, People, Nature*, held that "many hunter-gatherer band societies had both low levels of warfare and considerable gender inequality."

But, then, there came for Veblen, the lower barbarian (Neolithic) period, allowing humanity to develop a greater economic surplus in which the predatory nature of hunting was extended to warfare for the capture of slave women as "trophies" for sex and work, the general beginning of extensive private property. This early form of slavery itself in time extended to common "ownership-marriage." Veblen was partly confirmed here by the eminent French anthropologist Claude Levi-Strauss, who saw women as the principal merchandise in the early exchange of goods. But Veblen was incorrect in viewing Neolithic women as simply being the property of men. Although not men's equals, women at this time possessed much dignity and power, especially where matrilineality existed.[9]

With the rise of civilization, Veblen theorized the lot of women deteriorated rapidly, his example being their enslavement in Homeric Greece, "woman even becomes to serve as a unit of value" as "men consume what the women produce." Harris again confirmed Veblen generally here in stating that "both warfare and gender inequality increased with the development of the state," i.e., civilization. Ultimately, for Veblen, force and power decided the occupations of men and women (even among the socially oppressed)—the former fought, had egress to the gods as priests, hunted, and fished; the latter did the drudge work or were trophies of men.

Veblen also did pioneer work in deftly examining the relationship between social class and feminine beauty. Particularly did he indicate that leisure-class males, with their normal canons of waste and power, imposed a changeable ideal feminine beauty: For the Homeric Greeks, the "service element" being in vogue, the ideal woman was "robust, large limbed," consonant with a physically active lifestyle. In the European Middle Ages, the nobility favored women "exempt from all work," thus prizing "delicacy" of "face," "hands and feet," and "slender waist." For modern capitalists, so rich that their women were "above all imputation of vulgarly productive labour," feminine beauty partly reverted to the Homeric ideal of the athletic woman.

In the logic of women's oppression (again, the pace was set by the leisure class), Veblen masterfully related women's dress to "conspicuous consumption," "conspicuous leisure," and "invidious distinction." He began linking dress to class in both sexes. In comparing the dress of men and women in general, an obvious difference, for him was the truism that leisure-class women's dress was based on "exemption from or incapacity for all vulgarly was productive employment." Thus, for "respectable women" the impression was made "that the wearer does not and can not habitually engage in useful work," viewed as the "chief ornament," of the "household," a trophy and servant to glorify the husband's wealth and power in the community.

Specifically, Veblen presented numerous examples of this servitude so very widespread during his lifetime (and in varying degree today), like the "deformed foot of the Chinese," the "high heel, the skirt, the impracticable bonnet, the corset," which "disregarded...the wearer's comfort." He, then, related women's dress to that of domestic servants: Both displayed an "unnecessary expensiveness," but for wealthy women, the dress "goes farther in its elaborate insistence on the idleness, if not on the physical infirmity of the wearer." The corset, in particular, for him, made a woman incapable of useful work, while, at the same time, imposing a "mutilation" on her. Then, too, for him, from an aesthetic or good-taste perspective, the latest expensive women's style was deemed as the ultimate of beauty, only quickly, then, to be decreed as demodé; thus, canons of taste dictated to by wealth and leisure, based on waste and "futility," contrasted to the "loud" dress of working-class women.

These dress codes, for Veblen, prevented women from being "self directing" or to take part "in the affairs of the community, civil or industrial," on the pretext of avoiding the difficulties that men experience. In this respect, Veblen quoted Stanton: "All this fume and froth of emancipating woman from the slavery of man and so on is utter rot." She championed the efforts of the "New-Woman movement" to liberate women under "the double watchword, 'Emancipation and work'."[10]

Veblen's remarks on the present oppression of women under the hegemony of the leisure class were so pungent and cutting that the greatest snob of the time who reviled the stupidity of the masses, the "booboisie," H.L. Mencken, of course, frothed at the mouth. He gleefully revealed that women's wasteful expenditures were of such great proportion that men were "forced into renunciations—which brings Prof. Dr. Veblen's theory to self-destruction." Thus, "a rich man hangs his wife with expensive clothes" because "she intrigues him, that he delights in her, that he loves her and so he wants to make her gaudy and happy."[11] *Thus Spake* (the Nietzchean) *Zarathustra*! Veblen wisely did not reply, for who could best Mencken in the art of inane invective.

Other key works on women by socialists, beginning with Engels' *The Origin of the Family, Private Property and the State*, are now presented to better situate Veblen's contribution to this problem; modern socialist feminists, like Simone de Beauvoir, Shulamith Firestone, and Ann Ferguson invariably utilized this work as a basic reference.

Engels formulated that early human cultures were characterized by communist arrangements in which sexual intimacy transpired in the "primitive horde" or group marriage (indiscriminate mating), there being neither a distinct family as now known nor private property; later, however, sexual mating excluded close relatives. He also maintained that, although during the savage and early barbarian periods women were socially superior to men, with the increasing importance of hunting, men assumed the superior position. (Engels here was comparatively more accurate than Veblen.) The great reversal for women came, according to him, with the "overthrow of mother-right," with the domestication of animals and rise of war and attendant slavery, allowing men, now armed, an economic surplus from cattle and slaves. Thus it was that in marriage, women belonged to men, signifying patriarchy, the economic explanation being primary.[12] Here, Engels and Veblen agreed.

What would ultimately lead to the emancipation of women for Engels? Again, from a general socioeconomic perspective, it would be:

> When women can take part in production on a large social scale, and domestic work no longer claims anything but an insignificant amount of her time. And only now has that become possible through modern large-scale industry, which does not merely permit of the employment of female labor over a wide range, but positively demands it, while it also tends towards ending private domestic labor by changing it more and more into public industry.[13]

A landmark 20th century work on women, which deftly employed the insights of Marxian historical materialism, existentialism, and Freud, was Simone de Beauvoir's *The Second Sex*. Its aim was to understand women in the multifarious aspects of their lives, in the family, at work, in religion, myth, and literature under the impress of class society.

A socialist and existentialist, De Beauvoir affirmed that the ultimate liberation of women and of humanity would only come about with a socialist society in which men and women maintained their separate identities under a common fellowship:

> When we abolish slavery of half of humanity, together with the whole system of hypocrisy that it implies, then the 'division' of humanity will reveal its genuine significance and the human couple will find true form.[14]

In the why of women's inequality, De Beauvoir particularly accepted the insights of Engels' *The Origin of the Family*: That the Agricultural Revolution engendered an increasing economic surplus and labor division, spawning private property, war, slavery, the state, and women's subjugation. She also echoed Veblen in his distinction between "exploit" and "drudgery": "Maternity dooms woman to a sedentary existence, and so it is natural that she remain at the hearth while man hunts, goes fishing, and makes war."[15]

To the insights of Marxism, De Beauvoir added those of existentialism to the encounter. Importantly, this included the dimension of the "alterity" or the "other" between two unequal partners: Man, being physically stronger and more active than woman, dominated her as "a sexual partner, a reproducer, an exotic object—an Other through whom he seeks himself." But she asserted that with the advent of modern technology, differences in physical strength between the genders were meaningless.[16]

The recent and powerful women's liberation movement in America was greatly inspired by Betty Friedan's *The Feminine Mystique*, which cogently analyzed the calculus of women's oppression. The "feminine mystique," for her, was defined by men who employed it to keep women in a subservient position, to stay home, raise children, and be erotic objects, always to please others. Her prescription for change demanded that women actualize themselves in the larger world outside the home by becoming career oriented. Then, and only then, would they free themselves from men, in the process of which they would become more loving mothers and wives.[17]

A most important feminist-socialist critique of the 1970s by Shulamith Firestone, *The Dialectic of Sex*, insisted that socialism must be linked to feminism to achieve ultimate human liberation. She respected the work of Marx and Engels in propounding a historical materialism emphasizing the class struggle, culminating in the final one between the bourgeoisie and the proletariat. Furthermore, she devoted due recognition to Engels' *The Origin of the Family* for noting that the:

> Original division of labor was between man and woman for the purposes of childbreeding; that within the family the husband was the owner, the wife the means of production, the children the labor; and that reproduction of the human species was an important economic system distinct from the means of production.

Then, following in the footsteps of De Beauvoir's *The Second Sex*, Firestone developed the concept of "sex-class," of women themselves constituting a separate class because of their biological servitude involving the bearing and rearing of children. Her socialism included women having "full control of human fertility, including both the new technology and all the social institutions of childbearing and childrearing,"[18] in a Marcusian "cybernetic industrial state," in which "drudgery" was eventually eliminated, wages became obsolete, and work transformed into an informative and life-enhancing experience.[19]

The final socialist feminist to be examined is Ann Ferguson, a philosophy professor, whose *Sexual Democracy* again called attention to Engel's *The Origin of the Family* as a beginning reference for women's liberation. Then, presumably following Firestone, she enunciated her basic reading of present social reality under the rubric of "sex class," in which social class was expanded upon to include its female component, i.e, every social class, like working-class and lower-middle class, had a parallel female class attached to it.[20] The class alignments themselves were undergirded by the "capitalist patriarchal nuclear family" (CPNF), the basic socioeconomic and cultural unit of capitalism which subtly and otherwise exploited and oppressed women through an unequal exchange relationship of labor in the various family duties, like "domestic maintenance, children nurturance, and sexuality," which in the world of outside exchange was embedded in lower wages for women than for men.[21]

Although aware that in the past women had not been able to forge a common bond to transcend class lines, Ferguson believed that present socioeconomic and cultural trends are chipping away at the traditional CPNF, like high divorce rates, the necessity for women to work outside the home, usually at low wages, more relaxed sexual mores, and rise of state welfare systems that maintain poor women and their children. She furthermore asked for women's empowerment through progressive social legislation, like inexpensive abortion, national childcare, national health insurance, ownership of property, and the vote. In fighting for these reforms throughout the world, she claims that women, now the lower part of the workingclass in industrialized nations, will necessarily opt for socialism.[22] Capitalism itself, for Ferguson, objectively exploited working-class women because it required an inexpensive work force and reserve army of unemployed, including minority and increasingly white men.[23]

The formulations of Firestone and Ferguson on "sex-class," are not novel, anticipated by Veblen who also viewed each class as composed of a male and female part, each representing its own particular social psychology and concomitant codes of dress, work, and behavior, influenced by the power relations at whose apex is the dominant leisure class. But Veblen's formulations on gender did not ultimately separate sex and class as did those of Firestone and Ferguson. In the final analysis, Veblen, along with Marx/Engels and other mainstream socialists, had class overriding gender, insisting that males and females of the same class had more in common than with those of other classes.

In this vein, I agree with Teresa L. Ebert, a feminist and socialist, who maintained "the priority of production and class struggle in the emancipation of women and reaffirmed the solidarity of humanity on the basis of shared needs."[24] This view does not deny the assertions of Veblen and other socialists of the double oppression borne by women, that of sex and class, but posits that human liberation is the task of both working-class men and women, with other allies, to effect socialism that by definition would end the age-old divisions between the sexes. In this progression, any advance to ameliorate the position of women with respect to men is a step toward socialism. (Nevertheless, socialists should pay close attention to feminist socialists who are aware of the sexism in the New Left and of the undisputed fact that Marx and many other socialists, did not sufficiently stress the importance of overcoming divisions between men and women in attaining socialism, but, as observed, Engels is a pioneer in women's liberation.)

The socialist-feminists just discussed (they integrated gender oppression within the larger horizon of the class/caste one) have played an important role, along with the radical feminists, who stressed the primacy of women's oppression in the social diagram, like Germain Greer's *The Female Eunuch*, for instance, in women's liberation, a profoundly broad and pervasive movement to free women which began in the mid-1960s, part and parcel of the broader New Left assault on capitalism in the United States and elsewhere.

Through a bevy of organizations, like The National Organization of Women (it has many hundreds of local chapters), Nine to Five, and Emily's List, women have won important victories, as in the Title IX of the Education Amendments of 1972, which decreed that women have equality with men in educational programs, affirmative action legislation for work, rape-shield legislation empowering women to seek justice in the courts against male violence in incest, rape, batterment, and sexual harassment, public funding for children's daycare and women's shelters, and securing abortion, which the 1972 Supreme Court decision *Roe V. Wade* legalized.

The theoretical views and events just discussed should be viewed in the light of these recent American statistics: Women, in 2000 make up almost half of the market workforce, including 72 percent of married women, two principal factors contributing to this: The drop in real wages among most men since 1973 has literally forced more women into the paid work force, as has their desire for more or full independence from men. But women's earnings today are still about three-fourths of men's, despite the fact that their real earnings have actually risen in the past twenty years. To these developments and conditions, add the sexual revolution in the 1960s, with its more permissive attitudes toward premarital and casual sex, itself signifying women's greater equality. These elements, in turn, have increased divorce rates, doubling in the industrialized nations from 1970 to 1995. In 1995, for instance, the divorce rate in the United States is 54.8 out of 100 marriages; in Sweden, 41.8; England/Wales, 41.7; Canada, 38.3; and France, 31.5.

Social class intersects with sexual revolution, women's greater autonomy, and economic downturn to savage the working-class in higher rates of fatherless children, 22 percent of white and 68 percent of black children at birth, largely from the lower part of the workingclass. A half of black, a quarter of Hispanic, and a sixth of white families are headed by women, half poor, thus the "feminization of poverty."

This growing fatherless family poverty is related to existential problems, especially faced by poor female teenagers whose families cannot provide them with sufficient support. Many come from abusive homes with male predators or live in the streets seeking the protection of older males simply to survive, who usually get them pregnant and then abandon them. Tragically, their only traditional hope and purpose in life or for a tolerable socioeconomic survival is to have children and a mate.

From a socioeconomic perspective, most women are in the lower part of the occupational structure. It is a truism that in women's occupations, like clerical work, nursing, and primary and secondary education, earnings are lower than men's in industrial work, transportation, engineering, law, business management, and medicine. But this economic disparity is exacerbated by divorce (a year after divorce, men's standard of living goes up by 10 percent, women's down by 27 percent). Married women often usually have a non-career track of low-wage, part-time or full-time work to supplement their husband's income, usually the principal one for the family.

If work is measured by the new concept of "comparable worth," which holds that wages should approximate the intrinsic worth of a job, utilizing criteria like education and skill requirements, many low-paid clerical jobs invariably held by women should pay as much, if not more, for instance, than factory and building-trades work in which men predominate. Most men oppose this concept for it would impinge on their earnings and power.

The workplace itself has been hellish for women, about half reporting losing jobs by being peremptorily discharged or leaving of their own volition, because of sexual harassment. In 1995, for instance, the Equal Employment Opportunity Commission (EEOC), a watchdog for affirmative action, was besieged by more than fifteen thousand complaints from women charging sexual harassment at work, twice the number filed in 1991. In 1996, in a well-known case, EEOC charged Mitsubishi Motor Manufacturing of America for allowing egregious sexual harassment of two-thirds of its nine hundred women work force in its Normal, Illinois plant. Then, too, widespread sexual abuse in the military is now in the news. Women's socioeconomic inferiority continues into old age, their retirement income being generally insufficient, only three-fifths that of men, forcing many to work until they die.

To be sure, middle-class women are making economic gains: Of recent college-degree recipients, women comprise two-fifths of those in law and a third in medicine—now half the students in medical school—as well as more than half the BAs and MAs. Furthermore, women hold 40 percent of executive/administrative positions in the top five hundred corporations, although only 2 percent of top management and less than 5 percent on boards of directors.[25]

NOTES

1. On women in primitive societies, the Neolithic Age, and in civilization, see the general picture in Marvin Harris, *Culture, People, Nature: An Introduction to General Anthropology*, (New York: Harper & Row, 1988), Chapter 20. Also, see Barbara Watterson, *Women in Ancient Egypt* (New York: St. Martin's Press, 1991). Sarah B. Pomeroy, *Goddesses, Whores, Wives, and Slaves: Women in Classical Antiquity* (New York: Schocken Books, 1975), pp. 57-119 on Athenian women; pp. 149-226 on Roman women; p. 189 on the quotation. For modern women, see, for instance, Donald Meyer, *The Rise of Women in America, Russia, Sweden, and Italy* (Middletown, CT: Wesleyan University Press, 1987). Almost any college textbook on general history now covers the role of women in society.

2. Mary Wollstonecraft, *A Vindication of the Rights of Woman* (London: Source Books Press, 1971), pp. 173-84 on the malevolent influences of private property and class society on women; on "legal prostitution"; and, on women leading active productive lives; p. 206 on the battle between men and women.

3. John Stuart Mill, *Subjection of Women*, Introduction Robert Carr (Cambridge, MA: MIT Press, 1972), pp. 13-14. Written in 1861 and first published in 1869.

4. *Ibid.*, pp. 16-18 ff. and p. 80.

5. *Ibid.*, p. 100.

6. *Ibid.*, p. xxiv. Bertrand Russell, *Autobiography, 1872-1914*, 3 vols. (Boston: Little, Brown, 1967-69), I, 233.

7. On socialism and feminism, see Meyer, *Rise of Women*, pp. 83-90. Ellen Carol DuBois, "Woman Suffrage and the Left: An International Socialist-Feminist Perspective," *New Left Review*, No. 186, March/April, 1991, pp. 20-45.

8. Ann Ferguson, *Sexual Democracy; Women, Oppression, and Revolution* (Boulder, CO: Westview Press, 1991), p. 191 on the quotation covering Soviet law. Meyer, *Rise of Women*, pp. 206-37 on Soviet women. Veblen, *Leisure Class*, pp. 23-24, 52-54, 68-72, 106-08, 118-28, and 229-34. Harris, *Culture, People, Nature*, Chapter 20.

9. Veblen, *Leisure Class*, p. 34. Claude Levi-Strauss, *Structural Anthropology*, translated by Claire Jacobson and Brook Grundfest Schoepf (Harmondsworth, England: Penguin Books, 1972), p. 47. Harris, *Culture, People, Nature*, p. 432.

10. Veblen, *Leisure Class*, pp. 106-31; Stanton's quotation is on p. 230.

11. H. L. Mencken, *Prejudices: First Series* (New York: Alfred A. Knopf, 1919), p. 74.

12. Frederick Engels, *The Origin of the Family, Private Property, and the State* (New York: International Publishers, 1942), pp. 31-32, 50, 147-48 ff. The anthropology of Marx and Engels was deeply influenced by the American anthropologist Lewis Morgan. Not all of Morgan's and Engels' views on primitive society are correct—there are many variations in primitive societies concerning gender relations—but it is incontrovertible that once civilization begins, with the possible exception of the Minoans, women are almost always subordinate to men.

13. *Ibid.*, p. 147.

14. Simone de Beauvoir, *The Second Sex*, translated and edited, H.M. Parshley (New York: Vintage Books, 1974), p. 814.

15. *Ibid.*, pp. 58-66, and 77.

16. *Ibid.*, pp. 35-36, and 66.

17. Betty Friedan, *The Feminine Mystique* (New York: Dell Publishing, 1963), pp. 73-94.

18. Shulamith Firestone, *The Dialectic of Sex* (New York: Morrow Quill Paperbacks, 1970), pp. 5-11.

19. *Ibid.*, p. 266.

20. Ferguson, *Sexual Democracy*, pp. 167-69 and 194.

21. *Ibid.*, pp. 42-46.

22. *Ibid.*, p. 163.

23. *Ibid.*, pp. 164 ff.

24. Terry Anderson, *The Movement and the Sixties* (New York: Oxford University Press, 1995), pp. 312-17 on male sexism among the left. Roger S. Gottlieb, *History and Subjectivity: The Transformation of Marxist Theory* (Atlantic Highlands, NJ: Humanities Press, 1993), Chapter 9, "Socialist-Feminism," asserted that Marxists did not sufficiently stress the women's question. Teresa L. Ebert, "Toward a Red Feminism," *Against the Current*, Nov./Dec., 1996, p. 27.

25. On statistics and events discussed, the local/daily press and mass weeklies are good sources. See, for instance, *Cleveland Plain Dealer*, Nov. 14, 1991, pp. A1 and A6. *Akron Beacon Journal*, Aug. 27, 1991, p. D6; June 2, 1993, p. A9; May 17, 1996, p. A5. *U.S. News and World Report*, June 12, 1995, p. 10. *Newsweek*, May 20, 1995, p. 44.

XIII   Imperialism

THAT IMPERIALISM, "THE POLICY OF EXTENDING a nation's authority by territorial acquisitions or by the establishment of economic and political hegemony over other nations,"[1] is of major importance in history is to state the obvious. Empire building has been
associated with such "great" men of history as Alexander the Great, Julius Caesar, Peter
the Great, Frederick the Great, Napoleon Bonaparte, and Adolf Hitler. Imperialism itself,
as Veblen pointed out, was not only synonymous with war and oppression, but also with
patriotism and martial glory, deleteriously influencing social totality, including religion.[2]

Imperialism itself is so deeply ensconced in the human condition that it is an integral part of its religious systems. In the Judeo-Christian-Islamic tradition, for instance,
crusades against unbelievers are common. In the *Old Testament*, Yahweh, originally a
war god, ordered the Hebrews to extirpate their enemies without mercy, as of King
Sihon and his subjects, "including the women and babies."[3] Christianity and Islam have
followed in this tradition, with the crusade and *jihad* respectively, victory or defeat being
dependent on either God's favor or disfavor. Not surprisingly, religion, usually interwoven with nationalism, is still a significant force in current warfare (including guerrilla activity), between Hindu India and Moslem Pakistan, the Judaism of Israel and Islam of
the Arab states, Islamic Al Qaeda and the Christian West, and Catholics and Protestants
in Northern Ireland. Furthermore, there is the longstanding Christian animus against
Jews, resulting in almost innumerable slaughters and deportations in the last thousand
years, climaxed by the Holocaust perpetrated by Nazi Germany during World War II.[4]

In the founding Western civilization, the Greek, its prototypical *Iliad* well portrayed the mindset of an imperialist society, in which an insult to one of the leisure class
(the abduction of Helen, wife of King Menelaus of Sparta, by the Trojan prince Paris)

was sufficient cause (an excuse) for war. As Simone Weil, asserted in the "The *Iliad*: Poem of Might," "the true hero of the *Iliad* is might," a force "which makes a thing of anybody who comes under its sway," including not only those whom it killed or subjugated, but the conquerors themselves whose hierarchy of power further subordinated underlings to superiors. Furthermore, imperialism, for her, being inimical to human solidarity and balance, led the Greek aggressors to no less an object in mind than "all the riches of Troy, all the palaces, the temples and the houses as ashes, all the women and children as slaves, all the men as corpses."[5]

In Thucydides' *The Peloponnesian War*, Greek civilization was torn asunder by the rival imperialisms of Athens and Sparta, in which treachery and massacre were the norms in a world deifying force. A leading Athenian unflinchingly told his fellow citizens that:

> You should remember that your empire is a despotism exercised over unwilling subjects, who are always conspiring against you; they do not obey in return for any kindness which you do them...but in so far as you are their masters; they have no love of you, but they are held down by force.[6]

And, we should not neglect the importance of imperialism in Roman civilization that unified the various and discrete groups of Europe to bring about what is a distinctive Western Civilization. Often forgotten was that this accomplishment rested on brutal conquest with resultant widespread slavery.

In the last five hundred years, imperialism has been an indivisible part of capitalism. Its early variety was in the Commercial Revolution, from the 15th to the 18th centuries, when the state was under the basic control of a king-and-nobility complex, with capitalist commoners often playing a secondary role in Spain, Portugal and France. But in England and the Netherlands, capitalist entrepreneurs (the great ones being member of the nobility in England) were clearly in the ascendancy by the 17th century. With the rise of the Industrial Revolution in the 18th century and rise of finance capitalism and international cartels in the 20th, capitalism continued its earlier imperialism under new forms.

It was during the Commercial Revolution that most of the original inhabitants of the Americas were either worked to death in the silver and gold mines and plantations or slaughtered in revolts or died from disease brought by the Europeans, necessitating slavery. (On Native American populations decimated by the Spanish conquest: The island of Hispaniola, with a quarter million people in 1492, 500 in the 1540s; the Aztec-dominated areas, with 10 million in 1530, 1 million in 1600; the Inca-dominated areas, from 9 to 14 million in the 1530s, half a million in the 1630s.) The resultant labor shortage brought African slaves to America for the Portuguese, Spanish, Dutch, English, and French entrepreneurs to farm the first great international money crop, sugar—later, cotton; from 10 million for Philip Curtin, to 7 million for Ferdnand Braudel, to 50 million for Basil Davidson between 1500 and 1800.

The many centuries of African slavery in the West, including what is to become the United States, was the seedbed of modern racism. In this light, many of the prominent thinkers of liberalism either accepted slavery or owned slaves, although acknowledging it as immoral like Locke and Jefferson. But Smith opposed empire (and by extension, slavery), with its concomitant economic theory of mercantilism stressing the importance of colonies for wealth, affirming that free trade was less costly and more efficient than empire and interminable wars in creating wealth.[7]

But even before written history or civilization, war was not unknown. There is an argument between anthropologists as to the prevalence of war before the Neolithic/Mesolithic Ages or 10,000 years ago. According to Lawrence H. Keeley (*War Before Civilization*), there was ample evidence that even before this time, primitive societies often engaged in fighting, as in the Upper and Late Paleolithic Age, in what was Czechoslovakia as early as 24,000 to 35,000 years ago and in Gebel Sahaba in Egypt from 12,000 to 14,000 years ago. To be sure, Keeley, who attributed these early wars or skirmishes to economic reasons, like control of land areas to furnish food, opposed the views of mainstream liberal and socialist anthropologists, like Montagu and Marvin Harris, who affirmed that war basically occurred after the Mesolithic/Neolithic Age or after 10,000 years ago over property and its extensions, but not too frequently before, and that it was only with the advent of near-civilization and civilization that war and its train of enslavement and exploitation became norms of the human condition. All three assigned various levels of socioeconomic complexity for organized war, Keely allowing small groups to be more warlike than Montagu and Harris.[8]

Imperialism was a major concern for Veblen, as in *Imperial Germany and the Industrial Revolution* (1915) and *An Inquiry into the Nature of Peace and the Terms of Its Perpetuation* (1917), articles—"An Early Experiment in Trusts" (1904) and "Outline of a Policy for the Control of the 'Economic Penetration' Of Backward Countries and of Foreign Investments" (1917)—and a review of J.A. Hobsons' *Imperialism*.

In *An Inquiry into the Nature of Peace*, Veblen traced the genesis of imperialism to the New Stone Age when humanity reached the necessary technological level to ensure the survival of relatively large organized groups with a sufficient economic surplus to allow for "individual ambitions and gains." This presupposed, for him, some pre-existing unequal socioeconomic relationships inviting "invidious distinction," exacerbated by the advent of civilization, when social inequality became pervasive and steep.[9]

Veblen's early interest in the intricacies of modern imperialism was cogently revealed in a sympathetic review of Hobson's *Imperialism: A Study* (1902) in the March 1903 issue of the *Journal of Political Economy*. On the whole, Veblen agreed with Hobson that the tap roots of the new imperialism (that of the late 19th century when the great European powers carved out for themselves most of Africa) were associated with capital's drive to find outlets for new investments. But he disputed Hobson's thesis that the underconsumption of goods by workers forced capital to seek profit elsewhere, holding that since capitalists must form combinations, like Trusts, to prevent a ruinous competition over the price of goods, overproduction was squelched in the market sense. He, then, heartily applauded Hobson's characterizing imperialism as a "social pathology" that favored particular "business interests," as well as furnishing careers for the "military, clerical, academic, and civil-service circles" that economically drained their nations with higher taxes. He also endorsed Hobson's attacking the imperialist mindset for being antithetical to "popular government," and to "liberty and equality," and that the "Darwinian-jingo" justification of the "higher" white groups in conquering their non-white "inferiors" was based on a specious racism promoted by a crass economism and malevolent patriotic propaganda. The review finished on a pessimistic note, recognizing that since "the motive force of imperialism is a militant sentimentality guided by the business interests of a small class," there could be no "appeal to the common-sense of the community," for it was impossible under present circumstances to "gain a wide hearing."[10]

Soon after, in 1904, Veblen published the succinct but cogent "An Early Experiment in Trusts," a well-delineated exposition of an early Viking business organization in the 10th century, very much patterned on the model of the modern Trust to control output of production and better maximize profits by eliminating competition.

The Viking "trust" in the Baltic Sea area was not the product of spontaneous development. At first the Vikings simply engaged in "piracy" and the "slave trade," aided by technological factors and ample labor reserves, like better methods of "shipbuilding, navigation, and the manufacture of weapons," and excess "freehold farmers."

As early as the 6th century, there were loosely-knit Viking business combinations that already partly controlled local business traffic, which by the 9th century led to more economic cooperation among them. By the 10th century, under the enterprising robber-merchant, Palnatoki, the Vikings, now having more than six hundred ships, established a "trust." It was drawn into the dynastic politics of the area, the leading actor in the "Danish conquest of England," but disintegrated when attempting to incorporate Norway with Denmark.

This account admirably illustrated how in the course of trade, Viking business evolved from small- to large-scale operations, inevitably becoming entangled with dynastic machinations, including imperialistic ambition, the fusion of economics with politics being deftly explored.[11]

The most extensive critique of imperialism by Veblen was *Imperial Germany and the Industrial Revolution*, which delineated the principal elements of a German imperialism leading to World War I, blaming it more so for this than others. He located this pathology in uneven economic development: Prussian dynastic/Junker aggressive militarism, relying on the new power unleashed by rapid industrialization after 1871, competed with British and French imperialism, all dominating the pacific proletariat represented by socialism, unable to prevent their rulers from launching war.[12]

Preparation for war itself, for Veblen, dictated German economic autarky, "a self-contained industrial community," that, although less economically efficient than the more accepted free-trade model, enhanced war potential. (Short-term economic sacrifice would lead to long-term economic gain through conquest.) His description of this nexus between the military and industry is today called the "military-industrial complex," its ultimate aim being nothing less than economic, military, political supremacy.[13]

Perceptively, Veblen also related imperialism to the power of the rulers over their subjects. Successful war, for instance, reinforced. an "enthusiastic subservience and unquestioning obedience to authority."[14] Indeed, he anticipated George Orwell's *1984* in stating: "What is military organization in war is a servile organization in peace,"[15] tracing this slavishness to the Junkers' strategy of inculcating the masses, beginning with early formal education, with such sentiments as "romantic loyalty" and a "militant patriotism,"[16] based on "solidarity of prowess," to ensure Germany's "place in the sun."[17]

It was in this volume that Veblen observed two diametrically opposing social forces in the years just before World War I: On the one hand, a war-prone leisure class representing oppressive institutions;[18] on the other, the masses, workers and farmers, who, despite their "flunkeyism," were now subjected to the new industrial patterns fostered by "machine technology" and its "mechanistic conception" of social reality making socialist ideals possible, who might opt for revolution and return to primeval archetypes featuring equality and "free and popular institutions."[19]

In *An Inquiry into the Nature of Peace* (1917), Veblen continued the socialist themes so prominent in *Imperial Germany*: Along with Hobson and the influential work by Lenin, *Imperialism: The Highest Stage of Capitalism* (1917), he situated modern imperialism in the context of a dynamic and aggressive capitalism. (Veblen and Lenin were left-wing socialists, while Hobson, a liberal socialist, would nationalize only selected industries.) But he analyzed imperialism somewhat differently than Hobson and Lenin, placing less emphasis on underconsumption, that workers' wages inevitably lagged behind output, thus allowing for an excess of goods and profits to spill into foreign trade and investment, encouraging imperialism. But along with Hobson and Lenin, he envisaged imperialism as being largely driven by an economic nationalism under the ruling groups already described. The three also agreed that, although imperialism furthered the careers and interests of selected ruling groups and institutions, including business, and military, in the national ledger of profit and loss, military and administrative expenses often exceeded any profit.[20]

In this work, Veblen divided the leading imperialist nations into four categories: The very aggressive, new to a world-scale imperialism, Germany and Japan; the defensive, that would fight if provoked, France, Great Britain, and perhaps the United States; the followers of more industrialized and stronger allies, like Austria-Hungary; and the deficient in dynamic industrialization, like Russia—the last two doubtful aggressors.[21] Furthermore, he did not see any basic differences between the imperialism of authoritarian monarchies and democracies, but admitted that in the former nations it was much more difficult for anti-imperialist forces to dissent than in the latter.[22]

Again, Veblen deftly traced the connection between a jingoistic nationalism and imperialism, decrying the persistence of "patriotism," described as "a sense of partisan solidarity in respect of prestige," and "a spirit of particularism, of aliency and animosity between contrasted groups of persons."[23]

Prophetically, Veblen viewed Germany and Japan as the two likeliest nations to precipitate the next great war, or World War II,[24] which only the rise of socialism could prevent:

> The peoples of the quondam Imperial nations must come into the league
> [League of Nations] on a footing of formal equality with the rest. This they
> can not do without the virtual abdication of their dynastic government estab-
> lishments and a consequent shift to a democratic form of organization.[25]

Or, nothing less than the destruction of monarchy, the military, and large private capital formations through the abolition of "property" and the "price system" to come from a socialist revolution stemming from a "cleavage between those who own [property] and those who do not," would ensure peace[26]

War, itself, for Veblen, was inimical to the realization of socialism because it invariably reinforced a feudalistic and capitalistic mindset, based on "suspicion, duplicity, and ill will," whose antithesis, associated with modern technology and its "matter of fact" view prevailing over personal and class domination, was socialism.[27]

In his "Outline of a Policy," Veblen again related "commercial enterprise" with "national ambitions," specifically linking "economic penetration" to "investment in foreign parts"; to obviate it, he called for—tongue-in-cheek—nations not to back their investors in foreign ventures. Furthermore:

> Investment is made in the foreign country to get a higher rate of profits than at home; which draws a part of the available means of industry out of the country, or keeps up the rate on home investments, by keeping the productiveness of the country's industry down; which enhances or keeps up prices, and the cost of living.

These conditions, for him, only benefited the "interested business concern," involved in foreign investment, with any corresponding cash flow going to the coffers of the "well-to-do," employing it for more conspicuous consumption, which necessarily "limits the production of goods to meet the ordinary needs of the community."[28]

Veblen's general approval of Hobson's *Imperialism* and his support of the Bolshevik Revolution leads to examining Lenin's primary work on modern imperialism, *Imperialism: The Highest State of Capitalism*. For Lenin, large capital or monopoly was now inextricably intertwined with big-power rivalry and war:

> Imperialism is capitalism in that stage of development in which the dominance of monopolies and finance capital has established itself; in which the export of capital has acquired pronounced importance; in which the division of the world among the international trusts has begun; in which the division of all territories of the globe among the great capitalist powers has been completed.[29]

Furthermore, economic and political penetration went together. In this progression, Lenin, following Hobson and Rudolf Hilferding in *Finance Capital* (1910), argued that capital from the advanced capitalist nations, like Great Britain, France, the United States, and Germany, was inexorably drawn into their colonies and other less-developed areas by higher profits through inexpensive labor as well as abundant and cheap raw materials.[30]

This thesis was disputed by William L. Langer, a well-known American historian, who argued that much more capital was invested by the leading capitalist nations among themselves than their colonies and other underdeveloped areas in the early 20th century.[31] This, of course, was true then and now. But he failed to point out that capital invested in underdeveloped areas contributed to their economic malformation as they were usually condemned to be either producers of raw materials or agricultural products, or low-wage platforms of selected manufacturing goods, resulting in their being more subject to price fluctuations and economic downturns than their economic overlords. Moreover, he did not include the injurious economic role of their comprador elites whose economic and political interests intermeshed with foreign imperialists. Thus there was the seeming anomaly of large foreign debts incurred by poor nations to rich nations, while their elites deprived them of scarce capital by investing large sums of money in the advanced nations for safekeeping. Exceptions to this in the late 20th century were Taiwan and South Korea that became industrial powers with American aid in its fight against Communism, which incidentally also forced reforms, in agriculture, like breaking up large landed estates, and China with its strong government/mercantilism.

A continuing debate among socialists is whether capitalism and war are synonymous. For Hilferding in *Finance Capital* and Kautsky in his theory of "ultra-imperialism" in 1914, economic rationalization through oligopoly/monopoly and international cartels, despite decline of free trade, allowed the possibility for more international capitalist cooperation. But Hilferding, for instance, was acutely aware that peace had to contend with powerful imperialist/militarist forces in the leading nations equated with an anti-humanistic authoritarianism, infinitely stronger than liberal-capitalist democratic elements.[32]

Even more certain than Hilferding and Kautsky that capitalism led to war was Lenin who believed that the totality of national capitals overrode those of its international variety. His *Imperialism* unerringly predicted World War II, basically begun by the imperialism of the Axis powers. But he himself could also approvingly quote from Hobson of an "European Federation" under a capitalist elite dominating "tame masses." His account of imperialism was largely analogous to Veblen's in focusing on the ever-growing concentration of finance capital over the industrial variety, some of whose profits went to underdeveloped areas.[33]

George Lichtheim, a distinguished 20th century scholar of socialism, in *Imperialism*, also agreed with Veblen's fusion of nationalism and imperialism, asserting that "nationalism transformed itself into imperialism wherever the opportunity offered," and that the chief proponent of Western imperialism was the chauvinistic bourgeois press. Like Veblen, he also associated war and militarism with the traditional "more primitive, aggressive, and warlike impulses" that inhabited the "frontiers" of the West. The social groups anxious to fight consisted of the "landed gentry" and the "rural population" generally, while the basically pacific groups were "middle-class burghers and industrial workers." His "landed gentry" might be construed as having the traditional penchant of the leisure class for war, and his farmers or the "rural population" as still under the traditional mindset of the Barbarian periods. As for his middle class and workers, their pacifism might be linked to Veblen's emphasizing the matter-of-factness of the new machine technology. Although Lichtheim then claimed that the German bourgeoisie developed, along with a sizeable segment of the German working-class, a strong martial nature. (The most avid supporters of Nazism were the nobility—Junkers and their Nationalist Party—big business, and its lower-middle-class base. Most of the workers voted for the socialists and communists.) Finally, he agreed with Lenin's *Imperialism* that the world was divided "among the great international trusts."[34]

A pertinent question is whether wars spawned by 20th century imperialism have aided or hindered socialism? From a broad perspective, insofar as war machines buttressed the existent social and other relations in any society—in this following Veblen—they were inimical to socialism. But since modern war was especially injurious to the institutions of economically backward nations under assault, like China and Russia, in conjunction with the class struggle, it aided in bringing about their deformed socialism.

War itself certainly accelerated the march of technology, industrialization and invention, and even in a supposedly more pacific Great Britain, its iron and steel and other industries benefited from government contracts.[35]

In a manner often closely following Veblen and other socialists were the views in *Imperialism and Social Classes* of Joseph Schumpeter, a well-known Austrian-American economist and social commentator, who claimed that the rising capitalist class grafted itself upon the older warlike dynastic/feudalistic power structure, thus making it a bearer of a capitalist imperialism:

> Nationalism and militarism, while not creatures of capitalism, become "capitalized" and in the end draw their best energies from capitalism. Capitalism involves them in its workings and thereby keeps them alive, politically as well as economically.

As for the forces that opposed nationalistic imperialism, Schumpeter believed that they revolved around socialism:

> Socialists…exclude nationalism from their general ideology, because of the essential interests of the proletariat, and by virtue of their domestic opposition to the conservative stalking force.[36]

Veblen and Marx also shared many common views on imperialism, especially linking it in the modern period to the drive of capital to find ever more new investments and new markets. Veblen and Marx did not basically subscribe to the under-consumption theory which held that imperialism was mainly propelled because workers in the advanced capitalist nations received lower-than-normal wages, resulting in excess productive capacity at home, one remedy being to seek economic opportunities through imperialism. On the contrary, for them, capitalism sought normally to expand whenever the opportunity presented itself.

Marx's view of imperialism was also certainly aware of capital movements among nations, like English investments in the United States, particularly in railroads, after the mid-19th century. But what Marx focused on was the role of Western merchant capitalistic imperialism in the making of Western capitalism over many centuries, one of a predatory nature, ruthlessly extracting surplus-value from the inhabitants of their colonies and other places through slavery and peonage, then transformed into industrial and banking capital. Thus, it was, for him, that "commercial supremacy" brought about "industrial dominance," which, in turn, led to further "commercial supremacy." This pattern, holding that Western industrialization and economic supremacy was first made possible by exploiting the periphery, was not developed by Veblen, but continued by 20th century Marxists, like Ernest Mandel in *Marxist Economic Theory*.[37]

Parenthetically, Max Weber, the prominent German sociologist and contemporary of Veblen, in examining imperialism, emphasized its association with the exploitation of land and labor, with its being favored by big industry, related to the military machine and elite groups hungering after prestige and honor, Veblenian themes. He, then, insisted that imperialism's most resolute opponents were workers, except for those directly employed in war industry.[38]

Veblen's thesis that war/imperialism was a constant factor in human affairs, one now dominated by capitalism, and that only a socialist world could abolish exploitative relationships, was reiterated later by various Marxist scholars, like Harry Magdaff and John Bellamy Foster, who held that advanced capitalist nations not only economically, and, thus, politically, dominated poorer nations, but also economically competed among themselves to penetrate each other's markets. Furthermore, Foster was especially cognizant of widespread leisure-class conspicuous consumption.[39]

In the 20th century, imperialist rivalry and war became not only the greatest of all destroyers, but poisoned the domestic politics of nations in the guise of military-industrial complexes that consumed enormous amounts of resources. Since World War II, for instance, American military spending alone has hovered from 3 to 15 percent of the GDP. By the late 1980s, annual world military expenditures in billions of dollars amounted to 900. In 1998, military spending among the major powers in billions of dollars was: United States, 266 (380 in 2003); Russia, 54; Great Britain, 37; France, 40; Japan, 37; Germany, 32; and China, 37. With the end of the Cold War, it lessened to under 800 billion dollars in 2000, but has since risen.

Half of the federal budget today, including interest payments from past wars and veterans' benefits, is eaten up by the military. Total American military expenditures since the Second World War easily exceed 20 trillion dollars, 4 trillion dollars alone for developing nuclear weapons. More particularly, annual American military and related intelligence costs are still prodigiously high: The military budget in 2005 is 400 billion dollars, with clandestine and other military operations and intelligence gathering by the National Security Agency (NSA) and Central Intelligence Agency (CIA) adding another 26 billion dollars.

Despite the demise of the Soviet Union, an American presence throughout the world, annually still requires 90 billion dollars to "defend" Europe, and twelve aircraft groups, at 2 billion dollars each to operate. The military-industrial complex still employs 5 or so percent of full-time workers, including 1.4 million military personnel, many highly skilled, its corporations and workers forming a powerful political special-interest bloc.

In 2001, American military spending is increasing, spending for weapons to go up 50 percent in the next five years. Annually, federal research and development grants and subsidies to arms manufacturers are near 8 billion dollars, second only to agriculture, with another 3 billion dollars for military assistance to friendly foreign governments, and 7 billion dollars in arms sales. In 2001, President Bush is contemplating a 120 billion dollar "Star Wars" program, adding to the 70 billion dollars already spent.

Rival imperialisms and civil wars in the 20th century killed about 150 million civilians and military personnel! In the two major wars alone, World Wars I and II, about 13 million and 75 million respectively were killed, half in the latter being civilians (the wounded at least double those killed), including the Nazi racist imperialist systematic murder of Jews and Gypsies let alone Russians and others, in the many millions—the Holocaust. Since World War II, the epidemic of war and its train of oppression has continued, as anyone who reads the daily press can attest.

As for the material costs of 20th-century war, with all of their ramifications, they should easily be in the hundred-trillion-dollar range. The perils of war today also involve thermonuclear destruction that has receded with the end of the Cold War. This may only be a brief interlude, as the underlying causes making for war, classism and imperialism, still exist.[40]

With the end of World War II, two nations emerged as the world's superpowers, the United States and the Soviet Union, engendering a normal rivalry between their governments and their conflicting class ideologies, of a still messianic Communism, which subsided over time, opposed by capitalism and social democracy.

The respective imperialism of the United States and the Soviet Union reflected the aims of their governments and balance of class forces within them; the former, a conservative representative democracy led by a wealthy corporate elite and newly emerging military (the military-industrial complex), the latter, an authoritarian Communism run by a small anti-democratic and anti-civil libertarian elite.

Thus it was that American foreign policy was related to preserving not only American hegemony in the world, but also the expansion of capitalism. A cornerstone of this policy, stated in an unapologetic manner by George F. Kennan (diplomatic historian, ambassador to the Soviet Union, and key advisor to the State Department), was that a rich America would protect its power and privilege with alliances not based on the "luxury of altruism and world-benefaction," or "unreal objectives such as human rights, the raising of living standards, and democratization."[41]

To be sure, this view would allow the United States to support conservatives and at times even social democrats in a democratic Western Europe through the Marshall Plan and its military might to stop Soviet advances there. But in its dealings with poor/underdeveloped nations with rigid class structures, as in Latin America, United States foreign policy unequivocally allied itself with reactionary bourgeois and military elements, eschewing any pretense of democracy.

From a national/class perspective this was a rational foreign policy for objectively Soviet Communism, even much more so than an economically marginal Communist China, was the principal enemy of American capitalism: Soviet hegemony meant the demise of the upper bourgeoisie as its large property would be expropriated by the state. This thesis follows the one of William Appleman Williams, a noted American diplomatic historian, who held that the main contours of American foreign policy fashioned by its capitalist elite were in its early history based on territorial expansion and later on opening the world to American trade and investment.[42]

A brief background on American imperialism before World War II is necessary before observing it afterward to indicate its continuity. From its earliest history, the United States has been an expansionist nation: As an extension of a modern and aggressive Western European capitalism, it subjugated Native Americans, easily defeated Mexico, abolished slavery in the Civil War, and by the end of the 19th century was a world power thanks to its pre-eminent industrial strength, great natural resources, and large population. These ingredients allowed it to expand overseas with the advent of the Spanish-American War in 1898, annexing the Philippines, Puerto Rico, and imposing a protectorate on Cuba.

It was during this period that the views of Admiral Alfred Thayer came into vogue, who in *The Influence of Sea Power upon History*, and other works, saw that the future greatness of a large-island America rested on sea power to protect its commerce and colonies providing it with markets and raw materials. This manifested itself in the early 20th century particularly in the Caribbean and Central America, as three "progressive" Presidents, Theodore Roosevelt, William Howard Taft, and Woodrow Wilson, sent American troops there repeatedly to protect American power/investments.

In World War I, United States entry permitted Great Britain, France, and Italy to defeat Germany, Austria-Hungary, and Turkey, and to preserve the safety of American loans to the Allies. In World War II, again, with the Soviet Union and Great Britain, the United States was instrumental in defeating the Axis powers (Germany, Japan, and Italy), becoming a superpower.

Several examples of American intervention in the internal affairs of other nations will be given to indicate its general nature, before concentrating on its involvement in Vietnam and Latin America, where it is most apparent: The United States intervened massively to support the reactionary Kuomindang regime in China representing the landowners and comprador capitalists in their fight against Chinese Communism in the 1945-49 period. In Europe, it provided the Greek right, ensconced in the upper bourgeoisie and military, the necessary economic and military assistance to defeat the Greek left, heavily Communist in the 1947-49 civil war. In 1953, in Iran, the CIA was instrumental in aiding its generals to stage a coup d'état against the legitimate government of Mohammed Mossadegh when it nationalized the Anglo-Iranian Oil Company. In 1953, the CIA was an accomplice in the assassination of Patrice Lumumba, the first premier of the liberated Congo. In 1965, when President Achmed Sukarno of Indonesia veered leftward (he probably supported the Indonesian Communist Party's unsuccessful attempt to rid the army of conservative generals), General T.N.J. Suharto, with the aid of the CIA, killed hundreds of thousands of Communists, and soon afterward became president.

The most dramatic example of American imperialism after World War II was in Vietnam. The fall of Vietnam—the "domino theory"—might have led to that of the surrounding states, including Indonesia to Communism, a false premise. Vietnam, part of the French colonial system before World War II, was under Japanese rule during the conflict. After the war, the Vietnamese wished to free themselves, but the French refused to leave and, with massive American economic assistance, remained until defeated at Diem Bien Phu in 1954 by the Vietnamese Communists led by Ho Chi Minh.

The United States, then intervened militarily to prevent Communist annexation of South Vietnam through elections. Its basic thrust was to prop up a small ruling class, the mandarins, who owned half the land, and a middle class in the urban areas, opposed by Communist-led guerrillas supported by most of the peasantry and North Vietnamese.

Perhaps as many as one-fourth of the South Vietnamese supported the Americans, who literally bought them off through massive assistance to a large South Vietnamese army and government and presence of an American army whose peak strength there was 575,000 in 1968. Mountains of consumer goods brought by the Americans was the hall-mark of this "prosperity."

The war—it also spilled into Cambodia and Laos—was horrendously costly to the Indochinese as more than 3 million of them were killed and millions more injured (the United States dropped a greater tonnage of bombs on Indochina than all combatants did in World War II). American human and material losses were also high—58,000 military deaths, 300,000 wounded, a high suicide rate for returning military personnel, and with the inclusion of veterans' benefits and interest on the national debt, 676 billion dollars by the mid-90s.[43]

Foreign capital, especially from the United States and Great Britain, has played an important role in Latin America, as in Mexico, Argentina, Chile, and Cuba. (The last, dominated by American capital before its socialist revolution, nationalized large private property, including that of foreigners.) This heavy dependence on foreign capital, with its emphasis on the export of raw materials, has undoubtedly misshaped Latin American economic development, preventing the growth of a balanced industrial economy to sustain prolonged economic growth resting primarily on the increasing purchasing power of its domestic work force. Many Latin-American nations are tied to a monocrop/monocommodity export earnings: Colombia, 75 percent in coffee; Chile, 65 percent in copper; Venezuela, 90 percent in oil; and Honduras, 50 percent in bananas—with wild swings in prices making long-range economic planning difficult.

In the 1990s, private wealth in Latin America is highly concentrated, being in the hands of its leisure class and a few other privileged layers, the top 2 percent of the people having about 80 percent of it, itself related to steep income inequality—examples, in Brazil, the top 20 percent with 60 percent; in Mexico, 10 percent with 40 percent; and in Chile, 20 percent with 60 percent. Landownership, obviously, is also highly concentrated, a general estimate being that 10 percent own all arable land, specific examples being Brazil, with 1 percent having half and Guatemala, with 5 percent having four-fifths. Not surprisingly, the South American wealthy, fearing possible social revolution, send large chunks of their wealth abroad, more that 243 billion dollars by 1987, mostly to the United States.

The heavy dependence on the military and the great corruption and waste related to leisure-class hegemony by the early 1990s, has resulted in a large Latin American debt to First World governments/banks, much of it to the United State, with Brazil, Mexico, and Argentina each owing from 60 to 100 billion dollars. The IMF under American leadership has now forced these and other nations to repay this steep debt through higher export earnings, two-thirds of it being earmarked for this. In some nations, the problem of repaying debts is very high: In Peru, for instance, the national budget is composed of three equal parts—the first third to repay foreign debt, the second for the military, and the last for all other needs.

These conditions have resulted in lower living standards, the case of Mexico being instructive. In the 1980s, workers' real wages declined by about a half. The devaluation of the peso in December, 1994, again reduced real wages and salaries. In 1995, from a work force of 36 million, 10 million were unemployed, 15 million categorized as "unlicenced street vendors," barely surviving, and 10 million with regular jobs, half working for the government. In the meantime, 49 billion dollars has been lent to Mexico by the United States and the IMF at high interest rates to prevent economic chaos and to protect foreign investment—two-thirds of all investment capital in Mexico—most of it held by American investors. The crisis now is so deep and pervasive that even the higher reaches of Mexico's middle class, like lawyers, physicians, and accountants, are forced to hold second jobs.

The roots of this economic crisis lay in the boom and bust cycles of the Mexican economy tied to the fortunes of oil prices and corruption and favoritism promoted by a one-party system (it ended in 2000) dominated by elites that mismanaged a formerly large nationalized sector. It should also be noted that because of large-scale capitalist agriculture, the Mexican countryside is emptying, small farmers ever more migrating to overcrowded cities already plagued by high unemployment.

Mexican realities largely reflect those of the rest of Latin America, where half of the work force is either unemployed or underemployed, resulting in degrading poverty and malnourishment. Studies indicate, for instance, that two-thirds of Brazilians and half of Mexicans are undernourished.

United States intervention in Latin American affairs has continued unabatedly after World War II. After a successful social revolution in Cuba, led by Fidel Castro and Ernesto "Che" Guevara, that rapidly turned to a Communist solution to counter capitalist intransigence, the United States, breaking international law by interfering in the internal affairs of another sovereign nation, openly aided Cuban exiles in the ill-fated Bay of Pigs invasion of April 1961. Then, a nuclear holocaust was averted in the summer of 1962 when Soviet nuclear missiles sent to Cuba at Castro's request were withdrawn when President Kennedy threatened to destroy them.

The obsession to destroy the Cuban Revolution has been a constant aim of American foreign policy, lest it spread throughout Latin America. There have been numerous attempts by the CIA to assassinate Castro, even working with the American Mafia, which lost its gambling casinos and brothels there.

In 1964, when the Brazilian President Joáo Goulart was intent on making far-ranging socioeconomic reforms, the United States supported a successful coup d'état of generals against him by sending the Sixth Fleet off the Brazilian coast on the grounds of stopping increasing Communist influence within his government.

In Chile, where a large democratic socialist movement had been in place for decades, a democratic socialist, Salvadore Allende, led a popular-front electoral coalition, including Communists, to victory in 1970. His program proposed the nationalization of the American-owned Anaconda Copper Company and a social-welfare package to improve the living standards of the working-class. But Allende was opposed by the Chilean leisure class, including its military component (the sons of the middle class and wealthy formed the officer corps in the military).

President Nixon and Secretary of State Henry A. Kissinger were determined to topple Allende from power: They ceased economic assistance, insisting that foreign loans be promptly paid, but continued aid to the Chilean military, and with the covert assistance of the CIA and other American agencies encouraged the Chilean military to destroy Allende's government in 1973. Kissinger, in 1970, on Allende and his socialist coalition, stated: "I don't see why we need to stand by and watch a country go Communist because of the irresponsibility of its own people."

American intervention in Central America, of long-standing duration, continues. In Guatemala, after President Jacobo Arbenz in 1953 wished to expropriate lands of the United Fruit Company, the CIA, with the aid of reactionary Guatemalan army officers, attacked from Honduras, forcing him to resign. This action began four decades of civil war between the left and right, resulting in 200,000 deaths, more than 80 percent of them committed by right-wing CIA-backed death squads. In the Dominican Republic, after the fall of General Rafael Trujillo, the United States intervened in 1963 to forestall reforms by Juan Bosch, a popularly-elected president. From 1980 to the early 1990s, El Salvador was in the throes of civil war, resulting in 75,000 deaths, pitting left against right, the CIA intimately allying itself with its wealthy conservatives and military. In 1989, the United States again meddled with massive military force to dislodge General Manuel Antonio Noriega from power in Panama.

In Nicaragua, after the Sandinista National Liberation Front overthrew the dictatorship of General Anastasio Somoza in 1979, a client of the United States for many decades, the United States once more stepped in. As in the other instances, this interference was predicated to stop a bogus Communist threat, for the Sandinistas, left-wing socialists, not Communists, were supported by the Socialist International, comprising such democratic socialist parties, as the French, German, Spanish, and Swedish.

From its very beginning, President Reagan was determined to destroy this "Communist" revolution by imposing a trade embargo on Nicaragua and ordering the CIA to form a counter-revolutionary force of "Contras" to destabilize it. The CIA itself was caught in mining the harbors of Nicaragua, an illegal war act. When the World Court ordered the United States to pay for this crime, Reagan refused its jurisdiction. Ultimately, the Sandinistas lost power in a narrow electoral defeat, the basic reason being the wish of many Nicaraguans to simply end a murderous guerrilla war financed by America, resulting in the deaths of many tens of thousands.

Every one of these actions by the United States was against accepted norms of international law. Indeed, the United States not only trained the leading officers of its Central American client states, but repeatedly buttressed their right-wing rulers through CIA agents advising their military in their daily operations, which included deliberate mass murder of civilians, and if all else failed to stop popular forces, directly intervened with massive military force to defeat them. As Ralph *et al.*, in *World Civilizations* (a typical college textbook) affirmed: President Reagan's policy in Central America rested on the premise that American interests there "would take precedence over treaties, conventions, and international law."

These American actions were part and parcel of neo-Imperialism, i.e., the combined economic and political hegemony of the wealthy/industrialized capitalist nations of the North over the poor ones of the South. In economic terms alone, from 1982 to 1990, for instance, it resulted in this disparity—the North received 418 billion dollars more from the South for debt payments than it extended to the South in grants and other aid.[44]

Before embarking on a brief exposition of Soviet imperialism in Eastern Europe, the existence of the Soviet Union was an important factor in the rise of Chinese Communism and consequent decolonization in Asia (Indonesia, India, and Vietnam), Africa (Kenya, Algeria, Zambia, Mozambique, Angola), and in the Americas (Cuba).[45]

Soviet imperialism itself was associated with the Soviet Army's advance during the final stages of the Second World War into Poland, Hungary, Romania, Bulgaria, and East Germany. In Yugoslavia, under Josip Broz (Tito) the Communist-led partisans reflected a successful indigenous Communism. After a brief period of cooperation with opponents, socialists and others, for several years in the "People's Democracy" phase, the Communist parties of these nations (except for Yugoslavia which proceeded to

Communism rapidly on its own) consolidated their positions to becoming, for all intents and purposes, single-party states. They nationalized industry and collectivized agriculture, the latter's intensity and success being varied; in Poland, for instance collectivization never proceeded far, although it did so in Bulgaria and Romania. Furthermore, in challenging the traditional religious structures, with their often reactionary mindset, Communism aided progressive change, encountering much more opposition from a disciplined and international Catholicism than the discrete national churches of Eastern Orthodoxy.

In the realm of popular support, Communism, especially in Bulgaria, East Germany, independent Yugoslavia, and Czechoslovakia (in free elections in the last, its Communist party garnered 38 percent of the vote, emerging as the largest party), enjoyed much popular support, but less so in Romania, Poland and Hungary. After Communism imploded in 1989-1991, renamed Communist parties in Eastern Europe, usually using the name "socialist," did very well in every one of the nations mentioned, heading governments or being the main opposition parties.

On the whole, the Communist legacy in Eastern Europe has partially modernized an economically underdeveloped region, which included destroying its traditional large landowner/military/capitalist elites, which invariably disdained democracy and civil liberty. The exceptions to this generality were Czechoslovakia with its industry, democracy, and large working and middle classes, and East Germany whose large working class was strongly Communist before the rise of Nazism, although there was also some industry in Poland and Hungary with at least some semblance of a working class. Communism promoted industrialization, mass education, extensive social-welfare programs, like socialized medicine and old age pensions, increased women's freedom, and so forth, within a general socioeconomic equality.

The repressive and brutal aspects of Soviet Imperialism are not discounted: It was hostile to democracy and civil liberties, very harsh in dealing with the old elites, and if need be with workers, defeating the Hungarian Workers' revolt in 1956 with great loss of life, repeatedly interfering with Polish workers' struggles, particularly the Solidarity Union, and in squelching the "socialism with a human face" in 1968 Czechoslovakia. The one-party Communist Eastern European states controlled the media, education, and so forth. Nevertheless, there was always movement and change in these nations and when Communism expired there, it was replaced peacefully outside of Romania.[46]

In contrast to the fall of the Soviet Union, the internationalization of capital and privatization of nationalized property, especially after the 1980s, indicating the resurgence of bourgeois power, was related to free-trade areas, like the EU and NAFTA, as well as to international regulatory agencies like the IMF and WB. The almost free-trade element just mentioned is, of course, not entirely true. For instance, between the United States and Japan there are self-imposed quotas on automobiles from Japan—which the Japanese have obviated by building plants in the United States—and on semiconductors, and the trade blocs protect special interests groups, like agriculture and aviation.

Now, world capitalism is at its height with its international stock, bond, and money-market funds. TNCs themselves have interpenetrated one another, like Ford owning a third of Marzda, and have set up operations within the large trade blocs themselves, like Honda in America and Ford in Europe. The extent of this internationalization of capital since 1987 has increased by almost 10 percent annually.[47] Before World War I, Kautsky's theory of "ultra-imperialism," holding that competing national imperialism might reconcile in a general peace, proved to be incorrect because of World Wars I and II, but it now seems to be true. Furthermore, a war involving thermonuclear weaponry now promises the end of civilization and probably of humanity.[48]

The strength of international capitalism today may be illustrated by its rapid penetration of the former Communist states of Eastern Europe and the former Soviet Union. It first destroyed the Communist trade bloc or COMECON, obliterating long-standing trade links and causing economic chaos. Then, it prevented the new governments from borrowing money to restructure many of their relatively advanced industrial sectors to keep them in the hands of the state or workers, forcing them to accept free trade, including unregulated currency exchange, and imposing economic austerity by keeping wages low and gutting social services. Only then could these new governments receive Western aid through the IMF and the WB. (Only Poland was greatly helped, having half of its large foreign debt written off; its Communist planners had borrowed large amounts from the West to industrialize, a project which they mismanaged.)

It was under these circumstances that Western capital mostly from the EU purchased leading state industrial sectors in Poland, Hungary, and the Czech Republic at very low prices, 55,000 companies principally in chemicals, auto, telecommunications, cement, and glass. Western penetration of Eastern Europe led to these restraints: The foreign owners of the Hungarian cement industry forbade it from exporting to the West lest it impinge on long-term profits there. After General Electric bought Tungsram, a Hungarian electric company, it closed some of its divisions which its Hungarian managers saw as profitable, but apparently not enough so.[49]

To be sure, there is a double standard concerning business here. When capitalism is in danger of wholesale collapse or penetrates a socialist area, capitalist governments aid it. In the Great Depression, for instance, President Hoover launched the RFC to lend monies to failing big business—a program continued by the New Deal—while opposing federal relief assistance to unemployed workers, and in 1979, President Jimmy Carter bailed out an ailing Chrysler Corporation through government-guaranteed loans. The Export-Import Bank, a federal agency, now supports exports by providing loans and even insurance to American companies. For instance, in 1996, the government was involved with Westinghouse, Caterpillar, Boeing, and other companies in a 10-billion-dollar package of business with China. The EU also granted subsidies to its large transnational corporations invading Eastern Europe.

Imperialism is also complicit in the deliberate destruction of the ecosystem. Obvious examples of this were in Vietnam and Nicaragua. In Vietnam, the American military employed Agent Orange, containing dioxin, a powerful toxin, to defoliate large parts of its countryside, adversely affecting the health of its people. In Nicaragua, working through its proxies, the Contras, the United States encouraged a "scorched-earth" policy, including the deliberate destruction of projects instituted by the Sandinistas to protect the ecology.

But the greater damage of imperialism, and its leading institutions—WTO, IMF and WB—occurs during its normal operations in peacetime, in the guise of free trade and privatization which encourage TNCs to squander the resources of poor nations, resulting in the wholesale destruction of the ecosystem through widespread deforestation, accelerated extraction of minerals, and toxic dumping.[50]

In conjunction with rich-nation capitalist foreign investment in poor nations, like China, Indonesia, Thailand, and Mexico, the question of its overall effect, beneficial or not, in their economic development arises—this assumes no direct foreign intervention as that of the United States in Latin America. There is awareness here of the many variables that go into economic development, like rate of savings and building proper infrastructure—transportation, energy, educational, and other systems—with balanced and proportionate growth among various economic sectors. For instance, to what degree do somewhat higher wages that foreign companies pay to workers in China, Indonesia, and elsewhere benefit local economies? How much do capital/technology transfers help the recipient nation *in* its overall *economic* development?

From a long-run historical perspective, as observed, foreign investment in poor nations that do not have comprehensive plans for domestic development are a drain on their economies, largely warping them, but for those which do, like China and South Korea, despite the latter's recent economic setbacks, it spurs economic development. To be sure, economically advanced nations, like Japan, Germany, and France, had and have well-developed capitalist mercantilisms with strong state direction for economic development. Even a supposedly pro-laissez-faire United States imposed high tariffs for generations to protect its developing industries from cheaper foreign competition, encouraged almost unlimited immigration to keep wages down, tried to end the Great Depression, and now grants huge tax breaks and other subsidies to business.

We reiterate to emphasize this critical point: That ultimately the neo-imperialism of developed capitalist nations, with its IMF, WB, and other institutions, prevents poor nations from properly developing their economies for balanced and sustainable economic growth. In lending them money, the IMF, for instance, compels them to follow its directives on levying taxes and setting broad social policies, priority given to debt repayment and providing a favorable business climate for TNCs in their borders, like low or no taxes and docile labor forces without unions. But there is more, for poor nations, usually providing raw materials and/or being low-wage platforms for wealthy ones, are invariably hurt the most in worldwide economic downturns, preyed upon by the speculative frenzies of international capital. Thus it is that from 1980 to 1998, GDP median annual growth rates were 1.8 percent in developed nations, but 0 percent for developing ones, but if population-weighted for the latter, i.e., including China and India, 0.8 percent, since the two have much autonomy vis-à-vis neo-imperialism because of their policies and large populations.[51]

In 2000, from a world population of six billion, a fifth lives on less than a dollar a day in the poorer nations (the WB designates these people as living in poverty) and a third from 1 to 2 dollars a day (not in poverty according to the WB!), or half subsists on less than 2 dollars daily. In line with these statistics, the UN World Food Program in January 2001 reports that almost 800 million people are chronically malnourished—apparently the WB's criterion for poverty. Then, too, more than half the people do not have minimally adequate toilet facilities, at least a fourth do not have clean drinking water, and a fifth have no access to any health system. Also a billion people are illiterate, the majority living in India, China, Pakistan, Indonesia, and sub-Sahara Africa. In contrast to this is a poor Communist Cuba (GDP in 1999 at 1,700 dollars) that educates all of its children, has a tolerably good national healthcare system a comprehensive social-security system, adequate food supply, safe water and toilet facilities for 90 percent of its people, and a life expectancy of seventy-five years, among the highest in the world.[52]

NOTES

1. *The American Heritage Dictionary*, 2nd College Edition (Boston: Houghton Mifflin Co., 1982), p. 645.

2. Veblen, *Leisure Class*, pp. 22 ff., in which warriors and priests are the key members of the traditional leisure class; and pp. 192-216 on "Devout Observances."

3. On the quotations, see Numbers 33:53, Deuteronomy 7:7, 7:16, 2:33-36, and 3: 6-7.

4. On consequences for disobeying God, see Deuteronomy 28:15 and other parts of 28.

5. George Panichas, ed. *The Simone Weil Reader* (New York: David McKay, 1977), pp. 153-83, "The *Iliad*: Poem of Might."

6. Thucydides, *The Peloponnesian War*, translated, Benjamin Jowett, Introduction by H. Baldwin and Moses Hadas (New York: Bantam Books, 1965), p. 174.

7. See Michel Beaud, *The History of Capitalism: 1500-1980* (New York; Monthly Review Press, 1983), p. 19, which maintains that much of mercantilism is built on large, not small capital. On the number of slaves and slavery, see Ferdnand Braudel, *Civilization and Capitalism*, Vol. III, *The Perspective of the World* (New York: Harper and Row, 1984), p. 440. Philip Curtin, *The African Slave Trade: A Census* (Madison, WI: University of Wisconsin Press, 1969). Basil Davidson, *The African Slave Trade* (Boston: Little, Brown, 1961). Also, see Russell Thorton, *American Indian Holocaust and Survival* (Norman, OK: University of Oklahoma press, 1987).

8. Montagu, *Man*, pp. 105-06; Montagu, *Human Aggression*, pp. 256 ff. and 270-71; Harris, *Culture, People*, p. 361; Lawrence H. Keeley, *War Before Civilization: The Myth of the Peaceful Savage* (New York: Oxford University Press, 1996), pp. 25-39 and 111-41.

9. Thorstein Veblen, *An Inquiry into the Nature of Peace and the Terms of its Perpetuation* (New York: B.W. Huebsch, 1917), pp. 31-76.

10. Thorstein Veblen, Review of J.A. Hobson's *Imperialism: A Study*, *Journal of Political Economy*, March, 1903, pp. 311-14.

11. Thorstein Veblen, "An Early Experiment in Trusts," *Journal of Political Economy*, March, 1904, pp. 270-79.

12. Thorstein Veblen, *Imperial Germany and the Industrial Revolution*, Introduction by Joseph Dorfman (New York: Augustus M. Kelley, 1964), pp. 258-59.

13. *Ibid.*, pp. 242 ff.

14. *Ibid.*, p. 65.

15. *Ibid.*, pp. 81-82.

16. *Ibid.*, p. 253.

17. *Ibid.*, pp. 258-59.

18. *Ibid.*, p. 269.

19. *Ibid.*, pp. 268-69.

20. Cf. Veblen, *Nature of Peace*, pp. 26 and 72 ff. with Hobson, *Imperialism*, pp. 11-12 in Harrison M. Wright, ed., *The "New Imperialism": Analysis of Late Nineteenth Century Expansion* (Boston: D.C. Heath and Co., 1961); and, V.I. Lenin, *Imperialism: The Highest Stage of Capitalism* (New York: International Publishers, 1939), pp. 117-18.

21. Veblen, *Nature of Peace*, p. 79.

22. *Ibid.*, p. 156.

23. *Ibid.*, pp. 22, 31-76 are on patriotism. The quotations in this paragraph are respectively on pp. 31, 38, 39, and 45.

24. *Ibid.*, pp. 77-117, for instance.

25. *Ibid.*, p. 241.

26. *Ibid.*, pp. 362-67.

27. Veblen, *Imperial Germany*, pp. 268-69.

28. Thorstein Veblen, "Outline of a Policy for the Control of the 'Economic Penetration' of Backward Countries and of Foreign Investments," in *Essays in Our Changing Order* (New York: The Viking Press, 19347, pp. 361-82.

29. Lenin, *Imperialism*, p. 89.

30. *Ibid.*, pp. 62-63.

31. William L. Langer, "A Critique of Imperialism," *Foreign Affairs*, XIV, (October, 1935), 102-15.

32. Rudolf Hilferding, *Le Capital Finacier* (Paris: Editions de Minuit, 1970), pp. 431-454 ff. This work is originally published in German in 1910. On Kautsky's concept of "ultra-imperialism," see footnote 48 in this chapter.

33. Lenin, *Imperialism*, pp. 103 and 119.

34. George Lichtheim, *Imperialism* (New York: Praeger, 1971), pp. 81-87 and 119-20.

35. Eric J. Hobsbawm, *Industry and Empire: An Economic History of Britain Since 1750* (London: Weidenfeld and Nicolson, 1968), pp. 10-39.

36. Joseph Schumpter, *Imperialism and Social Classes* (Cleveland, OH: Meridian Books, 1961), pp. 95-96.

37. Marx, *Capital*, I, 822-33; the quotations are from p. 826. Also, see Karl Marx and Frederick Engels, *On Colonialism: Articles from the "New York Tribune" and Other Writings* (New York: International Publishers, 1972). Mandel, *Marxist Economic Theory*, II, 441-84, on imperialism.

38. Max Weber, *Economy and Society: An Outline of Interpretive Sociology*, edited by Guenther Roth and Claus Wittich, 3 vols (New York: Bedminster Press, 1968), II, 913-21.

39. Harry Magdoff, *Imperialism: From the Colonial Age to the Present* (New York: Monthly Review Press, 1978), pp. 237-61, for instance. John Bellamy Foster, *The Theory of Monopoly Capitalism: An Elaboration of Marxian Political Economy* (New York: Monthly Review Press, 1968), pp. 160-89.

40. On military spending, see *U.S. News and World Report*, March 6, 1995, p. 68; Robert L. Borosage, "All Dollars and No Sense," *Mother Jones*, Sept./Oct., 1994, pp. 41-44. On waste in military procure-

ment, see A. Ernest Fitzgerald, *The High Priests of Waste* (New York: W.W. Norton, 1972), pp. 282-332. On the wasteful and obsolete aircraft-carrier groups and ninety billion dollar annual cost to defend Europe, see Borosage, "All Dollars and No Sense," p. 3. On the cost of nuclear weaponry, see *Akron Beacon Journal*, July 13, 1995, p. A4. On jobs and the military-industrial complex and the annual expenditures of the CIA (3 billion dollars) and NSA (10 billion dollars), see *Nation*, Oct. 6, 1999, p. 5-6. *Akron Beacon Journal*, Oct.,16, 1997, p. A3. Total annual spending in the mid 1990s on clandestine-intelligence operations is about 26.6 billion; the CIA is forced to reveal this in October, 1997 by a lawsuit. On civilian and military deaths in the 20th century, see Gabriel Kolko, *Century of War: Politics Conflict and Society Since 1914* (New York: The New Press, 1994), pp. 103, 207-08; 315; Hobsbawm, *Age of Extremes*, pp. 34-35. Arlene Levinson, "20th is Century of Death," *Akron Beacon Journal*, Sept. 17, 1995, p. A2, estimates that in the 20th century, 200 million people perished in war, genocide, and politically caused famines, as in China in the 1960s. On omnicide, see Jonathan Schell, *The Fate of the Earth* (New York: Avon Books, 1992), pp. 17-91, especially.

41. William Appleman Williams, *The Tragedy of American Diplomacy*, 2nd ed. revised and enlarged (New York: Delta Books, 1972), pp. 19-89 on imperialism and the American character; p. 313 calls for an end of American imperialism based on frontier expansion and Open Door Policy on the basis that it "no longer bears any significant relation to reality."

42. On American imperialism in the early 20th century, see, for instance, Dana G. Munro, *Intervention and Dollar Diplomacy in the Caribbean, 1900-1921* (Princeton, NJ: Princeton University Press, 1964), pp. 160-216, for instance, on Nicaragua. On Kennan's remarks in 1948, see Noam Chomsky, *What Uncle Sam Really Wants* (Berkeley, CA: Odonian Press, 1993), p. 9. On the reactionary policies of American imperialism, resulting in mass slaughter and disregard of human rights, see Noam Chomsky and Edward S. Herman, *The Political Economy of Human Rights:* Vol. I, *The Washington Connection and Third World Fascism*; Vol. II, *After the Cataclysm; Postwar Indochina and the Reconstruction of Imperial Ideology* (Boston: South End Press, 1979), I, 1-40 is a "Summary of Major Findings and Conclusions." This work is a clear and convincing indictment of United States foreign policy throughout the world, including Vietnam, Iran, Indonesia, East Timor, and Cambodia.

43. On Vietnam, see Gabriel Kolko, *Anatomy of a War: Vietnam, the United States and the Modern Historical Experience* (New York: Pantheon Books, 1985). On the total human and material costs of the war for the United States alone, see *Nation*, Dec. 24, 1990, p. 793, and Feb. 18, 1991, p. 184. On the anti-Vietnam War movement, see, for instance Lawrence Lader, *Power on the Left: American Radical Movements Since 1946* (New York: W.W. Norton, 1979), pp. 195 ff. on the college teach-ins which began at the University of Michigan in March 1965. On massive public resistance to the war and the usual government duplicity on the war, see Howard Zinn, *Declarations of Independence: Cross-Examining American Ideology* (New York: Harper Perennial, 1991), pp. 123-46.

44. On United States imperialism in Latin America, see: For a typical college textbook, Philip Lee Ralph *et al.*, *World Civilizations: Their History and Their Culture,* 8th ed. (New York: W. W. Norton, 1991), II, 781-87. It includes U.S. complicity in overthrowing Allende and intervention against the Sandinistas; p. 810 on U.S. disregard for international law. On Kissinger's remarks on Chile, see *In These Times*, July 4-17, 1990, pp. 4-5. On recent U.S. involvement in Central America, see Walter LaFeber, *Inevitable Revolutions: The United States in Central America* (New York: W. W. Norton,

1983), pp. 5-18, 29-58, 64-92, 164-302. LaFeber, a distinguished historian of American foreign policy accurately indicates the reactionary meddling of the American elite in this region. Noam Chomsky, *Turning the Tide: U.S. Intervention in Central America and the Struggle for Peace* (Boston, MA: South End Press, 1985), pp. 85-170, again, well portrays U.S. imperialism here. Among the articles—some titles are not noted—whose statistics I use are: James Petras, *In These Times*, Feb. 18-24, 1987; Penny Lernoux, *Nation*, Dec. 12, 1987; H. Brand, "The World Bank, the Monetary Fund, and Poverty," *Dissent*, Fall, 1993, pp. 497-504; Christopher Whalen, "Going South," *Nation*, Jan. 23, 1995, p. 80. David Knox, "In Mexico, Economic Hardship Cuts Deep," *Akron Beacon Journal*, Oct. 22, 1995, pp. A1 and A12. On CIA involvement with mass murder in Nicaragua, see, for instance, Allan Nairn, "CIA Death Squads," *The Nation*, April 17, 1995, pp. 513 ff. On American determination to crush the Sandanista Revolution in Nicaragua, see, for instance, William I. Robinson and Kent Norsworthy, *David and Goliath: The U.S. War Against Nicaragua* (New York: Monthly Review Press, 1987), pp. 9-172, for instance. On the CIA, see, for instance, Bob Woodward, *Veil: The Secret Wars of the CIA, 1981-1987* (New York: Simon and Schuster, 1987). A prescient work on American imperialism from the 1970s to 1990s is by Michael T. Klare, *War Without End: American Planning for the Next Vietnams* (New York: Alfred A. Knopf, 1972), pp. 3-28, 88-240. On the economic figures involving the North's pillage of the South, see Tom Athanasiou, *Divided Planet: The Ecology of Rich and Poor* (Boston: Little, Brown, and Co., 1996), p. 214.

45. See, for instance, Hobsbawm, *Age of Extremes*, Chapter 7, "End of Empires," p. 203, which takes cognizance of the newly freed colonies of Western imperialism being attracted to the Soviet Union.

46. For an overview of Eastern European Communism in its various national settings, see F. Lee Benns and Mary Elisabeth Seldon, *Europe: 1939 to the Present* (New York: Appleton-Century Croft, 1965), pp. 217-53. On the fall of Eastern European Communism, see various articles in *Dissent* whose cover is "Revolution in Europe," Spring 1990.

47. On the dollar amounts of investments, see, *Akron Beacon Journal*, June 29, 1995, p. B6. On the foreign investment figures, see Julius, *Global Companies*, p. 40.

48. On Kautsky's concept of "ultra-imperialism," see Silber, *Socialism*, pp. 62-63; David McLellan, *Marxism after Marx* (Boston: Houghton-Mifflin, 1979), pp. 95-96; Ernest Mandel, *Late Capitalism* (London: NLB, 1975), pp. 332-34.

49. On Western economic penetration of Eastern Europe, see Peter Gowan, "Eastern Europe, Western Power and Neo-Imperialism," *New Left Review*, No. 216, March/April, 1996, pp. 129-52.

50. On the environmental ravages of imperialism and neo-imperialism, see Daniel Faber, *Environment Under Fire: Imperialism and the Ecological Disaster in Central America* (New York: Monthly Review Press, 1994), pp. 11-88 and 193-215. Foster, *Vulnerable Planet*, Chapters 5 and 6. Athansiou, *Divided Planet*, pp. 60-95 and 163-225, on the IMF, WB, and GATT in economically exploiting poor nations through the wanton destruction of their forests and other natural resources, with the complicity of their elites.

51. Robert Wade, "Showdown at the World Bank," *New Left Review*, No. 6, Jan/Feb, 2001, p. 135.

52. The statistics presented here are common knowledge.

XIV   The Riddle of Religion

RELIGION (FROM THE LATIN VERB *RELIGARE*, to bind together) is an old human institution, elements of which, like sympathetic magic in cave paintings of animals and fertility symbols and of female statuettes, with exaggerated sexual features, go back at least thirty thousand years. A complex social phenomenon signifying human dependence on some form of transcendent or supernatural being(s)/power(s), which unify human groups by institutionalizing codes of social behavior to aid individual and group survival, religion imparts meaning to individual/community life. It is also normally associated with celebrating and coping with life's important events, including crises, like birth, illness, marriage, and death, and protecting the community from external enemies or allowing for their conquest and extermination. Magic and prayer are usually involved in these proceedings, usually led by a priesthood involved with various mysteries. Before civilization, humans worshiped nature, related to animism, but with its advent, anthropomorphism dominated, of male and female gods and goddesses, and ultimately of one god or underlying force. A key element of religion is also related to some form of hereafter to soften the annihilation of death. Thus it is that the manifold roots of religion encompass the economic, social, psychological, and political elements of the human experience, traditionally allowing it to be intimately involved in every aspect of life, thus often bestowing upon it an authoritarian/totalitarian nature.

A traditional social totality itself demanded that religion itself, representing its underlying essence, be invariably organized in elaborate priestly hierarchies paralleled by hierarchically arranged invisible beings with visible manifestations to help or injure the individual/group. This is to be viewed from the perspective of an alienated world, especially with the advent of civilization, which for the masses is usually one of unrelieved socioeconomic misery and general injustice at the hands of the leisure class, in which religion largely becomes simply another alienation chaining humanity to the additional wall of religious differences, but religion itself as enunciated by the great prophets, like Isaiah, Buddha, Pythagoras, and Jesus of Nazareth, leads to an opening for human liberation in the form of the good society.

Not surprisingly, religion usually erects elaborate afterlife systems, based on a reward-punishment axis, on heaven(s) and hell(s) to maintain some sense of worldly justice, although again within the confines of caste and class. Believers of Judaism, Christianity, and Islam, for instance, are twice *born,* with resurrection after death, itself tied to final judgment for heaven or hell; there are also intermediate states like purgatory for Catholics. As for non-believers, Christians, for instance, traditionally believed that those living after the advent of Christ are condemned to hell.

But Hinduism and its offshoot Buddhism, allow for many human reincarnations before reaching *nirvana* (the Hindu version is attaining sufficient wisdom to end any attachment to the world of materiality; the Buddhist one is disinterested understanding of the human condition and its corollary of infinite compassion). Rebirth itself is related to *karma* or the moral cosmic law of accumulated good/bad actions, involving caste or *dharma* for Hindus and class for Buddhists; good moving the individual up the social progression, the bad, down. This locks individuals into a set of almost unalterable and oppressive socioeconomic and other relationships, perpetuated with a good conscience—predestination. In Hinduism, for instance, the more "virtuous" and powerful are at the higher reaches of socioeconomic and intellectual endeavors: The *Brahmans* (priests) at the top are followed by the *Kshatriyas* (kings, nobility, warriors), and *Vaisyas* (merchants, artisans, and free workers)—members of the top three castes are at least twice-born. The preponderance of economic power is in the hands of the *Kshatriyas* in large landed estates, although the bankers and merchants also have considerable wealth. The *Brahmans* themselves are quite wealthy, subsisting on fees for religious services and investments on land, in this regard being somewhat economically dependent on the *Kshatriyas* and wealthier *Vaisyas*. The overwhelming majority of the Hindu population is in the *Sudra* caste, of serfs and farm workers, that follows the leading three. At the bottom are those below the castes or *Dalits*, the "Untouchables," performing the most unclean and menial work, a fifth of the Hindu world. The caste system itself is legally outlawed in India in 1947, but tenaciously still exists, especially in the countryside.

The many-reincarnations belief of Hinduism and Buddhism, in allowing their believers to taste the various socioeconomic levels of society before being finally saved or liberated from the temptations of the "selfish body," i.e., not returning to the material world, seems more compassionate than that of the twice born religions presenting their adherents to only one chance for eternal salvation or damnation. But the many-reincarnations belief buttresses the status quo by counseling patience to social inequality/oppression.

Traditional Christianity, as an example of twice-born religions, itself has its own variant of the *karma* doctrine in the form of predestination. God, omnipotent and omniscient, for His (not Her) own reasons, saves some persons (a small minority) for heaven, relegating the others to hell. Why this is so is a mystery. Signs of election include being a Christian, but each Christian sect traditionally believes that its membership has priority in salvation. But Christian "free will" opposes predestination.

Salvation also is related to class: For very early Christianity, the rich are usually condemned to hell, while the poor enter heaven; for later Christianity, sin condemns one to slavery, according to St. Augustine; and for Calvinists, poverty is surely a sign of sin, a sensible idea if equal egress to the means of production is granted to all, which, of course, seldom happens. For some of 20th-century Christianity, under the impress of socialism, the rich and powerful are again not seen as paragons of virtue. As for some Christians stressing free will, they have to contend, why an omnipotent and omniscient God ends up by condemning most of humanity to hell. Their reply is that God can do anything; that even if He knows what will happen to one, individuals themselves do not. This view, however, has this truth: It reflects the antagonistic socioeconomic relations of class society and accompanying manifestations of alienation, which includes one's social station in an afterlife. Today, most Christian groups grant relatively easy access to heaven.

Religion itself for thousands of years has been challenged by philosophical materialism, at first, primarily in the Greek world, by the Milesian/Atomist school of philosophy, the first consistently materialistic school seeking a natural/rational or scientific explanation of the world, discarding the aid of any supernatural being(s). Its leading figures, who flourished from the 7th to the 4th centuries BCE, included Thales, Anixamander, Anaximenes, Parmenides, Anaxagoras, and Democritus, the last elaborating an atomic theory begun by predecessors. Heraclitus, although not a member of this school, an unusual mystic, is still honored by philosophical materialists. As for the principal Greek philosophers, Socrates, Plato, and Aristotle, the first two believed in a soul related to one god, the last was a deist, the gods being impersonal beings not concerned with humanity: But the three invariably emphasized human reason to comprehend present reality. This focus on reason led the Greek philosopher Euhemerus (c. 300 BCE) to theorize that the gods and goddesses were simply deified mortals. Among the educated classes of the Greco-Roman world, two leading philosophies prevailed,

Epicureanism and Stoicism, both materialistic; although gods existed in their systems, they were extensions of the physical world, having no concern with humanity, including any afterlife.

In the East, its central civilization, the magnificent Chinese one, engendered the principal philosopher of Asia, Confucius, whose basic materialism was related to human reason in understanding the cosmos; he was especially interested in social matters. As for religion, he respected its social aspects or customs, but as for an afterlife stated: "We do not know life; how can we understand death?"

In the West, the rise of Christianity eclipsed philosophical materialism as the Christian monopoly on education relegated it to the nether world. But the Renaissance beginning in Italy, with the rise of the bourgeoisie and science, led to the Enlightenment of the 17th and 18th centuries, replete with social criticism, including that of traditional religion. Its most audacious thinkers followed the Greeks in their atheism and deism, banishing a personal god from the cosmos. Leading figures in this regard were Henri Beyle, Baruch Spinoza, Voltaire, Diderot, and the Baron d'Holbach.

In the 19th and 20th centuries, especially with the continued rise of scientific and technological progress, and widespread national secular education, the views of philosophical materialism were again at center stage, with its criticism of religion conducted by leading social philosophers and scientists; Veblen participated in this assault, but before delving into his views, we observe those of Marx. For him, religion attempted to explain and alleviate the tragedy of alienated human existence in oppressive class society under the hegemony of the master classes, thus emphasizing the importance of an afterlife to resolve the tragedies and injustices of the present world:

> Religious suffering is the expression of real suffering and at the same time
> the protest against real suffering. Religion is the sigh of the oppressed crea-
> ture, the heart of a heartless world, as it is the spirit of spiritless conditions. It
> is the opium of the people.

Veblen followed Marx in viewing religion as usually a conservative force, one associated with the leisure class through the priesthood, one of its principal components. Some examples of this are the Constantinian Church in the Roman Empire and its heirs, the Byzantines and Russian Orthodoxy under the Czars; Catholicism with the Hapsburgs and Bourbons; Anglicanism with the English monarchy; and Lutheranism with the German Kaiser and Scandinavian kings. In the United States, religious conservatism, for instance, is intimately linked with American nationalism/imperialism and bigotry; in the last instance, it is only in 1995 that Southern Baptists have apologized for their ancestors' defense of slavery and racism to African-Americans.[1]

Basically, Veblen approached religion from a humanistic socialist perspective, profoundly influenced by the materialism and rationalism of the Enlightenment and 19th-century science. Although ridiculing religion ("if there is a difference between religion and magic, I have never been able to find out"; religious denominations are "chain-stores"; the local church being a "retail outlet"), he nevertheless, recognized its importance in human affairs, insisting on its intimate relationship with the economic and social organization of society and accompanying social psychology.[2]

An instance of this: In opposition to the "non-resistance and brotherly love" elements in Christianity, Veblen observed the rise of "pecuniary competition," as a result of increasing "handicraft" and "petty trade," which fractured the socioeconomic bonds of medieval society to usher in capitalism and the natural-rights outlook of the 18th century. This element, for him, representing such traits as "egoism, self-interest, or individualism," was egalitarian and revolutionary, with its emphasis on ownership of private property, subverting medieval social and economic privileges. Ownership itself at this time was still largely consonant with "workmanlike serviceability" and the "instinct of workmanship," with their correlative components of "mutual aid and serviceability to the common good."[3] This led to a radical lower-middle class Protestantism.

But the early period of capitalism, based on small private property and handicrafts, because of new technology and new "pecuniary relations," ultimately metamorphosed, for Veblen, into one of large industry and accompanying extensive labor division, in which the spirit of workmanship was not as intimately linked with the product of labor as before, lacking the close connection between "serviceability and acquisition" and the "use of wealth and the common welfare." Instead, the new enterprises were now based on an "impersonal, dispassionate" drive "for profit." Thus, a growing cleavage developed between the "natural rights of pecuniary discretion" and "brotherly love," which either led either to upper-class "ideals of emulation and status" or to a working-class "Christian principle of brotherhood."[4] The latter led to Christian Socialism.

Veblen conceptualized religion as operating in two general periods, the barbarian/predatory in a rural/agricultural setting, and the mechanistic/urban since the Industrial Revolution: The first thrived in the milieu of a socioeconomic structure characterized by deep social division, of "superior and inferior, noble and base,"[5] which being normally "predatory" or warlike was pervaded by an attitude of "devoutness,"[6] itself related to underlying elements of "personal wealth" and "invidious distinction."[7] The second, witnessing humanity's progressive mastery over nature, had belief in the supernatural markedly diminishing. But he noted that not only did the leisure class still cling to its religiosity, whose practices reinforced its "conspicuous consumption," but so did many workers and farmers.[8]

Thus it was, for him, that among Americans, for instance, religion was more ensconced in rural settings, as in the South, rather than in the urban North, and was almost universally practiced among the recently arrived and poverty-stricken immigrants from Southern and Eastern Europe—Catholics, Eastern Orthodox, and Jews—and by African-Americans. But he averred that artisans or skilled workers and middle-class adult males were less prone than others to attend church, although their women and children did. Furthermore, as between males and females, more of the latter were "religious," because of their traditional dependency on the former. Then, too, he witnessed the widespread prejudice among religions against one another in America, his example being that of Protestant Fundamentalism, as reflected in the evangelism of Billy Sunday, which also opposed modern theories of evolution ("such-like maggoty conceits are native to the religious fancy").[9] However, he approved that non-conformist Protestants had shorn their ministers of priestly powers and privileges, erecting simple and utilitarian churches devoid of costly conspicuous consumption.

To be sure, Veblen expected that, in the long run, religion would become ever more redundant before the advancing "matter-of fact" attitudes promoted by the new machine technology, invariably antithetical to magic, leading the groups most involved and influenced by its scientific views, the industrial workers, technicians, engineers, and scientists, to question the supernatural foundation of religion.[10]

In picturing religion as an institution used by the ruling classes to buttress their power and privileges, Veblen perceptively saw its relationship to waste as reflected in the "consumption of ceremonial paraphernalia," including "shrines, temples, churches, vestments, sacrifices, sacraments, holidays, attire, etc." The clerics themselves as part of the leisure class were thus normally exempt from "vulgar labor," befitting the "servants of an invisible master,"[11] who served chieftain and capitalist in bureaucracies to indicate their power to waste and to command.[12]

This waste was intimately involved with hierarchy which has its counterpart in heaven, for instance, among various Christian sects:

> Beyond the priestly class, and ranged in an ascending hierarchy, ordinarily comes a superhuman vicarious leisure class of saints, angels, etc.—or their equivalents in the ethnic cults. These rise in grade, one above the other, according to an elaborate system of status. The principle of status runs through the entire hierarchical system, both visible and invisible.[13]

Veblen also recognized the close ties between religion and sports, luck, and gambling involved in the "barbarian temperament." The principal aims here were not only to be luckier or more favored by the supernatural than opponents, but through such sterling barbarian qualities as "force and fraud" and "ferocity and astuteness," based on "invidious comparison," to inflict upon them a "more painful and humiliating defeat.[14]

On the whole, Veblen claimed that modern civilization, with its advanced technology, based as it is on the principles of science, was corrosive to religion. To this, he added that "the decay of the system of status," or rise of social and economic equality, would also lessen the power of a leisure-class dominated religion.

But Veblen did not underestimate the soft side of religion with its focus on "charity" and "social good-fellowship," which he equated with the enduring human elements of "human solidarity" and "sympathy." Furthermore, he was appreciative of religion's "aesthetic" dimensions and its allowing humanity a "sense of communion with the environment, or with the generic life process." In fact, these elements, for him, imparted to religion a "direction contrary to the underlying principles of the institution of the leisure class as already formulated."[15] This leads one to believe that, although an atheist, Veblen may have tolerated a socialist working-class religion resting on traditional virtues, as opposed to one based on inequality and exploitation.

Veblen and Marx, to be sure, were not the only socialist thinkers to demystify traditional religion. They were joined in this by other well-known 20th-century socialists in the Marxian tradition, like Karl Kautsky and Eric Fromm, who also applauded religion's positive social side. In *Foundations of Christianity*, Kautsky creatively employed a Marxian historical materialism to contrast an early Communist Christianity, based on mutual aid among the poor and oppressed, with a later one in the hands of the wealthy and powerful interested in "mastery and exploitation." For him, the authentic Jesus of Nazareth was the committed social revolutionary, who not only condemned the wealthy and powerful and expelled the moneychangers from the temple, but urged his followers to arm themselves ("Think not that I come to send peace on earth; I came not to send peace, but a sword."), not the one, transformed after his betrayal to the power structure, advising that "those using swords will get killed," the meek and mild Jesus. He then presented a rational, non-supernatural explanation of Jesus as the Messiah who gave hope to working-class mutual-aid societies of the period, so weak and alienated in their attempts to change society that they transformed their champion into a god who would soon return to destroy the world of wealth and power for one of justice and equality for his believers.[16]

Fromm continued the work of Veblen and other socialists in *Psychoanalysis and Religion*, principally contrasting the two primary, but antithetical, streams of the Judeo-Christian tradition, the authoritarian and humanistic: The former emphasized the importance of obeying a God of fear and retribution, justifying social and economic inequality by regarding the status quo as God-ordained; the latter insisted on the power of love, joy, and self-fulfillment, recognizing that, although human beings had limited powers, they could still change oppressive socioeconomic and other structures, like the Hebrew prophets urged.[17]

To this Marxian socialist perspective, we now add the insights of Mumford's anarchist vision of the critical importance in history of the "teachers of righteousness," like Isaiah, Pythagoras, Buddha, and Jesus of Nazareth, exponents of "axial religions," who stressed the autonomy, freedom, and integrity of the individual as against brutal socioeconomic structures or "mega-machine."[18]

That Veblen made a distinction between a capitalist- and socialist-oriented religion was not surprising, for as a student of history he could not but have observed its many manifestations. Indeed, during his lifetime, especially in the 1900-1920 period, the Protestant Social Gospel movement in the United States was greatly under the impress of socialism.

We now observe the influence of progressive and socialist elements in Christianity in the United States and elsewhere (the views of other religions in this respect are not observed, although they are not dissimilar) to confirm Veblen's views that religion importantly has a strong side involved with "human solidarity."

Comment has already been made on early Christian socialism/communism in history, including its American utopian tradition. In Europe itself, early modern manifestations of socialism associated with the working-class included the views of the French Abbé Hughes-Félicité Robert de Lammenais in the first half of the 19th century, who attacked the privileges of kings, nobility, and capitalists and feared that the Catholic Church's close association with them would cause the masses to leave it. His solution was for Catholicism to disassociate itself from the ruling classes by accepting the separation of church and state and by supporting a democratic and egalitarian society freeing the workers from their capitalist overlords through cooperative enterprises. For this and other views, he was excommunicated.

In mid-19th century England, the term "Christian Socialism" was first coined by two Anglican ministers, Frederick Denison Maurice and Charles Kingsley (both professors at Cambridge University; the first in moral philosophy, the second in history who also served as Queen Victoria's private chaplain for a year), and J. M. Ludlow, a lawyer. Their periodical, *The Christian Socialist*, condemned a selfish and predatory capitalistic ethic for one based on political democracy and worker-run cooperatives.[19]

The Protestant Social Gospel movement in the U.S. was especially influential in the 1900-1920 period, during the heydey of Veblen and American socialism. It continued the earlier Christian utopianism of the first half of the 19th century, although there were different social and economic settings characterizing the two movements: The first thrived in a basically rural milieu and was usually Protestant fundamentalist, while the second acted in the urban scene, coping with intense working-class poverty, generally accepting science and Darwinian evolution.[20]

An early exponent of this Protestantism, even disclaiming the socialist label, was Washington Gladden, a Congregationalist minister from Columbus Ohio's First Congregational Church. He fought for a world without racial and religious prejudice—deeply aware of the plight of African-Americans and the wrongs perpetrated on them by society and of prejudice between Catholics and Protestants—and took an active interest in alleviating working-class misery, to be remedied by extensive socialization of industry (mines, railroads, telephones and telegraph, gas, electricity, and water), and co-operative ownership of large business: "All the people should unite to furnish the capital and direct the work," a view reminiscent of Emerson's dictum uniting labor and capital. He was joined by Richard T. Ely, a professor of economics at Johns Hopkins, the University of Wisconsin, and Northwestern, a consistent friend of labor, supporting the eight-hour day, formation of labor unions, abolition of child labor, workers' compensation, and the nationalization of large industry, but allowing for small private enterprise.[21]

The best-known proponent of the movement was Walter Rauschenbusch whose father, Karl, a German Lutheran minister-missionary sent to America, became a Baptist and, then, a professor of German at the Baptist Rochester Theological Seminary. After graduating from a *Gymnasium* in Germany, he attended the University of Rochester, Rochester Theological Seminary, and the University of Berlin, concentrating on economics and theology, then, went to London to study industrial relations, meeting members of the socialist Fabian Society.

Thus it was that when Rauschenbusch became the pastor of the Second Baptist Church in New York City, a slum near Hell's Kitchen, to minister to working-class German immigrants, his interest in socialism quickened. (In addition to Christ and the Bible, the other important ethical-intellectual influences on his socialism included Marx, Bellamy's *Looking Backward*, George's *Progress and Poverty*, Leo Tolstoy, and the Fabians.) As early as 1900, he supported Debs' Presidential runs, although he never formally joined the SP.

The principal model of Rauschenbusch's socialism was primitive communistic Christianity as practiced in the Book of Acts, buttressed by belief that God worked in history for progress or the growing perfection of human beings and their collective institutions. In the coming of socialism, he assigned the primary role to the working-class because it suffered the most, the goodness-through-suffering theme.

In *Christianity and the Social Crisis* and *A Theology for the Social Gospel*, Rauschenbusch castigated capitalism as the greatest enemy of God, a system spawning great riches and its corollary of great poverty, "inherent in a social system that exalted profit and position above virtue, and an economy that taught us to approach economic questions from the point of view of goods and not of man." He deplored society treating people like things or commodities, encouraging a competitive spirit based on covetousness, invariably breeding fear and intolerance, in which the new machine technology, although leading to more economic abundance, also brought the specters of unemployment and maldistribution of wealth. His remedy called for a society of general social, economic, and political equality to socialize large property under the control of the producers, which, at the same time, allowed for small private enterprise. To achieve this goal, he recommended democracy and passive resistance; a model followed, for instance, by Martin Luther King, Jr., also a democratic socialist.[22]

The socialist impulse of the Social Gospel extended to the 1930s depression period. One of its leading figures Reinhold Niebuhr, a disciple of Rauschenbusch and well-known theologian, joined the SP, running once, unsuccessfully, on its ticket for the U.S. House of Representatives. He later became a left liberal, one of the founders of Americans for Democratic Action in 1940.[23] Norman Thomas, the chief spokesperson of the SP after Debs' death, running as its presidential candidate in 1928, 1932, 1936, 1940, 1944, and 1948, also entered socialism through the religious route, as a Presbyterian minister.[24]

Today, the Social Gospel tradition continues in American life through mainline Protestantism, Eastern Orthodoxy, and an enlightened social Catholicism. The National Council of the Churches of Christ in the United States of America, comprised of progressive elements of the first two groups, has a left-liberal, if not a moderate socialist, economic and social orientation. For instance, it envisages the possibility, with the recent spectacular development of technology/production, of "a world without hunger, nakedness or human beasts of burden," "participation" of the citizenry in the decision-making process in the various avenues of society, for all people "regardless of employment status" to have "an adequate livelihood," the vital importance of "human rights and freedoms," narrowing the income gap between the rich and the poor nations, and the diminution of the armaments race. It is unabashedly aware of the "hazards of great wealth," holding that private property is not an absolute right, and warns of the dangers of pollution.[25]

In Europe itself, the two foremost Protestant theologians of the 20th century, Karl Barth and Paul Tillich (both also active ministers), were firmly lodged in the socialist camp. Barth, depicted as the "red pastor" in his native Switzerland, wholeheartedly assisted the workers in their fight to establish unions and win higher wages and recognized the importance of politics, becoming a member of the Social Democrats.

Tillich's socialism was even more involved with his theology than Barth's. A chaplain in the German Imperial Army during World War I, utterly appalled by the death and destruction unleashed by forces of autocracy and capital, he became a left-wing socialist. In fact, in the work which he was most proud of, *The Socialist Decision,* he noted the critical role of Marx in developing a working-class consciousness, realizing that under capitalist economic arrangements workers were condemned to a continuing inferiority. In the tradition of Marx and Veblen he believed socialism would at once "liberate the workers from having to work for someone else's profit," educate them in understanding the complexities of the new technology, and remove the curse of purely repetitive work through technological innovation. In the tempestuous period after the collapse of Imperial Germany, just after the war, when Germany was on the brink of a social revolution, he rejected the Communists and reformist Social Democrats, only to endorse the revolutionary Independent Socialists. He also had the rare distinction of being the first non-Jew to lose his professorship at a Germany university with the advent of Nazism. With the aid of Niebuhr, Tillich came to America where he pursued a successful teaching career.[26]

We now examine the social concerns of Catholicism, the largest, indeed central, Christian group, from the late 19th century to the present. Catholicism's social doctrines have been fashioned by its long history of being part of the governing order in the West, much of it under the rule of the kings and nobility. Thus, its core social doctrines historically have been of a conservative nature, based on Aristotle and Aquinas, defending private property, the male-dominated patriarchal family, and socioeconomic inequality. But this view of the world is generally antithetical to capitalist "usury," unbridled economic individualism, and large trade and industry which signify the rise of the bourgeoisie, especially with the arrival of the Industrial Revolution.

Catholic social views often longed for the medieval past where everyone knew his/her place in villages/small towns, but where there was some sense of community, with the higher socioeconomic groups being involved in paternalistically looking after their socioeconomic inferiors under the rubric of "Christian charity." It should also be pointed out that in most of Catholic Europe, the Industrial Revolution came later than in England, allowing the mindset of the Middle Ages to continue. Thus, even the conservative side of Catholicism lodged in the papacy would decry capitalist evils, wishing to mitigate them, while still upholding the new inequality ushered in by capitalism.

The landmark papal encyclical on the socioeconomic ravages that capitalism inflicted on the working-class was *Rerum Novarum* (*Of New Things*), issued by the progressive Pope Leo XIII in 1891. (Encyclicals or papal letters are position papers on Catholic views, which, although not binding on Catholics, carry great weight among them. Only in matters of dogma, as in the Immaculate Conception of Mary, are popes considered infallible.)

To begin, he lamented the bourgeois destruction of the medieval craft guilds and the present clearly inadequate social services for the working class, "that workingmen have been surrendered, isolated and helpless, to the hard-heartedness of employers and the greed of unchecked competition." To this he added the evils of usury now common, and "that the hirings of labour and the conduct of trade are concentrated in the hands of a comparatively few; so that a small number of rich men has been able to lay upon the teeming masses of the labouring poor a yoke little better than slavery itself." Appealing to Catholic social justice, he urged employers not to see their workers as slaves, that work in itself is honorable, thus to treat them justly, including paying them proper or living wages, even not based on market-place bargaining, ending the brutality of children working in factories, and lessening the burden of women's factory work and even eliminating it. He, then, approved of the establishment of labor unions, with the right to strike, recognizing that the collective strength of workers was needed to improve their socioeconomic lot, thus, allowing for some form of institutional antagonism between labor and capital, but rejected the notion of a general class struggle advocated by socialists, especially Marxists. In this vein, he eschewed industrial violence injuring capital. Overall, he saw that labor and capital were interdependent, both needing one another. He also recommended local state-sponsored arbitration boards to settle particular industrial disputes concerning hours of work, sanitation, and so forth in the workplace.

Nevertheless, Leo XIII accepted socioeconomic inequality as part of the natural order of things; that, although God gave the earth to man, He left it up to human institutions to determine its distribution, an almost explicit social Darwinism, that natural inequality was a fact of life: "People differ in capacities, skills, health, strength; and unequal fortune is a necessary result of unequal conditions." Furthermore, he held that a perfectly just world could never exist on earth. In conjunction with his defense of private property, which he deemed inviolable, he averred that without it "nobody would have any interest in exerting his talents or industry."

Leo's defense of an alienated human nature tied to exploitative private property/human relations, including the family, was overdone, neglecting the powerful forces of mutual aid among the masses for a better and more just society. The upholding of this traditional order was itself part of the problem leading to inequality and its various aggressions/alienations. But Leo XIII demanded that private property also listen to the cries of exploited labor and render them social justice on the basis òf Christian charity, which for Aquinas required that people should share their bounty "without hesitation when others are in need." He also condemned an atheistic Marxian socialism. The significance of this encyclical was the formation of Catholic reform parties, as the Catholic Center Party in Germany and the Popular Party in Italy.

It should be pointed out that *Rerum Novarum* itself was influenced by the efforts of earlier and contemporary Catholic social activists concerned with ameliorating the lives of workers, as in supporting unions, like Count Albert de Mun in France, Bishop Emmanuel von Ketteler in Germany, and Cardinal James Gibbons in the United States. Gibbons, for instance, supported the Knights of Labor, the right to strike, worker-owned cooperatives, and state legislation to aid workers, like reducing working hours, better working conditions, and so forth.

Rerum Novarum was not only reaffirmed, but broadened. In *Quadragesimo Anno* (*On the Fortieth Year of Rerum Novarum*, 1931); Pope Pius XI repeated Catholicism's commitment to more social justice, urging that capitalists introduce profit sharing for workers in industry to promote greater harmony between them and workers. In this schema, he endorsed various forms of fascism, which through the corporate state sought to ensure social peace between labor and capital.

Pope John XXIII on the thirtieth anniversary of the last encyclical issued *Mater et Magistra* (*Mother and Teacher*, 1961), which focused on the responsibility of Europe and the United States to end poverty in the Third World. In *Pacem in Terris* (*Peace on Earth*, 1963), this progressive and humane pope stressed the indispensability for peace in the atomic age.

Pope Paul VI, a noted liberal scholar whose ideas were very similar to Pope John's, in *Populorum Progressio* (*On Progress for the People*, 1967), again declared that private property was not an unconditional right that had no responsibilities; in fact, there was no justification for one to retain "what he does not need, when others lack necessities." Furthermore, he broke new ground in asserting the necessity of "building a world where every man, no matter what his race, religion or nationality, can live a fully human life, freed from servitude imposed on him by other men or by natural forces over which he had not sufficient control," castigated the "international imperialism of money," and decried the increasing gap between rich and poor nations.

The present pope, John Paul II, the "Polish Pope," in various encyclicals, as *Laborem Exercens*" (*On Human Work*, 1981) and *Centesimus Annus* (*The One Hun-

dredth Year of Rerum Novarum, 1991), continued in this social tradition. He even allowed, as a last resort (when other avenues were precluded) for armed struggle against socioeconomic oppression. Although defending private property, socioeconomic inequality, free-market economics, and the profit system under capitalist auspices, he maintained that limits be placed on them, that they be subordinated to social justice and to work itself which played a central role in human development. In fact, he insisted on the "priority of work over capital" which "places an obligation in justice upon employers to consider the welfare of the workers before the increase of profits," and critical importance of unions in working-class life, which not only protected the "dignity" of workers, but allowed them "to gain broader areas of participation in the life of the industrial enterprise so that, with others and under the direction of others, they can in a certain sense 'work for themselves' through the exercise of their intelligence and freedom." Furthermore, in the spirit of human solidarity, he urged society to provide everyone with various social services to ensure their well being, including pensions, health insurance, and workers' compensation. Although the state had a responsibility to bring about social reform, unions also were to be involved in this process. He finally, echoing Veblen, attacked a "sinful" and wasteful Western consumerism in a world of great poverty.

These encyclicals were reflected in the United States by The National Conference of Catholic Bishops' pastoral letter in 1986, *Economic Justice for All*. It forthrightly declared that: "We feel the pain of our brothers and sisters who are poor, unemployed, homeless living on the edge," Catholics to "work actively for social and economic justice." It also affirmed that "we judge any economic system by what it does for and to people and by how it permits all to participate in it," and that "all people have a right to life, food, clothing, shelter, rest, medical care, education, and employment." Importantly, it also allowed for the "socialization...of certain means of production" and "cooperative ownership of the firm by all who work within it," posited that "full employment is the foundation of a just economy," and insisted that the "highest priority" now was to eliminate the poverty of those on welfare and the lowest income groups, a "social and moral scandal." Then, too, the letter gave proper recognition to labor unions and advocated the strengthening of civil liberties and democratic institutions. These measures themselves were to be undergirded by "an unalienable dignity that stamps human existence prior to any division into races or nations and prior to human labor and human achievement.[27]

To understand this heavily socialist document, some background is needed on Catholic Socialism. An early exponent was Charles Péguy, a French writer who synthesized a deep religiosity to an equally great love for socialism, his epic poem/drama, *Joan of Arc,* being dedicated to those working for the "universal socialist republic." In his *So-*

cialist City (*De la cité socialiste*, 1897), he sketched a democratic and open socialist society whose economic parameters emphasized cooperatives being run by workers, clearly in the tradition of Proudhon and Anarcho-Syndicalism.

Perhaps the most noted Catholic theologian of our century, the French neo-Thomist, Jacques Maritain, an intimate of Péguy, became a Christian socialist by the 1930s, inspired by *Rerum Novarum* and *Quadragesimo Anno*. In *True Humanism* (1936), Maritain's Christian Socialism cogently spelled out the need for a "certain collectivization of ownership" in large enterprises inasmuch as it protected human dignity and solidarity. In following Proudhon and Sorel, he affirmed the principle of economic democracy, involving worker ownership/management through unions, maintaining that labor was not to be regarded as simply a commodity by capital, and that socioeconomic arrangements be so organized that a worker's job was a right. Furthermore, within the context of a free and democratic society, a "pluralistic commonwealth" of competing ideologies, the new society would provide a comfortable standard of life for its citizenry. He disseminated his liberal/socialist ideas in America as a professor at Columbia and Princeton.

Another prime example of Catholic socialism was the personalist (personalism stresses the primacy of the individual) Emmanuel Mounier, the founder and editor of *Esprit*, the leading French Catholic journal, from 1932 to his death in 1950. He revered Péguy and was especially close to Maritain. Under Mounier, *Esprit* was engaged in a serious dialogue with Marxism/Communism.[28]

We should finally mention Simone Weil and her odyssey in life as another outstanding example of Catholic socialism, particularly of the Anarcho-Syndicalist variety. Weil, who died in 1943, was a leading French Catholic socialist in the 1930s. Her influence on the Catholic left in Europe, the United States, and elsewhere is now considerable, as on Pope Paul VI for instance. Although never baptized as a Catholic, this upper-middle class French-Jewish professor of Greek at a lycée, after several mystical experiences, in one of which she felt the presence of Christ, became a devout Catholic, thoroughly immersed in a Catholic milieu. Earlier, she had supported Communism, but, appalled by Stalinism, turned to Revolutionary Syndicalism, deeply involved in the Workers' Education Circle.[29]

In the United States itself, there is the ongoing well-known Catholic anarchist movement, the Catholic Worker (CW), founded in the early 1930s by Dorothy Day and Peter Maurin—its monthly journal, *The Catholic Worker*, which began publication on May 1,1933, is still going strong. Day, born into a middle-class Episcopalian family, joined the SP in 1916, became a reporter for the socialist *New York Call* and was then involved in the publication of *The Masses* and *The Liberator*. In 1927, she converted to Catholicism. Maurin, born into a poor French peasant family, was a member of the Christian Brothers for nine years, joined the *Sillon* (Furrow) movement favoring workers and unions, farmed in Canada for many years, then went to New York City in 1925, as an unskilled worker, where he eventually met Day.

The general socioeconomic views of the CW were heavily influenced by Kropotkin, Tolstoy, Martin Buber, the Jewish religious socialist philosopher who contributed to their newspaper, and the English Distributism of the Catholics Hilaire Belloc and Gilbert K. Chesterton, espousing a return to a medieval-like society of small towns and villages dominated by small producers/property, honoring work and devoid of large capitalism, including the charging of interest.

Specifically, Day and Maurin opted for a decentralized society whose socioeconomic parameters were based on the combination of small private property and its communal variety to ensure mutual aid in a communitarian setting featuring smallness. On farms and in factories, for instance, tools, land, buildings, and machinery (the last is kept to a minimum) were to be held in common, wage labor and assembly lines done away with, and crafts restored, freeing workers from meaningless/alienating work. Furthermore, they emphasized the importance of the new society's ending racism, anti-Semitism, all exploitation, and war. They were also pacifists, even refusing to fight in World War II. In the meantime, the CW has Houses of Hospitality, staffed by volunteers, to aid victims of capitalism, the unemployed and needy.

The importance of the CW on American Catholicism should not be underestimated, especially among Catholic intellectuals and members of the Church's hierarchy: Socialist and peace stalwarts, like Michael Harrington and Fathers Daniel and Philip Berrigan, the last two being imprisoned for their anti-Vietnam War activities, are closely associated with it.[30]

The importance of socialism within Catholicism is also well illustrated by the splendid work of the Maryknoll Order among workers and farmers in Latin America and by their outstanding publishing house, Orbis Books, a valuable resource of Catholic Socialism, emphasizing the social struggle in poor nations.

In Latin America, Catholic Liberation Theology, whose doyen is Gustavo Gutierrez, is now widespread, encompassing a large minority of the Catholic clergy, playing a leading role in establishing more than 200,000 Basic Christian Communities or mutual-aid groups. It was also much involved in the Sardinista Revolution in Nicaragua. Its theology, combining the revolutionary life of Jesus of Nazareth and revolutionary Marxist socioeconomic analysis, envisages a God of the poor and oppressed who encourages them to fight for a better life in the here and now.

An examination of Gutierrez's *A Theology of Liberation* (1973), one of the principal works of this movement, follows. To begin, Gutierrez categorically advocated a socialist solution to solve the manifold problems of contemporary society, one involving the "social ownership of the means of production." In socialism's construction, he quoted Che Guevara on the importance of not only increasing material prosperity, but in transforming the human person for the better. He also endorsed Marxian class struggle, which existed within the "church itself," today between the "oppressors" (the wealthy and their allies) and "oppressed" (workers and farmers), many of them living in "material poverty," a "scandalous condition," and in a "subhuman situation." As for "class enemies," it would be "necessary to combat them." In this regard, he asserted that "to love all men does not mean avoiding confrontations; it does not mean preserving a fictitious harmony." Indeed, the "liberation of the poor and the liberation of the rich are achieved simultaneously. One loves the oppressors by liberating them from their inhuman condition as oppressors." Anyone denying the existence of class struggle, for him, including the Church, only aided the "dominant sectors," thus no neutrality here. Indeed, he charged the Catholic Church in Latin America as being part of the present capitalist and "alienating" social system, of upholding its "dominant ideology," based on the "worst kind of violence—a situation which pits the powerful against the weak." Only by severing its ties with this power structure, with a "radical critique" of it, could Catholicism properly fulfill its mission on earth.

In this vein, Gutierrez examined the concept of sin in history, of an individual/collective nature, i.e., individual sin was related to the larger socioeconomic and other collective sins, to be "regarded as a social, historical fact, the absence of brotherhood and love in relationship among men, the breach of friendship with God and with other men, and, therefore an interior personal fracture." This "sin is evident in oppressive structures, in the exploitation of man by man, in the domination and slavery of peoples, races, and social classes," and is "the fundamental alienation, the root of a situation of injustice and exploitation." Only by overcoming this sin could humanity witness in history the "growth of the Kingdom," but it itself was "not the coming to the Kingdom, not of all salvation." Thus, although allowing for the existence of a socialist humanity, a supernatural presence was also needed for complete human fulfillment/liberation.

The ending of class oppression, for Gutierrez, was ultimately based on God's love for humanity which literally demanded that humans love one another, for following the Hebrew prophetic tradition, "man is created in the image of God." Individual and class oppression was thus an affront to God, indicating alienation from Him and the general community. The Bible, for him, was replete with denunciations of the wealthy oppressing the poor and insistence on a society of general equality and "common ownership of goods," as in Acts, instituting a proper *koinonia*.[31]

The radical Eastern Orthodox socialist tradition is represented by Count Leo Tolstoy and Nicholas Berdyaev. Tolstoy, the author of *War and Peace* and *Anna Karenina,* enjoyed the wealth, power, and culture of one born into the Russian nobility in the 19th century, advantages gained at the expense of the peasantry that until the1860s were serfs. In his middle years, Tolstoy experienced a religious conversion to imitate Jesus as a Christian anarchist, rejecting individual possessions, and identifying himself with the peasantry. He would change the world through non-violent resistance, by non-payment of taxes and refusal to serve in the military, actions based on Christian love. The ultimate aim of these pursuits was to establish cooperative communes, devoid of private property, where people lived and worked together on the basis of equality and solidarity. This pervasive radicalism resulted in his excommunication from the Russian Orthodox Church.[32]

Berdyaev was the outstanding Eastern Orthodox theologian of the 20th century. His controversial theology reflected an individualistic view of religion—a personalist—embedded in a mystical escahtalogical vision. He regarded himself as a member of both the Russian intelligentsia, in the legacy of Tolstoy and Dostoevsky in the religious realm, and of the Westernizer socialists, like Herzen, Belinsky, Chernishevsky, and Bakunin. He thus combined a deep religiosity to a basically anarchist perspective; he loathed. the authority of the state.

A rebel Marxist youth, Berdyaev repudiated the class of his parents (the nobility), for the working class and Marxism. Although he later rejected Marxism for religion, he remained steadfast in his socialist convictions, including the cooperative ownership of the means of production, decentralist patterns to prevent authoritarianism, the abolition of wage labor, and participatory democracy. The end result of this socialism would be the creation of a new working class, akin to the old nobility, where classlessness would still allow for some status differentiation. Berdyaev was expelled from the Soviet Union in 1922 because he refused to abandon his activities to propagate Christianity. He emigrated to France, becoming a close friend of Maritain and Mounier.[33]

To be sure, Veblen's prophecy of traditional religion's becoming progressively irrelevant, predicated on the increasing importance of science/technology, itself associated with the rise of the city and mass secular education, with the attendant mindset of philosophical materialism, is partly correct. Regular church attendance now in percentages for selected nations are: United States, 40; Ireland, 50 plus; 5 or less in Germany and Scandinavia; 27 in the UK; 20 in France; and 40 in Italy. In former Communist Eastern Europe/Soviet Union, 2 in Russia but more than 50 in Poland. Outside these areas, Communist China is officially atheist, but India is very religious. Indeed, as already observed, in the Islamic world, Catholic Latin America, and in Hindu and Buddhist nations, where religion is important, it itself must become ever more socialist to survive.

Other statistics on religion are in order: On acceptance of life after death for selected nations in percentages: The U.S. and the two Irelands, 80; Italy, 65; Poland, 60; West Germany, 55; former East Germany, 12; Britain, 50; Israel, 42. As for belief in God (not only a theistic one), for selected nations in percentages: the U.S. leads with 94; followed by Italy, the two Irelands and Poland, from the mid-80s to low-90s; UK and Israel, 70; West Germany, 65; East Germany, 32; Norway, 60; Russia, 54.

Belief in traditional Christianity in the U.S. itself varies widely, highly correlated with amount of general education, socioeconomic status, and region. For instance, in a survey after World War II, among four denominations, in percentages: (1) on belief in Jesus as God's divine son—Congregationalists, 40; Methodists, 54; Catholics, 86; Southern Baptists, 90; (2) on belief in life after death—Congregationalists, 36; Methodists, 49; Catholics, 75; Southern Baptists, 97; (3) on belief in the definite second coming of Jesus—Congregationalists, 13; Methodists, 21; Catholics, 47; Southern Baptists, 94.[34]

In discussing the major religions, we observed their double standard with respect to worldly wealth and power: Although their prophets have high ideals, once religions become well ensconced in the world they increasingly reflect the views of ruling elites. For instance, they allow their average adherents to engage in war and to succeed in business, thus permitting the economic exploitation of labor, including the employment of slavery—although Buddhists were admonished not to engage in the slave trade—and are not too kind to unbelievers or members of other religions, invariably condemning them to the fires of hell or to deferred salvation. Thus, it is neither surprising that when members of different religions wish to marry one another and have children, "religious" disputes usually follow, that various religio-social associations themselves invite conflict in business and other areas of life as they usually favor their co-religionists at the expense of others, and that religiously-inspired warfare among and within religious groups is a common occurrence.

Penultimate remarks on religion in the U.S.: The progressive elements of it have been catalogued, but the Catholic Church's position on abortion and sexuality is still reactionary, although 85 percent of Catholic couples use contraceptives and many approve of abortion, especially in the first trimester. This, of course is related to traditional cultures with their high death rates for children and to patriarchy.

But there is a conservative white Protestant fundamentalism, most of whose adherents are from the white working- and lower-middle classes, which is highly racist, homophobic, and sexist, opposition to abortion belonging to the last category. They staunchly resisted civil rights for blacks and other minorities. Their conservative leaders-ministers, all Republicans, are Pat Robertson, Jerry Falwell, Donald Wildmon, and D. James Kennedy. The Reverend Billy Graham does not endorse Presidential candidates, but he gave an unofficial nod to George W. Bush in the 2000 elections. To be sure, the many Black Protestant fundamentalists are on the left of the main political spectrum; Dr. Martin Luther King Jr. was a democratic socialist and many others are near socialists. The historically sharp socioeconomic and ethnic differences between the two groups explain their respective religio-political orientations.[35]

Ultimately, will alienated institutional religions escape their exclusiveness, with resultant bigotry and parochialism (the Unitarian Universalist Association has), and even unite to establish a world which the great religious prophets were pointing towards, a worldwide society of general equality, fraternity, and liberty based on pervasive democratic norms. Perhaps, but only if they become more spiritual or socialist.

NOTES

1. On religion in general, see Martin A. Larson, *The Religion of the Occident or The Origin and Development of the Essene-Christian Faith* (Paterson, NJ: Littlefield, Adams, 1961), a significant work demystifying religion. Harris, *Culture, People, Nature*, pp. 447-81, for an anthropological approach. Shepard, *Sociology*, pp. 433-57, for a sociological view. Bronislaw Malinowski, *Magic, Science, and Religion, and Other Essays* (Garden City, NY: Doubleday Anchor Books, 1948), pp. 17-148, for instance, on the similarities and differences between magic and science, along with other matters, as fear of death and its ties to religion, religion and community solidarity, and so forth. Sigmund Freud, *The Future of an Illusion* (Garden City, NY: Anchor Books, 1964), pp. 1-92, indicates that religion is an "illusion," its antidote being science. Erich Fromm, *Psychoanalysis and Religion* (New Haven, CT: Yale University Press, 1950), pp. 1-119, is a superlative commentary by a humanistic socialist and psychoanalyst on the components of religion. Emile Durkheim, *The Elementary Forms of Religious Life* (New York: Free Press, 1995), p. 236-41 and 418-48, on the connection between "religious evolution" and "social conditions," justifying present social structures, and so forth, society itself being the source of religion. On religion and invention, see David F. Noble, *The Religion of Technology: The Divinity of Man and the Spirit of Invention* (New York: Alfred A. Knopf, 1997), Chapter 1, for instance. On religions featuring multiple reincarnations, Hinduism is the principal source. On Hinduism, see, for instance, K. M. Senn, *Hinduism* (Baltimore, MD: Penguin Books, 1961); pp. 27-31, on the troubling problem of caste. On Marx's quotation in *Toward the Critique of Hegel's Philosophy of Law: Introduction*, see Easton and Guddat, *Writings of the Young Marx*, p. 250.

2. Dorfman, *Veblen*, p. 489, on the quotation noting the similarity between religion and magic; Thorstein Veblen, "Christian Morals and the Competitive System," *International Journal of Ethics*, Jan., 1910, pp. 170 ff. Heilbroner, *Worldly Philosophers*, p. 207

3. Veblen, "Christian Morals," pp. 178-79.

4. *Ibid.*, pp. 179-80.

5. Veblen, *Leisure Class*, p. 197.

6. *Ibid.*, p.215.

7. *Ibid.*, pp. 199-200 ff.

8. *Ibid.*, pp. 215-16.

9. Thorstein Veblen, "Dementia Praecox," in Thorstein Veblen, *Essays in Our Changing Order*, edited by Leon Ardzrooni (New York: The Viking Press, 1934), pp. 430-31 ff. (The quotation is on p. 431)—Veblen links the renaissance of Protestant Fundamentalists to World War I and its begetting more bigotry, as manifested by the Ku-Klux-Klan; and Veblen, *Leisure Class*, pp. 213-14.

10. Veblen, *Leisure Class*, p. 215.

11. *Ibid.*, pp. 204-10.

12. *Ibid.*, p. 202.

13. *Ibid.*, p. 207.

14. *Ibid.*, pp. 181-82 ff.

15. *Ibid.*, pp. 217-18 on the quotations.

16. Kautsky, *Foundations of Christianity*, pp. 235, 309-23 ff.: Luke 10:34, 12:49 ff. And Matthew 26:52 ff., for instance.

17. Fromm, *Psychoanalysis and Religion*, pp. 10-63, for instance.

18. Mumford, *Myth of the Machine*, I, 256 ff.

19. See O.J. Brose, *Frederick Denison Maurice, Rebellious Conformist* (Athens, OH: Ohio University Press, 1971). Brenda Colloms, *Charles Kingsley, The Lion of Eversley* (London: Constable, 1975). Peter N. Stearns, *Priest and Revolutionary: Lamennais and the Dilemma of French Catholicism* (New York: Harper and Row, 1967).

20. See, for instance, Donald Gorrell, *The Age of Social Responsibility: The Social Gospel in the Progressive Era* (Macon, GA: Mercer University Press, 1988).

21. Robert T. Handy, ed., *The Social Gospel in America: Gladden, Ely, Rauschenbusch* (New York: Oxford University Press, 1966), pp. 33-169, on Gladden; pp. 184-250 on Ely.

22. On Rauschenbusch, see Dores R. Sharpe, *Walter Rauschenbusch* (New York: Macmillan, 1942). See for instance, his *Christianity and the Social Crisis* (New York: Macmillan, 1914), pp. 44-92, in which Jesus of Nazareth is portrayed as a socialist.

23. On Niebuhr, see Gabriel Fackre, *The Promise of Reinhold Niebuhr* (Philadelphia: J. B. Lippincott, 1970), pp. 20-21. June Bingham, *Courage to Change: An Introduction to the Life and Thought of Reinhold Niebuhr* (New York: Charles Scribner's, 1961), pp. 163 ff.

24. On Thomas, see W. A. Swanberg, *Norman Thomas: The Last Idealist* (New York: Scribner's Sons, 1976), pp. 43-179, for instance.

25. See National Council of Churches of Christ in the United States of America, *A Policy Statement* (1966), 5 pp.

26. On Karl Barth, see Thomas C. Oden, *The Promise of Barth: The Ethics of Freedom* (Philadelphia: J. B. Lippincott, 1969), pp. 25 ff. on his socialism. On Paul Tillich, see his *The Socialist Decision*, translated by Franklin Sherman from German, Introduction, John Stumme (New York: Harper and Row, 1971), pp. 61 ff., 117 ff., and 157 ff. Wilhelm and Marion Pauck, *Paul Tillich: His Life and Thought* (New York: Harper and Row, 1976), I, 67 ff., on Tillich's socialism.

27. On Catholicism: On the encyclicals mentioned, see E.E.Y. Hales, *The Catholic Church in the Modern World: A Survey from the French Revolution to the Present* (New York: Image Books, 1960), pp. 193-212 on *Rerum Novarum* and *Quadragesimo Anno*. And, Michael Novak, *Freedom with Justice: Catholic Social Thought and Liberal Institutions* (San Francisco: Harper and Row, 1984), pp. 108-82, with much commentary by this conservative on Catholic social conservatism. He never once mentions Jesus of Nazareth or other Hebrew prophets! National Council of Catholic Bishops, *Economic Justice for All* (Washington, DC: National Council of Catholic Bishops, 1986), pp. v-xvi, 6-33, 65-105, 147-52. Also, for some of the more recent encyclicals issued by Pope John Paul II, see *In These Times*, Aug. 21-Sept. 3, 1991, p. 2; *Akron Beacon Journal*, March 1, 1995, p. A9.

28. Marjorie Villiers, *Charles Péguy: A Study in Integrity* (New York: Harper and Row, 1965). Jacques Maritain, *True Humanism*, translated by M.R. Adamson (London: Geoffrey Bles; The Centenary Press, 1938), pp. 156-204 as an example of his socialism. John Hellman, *Emmanuel Mounier and the New Catholic Left, 1930-1950* (Toronto: University of Toronto Press, 1981), pp. 200 ff. on sympathy for Marxism.

29. On Simone Weil, see Simone Pétrement, *Simone Weil: A Life*, translated from French by Raymond Rosenthal (New York: Pantheon Books, 1976). See, also, Simone Weil, *Oppression and Liberty*, translated from French by Arthur Wills and John Petrie (Amherst, MA: University of MA Press, 1973), pp. 83-108 on her good society, basically a socialist-anarchist one. Simone Weil, *The Need for Roots: Prelude to a Declaration of Duties Toward Mankind*, translated by Arthur Wills with a Preface by T.S. Eliot (Boston: Beacon Press, 1960), pp. 34-184 on her basically socialist-anarchist society.

30. On the *Catholic Worker*, Dorothy Day and Peter Maurin, see *Dorothy Day, The Long Loneliness: The Autobiography of Dorothy, Day* (New York: Curtis Books, 1972), pp. 193-316 on her *Catholic Worker* experiences, including her encounters with Maurin. Dorothy Day, *Loaves and Fishes* (New York: Harper and Row, 1963), is on the journal the *Catholic Worker* and the movement in general; pp. 28-41 on "Houses of Hospitality"; pp. 42-59 on "Communitarian Farms"; pp. 103-117, on Ammon Hennacy another key member of the movement. Arthur Sheehan, *Peter Maurin: Gay Believer* (Garden City, NY: Hanover House, 1959), pp. 90 ff. on his meeting Day and so forth.

31. Gustavo Gutierrez, *A Theology of Liberation* (Maryknoll, NY: Orbis Books, 1973), pp. 111 ff. on necessity for socialism in Latin America; pp. 236-37 on Guevara; 272 ff. on the class struggle; 265 ff. on the Church being part of the traditional power structure; pp. 175 ff. on sin; pp. 287 ff. on Bible's denouncing wealth, power, and privilege of the few at the expense of the many. Also, see, the brilliant

work of José Porfiro Miranda, *Communism in the Bible* (Maryknoll, NY: Orbis Books, 1987), pp. 1-85. For a Protestant view similar to Gutierrez's and Miranda's, see C.M. Kempton Hewitt, "The Marxist Jesus of Nazareth," in Louis Patsouras and Jack Ray Thomas, eds., *Essays on Socialism* (San Francisco: Mellen Research University Press, 1992), pp. 299-343. See, also, William K. Tabb, ed., *Churches in Struggle: Liberation Theologies and Social Change in North America* (New York: Monthly Review Press, 1986), with its many excellent articles, in which the similarity of interests between Marxism and religious socialism is evident.

32. Henri Troyat, *Tolstoy*, translated from French by Nancy Amphoux (New York: Doubleday, 1965), especially pp. 373-584 on Tolstoy's religious/anarchist quest.

33. Nicolas Berdyaev, *Dream and Reality: An Essay in Autobiography* (New York: Macmillan, 1951). Nicolas Berdyaev, *The Realm of Spirit and the Realm of Freedom*, translated by Donald A. Lowerie (New York: Harper and Brothers, 1952), pp. 57-63 on socialism. Nicolas Berdyaev, *Slavery and Freedom*, translated from Russian by R. M. French (New York: Charles Scribner's Sons, 1944), pp. 200-22 on his socialism.

34. On traditional religion's general decline, although it appears to be slightly gaining in Eastern Europe and the former Soviet Union with the fall of Communism, with statistics, see, *Time*, Aug. 9, 1976 (Gallup Poll); David Briggs, "Religion Enjoys a Revival," *Akron Beacon Journal*, May 22, 1995, p. A6; P. Ehrensaft and A. Etzioni, *Anatomies of America: Sociological Perspectives* (New York: Macmillan, 1969), pp. 272-85. Gordon Wright, *France in Modern Times: 1760 to the Present* (Chicago: Rand McNally, 1960), p. 557, "The Dechristianization of Rural France." H. Stuart Hughes, *Contemporary Europe: A History* (Englewood Cliffs, NJ: Prentice-Hall, 1976), p. 290, on Communism's destruction of Orthodox Christianity in Russia. *Akron Beacon Journal*, Jan. 16, 1998, p. A9—a recent poll in Russia has 46 percent of respondents as atheists.

35. On Christian conservatism in America, see Sara Diamond, *Not By Politics Alone: The Enduring Influence of the Christian Right* (New York: Guilford Press, 1998). Clark Morphew, "Conservative Christians back Bush," *Akron Beacon Journal*, Jan. 13, 2001, pp. A14 and A16. On the democratic socialist Martin Luther King Jr., see David J. Garrow, *Bearing the Cross: Martin Luther King Jr. and the Southern Christian Leadership Conference* (New York: William Morrow, 1986).

XV   Higher Education

NO AMERICAN ACADEMIC HAS MOUNTED A MORE effective critique of American higher education than Veblen in *The Higher Learning in America: A Memorandum on the Conduct of Universities by Businessmen*. When he wrote this work in the first decade of the 20th century, higher education in America was elitist, only 2 percent of the people having it; in fact, when he attended college in the 1870s and early 80s, only 1 percent had it, and the number of graduate-school students was minuscule, only 399 in 1875, rising to 5000 in 1900.[1]

Not surprisingly, when Veblen was student and professor, higher education was under the impress of a pervasive conservatism. At Carleton, a not atypical American college, the curriculum, mostly taught by devout New England Congregationalists, was based on a conservative biblical interpretation of society, buttressed by Scottish Common Sense Philosophy whose principal figures were the Scot philosopher, Sir William Hamilton, greatly influenced by Aristotle and Kant, and his chief American acolyte, James McCosh, president of Princeton. In economics, this conservatism was followed by the text of Weyland's *Elements of Political Economy*, based on the classical economists Evolution itself was staunchly resisted at Carleton because it would undermine biblical literalism. Even the leading social Darwinist, Spencer, was denounced as a dangerous radical, subverting traditional religion, considered the core of morality and conservatism.[2]

Traditional conservative religious views themselves were so strongly entrenched that even at an elitist Yale in the 1879-81 period, when Veblen's economics professor, Sumner, a recent convert to Spencerism, employed Spencer's *The Study of Sociology* as a text in a sociology course, Yale's pious President Porter objected, but the issue was ultimately resolved in favor of academic freedom.[3] This event signified that upper-class conservatism was now firmly anchored in evolution and a conservative social Darwinism, not in Christian fundamentalism.

When Veblen attended Carleton in the 1870s, his education scarcely differed from the description of American higher education in the first half of the 19th century offered by Richard Hofstadter and Walter P. Metzger (both eminent Columbia University history professors) in *The Development of Academic Freedom in the United States*: "Paternalistic and authoritarian…students took prescribed courses and recited their lessons by rote; professors acted like schoolmasters, drillmasters, and prisonkeepers."[4] Although a few courageous students and professors challenged the prevailing practices and prescriptions, they could not stem the juggernaut of traditional religion and conformity imposed by boards of trustees (40 percent clergymen, the remainder, from business and the professions closely allied to them) and presidents who invariably did their bidding.

In this intellectually authoritarian milieu:

> The professor was…dependent on student fees and yet the inquisitor of student morals, he took on the uncertain authority and something of the status of the nursemaid.

The "nursemaid" professors were clearly subordinate to and often held in contempt by the board of trustees who were invariably "officious, meddlesome, and often tyrannical," toward them, usually "prescribing the work of the classroom, writing the laws of student government, shaping the curriculum, subjecting the private lives of teachers to scrutiny and espionage."[5]

An examination of Veblen's *Higher Learning* now follows. Veblen first presented a yardstick of what a university should be: "A university is a body of mature scholars and scientists, the 'faculty,'—with whatever plant and equipment may incidentally serve as appliances for their work in a given case." Faculty themselves taught and learned as equals in a cooperative environment without any thought for economic reward, consonant with his basic view of human nature in which two of its primary propensities, "idle curiosity" and "workmanship," far outweighed pecuniary or other considerations in the pursuit of truth and knowledge. The university's other half consisted of students, regarded as apprentices, learning in a noncompetitive setting, but one requiring them to master the necessary curriculum.

Veblen himself squelched competition in his classes by rewarding all students with a grade of "C," reflecting his belief that the increasing impress of science and technology was "matter-of-fact." Thus it was that his ideal intellectuality did not thrive in a competitive business climate, pitting faculty members against one another or fostering untoward competition among students. He would end "invidious distinction" for an intellectuality ultimately based on cooperation and basic equality. The university itself, like a free and autonomous body, would be free from all outside interference.

We may add that Veblen's progressive views of a cooperative education were consonant with those of Dewey, as in *The School and Society*, and those of the present cooperative learning (CL) movement whose ranks include educator/psychologists David W. Johnson, Roger T. Johnson (brothers) and Alfie Kohn. The last, in his well-regarded *No Contest*, promotes CL on the basis that competitive education, with its boring memorization, hinders learning by causing undue anxiety, repeated humiliations, and subsequent defeatist attitudes and anger, along with lower self-esteem for students with low(er) grades, with consequent loss of interest in academic work. Instead, students learn in an interdependent relationship, usually in groups of two or three, ensuring that before an assignment is completed, it is understood by all, enhancing intellectual curiosity and enthusiasm. In many studies conducted on the validity of CL, excellent results are obtained.[6]

Veblen, then, importantly contrasted his ideal university with the one under the impress of an authoritarian capitalist bureaucracy: The board of trustees controlled the budget and elected the president, who appointed other top administrators, who, in turn, were propped up by an extensive faculty committee system, the importance of a committee being measured by its proximity to administrators and president. This system, resting on "bureaucratic organization" or "bureaucratic officialism," invariably represented business interests and principles in exercising control over the various aspects of education, including the grading system, faculty promotion, course offerings, and penalties imposed on students. In particular, the college administration implemented this discipline through a "persistent and detailed surveillance of the work and life of the academic staff," which invariably hampered its initiative and independence to maintain a vibrant intellectuality.

Furthermore, Veblen indicted the university for largely becoming a "business house" of "merchantable knowledge" whose basic purpose was to serve business, thus often subverting the ideal academic values of work and knowledge for those of "nugatory intrigue" and mere "pedantry."[7] But even more than this, he held that the university, as a corporation possessing great wealth, was itself a major capitalist institution, intertwined with the survival of capitalism itself.[8]

Two different views of Veblen's *Higher Learning* by two well-known academics of the left: Beard in *The Dial* in 1918 and Riesman writing in the conformist 1950s: For Beard, the university, indeed, was deformed by its close ties to the wealthy whose large grants and endowments allowed them considerable leverage in its affairs, a condition that could not be changed under present circumstances.[9] For Riesman, Veblen's work was "an effective caricature of academia" which "has not been equaled,"[10] but this "caricature" sadly often approximates the reality today, especially for part-time instructors.

A companion volume to *Higher Learning* was Sinclair's *The Goose-Step* (1923), the title based on the goose-step of the German military. This work, contrary to Veblen's, eschewed generalizations and indicted by name the plutocracy and their control of various universities, like Harvard, Columbia, and University of Pennsylvania, through administrators, like President Nicholas Murray Butler at Columbia. (Sinclair's tome was as thorough an exposé of classist American universities in the first two decades of the 20th century as Myers' *History of the Great American Fortunes* was on the rise of large capitalists during the Gilded Age.) Then, too, he well explored the subordination of the professoriate based on fear of losing their positions and means to support themselves to college administrators in case after case, and how socialists, like Veblen and Nearing, were harassed, losing or being denied teaching positions.

Veblen himself was prominently mentioned by Sinclair as the author of *Higher Learning*, which he defended against a Columbia University professor, Brader Matthews, who unfavorably reviewed it in *The New York Times*, and praised Veblen for being on the staff of The New School for Social Research in New York, a progressive institution of intellectual ferment.

A prophetic passage in Sinclair's work urged college teachers to organize themselves, to join the American Association of University Professors (AAUP) and the American Federation of Teachers (AFT) to fight for academic freedom and higher salaries. Indeed, he stressed that college teachers should consider themselves as "intellectual proletarians," and "the quicker they realize it the better for them."[11]

College conservatism for Veblen, itself reflected a conservative society under the impress of the leisure class, the obvious arbiters of social conventions, enjoying a "sentimental deference" from the people at large that was "massive, profound, and alert." This mindset specifically included most workers, docile and replete with "filial piety" in supporting "patriotism and property," and by extension a "government for business ends," and the engineers who regarded themselves as being merely "employees." These attitudes were characteristic of a general "commercialized frame of mind," itself an "outgrowth of many generations of consistent training."

Veblen, of course, followed closely his professor at Yale, Sumner, in these remarks, who in the class-struggle scenario between proletariat and bourgeoisie, conferred the advantage to the latter because of the former's being bound to tradition: "They are conservative. They accept life as they find it, and live on by tradition and habit," further noting that for the masses "patriotic emotions and faiths are its favorite psychological exercises," and that national interests were basically interpreted by a "ruling clique which the rest are compelled to serve."[12]

The views of Veblen and Sumner on elite hegemony, including cultural, over the masses is a truism shared by many prominent thinkers throughout the ages, like Plato, Marx and Engels, Antonio Gramsci, and Moore Jr. In Plato's *The Republic*, the "noble lie" justified a basic two-class social structure under the tutelage of the God-chosen guardians regarded as superior beings by the common herd, farmers and workers.[13] In *The German Ideology*, Marx and Engels noted that "ideas of the ruling class are in every epoch the ruling ideas; i.e., the class which is the ruling material force of society, is at the same time its ruling intellectual force."[14] They were followed by the first-rate Italian Marxist, Gramsci, who made many invaluable insights on the problematic of economic power and its bearing on general culture. For him, the rulers not only normally dominated the economic, social, and political structures, but also the superstructure, consisting of the law, religion, education, and so forth, which reflected and reinforced their authority, allowing them to maintain power and privilege without exercising undue coercion. This economic/cultural hegemony presented a formidable challenge to the working class and socialism, necessitating a long and patient struggle to change social attitudes and beliefs.[15] Today, Moore Jr., in *Injustice: The Social Bases of Obedience and Revolt*, observes that the dominant groups, because of their cultural preeminence, largely interpret "what is socially necessary."[16]

Before proceeding further we should mention two noteworthy volumes of rather recent scholarship which delved into the problems of the modern American university, including the vital one of academic freedom, both cognizant of Veblen's views: The first by Hofstadter and Metzger, *The Development of Academic Freedom in the United States*, Part II, "The Age of the University," being by Metzger; the second, a companion volume by Robert M. MacIver, a professor of political philosophy and sociology, Columbia University, *Academic Freedom in Our Time*.[17]

Metzger directly dialogued with Veblen's critique of higher education in America, claiming that Veblen presented this dichotomy on higher education in America: On the one hand, there was an ideal of the disinterested scholar searching for truth; on the other, the demands of business to employ the university for its ends to make a profit and preserve the status quo. It was this business-culture element which, for him, allowed Veblen to view the university as becoming ever more authoritarian, simply viewing professors as mere employees, endangering academic freedom and inviting intellectual conformity.

Although Metzger believed that "Veblen's indictment contained an element of truth and yet conveyed an erroneous impression," he still maintained that business organization bureaucratized the university "into a graded hierarchy of ranks" inevitable with bigness and specialization, a danger that might "deaden the spirit of the university by burdening it with procedures and tying it to routines," and that university size became equated with "reputation" and "power." But he, then, claimed that this very bigness and bureaucratization strengthened the role of college faculty, permitting them to better fight for academic freedom and tenure with its economic stability/rewards. Nevertheless, he was aware that nonconformity was punished by various devices, like delaying or refusing tenure and promotion or through daily harassment.

As for college presidents or Veblen's "Captains of Erudition," Metzger admitted that many of Veblen's barbs against them were accurate: That in wishing to increase their own and their university's power (raise more money, have more students and a larger physical plant), they acted like businessmen, many being mere "Rotarians." But he faulted Veblen for not seeing that these presidents, "energetic missionaries" of higher education, often protected the faculty's academic freedom from business and other interests, thus viewing them as mediators between academic life and the outside world.

Metzger also agreed with Veblen's assertion that professors were simply mere employees of business through its control of boards of trustees, averring that this had always been so. Furthermore, he lamented the "profound dissatisfaction and the deep-seated feeling among professors that their profession had lost caste" during Veblen's lifetime; that as against the "enormous returns that *accrued* to business, the professor's *emoluments* seemed small"; this despite the fact that by the end of the 19th century, they "had an average income 75 percent higher than that of clerical workers, 75 percent higher than that of Methodist and Congregationalist ministers, 300 percent higher than that of industrial laborers." But then, he noted that because of inflation, professors' salaries slipped downward by the 1920s, but still "higher than that of social workers, ministers, journalists, and librarians."[18] This, of course, indicated that most professors were lower-paid professionals, as is usually the case today.

In MacIver's work, Veblen was a leading character. In agreement with Veblen, MacIver wished for an academic environment in which "the student is freely permitted, indeed encouraged, to think for himself, to question, to discuss, and to differ," in the context of being "the junior partner of the teacher." Also, in following the guild spirit of

Veblen, and Dewey's *The School and Society*, he would minimize rote learning for one based on dialogue (and by implication, on learning by doing) and reduce the competitive, one-dimensional view of education that evaluated academic competence largely on formal testing.[19]

Then, again following Veblen, MacIver decried the lack of autonomy of American universities, pointing out that, although universities in Western Europe were under state aegis, they, nevertheless, were self-governing entities run by the faculty, without boards of trustees. He contrasted this condition with the typical American university in the 1940s, in which a board of trustees appointed a president, who selected the deans, who chose the department chairpersons.[20] With good reason, he disapproved of the power of administration over teaching staff. This, of course, is no longer always true because in many schools faculty input is substantial in choosing department heads and other administrative positions, although their capacity is often only advisory. But this greater power of teachers can only be explained by a paradigm of conflict with pits them against status quo administrators.

That leisure-class dominance and ideals are still pervasive in American university circles is axiomatic: Boards of trustees are overwhelmingly drawn from the wealthier business groups; administrators, by force of circumstance, are almost invariably of a conservative bent; the commercialized sports complex, usually interwoven with clerical and military ceremony, thrives; large corporations are ever more involved in funding research in science, business, and even in the liberal arts through partnerships or foundations; the military presence is widespread through the Reserve Officers Training Corps; and religious groups have a decidedly strong presence in various activities. All of these elements, with the partial exception of the religious one, basically left liberal in the mainline universities, but invariably conservative in fundamentalist Protestant colleges, indicate that large and influential sectors in higher education are hostile to socialism.

To be sure, socialist scholars have often suffered under this conservatism: Edward W. Bemis of the University of Chicago lost his position for supporting Debs and the American Railway Union in the Pullman strike; and Edward A. Ross, a noted sociologist and economist, was compelled to resign at Stanford University for favoring Debs and a moderate socialism which included the municipal ownership of public utilities (gas and water socialism).

Veblen himself in *Higher Learning* specifically mentioned Nearing's dismissal from the Wharton School of Commerce, University of Pennsylvania, in 1915, for activities on behalf of the working class, noting a common Philistine excerpt from the *Minneapolis Journal*, August 11, 1915, indicating that Nearing broke the trust of millionaire donors to colleges/universities. He, also, observed that universities "will not aim to alienate the affections of the large businessmen of a ripe age, by harbouring specialists whose inquiries are likely to traverse these old-settled (conservative) convictions in the social, economic, political, or religious domain."

Academic freedom was further assaulted in the 1917-18 period with America's entry into World War I. Some of the well-known scholars who lost university positions for opposing the war included Professors Nearing at the University of Toledo; William A. Schaper, Chairperson of the Political Science Department, University of Minnesota; two at Columbia University, J. McKeen Catell in Psychology, and Henry Wadsworth Longfellow in English. Also at Columbia the noted historian Beard was accused of condoning treasonable speech, but, although he successfully defend himself, he resigned in disgust.[21]

University teachers, of course, defended themselves against these attacks on academic freedom. To this end, they formed the AAUP in 1915, which despite its early elitism favoring associate and full professors, has greatly contributed to maintaining academic freedom by insisting on teachers' involvement in university governance and a tenure-track system to at once protect their academic freedom and economic security. Important in this is its Committee A on Academic Freedom and Academic Tenure.[22]

The last two great outbreaks against academic freedom occurred during the Second Red Scare of 1947-1958 and the fight to end the war in Vietnam, especially in the late 1960s and early 1970s. Soon after World War II, with the Republican capture of Congress in the 1946 elections, they orchestrated a hysterical campaign against Communists in government, the movie industry, education, and military, in which socialists and even liberals were suspected of aiding them. Not wishing to appear unpatriotic (the Cold War was on), the Democrats, although reluctantly, joined in the witch-hunts. Loyalty boards investigated millions, leading Communists were jailed under the 1940 Smith Act, and thousands lost their government, Hollywood, and teaching positions. In academia, notable witch-hunts at the University of California and the State of Washington systems met considerable resistance from the professoriate, but universities that cravenly capitulated to the hysteria included the University of Illinois, Penn State University, and The Ohio State University. Scores of faculty were dismissed as fear descended among those teaching in the humanities and social sciences. Again, during the Vietnam War, anti-war protests in academia met determined resistance from conservatives in the university hierarchy. (Much material on this is in MacIver's work, part three, "The Lines of Attack on Academic Freedom," which comprises one-third of the volume.[23] MacIver, unequivocally for academic freedom, quoted Commager that conservatives attacking free speech are un-American.[24])

The next problem concerns the relationship between higher education and class. Generally, for William Sewell in 1971, students from the upper-middle class to the wealthy, have these advantages over lower-middle and working-class ones: "An almost 4 to 1 advantage in access to college, a 6 to 1 advantage in college graduation, and a 9 to 1 advantage in graduate or professional education." In 1989, according to Daniel Levine and Robert Havinghurst in *Society and Education*, the typical student from the two wealthier classes attended colleges, while this was not true for the two lowest classes. Indeed, Katha Pollitt of *The Nation* reported that the poorest fourth of the population sent only 8 percent of its children to college. Out of fifteen million students attending college in 2000, 40 percent, invariably from the bottom two classes, especially the lowest or working-class, went on a part-time basis. By 2000, as percentage of population over age twenty-five with college education, 25 had two and less years and 25 at least four, with blacks at 17. Colleges/universities are a big industry in contemporary America, generating 200 billion dollars in revenue in 1995.

As already observed, most of the college graduates now form the large mass of lower mental labor (teachers, nurses, engineers, and computer specialists), having all the prerequisites to become proletarianized because their increasing numbers relatively cheapens their labor. Thus, although in the lower-middle class, they are an increasing part of the working-class/lower-middle class majority of mass society and should become more receptive to socialism.

To be sure, reflecting American class society, there is a class system in American higher education itself, tellingly spelled out annually in the *U.S. News and World Report's* "America's Best Colleges" guide. Its "1996 Annual Guide" lists the 229 national universities in this order: The top twenty-five, including Harvard, Princeton, Yale, Stanford, Columbia, Massachusetts Institute of Technology (the top six), followed by the next twenty-five, and second- to fourth-tier schools. Then, there are 161 national liberal arts colleges, with twenty-five leading ones, the next fifteen in order of prestige, then those from the second to fourth tiers. There is, also, a listing of the chief hundred regional colleges and universities from a total of 505 in this category.

Today, there are rising socioeconomic tensions in academia. To begin, paralleling the class system of American higher education, there are the increasing socioeconomic differences within the larger educational complexes between graduate-student teachers and adjunct teachers (more than two-fifths of college instructors are part-timers condemned to economic marginalization), on the one hand, and tenure-track ones, on the other. Today up to 70 percent of college teaching is done by graduate students and contingent teachers, as is 90 percent of grading. Indeed, in the last twenty-five years, graduate-student teachers have increased 40 percent, while tenure-track ones have declined by 10 percent. Furthermore, in this period, salaries of full professors have declined by 5 percent despite expanding student enrollment. The key response to these developments is increased unionization for regular faculty and for graduate student teachers/assistants, the latter now covering 20 percent of them, an indication of an intensified class struggle occurring within the confines of proletarianized mental labor.

It should also be noted that tuition and other costs for college students (room, board, and books) are now rapidly rising. In 2000, they are more than 35,000 dollars annually in the Ivy League private schools, 25,000 dollars in other private colleges, 12,000 dollars in four-year public ones, and 6,000 in the two-year variety, the last includes transportation costs.

Eighty percent of college students now are in the undergraduate divisions of public universities, many of which have two-year branch campuses, and two-year technical colleges, their students being largely from the upper working-class. The cost of attending these schools is usually only a small fraction of the more costly ones, but still quite expensive, forcing most students to work at outside jobs: for instance, more than 90 percent of the students at the Stark Campus of Kent State University in Canton, Ohio do so from twenty to forty or more hours a week. Overall, about half the nation's high-school and college students have outside work, making it all the more difficult for them to do justice to their studies.

This, of course, is part of the general malaise of public school education, grossly underfunded in many school districts, well described, for instance, by Jonathan Kozol in *Savage Inequalities*. Thus, not surprisingly, in Japan, which has more socioeconomic equality and more interest in education than the U.S., average high school students would rank in the top 5 to 10 percent of those in America.

That socioeconomic success is correlated with higher education and where it is acquired is axiomatic, critically involving friendship and networking. In 1998, for instance, the annual earnings in dollars of those with less than a high-school education was 16,000; high school, 23,500; bachelor's degree, 44,000; and post-graduate education, 63,000. For top positions in corporations and government, the leading twenty-five universities furnished 54 percent in the first category and 42 percent in the second. Furthermore, a study of 3,500 senior managers indicated. that those with an Ivy-League degree earned 32,851 dollars more in 1992 and received more promotions than those from other colleges.[25]

A recent work by Lawrence C. Soley, a professor of communication at various universities, *Leasing the Ivory Tower*, confirms Veblen's charge that universities are largely businesses involved with "merchantable knowledge," especially true in the sciences/medical/and business colleges, although not unknown in other areas. He again asserts the truism that the trustees of colleges/universities are usually successful business people, corporate executives being the "largest single group," and that university presidents and deans are usually politically conservative. (A prerequisite for being a college president is to raise funds from business.) Some of these presidents are notorious for attacking academic freedom, especially in the Social Sciences and the Humanities, the most known being John Silber of Boston University. The annual dollar salaries, including benefits and bonuses of these presidents are substantial, the average leading research schools in 1991 being 141,000 (for the top fifteen or so it is in the 300,000 range), those of smaller private universities being about 114,000. This income is supplemented by sitting on corporation boards and normally receiving fringe benefits as free housing, travel, and entertainment expenses, including membership to exclusive private clubs. By 2000, these incomes have doubled.

Many professors themselves become very successful entrepreneurs, especially in the business and science departments, receiving research grants from and being consultants to the federal government and private corporations. Their annual combined income is often in the many hundreds of thousands of dollars.

In the Social Sciences and history, there has been a proliferation of well-funded (from corporations and wealthy entrepreneurs) right-wing think tanks (there are dozens of them), like the Hoover Institution at Stanford University, the John M. Olin Institute for Strategic Studies at Harvard University, and the Center for the Study of Public Choice at George Mason University, that closely cooperate with off-campus conservative think tanks, like The Heritage Foundation, The American Enterprise Institute, the Cato Institute, and Center for Strategic and International Studies. The annual expenditures of only one of the larger ones exceeds the combined total of those on the left! In addition, the conservatives have almost a monopoly of endowed chairs, funded by corporations and wealthy individuals, and there are now about a hundred "free enterprise chairs" in American universities, many in major ones.[26]

Despite the vast amount of monies devoted by conservatives to influence higher education, the professoriate is basically liberal, with a sizable left-liberal element. According to a Carnegie Foundation report, as between conservative and liberal professors, the latter are twice as numerous as the former, this advantage increasing by three to one for those under age forty. Indeed, the conservative business presence is somewhat counterbalanced by more than 350 African-American and 500 women studies programs: The former includes such prestigious African-American research centers as Harvard's W. E.

B. Dubois Institute, the University of Virginia's Carter C. Woodson Institute, the University of Pennsylvania's Center for the Study of Black Literature and Culture, and the University of Rochester's Frederick Douglass Institute. That these programs are part of the left's assault on conservatism is axiomatic. But this is not all, because in departments like philosophy, history, sociology, art, and literature, there are now legions of liberal/left professors, many holding prestigious positions in leading colleges/universities.[27]

From the aftermath of World War II to the present, there were four significant mass movements to change the status quo: Civil Rights, war against poverty, to end the Vietnam War, and affirmative action. In all four, the university left played leading roles. Many of the activists in these struggles were part of the counterculture in the 1960s and 70s, a complex cultural phenomenon which involved college students and others living on the periphery of college campuses. The New Left, principally the Students for a Democratic Society (SDS) was its politicized arm.

Generally, the counterculture/New Left was against the "system," or present capitalist society. Like Veblen, they railed against a consumerist society which negated individualism for business conformity and economic success. Their individuality was against class and racist oppression, having great empathy for African-, Native-, and Hispanic-Americans. Millions of them, lived in communes, spontaneous mutual-aid groups whose members lived together, sharing expenses.

In the political realm, the SDS opted for a socialist society which would have warmed the heart of the Wobbly Veblen, one based on participatory democracy, ownership and control of industry by the working class, an end to a wasteful armaments race and war in Vietnam.[28]

The rise of the left in the universities has met opposition from conservative scholars who lament the new militancy of leftists in general. Three rather recent examples will be presented. The first by the well-known conservative ideologue, Russell Kirk in the late 70s, and two in the 90s by Roger Kimball and Dinesh D'Souza.

Kirk, in *Decadence and Renewal in the Higher Learning,* unrelentingly opposed the new progressive trends. An unmitigated snob, he was appalled by the stupidity of the masses, the "banality and crass commercialism of TV," the drug culture, and of students occupying university buildings, likening them to "educational Luddites." This criticism has some validity, but neglects to mention that in a socially deeply divided society, workers and minorities must express their malaise in some such manner; we do not live in a utopia. Indeed, the cultural junk thrown at working-class youth, reflecting their alienation, may be utilized by them to change society.

Basically, Kirk envisaged the university from a mythical historical perspective, as simply an institution to preserve and extend the knowledge and culture of the past, neglecting to observe that it was also used by the leisure class to train its superior cadres and to buttress its cultural hegemony.

There were, to be sure, the usual excesses in the student sit-ins and demonstrations in the 60s and early 70s, but the media and Kirk overemphasized them, both rather oblivious to the deeper causes for the student revolt—American imperialism in Vietnam, racism, and social problems endemic in classist societies.

Kirk's conservatism, however, did not stop with the student revolt, also deploring more students enrolling in college, thus eroding traditionally high academic standards. It is undeniable that many working-class students entering college are not academically well prepared, but this has nothing to do with general intelligence, but everything to do with class oppression. The New Left, obviously aware of this, attempted to change the balance of forces within the university by promoting a more egalitarian culture that by its very nature had to bring in the mass culture in varying degree to make the traditional college education more relevant to social layers not previously exposed to it. Education itself should not only extend learning, but change the world, a thesis that Kirk studiously ignored, as befits his conservatism.[29]

Kimball's *Tenured Radicals* is a highly entertaining work which unstintingly attacks the academic left for daring to overturn the status quo. Kimball claimed that this was performed by the left's assaulting the accepted canons of what is significant in Western culture and of their being obscurantist and elitist. He was also envious of the left's cultural hegemony in many areas of learning/culture, as in deconstruction studies and art criticism: In this area, he unleashed a long diatribe against a premier left intellectual art journal, *October*, for perpetuating the élan of the early Bolshevik Revolution. He also regretted the rise of leading left academics, like Stanley Fish at Duke University, chairperson of its English Department, and a professor of law there. Fish himself was accused of being instrumental in appointing prominent academic leftists to the English Department. Furthermore, Kimball solemnly informed us that Cornell West, a prominent black academic and socialist, admired the French Marxist Louis Althusser, who loses all credibility for murdering his wife, and Herbert Marcuse. These inroads by the left probably signaled the end of the world! This work was funded by the John T. Olin Foundation.[30]

D'Souza's *Illiberal Education* was a screed attacking the rise of the left in some departments in academia, including its influence in African-American and women's studies. D'Souza was perturbed that in attempting to defend themselves from racism and sexism, blacks and women were forcing higher education to follow "political correctness," as if this were a crime. But was he not aware of the attacks on the left, blacks, and women in American society since its inception?

To be sure, there was some truth in D'Souza assertion that some black and feminist scholars had exaggerated notions of black importance in Western civilization and centrality of gender in explaining the human condition. His faulting affirmative-action programs for discrimination against Asian-Americans also had obvious truth, but he failed to point out that blacks often had very competitive SAT scores, and that colleges/universities bestowed preferential treatment to the children of alumnae and of the wealthy for admission. This work also received monies from the John T. Olin Foundation.[31]

Notes

1. Thorstein Veblen, *The Higher Learning in America: A Memorandum on the Conduct of Universities by Business Men* (New York: Augustus M. Kelley, 1965)—first published in 1918. Brinkley, *American History*, II, 562.

2. Dorfman, *Veblen*, pp. 17-36 on Veblen at Carleton.

3. *Ibid.*, pp. 33-44.

4. Richard Hofstadter and Walter P. Metzger, *The Development of Academic Freedom in the United States* (New York: Columbia University Press, 1955), p. 279.

5. *Ibid.*, pp. 304-05, on the various quotations.

6. Veblen, *Higher Learning*, pp. 5 and 18. On the horrendous problems that working-class children, especially those from the lower half of the working class have in public schools, often woefully underfunded, see for instance, Jonathan Kozol, *Death at an Early Age* (Boston: Houghton-Mifflin, 1967); and Jonathan Kozol, *Savage Inequalities: Children in America's Schools* (New York: Harper Perennial, 1992). Also, see John Holt, *How Children Fail* (New York: Pittman, 1964). John Dewey, *The School and Society* (Chicago: University of Chicago Press, 1943), pp. 63-94. Alfie Kohn, *No Contest: The Case Against Competition* (Boston: Houghton Mifflin, 1986), pp. 197-245.

7. Veblen, *Higher Learning*, pp. 85-134 and 220 ff.

8. Veblen, *Leisure Class*, p. 145. Hofstadter, *Anti-Intellectualism in American Life*, pp. 262-63, states that Veblen's *The Higher Learning* condemns the business college of the university and divinity schools to the lower depths, as being outside the purview of the university.

9. Charles A. Beard, "The Hire [*sic*] Learning in America," *The Dial*, Dec. 14, 1918, pp. 553-55.

10. Riesman, *Veblen*, p. 100.

11. Upton Sinclair, *The Goose-Step: A Study of American Education* (Pasadena, CA: The Author, 1923), pp. 18 ff., 163-64, 243, 297, 308, 375, 424, 455.

12. See Veblen, *Engineers and the Price System*, pp. 150-62; Sumner, *Folkways*, pp. 51 and 64; William Graham Sumner, *War and Other Essays* (New Haven: Yale University Press, 1911), p. 45.

13. Plato, *The Republic*, pp. 123-25.

14. Marx and Engels, *German Ideology*, p. 39.

15. Quintin Hoare and Geoffrey Novell Smith, editors and translators, *Selections from the Prison Notebooks of Antonio Gramsci* (New York: International Publishers, 1971), pp. 228-45.

16. Moore Jr., *Bases of Obedience and Revolt*, p. 42.

17. The Hofstadter and Metzger work has been already mentioned. Robert M. MacIver, *Academic Freedom in Our Time* (New York: Gordian Press, 1967). Earlier published by Columbia University Press in 1955.

18. Hofstadter and Metzger, *Academic Freedom*, pp. 452-67, on the various quotations and statistics.

19. MacIver, *Academic Freedom*, p. 206 on the two quotations. John Dewey, *Democracy in Education: An Introduction to the Philosophy of Education* (New York: Free Press, 1966), pp. 83-99, urges that democratic ideals demand that education be so constructed as to involve the citizenry into meaningful social and political participation in the community.

20. MacIver, *Academic Freedom*, pp. 68-69, on the two quotations.

21. Hofstadter and Metzger, *Academic Freedom*, pp. 413-67, entitled "Academic Freedom and Big Business." Veblen, *Higher Learning in America* (New York: B.W. Huebsch, 1917 edition), pp. 184-85 for quotation on Nearing and excerpt from the *Minneapolis Journal* which he comments on.

22. Hofstadter and Metzger, *Academic Freedom*, pp. 396-412.

23. MacIver, *Academic Freedom*, pp. 123-200, for instance.

24. *Ibid.*, p. 195. Henry Steele Commager, "Who Is Loyal to America?" *Harper's Magazine*, CXCV (Sept. 1947), 198-99. For a detailed coverage of the witch-hunts against Communists in America, see David Caute, *The Great Fear: The Anti-Communist Purge Under Truman and Eisenhower* (New York: Simon and Schuster, 1978); on various witch-hunts, see, for instance, pp. 403-45 in secondary and higher education, pp. 349-400 in labor unions, pp. 487-538 in Hollywood and entertainment in general.

25. On socioeconomic inequality and higher education, see William H. Sewell, "Inequality of Opportunity for Higher Education," *American Sociological Review*, No. 6, Oct., 1971, pp. 793-809. Daniel V. Levine and Robert J. Havinghurst, *Society and Education*, 7th ed. (Boston: Allyn and Bacon, 1989), pp. 58-62. On the 8 percent figure attending college for the bottom fourth of the class chain, see Katha Pollitt, "Don't Blame Me, I Voted for Nader," *The Nation*, March 3, 1997, p. 9. On college and graduate-school rankings, *U.S. News and World Report* issues annual ones. On more graduate student teachers at low salaries, more unionization, and so forth, see Gordon Laffer, "Graduate Student Unions Fight the Corporate University," *Dissent*, Fall 2001, pp. 63-70; and Larry Hanley, "Troubled Times for Public Higher Education," *Dissent*, Spring 1996, pp. 67-79. On Stark Campus students, my polls from 1968 to 1994. On horrid school conditions for inner-city children, see Kozol, *Savage Inequalities*, pp. 1-32, for instance. On Japanese high-school students doing better than their American counterparts, see Hedrick Smith, *Challenge to America*, Part II, "The Heart of the Nation" (Films for the Humanities and Sciences, 1994). On elite higher education and its graduates, see Lionel S. Lewis and William Paul Kingston, "The Best, the Brightest and the Undergraduate Elite

Institutions," *Academe*, Nov.-Dec., 1989, pp. 28-33. On income and education, see *The New York Times 2001 Almanac* (New York: Penguin, 2000), p. 358. On corporate and government leaders, see Lewis and Kingston article in *Academe*. On the economic advantage in attending Ivy League Schools, see *Akron Beacon Journal*, Sept. 26, 1995, p. D4.

26. Lawrence C. Soley, *Leasing the Ivory Tower: The Corporate Takeover of Academia* (Boston, MA: South End Press, 1995), pp.20 ff., 40 ff., 57-153.

27. On the ratio of liberal to conservative professors, see *The Condition of the Professoriate*, Carnegie Foundation, Washington, D.C., 1989, p. 143. On the number of African-American studies, see Christopher John Farley, "African Culture Resurges on Campus," *USA Today*, Nov. 21, 1989. On the number of Women's Studies, see "Report of the Committee on the Status of Women in the Academic Profession," by American Association of University Professors, *Academe*, July-August 1989, pp. 35-39. On the large numbers of left professors in the humanities and social sciences today, see Seymour Martin Lipset, *Rebellion in the University*, with a New Introduction by the Author (New Brunswick, NJ: Transaction Hooks, 1993), pp. xiii-xxiv.

28. There is a plethora of works on the New Left and the 1960s and after. Some of the more recent include: James J. Farrell, *The Spirit of the Sixties: The Making of Postwar Radicalism* (New York: Routledge, 1997). Anderson, *The Movement and the Sixties* Chapter 2, pp. 87-130 "The Movement and the Sixties Generation," and Chapter 5, pp. 241-91, "Counterculture," are particularly interesting and informative. Stanley Aronowitz, *The Death and Rebirth of American Radicalism* (New York: Routledge, 1996), Chapter 2, pp. 57-90, "The New Left: An Analysis," is a good account of the movement. Seymour Martin Lipset, *Rebellion in the University* (Boston, MA: Little, Brown, 1972), pp. 80-123 on the family backgrounds of New Left student-activists, many from politicized upper-middle class families, many Jewish. An important guru of the New Left representing a libertarian neo-Marxism is Herbert Marcuse, a German-Jewish refugee professor, author of *Counterrevolution and Revolt* (Boston: Beacon Press, 1972); *One Dimensional Man: Studies in the Ideology of Advanced Industrial Societies* (Boston: Beacon Press, 1964). Staughton Lynd, *Inside Our Hope: A Steadfast Radical's Thoughts on Rebuilding the Movement* (Ithaca, NY: ILR Press, 1997), Part III, pp. 141-231, "Solidarity Unionism," is mostly on the Youngtown-Pittsburgh area workers' struggle to save the steel mills and ends with thoughts on the internationalization of capital and on the Webbs, Lenin, and Rosa Luxemburg. Lynd's message of hope is that as long as there is oppression, the struggle for liberation continues.

29. Russell Kirk, *Decadence and Renewal in the Higher Learning: An Episodic History of American University and College Since 1953* (South Bend, IN: Gateway Editions, 1978), pp. 127 and 225 on the quotations; pp. 275-79 on the reading lists; pp. 150-63 on his snobbery.

30. Roger Kimball, *Tenured Radicals: How Politics Has Corrupted Our Higher Education* (New York: Harper and Row, 1990), pp.63-67 and 76-115, for instance.

31. Dinesh D'Souza, *Illiberal Education: The Politics of Race and Sex on Campus* (New York: The Free Press, 1991), Chapters 2, 4, 5, 6, 7, for instance.

XVI   Historical Progression

THAT VEBLEN PICTURED HISTORY AS COMPRISING various discrete elements is axiomatic, as already adduced form the preceding chapters. From a broad perspective, he theorized that human interaction with nature, resulting in an ever more sophisticated technology or economic organization, brought about attendant changes in class alignments, the two influencing individual and social psychology, in which conflict between individuals, classes, and nations became the norm, thus his tying the economic with the anthropological/sociological and psychological. From a broad historical perspective Veblen's historical progression is a synthesis of Darwin's evolutionary biology and Marx's economically based class struggle.

To be sure, this perspective was very similar to that of America's progressive historians in the early 20th century—Frederick Jackson Turner, Beard, Vernon Louis Parrington (an English professor), and James Harvey Robinson (Beard and Robinson were colleagues of Veblen at the New School for Social Research)—whose historiography emphasized the importance of science and its methods, including the validity of evolution, and increasing importance of advanced technology leading to the rise of large working and lower-middle classes that in the long run would be predisposed to some form of socialism.[1]

Veblen saw the earliest historical period in the nebulously long "savage" one, in which humanity's primitive technology compelled it to gather and hunt food in various proportions, at first by stones, then the spear and bow and arrow for big-game hunting. The latter improvement, for him, (slight by our standards, but of great significance to primitive groups), ruptured dependence on foraging for food and hunting small animals, and in conjunction with natural selection, permitted male hunters, not burdened with bearing children, to become ever more larger and swifter than females, consigned to the care of children, foraging, and hearth. The next level of Veblen's historical schema was the "lower barbarian" period or New Stone Age, beginning about ten to twelve thousand years ago, "from primitive savagery to barbarism," when human groups of the "predatory habit of mind," i.e., those either engaged in "war or the hunting of large game or both," evolved into status societies. This condition, for him, was related to a higher productive level, resulting in increasing labor division, exacerbating the earlier one between the genders, in which "some employments," of "exploit" (as of military leaders and priests) became "more worthy" than "menial" others, or ordinary work performed by women and lower-status men. Underlying this dichotomy was "personal force." But although this labor division, which obviously involved status groups, was rather marked, class divisions as yet had not developed.

In the progression in which primitive cultures, peaceful and egalitarian, developed a war-prone and class society, Veblen intertwined the technological and social: The Agricultural Revolution assumed a primary role in the process ("the crop plants appear to have come earlier than the domestic animals" and that "with tillage necessarily goes a sedentary manner of life"), which decisively increased the food supply and possibility of acquiring a surplus from another's labor. Advancing technology in agriculture was matched with better weaponry (like swords and battle axes), in conjunction with continuing war activity enslaving the losers' women, beginning the general subordination of women in a sexual-economic manner, and of male division/conflict on the basis of strength, to bring about the development of private property. In this pattern, for him, the enslavement of women was a primary factor. Once private property itself was well advanced, it engendered a further conflict within the society "between men for the possession of goods," based on "emulation" and "invidious distinction" for more "honor" and "self-respect." With the transmission of property to descendants, classes rapidly formed, characteristic of "civilization," with its extensive labor division and great socioeconomic and other inequalities, at the apex of which was the leisure class ruling the state.

Once the class/tribe and state complex is in place, it was possible to acquire wealth and power through not only economic but political means; the two, of course, were related and usually came in a bundle, although, depending on the historical period, one element might be more important than the other. For instance, imperialism was an obvious means of acquiring more wealth and power, as indicated by the success of the Roman Empire under its caste/class system, the patricians or Roman nobility representing the sword. This continued with the European nobility under feudalism, monopolizing the means of violence, and under capitalism by a nobility and capitalist combination.

The rise of the state/civilization encompassed, for Veblen, the higher barbarian period/culture which endured to the European Middle Ages (from fifty-five hundred years ago to six hundred years ago); with its advent his leisure class was now firmly in place. In this period, two leading antagonisms occupied center stage: war among various groups and internal status/class struggles, principally between the leisure class, with its dependents, and the rest of the people, particularly farmers and workers, "in chronic dissatisfaction," without the property/honor of the higher classes.[2]

These first three Veblenian stages of human history significantly posited that early peaceful cultures through technological changes would be transformed into war-driven and antagonistic societies. But Veblen believed that since primary human propensities were peaceful and cooperative, this "good" part, as technology advanced, would generally lead to less warlike societies in the next or capitalist stage and even more so under socialism.

It should be noted that Veblen's progression on the rise of class society/state somewhat differed, but not significantly, from that of Marx/Engels. Both agreed on the critical tie between economic surplus and private property in the formation of increasing labor division and subsequent rise of status groups and classes, but Veblen, contrary to Marx/Engels, more emphasized the capture of enemy women as slaves.

Veblen's historical pattern was also close to Ward's, who claimed that although early humanity was egalitarian and fraternal, the rise of private property invariably led to socioeconomic and political inequalities, which, in their wake, engendered war, the subjection of women and slavery. The modern period itself was characterized by big industry, with the bourgeoisie emerging as the exploiting class, as "wealth passed into the hands of the industrial leaders, and the great economic struggle began."[3]

The historical drama from primitive society to villages in the New Stone Age to civilization, as developed by Veblen, Marx, Ward and others, is now the common wisdom of historians and social scientists. A typical example in a history textbook by Philip Lee Ralph, et al., World Civilizations, follows: The authors had "hunter gatherers" in Western Asia developing agriculture and domesticating animals, allowing for "surplus production" and permanent settlements or villages, associated with a large increase in population and growing labor division. Warfare now began for "there was loot in a village." Over a period of time, as villages were amalgamated through war, an upper class of full-time military and priestly (religion was seen as a socially unifying factor) functionaries emerged, ruling the underlying village population from cities, in the process of which there developed a system of writing for "record-keeping." Unflinchingly, the authors accepted that this process was based on "subduing and exploiting others."[4] (This progression should be slightly modified by Keeley's [War and Civilization] assertions of war in the Upper/Late Paleolithic Age, indicating that less complex levels of social organization and accompanying lower economic surplus were also capable of resulting in war.)

The period following the higher barbarian one, for Veblen, was the current one of capitalism, which arrived upon the scene six or so centuries ago. He divided it into two phases: The first, or what was commonly known as the Commercial Revolution, from 1400 to 1700, and the second, from the 18th century Industrial Revolution in England to the present. It was in the second phase, for him, that an accelerating technology again decisively changed the contours of society and its basic direction:

> In the modern industrial culture, industry and industrial products have pro-
> gressively gained upon humanity, until these creations of man's ingenuity
> have latterly come to take the dominant place in the cultural scheme; and it is
> not too much to say that they have become the chief factor in shaping man's
> habits of thought.[5]

It was in this period that advancing technology, for Veblen, increased the class struggle between labor and capital, perhaps culminating in socialism. In this scenario, both Veblen and Marx held that capital's drive to constantly reduce the per-unit cost of production was of primary importance. It resulted for them (more explicitly for Marx than Veblen) in a proletarian class struggle against capital within the parameters of technological development and concomitant new organization to better control labor by relatively deskilling and cheapening it, like the introduction of the factory system, itself a vital component in destroying the craft guilds and relative autonomy of skilled labor, along with prohibiting and vitiating the power of unions in factories through government action. But in the long run, both agreed that new technologies ultimately were the seedbed for socialism as they bring about an ever expanding and more militant workingclass.[6]

Veblen himself had much to say about the main outlines of the next historical stage, of socialism, which he regarded as a broad and complex phenomenon in the process of formation, unleashed by a pervasive machine technology, with its matter-of-fact view of social reality. This exacerbated for him, the principal class struggle, between labor and capital or "those employed in the industrial and those employed in the pecuniary professions," sharpened by the factory setting, which brought workers together in close proximity to one another, normally developing among them a strong "sense of solidarity."

Thus it was, for Veblen, that there was a rising "socialistic disaffection" in his day in "the more important industrial towns" which contained "the effective nucleus of the socialistic malcontents," composed "of the more intelligent body of workmen in the highly organized and specialized industries," or skilled workers in the "mechanical trades." But he did not limit socialism to the industrial cities alone, noting its "inroads among the rural population of the American prairie region, where a mechanically organized and standardized method of farming prevails, with a large use of mechanical appliances."

Veblen also examined European socialists searching for votes among farmers and office workers: To appeal to farmers whose "habits of life" rested "on the ancient levels of handicrafts...and prescriptive custom," favoring the status quo, socialist parties invariably compromised their ideals. As for office workers becoming socialists, he observed a remote possibility, although they were reformists, interested in "social settlement, Prohibition, Clean Politics, Single Tax...Christian Science, New Thought, or some such cultural thimblerig." Indeed, for him, "accountants and office employees were nearly as conservative as clergymen and lawyers," in close proximity to the conservative business community. (As Mills pointed (out in *White Collar*, in 1900, office workers earned twice the amount of blue-collar workers and had twice their education, eight years to four.) He also placed "politicians," "soldiers," and "men of fashion" in the conservative or status quo camp, for they emphasized the importance of "proprietary rights," of "ownership," and he was also aware of socialism's unpopularity with unskilled workers (recent arrivals from the countryside),with rural/small town inhabitants, and with "half-civilized or barbarous countries." In these observations, the penetration of an advanced machine technology on the popular consciousness was the key ingredient for socialism.[7]

The older "Bolshevik" Veblen often commented on the bitter class warfare between labor and capital, a good example being in his *Absentee Ownership and Business Enterprise*:

> In the negotiations between owners and workmen there is little use for the ordinary blandishments of salesmanship. The two parties to the quarrel—for it is after all a quarrel—have learned what to count on. And the bargaining between them therefore settles down...into a competitive use of unemployment, privation, restriction of work and output, strikes, shut-downs and lockouts, espionage, pickets, and similar manoeuvres of mutual derangement, with a large recourse to menacing language and threats of mutual sabotage.[8]

This includes "sabotage that runs into violent offense against persons and property."[9]

On the subject of class complexity, Veblen mentioned, in addition to a capitalist elite, an upper-middle class, presumably of the higher professionals and other relatively prosperous businessmen; a lower-middle class of farmers, small business, and lower brain workers, like office workers; and a working class of skilled/unskilled workers. At the very bottom of his class progression stood a relatively large "underfed class" of "lower-class delinquents" (Marx's *lumpenproletariat*), compelled to "a closely enforced struggle...to meet its daily needs," condemning its members to becoming criminals, prone to idleness, gambling, and sports whose mindset closely resembled that of the leisure class. Veblen's class model, however, had an enduring polarity between producers—the working-class, including technicians and engineers, the latter, a large part of the upper-working and lower-middle classes—and leisure-class parasites.

Veblen, as already observed, contrary to Marx, did not present a coherent theory of capitalist exploitation of workers that in the process would enlarge the working-class as it merged with the lower-middle class to become one, which increasingly encompassed both manual and intellectual labor. Veblen's working-class/lower-middle class alliance through the rise of mass technology with increasing technicians/engineers component was close to that of Marx.

The class model proposed by Veblen, like those delineated by most of his contemporaries and before (Marx is an exception here, often offering specificity; for instance, in *Capital*, he presented the number of servants as opposed to industrial workers in Britain in the 1860s) was inexact on the size and composition of classes. Furthermore, he failed to confront the problem of class amorphousness, involving intermediate classes, related to Marx's concept of transition classes, as in *The Eighteenth Brumaire of Louis Bonaparte,* of individuals simultaneously occupying two class positions. For instance, was a skilled worker in the working-class or in the lower middle-class, especially if he had greatly profited from savings in the stock market, or in neither of them?[10]

Veblen's largely two-class polarity social model was not novel in socialist thought, following that of Marx and Engels; but unlike Veblen, they regarded entrepreneurs as playing a creative role in the amassing of capital, although well aware of capital's linkage to "conquest, robbery, and murder." But other socialists, like Saint-Simon (technically, not one) and Fourier, and a large segment of the American frontier tradition were more in agreement with Veblen's schema of antithetical classes divided along the basis of parasitism and usefulness.[11]

Socialists, like Veblen and Marx, were not the only ones to employ the concept of social class in understanding social reality. Leading conservative thinkers, for instance, during Veblen's lifetime also certainly did: Sumner; the Italian sociologist Gaetano Mosca; the Italian economist/sociologist Vilfredo Pareto; and Weber—the "four."[12] The four posited that small elite groups ruled society, in which the majority of the people, the masses, were dissatisfied and turbulent.[13] For Sumner, there were three classes—a capitalist elite, a middle class, and a minority proletariat. For Mosca and Pareto (although they too were aware of social complexity), the elite was generally contrasted to the masses. For Weber the ruling elite of Kaiser, army, and state bureaucracy (the wealthy bourgeoisie was not included) in Germany governed a society in which status groups took precedence over classes in daily conflict; although he saw a middle class of professionals and others between masses and rulers.[14]

The four did not deny the reality of the class struggle: Sumner apprehensively envisioned future America in the grips of a rising socioeconomic misery leading to increased class conflict between the proletariat and bourgeoisie. For Pareto and Mosca, the class struggle was an equally valid phenomenon between rulers and ruled. For Pareto, as an example, the class struggle necessarily did not proceed toward the goal of a classless society, but was interminable, as revolutionary elites of more able individuals, frustrated by the older elites in their drive to join them, used/led the dissatisfied but incompetent masses against them. In his circulation of elites, velocity of change increased during a successful revolution. The four presented this gloomy prognosis for socialism: Should it assume power, an elite would still manage society and deny universal equality. Weber, for example, emphasized that large-scale industry and labor division bureaucratized society—even under socialism—negating the principle of equality.[15] Ultimately, the four based class or status inequality on either a quasi- or strictly biological inequality, and the normally acquired advantages from inherited wealth and power.[16] For them, there was ultimately only contempt for the helpless masses, but admiration for the rulers.

To better understand any historical period, one should determine the primary class struggle, i.e., the steepest general class polarity, itself not always acute. This is because the peasants and workingclass are habituated to the subordination of enforced cooperation with the master classes, burdened by labor division and scarcity realities and divided by ethno-cultural differences. As for individual rebellion and small-scale revolt, they are usually quickly and ruthlessly crushed by governing elites. Indeed, in the short run, individual disagreements and status differences within classes occupy individual attention much more than any class struggle; indeed master-class hegemony is often pictured by the masses as eternal or almost so. Even so, for proper historical understanding, individual and status conflicts should be viewed within the context of the larger social oppression and class struggles against it.

In the larger sweep of history, class conflict, even when not acute, is still constant (Marx and Engels in *The Communist Manifesto* recounted the universality of the class struggle, "now hidden, now open"): In Hebrew Civilization, for instance, its Prophetic Revolution, including biblical Codes of Deuteronomy and Leviticus, and early Christian Communism, could not be understood without assuming it. The Greco-Roman world itself was replete with the class struggle of the masses against their rulers: For instance, the principal Greek philosophers, Plato and Aristotle, were much aware of it—Plato's *The Republic* was predicated on ending it and Aristotle's *The Politics* had it as the central category for understanding politics, reflecting a well-delineated one between the average citizenry and aristocracy/capitalists. In Rome, the class struggle between plebeians and patricians and between slaves and citizenry (the great revolt of Spartacus comes to mind in the latter instance) was certainly not fiction. (These class struggles were well described by G.E.B. De Ste. Croix in *The Class Struggle in the Ancient Greek World* which included the Roman and Hebrew experiences.)[17] In the Middle Ages and beyond, the class struggle between peasantry and nobility resonated with the 14th century peasant revolts, of the Jacquerie in France and of the English one, and of the early 16th century German Workers' and Peasants' Revolt.

Indeed, with the rise of industrial capitalism in the last three or so centuries, political activity among the peasantry and working-class has quickened, especially in the 20th, one characterized by war, revolution, and rapid technological development (technological advances necessarily intensify class struggle for socialism) whose milestones in strengthening socialism include three Russian Revolutions, 1905 and two in 1917, the Chinese Communist triumph in 1949, socialist revolutions in the Third World, and the rise of social democracy in Europe, Japan, India, South Africa, and elsewhere. But there is also the implosion of the Soviet Union and its Communism, effected by a nascent bourgeoisie, to be considered.

NOTES

1. On the Greek philosophers, see, for instance, Matthew T. McLure, *The Early Philosophers of Greece* (New York: Appleton-Century, 1935) and Andrew Thomas Cole, *Democritus and the Sources of Greek Anthropology* (Cleveland, OH: Western Reserve University Press. 1967). On Vico, Condorcet, Hegel, Comte, and Marx, see Patrick A. Gardiner, edited and Introduction, *Theories of History* (New York: The Free Press, 1959). On Turner, Beard, and Parrington, see Richard Hofstadter, *The Progressive Historians: Turner, Beard, Parrington* (New York: Vintage Hooks, 1970), pp. 47-164, 167-346, 349-434. James Harvey Robinson, *The New History: Essays Illustrating the Modern Historical Outlook* (New York; Macmillan Co., 1918).

2. On Veblen's view of early historical change, see *Leisure Class*, pp. 21-40. On Veblen's description of the Agricultural Revolution, see *Place of Science*, pp. 480 ff.

3. On Marx's view of early man, see, for instance, Shaw, *Marx's Theory of History*, pp. 114-18. Also see Engels, *Origin of the Family*, pp, 47-48 on the advent of agriculture and domestication of animals leading to an economic surplus and slavery. On the differences between Marx/Engels and Veblen on the rise of social oppression, see Diggins, *Bard of Savagery*, pp. 64-69. Also, see Ward, *Pure Sociology*, pp. 273-79 whose views of early humanity are very similar to Veblen's. On Marx's/Engels' appraisal of primitive societies, which compare favorably with those of contemporary anthropology, see Mandel, *Marxist Economic Theory*, I, 23-94.

4. Philip Lee Ralph *et al.*, *World Civilizations: Their History and Their Culture*, 8th ed. (New York: W.W. Norton, 1991), I, 14-26.

5. Veblen, *Theory of Business Enterprise*, pp. 302-400. For the long quotation, see Veblen, *Place of Science*, p. 17.

6. Marx, *Capital*, I, 353-488, for instance.

7. Veblen, *Theory of Business Enterprise*, pp. 321-53.

8. Thorstein Veblen, *Absentee Ownership and Business Enterprise: The Case of America* (New York: Augustus M. Kelley, 1964), p. 406. (First published in 1923.)

9. *Ibid.*, p. 407.

10. On Veblen and social classes, see especially, *Leisure Class*, pp. 22 ff., 87 ff., and 155 ff.

11. Marx and Engels, *Communist Manifesto*, pp. 11-19 on a two-class model in which capitalist entrepreneurs are creative. Marx, *Capital*, I, 784-87, on the predatory nature of capitalism. Manuel, *New World of Henri St.-Simon*, pp. 252-53 on Saint-Simonian idlers and producers. Manuel, *Prophets of Paris*, p. 217 on Fourier's parasites. Hofstadter, *Age of Reform*, pp. 60-119 on the Populists.

12. On Sumner, see M.R. Davis, *William Graham Sumner: An Essay of Commentary and Selections* (New York: Crowell, 1963). On Mosca, Patero, Weber, and Michels, see H. Smart Hughes, *Consciousness and Society: The Reorientation of European Thought, 1890-1930* (New York: Alfred A. Knopf, 1961), Chapter 7. On Pareto and Mosca, see James H. Meisel, *Pareto and Mosca* (Englewood Cliffs, NJ: Prentice-Hall, 1965). On Weber, see W.J. Mommsen, *The Age of Bureaucracy: Perspectives on the Political Sociology of Max Weber* (New York: Harper and Row, 1974).

13. On ruling elites (combinations of warriors, religious leaders, and capitalists), those generally agreeing with Veblen as to their composition include: Sumner, *Folkways*, p. 64; Gaetano Mosca, *The Ruling Class*, translated by Hannah D. Kahn (New York: McGraw-Hill, 1939), pp. 50-69; Vilfredo Pareto, *Mind and Society*, translated by Andrew Bongiorno and Arthur Livingstone, edited by the latter, 4 volumes, (New York: Harcourt, Brace and Co., 1935), III, 1423-31; Max Weber, *Economy and Society: An Outline of Interpretive Sociology*, eds. Guenther Roth and Claus Wittich, 3 vols. (New York: Bedminster Press, 1968), II, 941-1003. For Mosca, Pareto, and Weber, bureaucrats are ancillaries of elites.

14. On class structure: Summer, *Folkways*, p. 47; Mosca, *Ruling Class*, pp. 110-19, on "class distinctions"; Pareto, *Mind and Society*, III, 1427: "The least we can do is to divide society into two strata: a higher stratum, which usually contains the rulers, and a lower stratum, which usually contains the ruled." Weber, *Economy and Society*, I, 302-07, on "status groups and classes" indicates many.

15. On the acceptance of the class struggle: William Graham Sumner *Earth-Hunger and Other Essays* (New Haven: Yale University, 1913), p. 289. Mosca, *Ruling Class*, pp, 199-221, on class and revolution, in which economic discontent and other factors propel the masses to revolt. Pareto, *Mind and Society*, III, 1431 ff. Vilfredo Pareto, *Les systemes socialistes*, 2nd. ed., 2 vols (Paris: M. Giard, 1926), I, 16 ff., which accepts Marxian class struggle, but which links it to outside elites leading the masses. Weber, *Economy and Society*, II, 930-32, stresses the importance of status struggle in social conflict.

16. On the biological superiority of the wealthy to the masses, see Summer, *Earth-Hunger*, pp. 351-52. On elite groups passing on their economic, cultural, and other advantages to their offspring, making for general social stability, see Mosca, *Ruling Class*, pp. 5-69.

17. G.E.M. de Ste. Croix, *The Class Struggle in the Greek World: From the Archaic Age to the Arab Conquests* (London: Gerald Duckworth, 1981), Chapter 5, "The Class Struggle in Greek History on the Political Plane," pp. 278-326; Chapter 6, "Rome the Suzerain," 327-408, for instance.

XVII Critiques of
and Importance of Veblen

Critiques

REPRESENTATIVE CRITIQUES OF VEBLEN across the ideological spectrum, including different views among socialists, as well as his importance as thinker are now presented. (For a comprehensive examination of critiques on Veblen, see Rick Tilman's admirable *Thorstein Veblen and His Critiques, 1891-1963.*)

The definitive work on Veblen is by Joseph Dorfman, *Thorstein Veblen and His America* (1934), published in the midst of the Great Depression. Dorfman, a professor of economic history at Columbia University from the 1930s to 1970s, is also author of *The Economic Mind in American Civilization*, a noteworthy five-volume work (1946-59). His study on Veblen, of 556 pages, not only delved deeply into his life and works, often quoting lengthy excerpts from them, summarizing them and placing them within the context of the time, including reviews on them and resulting intellectual controversy, but also presented a plethora of material on the general economic, social, and political life of America, particularly of its radical liberal and socialist elements, well illustrating Veblen's America and Veblen's interaction with it. In this work, Dorfman emerged as Veblen's alter ego.[1]

A conservative view on Veblen is by Lev E. Dobriansky, a professor of history and economics at Georgetown University, and ambassador to the Bahamas, from 1982 to 1986, under the Reagan administration—*Veblenism: A New Critique* (1957). He basically viewed Veblen from the prism of a conservative Catholic Thomism, which, although disagreeing with his atheistic and socialist orientation, recognized his genius.

Dobriansky asserted, for instance, that Veblen's views on the establishment of early civilization—-technological advances leading to the formation of status groups/classes resulting in warfare and property/slavery—were "fictional," on the basis that it turned the peaceful savage into a predator and exploiter of other humans, "an exceedingly strange mutation for a peaceably conditioned people to become strangely warlike." He obviously was incorrect for the historical process leading to civilization, as already observed, is well understood by employing current anthropological data.

In the economic realm, Dobriansky faulted Veblen's wishing to abolish the price system, equated with Veblen's penchant for a society of "millennial...abundance"; without such a device he pictured society as "devoid of economic efficiency since prices accurately measured the social utility of investment and production." But Veblen, as has been observed, had local worker councils working closely with various coordinating bodies to adjust production and investment. (Price mechanisms themselves for the sake of economic efficiency are not antithetical to a socialist society.) What Veblen opposed was a capitalist price and investment system that resulted in depressions and such current practices sabotaging the economic system as Savings and Loans frauds and LBOs.

In the political realm, Dobriansky was perturbed by the criticism that Veblen directed against nationalism/patriotism and representative government under capitalist auspices. He himself perceived contemporary government, presumably the American, as defending individual rights and freedoms, but did not mention that they were traditionally opposed by wealthy conservatives and that it was progressive elements of the bourgeoisie and the workingclass which fought for them. But Veblen's unpardonable sin, for him, was to confiscate great wealth. To be sure, Dobriansky's conservative Catholicism would allow for a "social minimum."

On where to place Veblen in the socialist spectrum, Dobriansky was at least accurate in situating him in the anarchist stream, as an advocate of "idealist anarchy" and "anarchic technocracy," in the spirit of guild socialism in which technical expertise was valued.[2]

A most engaging and witty work on Veblen was David Riesman's *Thorstein Veblen: A Critical Interpretation* (1953). A Harvard sociologist, perhaps best known for *The Lonely Crowd*, he especially delved into the problems of higher education, as *On Higher Education*. As a member of the liberal left, he was critical of remaking society too rapidly, like the Communist experiment in the Soviet Union. But his admiration for the Wobbly Veblen was clearly abundant. In writing this work in the early 1950s, during the midst of a Cold-War anti-Communist hysteria, like a cautious liberal academic, Riesman critiqued Veblen under the mantle of the conventional truisms of the times, portraying him as being a utopian eccentric, gently chiding him for this and downplaying his support of Communism, which, in any case, was not Stalinist.

To be sure, Riesman, at times, was rather harsh toward Veblen, accusing him of opting for a technocratic/socialist society resembling Aldous Huxley's *Brave New World*, a society which neither Veblen nor Huxley endorsed. Veblen's syndicalism, which demanded active and pervasive worker involvement, necessitating the need for extensive education and brief work day, had no similarity to *Brave New World*, although today's monopoly capitalist society certainly resembles it closely. Furthermore, Riesman employed a specious *ad hominem* argument in objecting to Veblen's characterization of capitalists as parasites. But he presented many brilliant insights into Veblen's views on many areas, as in education and economics.

Riesman also unfortunately culturally sanitized Veblen by focusing unduly on Veblenian "conspicuous consumption," which supposedly had the leisure class and its dependents feel guilty and to more empathize with workers and women, thus their love for blue jeans, rejection of Cadillacs, more utilitarian women's dress, and glorification of toy trains. He himself was part of a Veblenian crusade as an undergraduate at Harvard, railing against construction of wasteful Georgian-style buildings. In fact, he devoted much more time to this and the other trivia in his critique than with Veblen's views of the Communist Revolution in Russia and other serious matters.[3]

Douglas Dowd, a professor of economics at Cornell University, in *Thorstein Veblen* (1966), wrote a most informative and interesting study on Veblen's many contributions to economics and the social sciences. He regarded Veblen as "America's most noted economist," the "wittiest of America's social scientists," and "America's most controversial social scientist."

On Veblen's ultimate socialist position, Dowd correctly maintained that despite oscillations between "worker control of a decentralized industrial economy" and one that "requires a high degree of centralized coordination" due to the demands of a "modern industrial technology," Veblen, on balance, favored the former position, close to British guild socialism. There is no contradiction between worker control and some form of "centralized coordination." It is possible to combine both of these elements by insisting on a pervasive participatory democracy of technical and cultural co-equals in which planners would have no advantage over the rest of the people, for planning itself requires the input of many layers of expertise.[4]

In *The Bard of Savagery* (1978), John P. Diggins, an historian, superlatively explored the many dimensions of Veblen's character, times, and thought. His forte, however, was in the realm of the last, tackling with great sophistication many of the controversial elements of Veblenism: As why peaceful humanity became warlike and predatory, dichotomy between workers and the leisure class, alienation, roles of contemporary working-class intellectuals and engineers in the socialist equation, criticism of Classical Economics, capitalist cultural hegemony, the gender problem, primacy of technology or the machine, higher education, and imperialism. In covering these problems, he at times compared the insights of Marx, Weber, and Mill, among others, with those of Veblen, while describing the contributions of Weber, Franklin, and Alexis de Tocqueville, among others, on the "Spirit of Capitalism."[5]

Another work on Veblen that appropriately appreciated his genius, but forcefully argued with him at times was *The Values of Veblen* by Bernard Rosenberg, a sociologist and a founding editor of *Dissent*. Importantly, he identified a strong Weberian element in Veblen—he properly stated that Veblen himself never read Weber—less optimistic that socialism could be rapidly achieved in contradistinction to the more optimistic Marx.

Other areas on Veblen examined by Rosenberg: In Chapter Six, "The Leisure Class," he almost invariably agreed with Veblen's insights, combining economic, social, and psychological factors in the making of elites, but believed that Veblen was too harsh towards sports, aiding to relieve aggression, especially among poor working-class youth. In Chapter Seven, he waxed rhapsodic in describing the importance of Veblen's *The Theory of Business Enterprise,* viewing it as the "most influential polemic Veblen ever wrote." He also praised Veblen's *The Higher Learning in America* ("Veblen's most important book"), agreeing generally with its main outlines, including the increasing bureaucratization and business control of higher education.

At times, Rosenberg was incorrect in some minor criticism of Veblen. For instance, he disparaged Veblen's "parental bent" by remarking that in primitive societies infanticide was the norm, and that within this context no remorse was evinced by the mother, failing to point out that without this practice, humanity could not have survived. That the older generations nurtured the younger ones was simply a truism, despite cruelties. I also disagree with Rosenberg's assertion that Veblen was against a classless socialist society, but for one dominated by the bureaucrat in the university, factory, and office: Along with Marx and Engels, Veblen recognized that socialism would have normal status differences in its first stage but mental and manual workers would cooperate in a democratic manner and with the further development of technology there was no reason why the dichotomy between these two labors could not be erased.

As for the Soviet Union, Rosenberg saw that it did not follow the prescriptions of Marx and Veblen to establish a workers' democracy for socialism, thus degenerating into a bureaucratic absolutism, lacking any popular participation and civil liberties. This scenario was related to sharp class divisions, themselves part of its economic backwardness, allowing many of the higher bureaucrats in mental labor to favor capitalism. Finally, in the area of war and peace,he generally agreed with Veblen on the possibility for peace, continuing progress in technology, end of feudalistic remnants, and further development of capitalism.[6]

In Commager's magisterial *The American Mind* (1959), the encomiums thrown at Veblen were almost never ending. (Commager, an eminent American historian, was a professor of history at Amherst College, among other places.) In Chapter Eleven (one of twenty) of the work, "Thorstein Veblen and the New Economics," Veblen emerged as one of the main protagonists against capitalism. But even in the introductory section of the chapter before covering Veblen, Commager, in a Veblenian mode declared: "That the control and exploitation of natural resources by private individuals or corporations was concentrating wealth and power in the hands of the few"; that big business was "thrusting small business into a hopelessly subordinate position," and that "finance capitalism...was shifting the control of industry from the builders to the bankers and converting the directorates of many corporations into a tightly knit structure"; that economic depression was "capitalistic sabotage," or "a conscientious withdrawal of efficiency." He, thus, joined Veblen in attesting to the "irrelevance of *laissez faire* to the realities of modern industrial society," particularly in *The Engineers and the Price System*, with its stress on the economics of production vindicated by its success during World War II. Furthermore, again following Veblen, he condemned the present socioeconomic system. On property, it "would have recognized the changing character of property dictated by the widespread use of the corporate device"; on competition, it "would have adjusted itself to the realities of competition between great corporations and individual workingmen, but economists maintained the fiction of perfect competition"; on economic control, "the transfer of power from industrialists to financiers." Furthermore, he opined that those against social welfare and wage legislation, and who saw "the state as necessary evil," were mistaken; and he lamented the "propaganda of the National Association of Manufacturers and the practices of advertisers who exalted the worst manifestations of individualism, pandered to the worst instincts of jealousy, snobbery, and fear, and reduced competition to its most primitive form." In addition, he recognized that "Veblen's most important contribution was his demarcation of the antagonism between industry and business...or of the engineers and the price system," or the "production of goods...[and] pecuniary gain," dichotomy between "machines...inordinately productive" and capitalists "required to articulate production to profit," whose antithetical elements led to depression. As for the roots of Veblen's criticism of capitalism, Commager pictured Veblen as more of a son of the "Middle Border" and of its "agrarian radicalism than of eastern progressivism or of the revolutionary economics of central Europe."

In the area of intellectuality, Commager was greatly impressed by Veblen's vast erudition: "For he brought to the study of economic institutions and conduct not only history and anthropology but philosophy and psychology." And his praise for the *Theory of the Leisure Class* was boundless: "His *Theory of the Leisure Class* was the most penetrating commentary on the psychological basis of economic institutions that had yet been made." He, also, noted the importance of Veblen's *Theory of Business Enterprise* in influencing the work of the progressive economist, John R. Commons. In general, for him, "Veblen took nothing for granted, questioned everything, and was merciless," and "his rebellion went so deep that it confounded even dissenters," and "he invoked not only a new philosophy but a new vocabulary."[7]

In *Thorstein Veblen and His Critics*, Tilman admirably examined the many critiques of Veblen, ably defending Veblen: They principally included those by the institutional economist, Commons, on the moderate left; Talcott Parsons, a conservative/functionalist sociologist; Marxist philosophers and economists, like Theodore Adorno, Paul Sweezy, Leo Huberman, and Paul Baran; Riesman; Rosenberg; and Dobriansky.[8]

Veblen, regarded by many pundits as America's premier social and economic thinker, did not escape from the wrath of the great iconoclast of American letters who never met a public figure whom he liked, H. L. Mencken. In *Prejudices: First Series* (1919), his ire toward Veblen reached its nadir. He complained that he was forced to read Veblen in 1918 when he replaced Dewey as the darling of the intellectuals: "He was all over the *Nation*, the *Dial*, and *New Republic* and the rest of them, and his books and pamphlets began to pour from the presses, and the newspapers reported his every wink and whisper, and everybody who was anybody began gabbling about him." And, "all the reviews were full of his ideas." Indeed, "there were Veblenists, Veblen clubs, Veblen remedies for all the sorrows of the world." Although he thought that Veblen's style was "clumsy, affected, opaque, bombastic, windy, empty," and "without grace or distinction," after many pages of balderdash against Veblen, he admitted that of the professoriate: "Veblen is not the worst. Veblen is almost the best."

Not to be outdone by the anarchist Veblen in his attacks on society, Mencken mocked the average people "for their idiotic ideas" and willingness to "follow platitudinous messiahs," took a swipe at the "plutocracy," characterized as "ignorant, hostile to inquiry, tyrannical in the exercises of its power, suspicious of ideas of whatever sort," and for good measure blasted the professoriate and intellectuals, calling them "intellectual eunuchs" who were "always in great fear of it [the plutocracy]."[9]

The aim is now to present representative views of what prominent American Marxists think of Veblen, focusing on the July-August, 1957 double issue, devoted to him in *Monthly Review: An Independent Socialist Magazine* (*MR*)—the leading Marxist journal in America, along with *Science and Society*. Its editors, Leo Huberman, Harry Magdoff, and Sweezy, and other contributors, like Paul A. Baran, Williams, and Nearing, are internationally known.

In the "Review of the Month," Huberman and Sweezy, readily admitted that Veblen was not a Marxist for "the differences are too obvious, too big, and too persistent to be considered of merely secondary importance," although "Marx was one of the decisive factors in shaping his intellectual development." But their praise for Veblen's work was abundant: "Veblen: he was a rebel, a man of the left." Indeed, they pointed out three essential points of agreement between Marx and Veblen: (1) of Veblen's "absentee ownership," with Marx's "capital"; (2) of capitalism's unreformability, with its contradiction of "private property in the means of production" toppling it; (3) of abhorrence to nationalism/patriotism, inevitably used by the bourgeoisie to buttress their power, with "militarism and imperialism." Furthermore, they pictured Veblen as a staunch supporter of the Bolshevik Revolution and Communism in the Soviet Union.[10]

A most interesting critique of Veblen's *The Theory of the Leisure Class* was by Baran, an economist at Stanford. He basically blamed Veblen for not differentiating between the various "upper classes" in history with respect to their "different social relations, different share of different social outputs produced in different stages of the development of productive resources." He also disapproved of Veblen's over-reliance on "biological-psychological" explanations in understanding history. Ultimately: "Although he [Veblen] did not manage to attain a full understanding of the process of historical change, he frequently came close to it. Had he gone further, he would have transcended himself and taken the decisive step to materialism and to dialectic."

Baran's analysis of Veblen is debatable. That Veblen closely pursued the nature-of-human-nature arguments was undeniable, but had to do so because of the wide interest in social Darwinism among academics during his lifetime—it reappeared in the 1980s and 90s as part of a rising American conservatism. That Veblen failed to explicitly differentiate among the different modes of exploiting slaves, serfs, and workers did not indicate that he was unaware of them but that he simply took them for granted. In fact, when Veblen discussed the possibility of a working-class socialist revolution, he associated it with the new conditions brought about by capitalism, like "absentee ownership" and recurring depressions, obviously related to exploitation of workers.

As for Veblen's materialism, Baran should not have questioned it for reasons already discussed. Although Veblen was not a believer of the dialectic, his Darwinian evolutionary beliefs certainly allowed for the class struggle between workers and bourgeoisie and the possibility for socialist revolution. Indeed, in the light of 20th-century developments, Veblen's more skeptical approach for rapidly achieving socialism was more accurate than Marx's.[11]

IMPORTANCE

Veblen's importance as a thinker may be measured by the following: Lev E. Dobriansky in *Veblenism* noted that "most probably no other social thinker, except Marx, has received such a wide range of varied commentary as Thorstein Veblen."[12] For C. Wright Mills, one of the bright stars of recent sociology, "Thorstein Veblen is the best critic of America that America has produced."[13] For Douglas F. Dowd, a professor of economics at Cornell, Veblen was not only "America's most controversial social scientist," but also "America's most noted economist."[14] Commager's definitive *The American Mind* awarded proper attention to Veblen, and recognized the importance of *The Theory of the Leisure Class*, already observed.[15] In Richard Hofstadter's *Social Darwinism in American Thought*, which examined a significant segment of American intellectual thought from the late 19th to the early 20th centuries, Veblen was accorded the importance given to Spencer, Sumner, Ward, William James, Dewey, and John Fiske.[16] In Daniel Aaron's *Men of Good Hope: A Story of American Progressives*, one of its nine chapters was devoted to Veblen.[17] In Morton White's *Social Thought in America: The Revolt Against Formalism*, the five most frequently cited individuals were Charles A. Beard, Dewey, Oliver Wendell Holmes, Jr., James Harvey Robinson, and Veblen.[18] Charles A. Beard and Mary R. Beard, in *The American Spirit: A Study of the Idea of Civilization in the United States*, insisted that: "After Veblen had spoken, no American student of economics who had passed beyond sheer sciolism could fail to associate civilization with economic thought."[19] In David W. Noble's *The Progressive Mind, 1890-1917*, the leading personages were Veblen, Charles A. Beard, Charles H. Cooley, Dewey, Sumner, Ignatius Donnelly, Walter Rauschenbusch, and Frederick Jackson Turner.[20] Staughton Lynd's *The Intellectual Origins of American Radicalism* depicted Veblen and W.E.B. Du Bois as the two ablest synthesizers of Marxism and American radicalism.[21] In Robert L. Heilbroner's *The Worldly Philosophers: The Lives, Times, and Ideas of the Great Economic Thinkers,* one of its eleven chapters was devoted to Veblen who occupied a separate chapter along with Smith, Marx, and Keynes. His admiration for Veblen was obvious: "He was seeking to penetrate to the true nature of the society in which he lived."[22]

Notes

1. Dorfman, *Veblen*.

2. Dobriansky, *Veblenism*, pp. 8 ff., 236 ff. and 368, for instance.

3. Riesman, *Veblen*, pp. 8, 32, 36, 43, 96-98, 116, 123, 130, 136-39, 170-86, and 108.

4. Dowd, *Veblen*, pp. xi-xvii, for instance.

5. Diggins, *Bard of Savagery*, chapters indicated.

6. Rosenberg, *Values of Veblen*, pp. 9-27, 47, 52, 81-90, 112.

7. Commager, *American Mind*, Chapter 11.

8. Tilman, *Thorstein Veblen*, pp. 168 ff., for instance, on Parsons.

9. H.L. Mencken, *Prejudices: First Series* (New York: Alfred A. Knopf, 1919), pp. 59-82 are entitled "Professor Veblen."

10. Leo Huberman and Paul M. Sweezy, "Review of the Month," *Monthly Review*, July-Aug., 1957, pp. 65-72.

11. Paul A. Baran, "*The Theory of the Leisure Class*," *ibid.*, pp. 83-91.

12. Dobriansky, *Veblen*, p. 24.

13. Veblen, *Theory of the Leisure Class*, p. vi, in "Introduction" by Mills.

14. Dowd, *Veblen,* pp. xv-xvi.

15. Commager, *American Mind*, p. 242 .

16. Richard Hofstadter, *Social Darwinism in American Thought*, revised ed. (Boston: Beacon Press, 1955), pp. 243-48, Index.

17. Aaron, *Men of Good Hope*, Chapter 7.

18. Morton White, *Social Thought in America: The Revolt Against Formalism* (Boston: Beacon Press, 1957), pp. 297-301.

19. Charles A. Beard and Mary R. Beard, *The American Spirit: A Study of the Idea of Civilization in the United States* (New York: Collier Books, 1962), p. 43.

20. David W. Noble, *The Progressive Mind, 1890-1917* (Chicago: Rand McNally College Publishing Co., 1970), pp. 191-96, Index.

21. Staughton Lynd, *The Intellectual Origins of American Radicalism* (Cambridge: Harvard University Press, 1968), pp. 168-69.

22. Heilbroner, *The Worldly Philosophers*, Chapter 8, "The Savage World of Thorstein Veblen," p. 208 on the quotation.

Index